SOCIAL THEORY AND PSYCHOANALYSIS IN TRANSITION

SOCIAL THEORY AND PSYCHOANALYSIS IN TRANSITION

Self and Society from Freud to Kristeva

Second Edition

Anthony Elliott

FREE ASSOCIATION BOOKS / LONDON / NEW YORK

This edition published in Great Britain in 1999 by
Free Association Books Limited
57 Warren Street, London W1P 5PA

ISBN 1 85343 445 0 (hbk); 1 85343 446 9 (pbk)

A CIP catalogue record for this book is available from the British
Library

Produced for Free Association Books Ltd by
Chase Production Services, Chadlington, OX7 3LN
Printed in the EC by T.J. International Ltd., Padstow

Contents

Acknowledgements

During the preparation of both editions of this book, numerous readers of the manuscript offered critical comments on particular chapters, and I have endeavoured to incorporate their suggestions wherever possible. I am especially grateful to Anthony Giddens and John Thompson, both of whom helped to shape the concerns of this book, and have always advised me well. Particular thanks are due to David Stonestreet at Free Association Books, for all the help he has given me in preparing this edition. It is now also a pleasure to acknowledge one of the first edition reviewers, Jeffrey Prager at UCLA, whose report served as a significant influence on the book. My greatest debt is to Nicola Geraghty. In helping to prepare this edition for publication, she devoted considerable time to the project, and made many important contributions. I am immensely grateful for her help and support.

Anthony Elliott
December 1998
University of Melbourne

For Nicola

Preface

When I began writing *Social Theory and Psychoanalysis in Transition* in the late 1980s, the question of human subjectivity and of self-identity had reappeared as a fundamental issue in social theory in particular, as well as the social sciences more widely conceived. By the time the book was published in the early 1990s, psychoanalytic theory had become an increasingly important and fruitful resource for the analysis of the self, self-identity and subjectivity in critical social theory. Lacan's Freud was, and in many disciplinary approaches remains, the dominant psychoanalytic discourse for understanding the constitution of the subject in the analysis of social and cultural processes. Yet the critique initially sketched in *Social Theory and Psychoanalysis in Transition* sought not only to demonstrate that the relation between society and the psyche was considerably more complex and creative than was generally recognized in Lacanian-orientated social theory, but also to examine other theoretical attempts to understand the interweaving of our psychic and socio-historical worlds.

The critiques of the relations between self and society which I analyse in this book are developed from three key standpoints. These are (1) critical theory, with its emphasis on the importance of psychoanalysis, political theory and philosophy for emancipatory thought; (2) post-structuralist interrogations of the production of subjectivity and identity; and (3) various feminist readings of psychoanalysis and of masculinist assumptions in Western social theory. In considering these standpoints, I put forward the argument that Freud and psychoanalysis are of considerable importance for charting both intimate, psychic processes and social-historical developments in the present age. I try to demonstrate the multiplex ways in which these standpoints allow us to grasp the complex, contradictory forms in which culture impacts on the process of self-formation, including the production of novel structures of cognitive and emotional coercion with new forms of social regulation. Against the backcloth of the critique that I develop, the elements of a more constructive account of the relations between self and society are offered. For in suggesting that various versions of social theory have falsely downgraded the personal and political impact of the unconscious in social relations, my primary concern is to trace Freud's arguments concerning the creative uses that the mind makes of fantasies and identifications, to link such internal fabrications to the making and remaking of society and culture, and hopefully to contribute to a broader dialogue between social theory and psychoanalysis.

It is my view that the social conditions in which we now live – in which forces of globalization, privatization and postmodernization increasingly impact upon our lives and our relations with others – render the task of developing a sophisticated theory of the human subject politically urgent. It is especially from this angle that the import of Freud and psychoanalysis for grasping the permeability between the self and the social world brooks large. The interdisciplinary project of social theory, infused by the conceptual insights and challenges of Freud and psychoanalysis, provides critical perspectives on the production of subjectivity and identity, on sexuality and gender, and on society, culture and technology. Today, this sort of interdisciplinary work is especially significant for grasping how subjectivity and identity are being reconstituted within a global context of economic uncertainty and ambivalence, in which the advent of new communication technologies and unpredictable political turbulence have produced novel forms of culture and social reproduction.

However, while *Social Theory and Psychoanalysis in Transition* develops an approach to social theory of a very definite type, combining an emphasis on human creation from psychoanalysis and a conception of social domination from critical theory and post-structuralism, there are many who remain sceptical of, or who have simply backed away from, the common ground opened up by recent exchanges between psychoanalysis and contemporary social thought. I refer here not only to recent attacks on psychoanalysis within the academic community, but also to the Freud-bashing and the culture wars which have dominated public and media debate of late. For much of the anti-subjectivist rhetoric that has influenced those working in the social sciences and the humanities throughout the 1990s, ranging from structural-systems analysis to certain versions of discourse theory, reflects a preoccupation with external forces as determining personal subjectivity, as well as a profound lack of interest in issues surrounding the complexity of the psyche and the self. This anti-subjectivist stance has been especially prevalent throughout various sectors of popular culture, in which questions about personal distress, depression or trauma are increasingly cast as a consequence of either oppressive social conditions or political structures. 'We live', writes Jeffrey Prager, 'in an age that, though profoundly psychological in its talk about the influence of traumatic pasts on the present, has created a particularly antipsychological psychology. It is an age that externalizes the self and, in so doing, subdues subjectivity.'[1]

In my view Freud and psychoanalysis, when integrated into a comprehensive social theory, provide models for understanding the richness and complexity of the psyche, penetrating critiques of the nature of the self, and resources for the development of a dialectical critical theory capable of grasping the radically imaginative and creative interplay between self and society. In short, a counter-discursive, and indeed political, strategy for combating current discourse which 'externalizes the self'. Several of the issues I raise in this preface are not discussed in the detail which they deserve, in part because of limitations of space, and in part because they are discussed in detail throughout this book. Although selective and partial, however, I shall consider here a number of recent developments in social theory and the social sciences which touch on questions of subjectivity and identity, as well as their relation to the production of society. I shall try to indicate throughout the central interest of Freud and of psychoanalysis to these recent debates.

Freud, Psychoanalysis and Social Theory

It is now seventy years since Freud published his seminal book, *Civilization and its Discontents*. In that book, Freud was concerned with repression. He argued that the repression of violent aggression, and the guilt it engenders, is *the* fundamental problem of modern societies. Freud understood society as a kind of trade-off: unfettered sexual desire and the satisfaction of violence are sacrificed for a sense of collective security. Self-expression is limited in the name of social order. 'Civilization', Freud wrote, 'is a process in the service of Eros, whose purpose is to combine single human individuals, and after that families, then races, peoples and nations, into one great unity.'

From a contemporary vantage point, to speak of culture in terms of unity or order sounds somewhat quaint. Against the backdrop of global economic uncertainty and multiculturalism, Freud's cultural analysis looks increasingly out of date. In the current political climate, the freedom of the individual now reigns supreme. As Margaret Thatcher famously put it, 'There is no such thing as society' – a comment that in one stroke defined our new era of privatization and deregulation. One way of understanding these social changes is that the 'cultures of discipline' which dominated during Freud's era have given way to today's 'cultures of desire'. The radical individualism of our age is one in which retail therapy rules, catering as it does to our endless cultural thirst for new sensations, appetites, cravings and products. Indeed, Zygmunt Bauman, the Polish sociologist, has recently argued that if Freud were writing *Civilization and its Discontents* today, he would need to reverse his diagnosis.[2] In today's world, the most common types of psychic troubles, anxieties and discontents are those of individual addiction – from drugs through gambling to episodic sex.

Where does this leave Freudian theory and its cultural legacy? According to some critics, especially in the US, Freud is finished. End of story, or so some would like to think. Frederick Crews, self-appointed guru of the revisionist anti-psychoanalysis movement, has been a powerful voice on this issue.[3] A former Freudian literary critic, Crews is out to demonstrate the intellectual fraud and pseudo-epistemology of his once beloved, but now spurned, master. He charges psychoanalytic theory, following Adolf Grünbaum, with a lack of scientific rigour, and declares key Freudian concepts – such as repression, the dynamic unconscious, transference and free association – bogus. Crews's debunking of the scientistic credentials of psychoanalysis undoubtedly reflects a rising anti-Freudian spirit of the times. As Tom Wolfe writes in a sharp polemic: 'Freudian psychiatrists are now regarded as old crocks with sham medical degrees, as ears that people with more money than sense can hire to talk into.'[4]

Ever since Freud first went public with his ideas on sexual repression and the unconscious, the scientific status and therapeutic benefits of psychoanalysis have been sharply contested, in both the public realm and the academic community. The recent Freud-bashing, however, has gone much further, with some critics arguing that psychoanalysis neglects issues of sexual abuse and others holding the father of psychoanalysis responsible for the ubiquity of recovered memory movements. I cannot go into detail here about the dramatic oversimplification of Freud in these scorching attacks. More interesting, I think, is the question of why, in our particular cultural moment, Freud-bashing should have become so widespread. How, as psychoanalysis passes into its second century, a kindergarten version of Freud has risen to public prominence is an important, though largely undebated, issue.

In terms of understanding Freud's enduring importance, however, there is a point of much deeper cultural significance, a point missed by much of the recent Freud criticism. Fifty years after his death, and notwithstanding the ongoing debate about the scientific status of psychoanalysis, Freud's intellectual and cultural influence remains profound. One reason why this is so (and there is no other way of putting it that does not sound like a cliché) is that Freud was a great thinker. His work at once embodies and points beyond the contradictions of his time. He created a language to describe the repressed unconscious as we have come to know it, and to the extent that contemporary men and women have (preconsciously) shaped their lives in and through the prose of psychoanalysis, Freud holds a pivotal place in the fabrication of the modernist epoch. In examining the deep fantasies of the self – anxieties about otherness, about envy and hatred, about need and desire – Freud demonstrated that a world of secrets, doubts, lies and fictions lurk within our individual and social lives. In introducing the notion of repression, Freud identified the submerged, hidden identities that imbued peoples' lives with a sense of fear, anxiety or shame. It was Nietzsche who spoke of the importance of time to our own self-understanding. But with Freud time is interwoven with pain, depression and mourning as key ingredients of what makes us fully human. The capacity of people to bear guilt and tolerate periods of depression is essential to personal growth and change. But self-understanding requires attention to the inner world, and this of course takes time – a scarce 'commodity' in our speed-driven information age.

The cultural reception of Freud and psychoanalysis, it seems to me, is split between competing modes of rationality, these being modern and postmodern, traditional and post-traditional – and this is a standpoint I have developed at length elsewhere.[5] In the modernist frame of reference, Freud's naming of the unconscious wishes, fantasies and anxieties that circulate at the borders of our personal and social life are often reacted to as threatening or overwhelming. The danger, sometimes treated as catastrophic, is that the dynamic unconscious threatens to subvert our cultural impulse for order, boundaries, mastery, classification and structure. Things go differently with the postmodernist mode of cultural reception. Here we find an acceptance of the tensions and contradictions of contemporary cultural life, accompanied by a recognition of plurality, ambivalence, ambiguity, contingency and uncertainty.

I have encountered these conflicting, yet interlocking, modes of cultural reception in respect of my own research on Freud and psychoanalysis in various guises, and for the purposes of the present discussion I think it is worth elaborating upon this briefly. Reviews of *Social Theory and Psychoanalysis in Transition* took up a very broad range of intellectual, psychoanalytic and political concerns, ranging from debates in contemporary critical theory, post-structuralism and postmodernism to the politics of social movements and the cultural implications of identity politics.[6] While the book was welcomed in many quarters for promoting a more informed psychoanalytic dialogue between French and German currents of social thought, several reviews raised some of the following criticisms:

- that I had failed to engage with, and draw from, psychoanalytic schools of thought other than traditional Freudian theory and Lacanian theory;
- that I had focused only upon conceptual disputes, and had thus ignored developments in clinical research and psychoanalytic practice;
- that I had privileged the application of psychoanalysis in the social sciences to social and political theory, and had thus ignored a range of developments in media studies and popular culture.

While I have some sympathy with these mild and more intensive critical comments, it is probably worth pointing out that the book made no claim to examine traditions of social thought other than those deriving from the application of psychoanalysis in critical theory, post-structuralism and feminism. (I might also add that, given that I drew from both object-relational and Kleinian theory, as well as extensively from Cornelius Castoriadis's interpretation of Freud, it is inaccurate to claim that the book only engages with Freudian and Lacanian approaches.) In the light of the foregoing comments concerning cultural reception, however, what is interesting about such critical remarks is that they reflect a curiosity, indeed an intellectual demand, for enlarging the space of the psychoanalytic imagination. To the extent that the demand is to embrace and learn from the plurality of competing psychoanalytic approaches to social processes and cultural life, we find an engagement with a psychoanalytic outlook that had previously been denied in a range of disciplines. Although I am suggesting that some of these criticisms were misplaced in terms of assessing the objectives of *Social Theory and Psychoanalysis in Transition*, the cultural influences informing these reviews clearly press for the extension of divergent conceptualizations – more openness, more debate, new angles of vision.

Compare and contrast such sentiments with a review published in the *Times Literary Supplement* of an edited book that I subsequently published, *Freud 2000*.[7] In certain respects, this book was an extension of the sort of interdisciplinary research concerning the relations between self and society in the present age that I argued for in *Social Theory and Psychoanalysis in Transition*. The contributors, a group of international scholars from various disciplines, engaged with the issue of what Freud and psychoanalysis have to offer intellectual debate and cultural criticism today. The *TLS* review, entitled 'The end of Freud?', by Andrew Scull, a professor of sociology in the US,

sharply criticized the book on the grounds that, as far as psychoanalytically informed social critique goes, 'a united front cannot be
found'.[8] The shift in approach here is self-evident. Whereas some
critics of *Social Theory and Psychoanalysis in Transition* urged for a
greater contrast and further comparison of psychoanalytical theory,
this critic of *Freud 2000* found various divergent perspectives on
Freudian theory too much to tolerate. As Scull wrote: 'We
encounter, as we wander through *Freud 2000*, an early and a late
Freud, a Lacanian Freud, a modernist Freud, a postmodernist
Freud, a humanist Freud and an anti-humanist Freud, a scientific
Freud and an anti-scientistic, heuristic Freud, even, Lord help us, a
feminist Freud, not to mention legions of neo-Freudian deviationists
and object relationists clinging tenuously to the mantle of the
master.' The problem for Scull is that Freudian criticism generates
too much noise, too many approaches, too many perspectives.
Although his argument is that this diversity reflects badly on the
conceptual unity of Freud's theoretical edifice, my point is that his
horror of heterogeneity ('even, Lord help us, a feminist Freud')
shapes the ill-tempered and vitriolic tone of his review.

While the prevailing climate of our culture has been distinctively
anti-Freudian in recent years, then, what I am suggesting is that a
psychoanalytic approach to sociological matters permits the deconstruction of crippling dualisms, and thus opens other intellectual and
cultural possibilities. In contrast to the binary oppositions of
Freudian versus anti-Freudian, modernist versus postmodernist,
traditional versus post-traditional, the problematic of cultural
production can be tackled from a psychoanalytic viewpoint as one of
ambivalence, ambiguity, plurality, multiplication and difference.
Psychoanalysis offers itself to the world not just as a therapy (as the
anti-Freudian revisionists so often assume), but also as a theory of
human subjectivity and social reproduction. Certainly it is the case
that therapy and theory cross and tangle; the point of theory, as
Freud often stressed, is to illuminate and guide therapy. Yet concentration upon the theoretical insights of psychoanalysis, especially as
far as social theory is concerned, highlights the continued relevance
of Freud for analysing the intersections between subjectivity, society
and culture. Whatever the fluctuating stock market fortunes of
psychoanalysis in the area of mental and public health, Freud's
impact has perhaps never been as far-reaching as it currently is within
public and academic debate. Psychoanalysis today is used by social
and political theorists, literary and cultural critics, by feminists and
postmodernists, such is its rich theoretical suggestiveness and
powerful diagnosis of our current cultural malaise. For example, if
one turns to some of the most interesting work that has been done in

contemporary philosophy, from Paul Riceour to Richard Rorty, we find a strong engagement with Freud. This is also obviously true of various versions of feminism. So-called 'third wave' feminists, such as Julia Kristeva and Luce Irigaray (both of whom are practising psychoanalysts), refer to Freud continually. Freud's doctrine of repressed desire, in particular, has provided for a new cultural emphasis on sexuality, the body, feeling and emotion. The affirmative politics of the countercultural movements, informed by the writings of Norman O. Brown and Herbert Marcuse, as well as various strands of identity politics, have drawn from Freud's legacy. Even the discourse that has caused so much alarm and lament inside and outside of academic circles – postmodernism – contains critical and descriptive terminology that reflect a Freudian debt. Jean-François Lyotard, widely considered the supreme analyst of postmodernism, remarked that his radical proclamation about the 'end of modernity' arose from concepts borrowed from Freud: 'remembering', 'repeating' and 'working through'.

In my view, there can be little doubt that the motivating force for this turn to Freud is as much political as it is intellectual. In a century which has seen the rise of totalitarianism, Hiroshima, Auschwitz and the possibility of a nuclear winter, cultural critics and intellectuals have demanded a language which is able to grapple with modern culture's unleashing of its unprecedented powers of destruction. Freud has provided that conceptual vocabulary. Freudian psychoanalysis continues to represent a profound response to the crises of modernism.

Current Debates in Psychoanalytic Social Theory

Since this book was originally published, there have been a number of substantial developments in the utilization of psychoanalysis in social theory for the analysis of self-identity and social relations. While I cannot do justice to the richness and complexity of recent advances in psychoanalytic research and theory in the following pages, my remarks will hopefully serve to underline the relevance and utility of psychoanalytic thinking to current debates over subjectivity and culture in the social sciences and the humanities.

Broadly speaking, there are three major directions in psychoanalytically orientated social theory which are especially relevant to the fuller theorization of self and society in the present age. The first relates to *pre-Oedipal processes*; the second concerns *intersubjectivity*; and the third connects to *postmodernism*.

Whereas Freud and Lacan see an essential affinity between Oedipal or symbolic processes and the constitution of identity, research into early infant development has tended to shift the focus of psychoanalytic social theory towards pre-Oedipal development and preliminary imaginary fabrications of the self. This research focuses upon the earliest or most primitive phases of psychic development in the infant–mother dyad, and there is particular concentration on issues of separation, individuation, and of the self and primary narcissism.[9] The role of primal fantasies and primary repression in pre-Oedipal development has become a major focus for understanding the individual subject's subsequent psychic investment in both the imaginary order (the mirror phase, for example) and the symbolic order (language, logic, rationality). The psychoanalytic work of Melanie Klein, D.W. Winnicott and Wilfred Bion is foundational in this respect, and in recent research the contributions of neo-Lacanians such as Jean Laplanche, Luce Irigaray and Julia Kristeva, relational theorists such as Thomas Ogden, Stephen Mitchell and Charles Spezzano, as well as innovators such as Francis Tustin and Christopher Bollas, have been crucial. The problem of the relationship between omnipotence and decentring has been especially important in the light of such research, primarily as the dangers of omnipotence and omniscience are increasingly seen as relevant to discussions concerning democracy, justice, autonomy, nationalism, ideology and globalization.

This leads, secondly, to the issue of intersubjectivity within psychoanalytically informed critical and feminist theory, as well as within contemporary psychoanalysis more broadly.[10] In contemporary theory, the term 'intersubjectivity' is often associated with Jürgen Habermas's theory of communicative action. However, as Jessica Benjamin notes, 'Habermas provided an entry into intersubjectivity, but without sufficient attention to the subject's destructive omnipotence.'[11] Benjamin's approach to rethinking intersubjectivity, which I rely on in various parts of this book, stresses that the subject is intersubjectively constituted within the social and cultural environment in which the individual is embedded, while simultaneously granting due recognition to intrapsychic processes of identification and projection. As she puts this, 'the embrace of intersubjectivity does not constitute a transcendence of the intrapsychic, but rather a modification and addition to it'. Such an intersubjective perspective arises from a revaluation of the affective and communicative relations between the infant and the mother that I noted above. In short, the idea is that the pre-Oedipal mother plays a more central and determining role in processes of intersubjective communication than traditional psychoanalytic theory postulated. From this angle, internal mental space is constituted and reproduced through an affective dialogue with other persons, a dialogue from which frames of meaning and affect come to be created and structured. Intersubjective relations are inscribed internally in our desire, in our psyches; and the task of a critical social theory is to analyse the multiplex forms in which social and political relations permit the individual subject to recognize or deny specific differences of the other, as well as cultural difference more generally.

Finally, psychoanalytic social theory has been revitalized through its engagement with postmodernism. The rise of postmodernism as a paradigm for the social sciences and the humanities – with its anti-individualist bent, its sensitivity to communal differences, its stress on heterogeneity, ambiguity and ambivalence, and its openness to differences and alternative viewpoints – is based not so much on a rejection of modernity and modernism (although in its cruder versions this has sometimes been the case), but rather on a radical and reflexive engagement with the modernist drive for world mastery, control, ordering and domination. Postmodernism has, in part, served to delegitimatize the claims of instrumental reason to mastery and control in favour of contextual, constructivist and anti-foundational views of subjectivity, knowledge, language and of social and political reality. Not surprisingly, this postmodernist impulse has influenced both psychoanalytic theory and psychoanalytically informed social theory. Here a range of postmodern discourses concerning shifting and fragmented identities, the need to listen to otherness, as well as the fostering of concern for difference parallels recent psychoanalytic research on the multivalent psychic modes of subjectivity, intersubjectivity, social relations and culture more generally. From this angle, some have spoken of a *postmodernization of psychoanalysis*.[12] While postmodern psychoanalytic theory is emerging as a radical discourse both inside and outside of the academy, I think it is important to also stress the extent to which we can now speak of a *psychoanalysis of postmodernity*.[13] By using the term 'postmodernity' I mean to highlight the emergence of a social system in which a proliferation of media simulations, a radicalization of communication technology, a thoroughgoing globalization of economic and social activity, and a multiplication of world-views comes to dominate cultural relations. Although space precludes a detailed analysis of these socio-historical developments, there can be little doubt that psychoanalysis has contributed significantly to our understanding of the complex, contradictory ways in which self and society are reconfigured in the postmodern epoch. Very often this has been achieved through the mapping of psychoanalytic terminology onto processes of, say, decolonization or simulation in order to foster an appreciation of how postmodernism promotes an increasingly reflexive, differentiated culture. In other approaches and discourses, psychoanalysis has been used to explore the overt conflicts between modernity and postmodernity.

Over the past few decades, as this book graphically details, social theory has drawn profitably from Freud and psychoanalysis. Current developments in psychoanalytic research, I have suggested, are likely to influence debates in social theory and the social sciences on a range of issues – to do with subjectivity, intersubjectivity, sexuality, gender and cultural forms. It is my hope that *Social Theory and Psychoanalysis in Transition* provokes scholars and students engaged in this productive dialogue.

Introduction

How do human beings create a sense of self that is sustained, consolidated, and refashioned across time? What role does unconscious sexuality and phantasy play in this fabrication of the self? What are the relations between sexuality, gender-identity and forms of social power? How are we to understand the complex relations between self, society and contemporary modes of domination? How do the psyche and social field interlace? In critical social theory, in the current period, there is an immense interest in psychoanalysis as a basis for confronting, discussing and reframing these concerns. Psychoanalysis has inspired a fundamental transformation in social theory in respect of issues related to how forms of political domination and exploitation become interwoven with the constitution of the self. Yet although social theorists agree that these connections between desire and domination are a good deal more complex than was previously realized, there is a striking lack of consensus about how best to approach issues about the self and human subjectivity more generally. Contemporary debates in social theory and psychoanalysis exhibit a range of theoretical positions and interests – discourses which influence social and emancipatory critique in distinctly different ways. This book explores various theoretical perspectives on the relationship between the psyche and the contemporary social world and in particular considers the importance of psychoanalysis for opening new interpretative strategies for critical social theory in relation to the self, self-identity and subjectivity.

In general, this book is written in the belief that contemporary elaborations of social theory and psychoanalysis stand in need of a radical rethinking. To carry through such an endeavour, it is necessary to begin from a detailed appraisal of the work of those writers who have established the principal terms of reference for thinking about the interconnections between the psyche and social field. In this respect, the theoretical approaches of the critical theory of the Frankfurt School on the one hand, and Lacanian, post-Lacanian and other associated post-structuralist positions on the other, stand out as the most prominent intellectual and institutional evaluations of the

1

self and society. Indeed, they represent the two broadest program-matic approaches in social theory to these questions and issues. Through different political vocabularies of moral and emancipatory critique, these approaches highlight that modern social processes interconnect in complex and contradictory ways with unconscious experience and therefore with the self. The aim of this book is to analyse the interconnections posited by these approaches, to explore their key conceptual weaknesses, and to contribute to the task of rethinking how certain problems might be remedied. In this latter respect, I believe that my approach departs considerably from many existing works in the field.[1] In this introductory section, I shall briefly outline the theoretical standpoints I examine and summarize some of the central claims that are developed in this study.

The problem of human subjectivity, not as some pre-given substance but rather as a reflexively constituted project, has emerged as a fundamental issue in social theory at the turn of the twenty-first century. The postmodern celebration of the 'death of the subject' and arrival of a 'post-ideological condition', while fashionable for some time in certain quarters, are shown by current world events to be without the flimsiest political warrant. As several contemporary critics have argued, the postmodernist deconstruction of subjectivity as sheer difference and heterogeneity is in many respects an ideolog-ical ruse of the late capitalist economy itself, masking the complex and contradictory ways in which men and women seek to appropriate and exert control over the conditions of their lives.[2] Against the postmodern destruction of the principle of subjectivity, there is a conceptual need now, perhaps greater than ever, to develop a more realistic conception of the self and contemporary social experience, to reach a more differentiated and graduated account of human subjectivity, and to assess what enabling aspects of our subjecthood are of political value within today's social and institutional frame-works. In this connection, I argue, the theoretical import of psychoanalysis brooks large. While focusing on the fragmented qual-ities of human experience through the disruptive effects of unconscious desire, psychoanalysis also powerfully accounts for the critical reappropriation of meaning in social life. Representation, phantasy, identification, pleasure: these are the essential and primary foundations of all human social activity. The theory of the human subject proposed by the theory of the unconscious demonstrates that the psyche is forever thrown off-centre in relation to itself through its traumatic insertion into the socio-symbolic order of modern soci-eties. Yet from a social and political angle, this decentering of the subject is significant since it allows for a reflexive involvement with the self and others. The law of social relations is at once the source of the desiring subject and is actively reshaped by the creative dynamics of desire itself. And it is for this reason, I suggest, that the tracing out of the subject within psychoanalytic terms of reference is of signal importance for social thought. In the contemporary debates on the nature of human agency, on the possibilities for social and political transformation, and on modernity and postmodernism, the question of the nature of the psyche is essential for the analysis and understanding of human subjectivity.

The opening chapter on Freud and social theory argues for the relevance of psychoanalytic concepts to subjectivity and social processes, forming a framework of critique for the whole of the study. I argue that Freud's discovery of unconscious representation and affect, coupled with his examination of the anchoring of authority and domination at the heart of psychical life, makes psychoanalysis the most suggestive and provocative discourse on the 'deep conflicts' of the self currently available to social theory. In suggesting this, however, I also identify important theoretical limits in the psycho-analytic approach. Freud's social and cultural writings, however insightful some of his observations might be, were set within what now seem to be rather dubious sociological and anthropological frameworks that typified characteristics of nineteenth-century thought.[3] There is consequently a great deal in Freud's work that needs to be substantially revised or, in some cases, discarded alto-gether. The reductive status accorded to the social by Freud is of fundamental significance in this respect. Many of Freud's descrip-tions of social phenomena as deriving from psychical displacements, defences, and compensations tend toward a universalism which negates the social and historical specificity of self-identity. While Freud's characterization may be accurate from a psychical angle, his theoretical claims often ignore the point that the sublimation of desire only exists within a meaningfully demarcated area of culture that is created by society. It is a serious mistake, I argue, to conflate the psychic and social fields in such a way. Reality cannot be assumed as simply natural or given as Freud often implies (a position which unfortunately has been further advanced in Lacanian and post-structuralist theories), but is constituted through ideological power relations. The content of the reality principle, as Herbert Marcuse argues, is structured within the dominant social practices and political relations instituted by society. Similarly, the sexual stereotypes and biases that inform Freud's account of sexuality demand a radical deconstruction and critique. Thus, in several chapters, I discuss recent feminist criticism and reinterpretation of psychoanalytic theory in order better to conceptualize the constitu-tion of gender-identity and sexual division.

Notwithstanding these problems, I argue in Chapter 1 that Freud's work need not be formulated (though it undeniably has been in many social-theoretical reformulations) in a deterministic and ahistorical fashion. There are several features in my approach to rethinking Freud which need to be mentioned at this point. Very briefly, I argue that, while the concept of repression designates a major limit to the knowledgeability of human subjects, we can also see in the concept of the *primary unconscious* the basis for a creative and reflexive involvement with the self and self-identity. The primary unconscious, as discussed by Freud, is the key psychical mechanism through which human beings establish an imaginary relation with the self, others, received social meanings, and society.[4] Following the interpretation of Freud developed by Cornelius Castoriadis, I analyse the nature of the primary unconscious as an endless emergence of representational forms, drives, and affects – understood as an imaginary dimension of subjectivity, the dimension through which human beings create themselves anew and the potential shape of their society.[5] The import of this definition, to be elaborated in subsequent discussion, is of considerable significance when contrasted with other approaches to the unconscious in social theory. This is so, I believe, since it emphasizes that the unconscious creates in the fullest sense of the term (as self-imagination) and indicates that psychical reality cannot be reduced to more general determinations – as with currently popular notions of 'structure' and 'language'. The latter half of this opening chapter poses the problem of the connection between the individual psyche and the socio-symbolic order of modern societies. In examining the trajectories of the psyche's entry into society, I try to reframe the complexity and ambiguity of Freud's view that there is an internal connection between the dynamics of unconscious desire and the repression and domination of the social order. Central to this discussion is my claim that repressed desire is constituted at the intersection of force and meaning within the social-historical world.

Many theorists of advanced capitalist society argue that a persuasive feature of modern social life is its ever-increasing capacity to enmesh human subjects in destructive relations of power, in situations of conflict, in processes of domination. For the neo-Marxists of the Frankfurt School, everyday consciousness has become profoundly disfigured through the objectifying aspects of science, technology and bureaucracy. What is at stake with the advent of these manipulative pressures of the rationalized world of advanced capitalism, the Frankfurt School argue, is a major alteration in the way that human subjects are constituted. Some of the main features of this view are discussed in Chapter 2. There I present a relatively schematized account of the theories of Herbert Marcuse and Theodor Adorno, assessing their analyses of the fragmentation and destructive tendencies of the modern subject. By 'fragmentation' Marcuse and Adorno mean that the process of individuation is the result of an unconscious drive for self-preservation that paradoxically leads to the dissolution of the human subject's capability for autonomous and creative action. Indeed, the individual in modern times is increasingly left with only its narcissistic appearance, having repressed its subjectivity as other. In particular, attention is devoted in this chapter to the view developed by Marcuse and Adorno that the self is brought under a self-regulated system of totalitarian control, engulfed within the heightening force of a hegemonic ideology. Through a consideration of the theory of internalization, upon which their analyses of the fragmentation of the subject are founded, I show that their argument is highly problematic in several respects. Among other things I contend that Marcuse's and Adorno's view of subjectivity and self-identity is unduly narrow and restrictive, premised as it is upon a rather dubious interpretation of the Oedipus complex and trapped within a dualist framework of subject and object. While Marcuse's and Adorno's account of the destructive transformation of the self in modernity is powerful, I argue that it fails to capture the complex and often contradictory ways in which repressive forms of self-identity are put into question, refashioned and changed.

Despite this rather gloomy analysis of how subjectivity becomes retrogressive in modernity, the Frankfurt School has invoked psychoanalysis as an important strategy for emancipatory critique. Central to these concerns is a conceptual focus on the repressed needs, dispositions and desires of human beings as prefigurative of an alternative social order. On this view, the desires and beliefs which human subjects currently hold, however illusory or distorted, are not taken to be discontinuous with the transformation of self and society. Chapter 3 examines some of the psychoanalytic themes that are developed in contemporary critical theory to support this emancipatory critique. It offers an outline of Marcuse's imaginative proposal that the contours of an alternative social rationality are already prefigured in the hidden depths of the unconscious – emerging surreptitiously in 'the return of the repressed' – and takes up a critical dialogue about the role of repressed sexuality in political communication. The chapter then turns to consider the thematically related work of Jürgen Habermas, examining the conceptual shift in critical theory from instrumental domination to the distorting effects of symbolic interaction, or what Habermas now calls 'communicative action'. There I try to unravel the main threads of Habermas's linguistic critique of the subject, analysing his incorporation of theories ranging from Anglo-American ego psychology to Alfred Lorenzer's work on distorted communication. In distilling the limits of an internal integration of reason and desire through communicational praxis, I link recent feminist and psychoanalytic appraisals of Habermas's work to certain problems confronting the transformation of the self in modern society.

Many analysts recognize that the study of language as it impacts upon the psyche involves more than a purely intersubjective dimension: it is a formal, structuring power that actually constitutes the human subject and the shape of desire. For Jacques Lacan, the *structure* of language is what founds the repressed unconscious, the speaking subject being grounded upon those metonymic substitutions around which desire forever circulates. The work of Lacan, which has had an immense influence upon current social and cultural criticism, is addressed in Chapter 4. This chapter provides an exegesis of Lacan's account of the imaginary – that it is the inevitable 'loss' and 'lack' of psychical life which generates imaginary constructions of concealment. In outlining Lacan's theory of the 'mirror stage', I focus on the double function of the imaginary to conceal an ontological 'lack' and to constitute the self through processes of misrecognition. I then examine Lacan's influential reformulation of the conscious/unconscious dualism as a linguistic relation – his axiom that 'the unconscious is structured like a language' – as the basis for a symbolic order instituting sexual difference, individuation, meaning and phallic law. In the latter half of this chapter, I offer a series of critical observations on both of these aspects of Lacan's work. Through a review of contemporary debates on Lacan's notion of specular selfhood, I argue that not only is his account of the imaginary inadequate, failing to capture the active psychical processes through which the self is formed, but also that his account has no conceptual grasp of the complexity and creativity of human subjectivity. Against the ontological primacy that Lacan grants to 'lack', I try to show that all forms of absence and loss can only be registered *through* the unconscious imaginary. 'Lack' as such does not predetermine subjectivity; rather it is the imaginary dimensions of psychical life which create a relation to 'loss' and 'lack'. I also call into question Lacan's application of structural linguistics to the unconscious. Reviewing Freud's theory of the primary processes, as well as Jean-François Lyotard's critique of Lacan, I argue that the basic structures of language are entirely different in scope from unconscious representation. These considerations are of considerable importance to rethinking the impact of the social field upon the psyche, I argue, since Lacan's structuralist method makes no room for the historical and cultural relativity of the law, nor for its political reformulation in less repressive forms.

Whatever the conceptual shortcomings of Lacan's work, the idea that the autonomous ego of humanist thought is actually a narcissistic imaginary construct has been taken up by many social and political theorists in recent decades. Chapter 5 assesses these developments in social theory, critically analysing the application of Lacanian thought to the study of ideology, politics and cultural reproduction. The chapter reviews Louis Althusser's application of Lacan's category of the imaginary to the notion of ideology, focusing on how the dominant ideologies of modern societies are reproduced and sustained. In examining Althusser's exploration of the relations between desire, language and ideology, I extend my criticisms of the Lacanian arguments upon which they rest. Among other things I contend that Althusser's structuralist approach to the unconscious seriously downplays the contradictory features of human passion within ideological struggle, and spuriously extends one particular mode of self-identity to all forms of self constitution in modern culture. If Althusser applies Lacan's doctrines to ideology in particular, Ernesto Laclau, Chantal Mouffe and Slovoj Žižek apply it to the social field in general. Extending the Lacanian notion of the imaginary as a narcissistic concealment of 'lack' that is always doomed to failure, these writers argue that society and all symbolic forms must be critically deconstructed as attempts to deny the antagonistic structure which is at the heart of cultural forms. In considering this argument, the chapter develops a critical assessment of their deployment and extension of Lacanian concepts – such as the notion of the real order, the function of 'suture' within the imaginary, the concept of antagonism – for the analysis of ideology and political domination. I argue that, despite the provocative nature of their concerns, their theory of subjectivity and desire remains unconvincing, presenting an account of social relations which is as sweeping as it is unfounded within specific political contexts.

The question of sexual division and the sex/gender distinction is one that remains highly problematic for social theory. The mainstream sociological view that a culturally constructed sex role is added to biological gender – through socializing influences such as parents, education, the media, and so on – is weak in explaining both sexual 'deviations' and how sexual identities come to change across time. Psychoanalysis has considerably enhanced our understanding of these issues by drawing attention to the complex links between the unconscious formation of psycho-sexuality and the broader encompassing influences of society. In this respect, the Lacanian premise of a symbolic, paternal law (the Name-of-the-Father) which structures all linguistic signification and gender identity has decisively influenced the terms of debate for feminist concerns with our unequal sexual world. In Chapter 6 I critically examine the current psychoanalytic feminist dialogue with Lacanian theory, particularly the French post-Lacanian feminist theories of sexual difference. To situate the relevance of Lacanian doctrine in relation to issues of gender, the chapter reviews the first major arguments for psychoanalytic feminist theory developed in the English-speaking world by Juliet Mitchell. I argue that Mitchell's use of Lacanian theory for an account of gender relations is ultimately problematic since she presents the repressive force of the symbolic as a monolithic structure, generating a static view of sexual relations and society as its result. The chapter then considers the writings of Luce Irigaray and Hélène Cixous, outlining their critical feminist deconstruction of the psychoanalytic account of sexuality. I argue that, while rightly focusing on those implicit assumptions of psychoanalytic discourse which reinforce gender hierarchies, their approach fails adequately to explore the repressive construction of sexual division because of the residual essentialism in their work. The remainder of this chapter is devoted to the work of Julia Kristeva, whose theory of the semiotic dimension of language offers an interesting critique of Lacanian premises concerning the determination of gender in modern culture. As an order of affects derived from the primary relationship to the maternal body, the semiotic for Kristeva is an ongoing source of subversion within the symbolic order. Yet while exposing the shortcomings of the Lacanian symbolic as a universal, monolithic effect of language as such, I try to show that Kristeva's account of the sources of self-transgression remains ultimately bound to the repressive language system which she seeks to question and undermine.

The foregoing introductory comments anticipate what I shall argue are the central problems that need to be addressed in social theory and psychoanalysis. To develop a more adequate account of the interconnections between the psyche and culture it is necessary to reconnect human subjectivity to the social and historical contexts in which it emerges. It is necessary to consider in detail the nature of the psychical development of the individual subject, of the considerable problems inherent in the transformation of the relations between the unconscious and consciousness, without presuming in advance that the self is a 'derivative' construct. It is necessary to consider the complex processes through which the individual subject opens out to a self, to others, to social reality, to existential issues and to collective moral questions. In contrast to much contemporary theory, it is necessary to consider in some other way the nature of unconscious representation in relation to drives and affects; not as substitutes for an ontological 'lack', but as the productive basis of subjectivity, the imagination, and self-transformation. It is necessary to consider realistically how the figuration of the law of human relationships interlaces with the social, political and historical realities of the global world order in which we now live. This list of concerns is a formidable one, and I certainly do not want to claim that they can be resolved easily. But daunting though such a rethinking may be, I do argue that this enterprise need not lead to a return of the 'autonomous ego' – as many post-structuralist and postmodernist thinkers seem to think – but rather to a critical re-evaluation of the relationship between subjectivity and desire. The broad purpose of this book is to contribute to such a re-evaluation which, although informed by ideas drawn from the approaches analysed, differs from them in a substantive way.

In this respect, a fundamental theme which I try to develop in this book is the productive foundation of the imaginary in human subjectivity and its parallel role in social life more generally. The idea that the imaginary is a derived phenomenon, an endlessly multiplying network of mirrors without psychic interiority or depth, is probably the pre-eminent outlook in current discussions of the self and postmodernity. For postmodern thinkers, the self is little more than image, simulacrum, blank fiction. On a psychoanalytical plane, this view is endorsed by the Lacanian argument that the imaginary is an *illusion*, a narcissistic misrecognition deriving from the inevitability of the other as 'mirror'. Similarly, in the approach of the Frankfurt School, the imaginary is seen as an 'effect' of some anonymous system of technological reproduction, structured through the organizing principles of advanced capitalist society. I think that such a judgement of the role of the imaginary is quite wrong. To see another human being as merely an 'object' or 'thing' (the depersonalization of which the Frankfurt School speak), or to see the self as 'signifier' and subjected to the hegemonic force of the law (as argued by Lacanians and post-Lacanians), requires not a closing down of the imaginary but an *extension* of it. While the unconscious imaginary is enmeshed within destructive political relations of power and force, it derives from an order of representations that cannot be understood on the basis of the social field alone. The imaginary nature of the unconscious, as I try to show, is at once a constitutive source of human practice and agency, as well as a force locating human subjects within unacknowledged conditions of action through the barrier of repression. It represents on the one hand a fundamental basis of innovation and creativity, and on the other an inscription of the subject within the oppression and domination of the social order.

Against the currently fashionable view that the unconscious is a linguistic system which can be deconstructed through formal logic, I argue that a critical conception of repressed desire must return to certain traditional paths and emphases as outlined in Freud's theory of the psyche. The unconscious, I want to claim, is a matter of individual and collective 'representational activity' rather than of 'language' – the productive effect of representational forms, drives and affects. As the *other side of language*, the unconscious plays a central organizing role in the constitution and reproduction of subjectivity within contemporary power relations and social interests. But it is not therefore to be seen as some passive by-product of the social field. The relations between psychical reality and social interests are complex, contradictory ones, in which unconscious dynamics work to process and transform ideological relations of the social field through condensation, displacement, and reversals of affect. It is necessary to think through how this unconscious order of representation intersects with modern social processes, this time through some other framework than a monolithic law which subjugates individuals either through the formal devices of 'language' or as an effect of the 'administered world'.

In general, I argue throughout the study that an adequate theory of the psyche and social field should seek to comprehend three central points. It should recognize (1) that the nature of the unconscious is a constitutive imaginary dimension of psychical life and subjectivity, a dimension through which the subject 'opens out' to the self, others, reason and society; (2) that on an individual and collective plane, human subjects are never passively 'shaped' by the symbolic forms of society, but actively receive such significations and creatively reconstitute them through representational activity; and (3) that the reception of symbolic forms takes place within specific social and ideological relations of domination and power.

A possible source of confusion about the imaginary and creation as it interconnects with self and society needs to be clarified at this point. The creative self-making of society, which I shall argue derives central impetus from the primary unconscious, cannot itself determine the political and ethical values which are instantiated through such creations. If the late modern world has extended the possibilities for self-development through the creation of a global world order, mass communications, and new forms of personal relations and sexuality, it has also radically extended the boundaries of human misery and destruction.[6] The possibilities of total annihilation through nuclear holocaust, the looming threat of ecological disaster, the brutal repressiveness of many political regimes – these too are created products of our contemporary experience. Yet if it is the case that the imaginary creations of the self and society can be carved out in such counterproductive ways, it is still necessary to insist that the 'openness' of collective possibilities, and the enactment of a desirable future, can only emerge against the backdrop of the imaginary capacity of human beings for critical reflection and self-transgression. Such a conception of the imaginary as a process of self-transformation gives rise to a number of important political and ethical issues which will be discussed in the concluding chapter.

This book does not claim to be the first to point to the more creative and active features of the imaginary and human subjectivity as it interconnects with the social-historical world. The positions of Cornelius Castoriadis and Julia Kristeva in psychoanalytic social theory, Paul Ricoeur, Manfred Frank and Richard Kearney in philosophy, and Anthony Giddens in sociology, to list only a few writers, all focus (in very different theoretical ways) on the constitutive and creative dimensions of subjectivity in relation to questions of social and historical research. My aim is rather to focus on those points of intersection between subjectivity, the unconscious and modern social processes as developed in social theory, to identify problems and gaps in the existing approaches, and to contribute to a more adequate theory of the connections between the psyche and social field.

Thus, to summarize the threefold purpose of this book:

1. To serve as a critical introduction to some fundamental concepts and issues in social theory and psychoanalysis, focusing upon developments in contemporary critical theory, Lacanian and post-Lacanian thought, the theories of structuralism and post-structuralism and feminist appropriations of psychoanalysis.
2. In general, to insist that the interconnections between the psyche and social field, the self and society, have not yet been formulated in an adequate fashion, and must be substantially rethought.
3. To contribute to the task of reformulating key problems in social theory and psychoanalysis, developing an approach sufficiently alert and sensitive to the psychological processes of the self and human social relationships, deployments of ideology and power, and the analysis of sexuality and gender divisions. In this connection, I argue that social theory must recognize, as it has not done hitherto, that the nature of the unconscious is a constitutive and creative source of human subjectivity.

1 Subjectivity and the Discourse of Psychoanalysis

Freud and Social Theory

This chapter traces three central themes in Freudian psychoanalysis: the nature of the unconscious, the formation of selfhood and the structure of the social order more generally. The various attempts this century to connect a critical theory of society with Freudian psychoanalysis have articulated the problematic of posing mediations between social phenomena and our psychic, more 'private' experience. While few today would want to claim strict adherence to Freud's solution of the dialectic between individual desire and the social-historical world, his formulations of this dilemma, and his more general discoveries, strongly pervade a number of major traditions of social and political thought. That this should be the case is not surprising. Traditional philosophical and sociological problems concerning the genesis of the self, the nature of subjectivity and its relation to the social world, the interconnections between reason and desire and the like are theorized in Freudian psychoanalysis in an illuminating and provocative fashion. In its archaeology of the human subject, Freudian psychoanalysis seeks to address the multifarious ways in which psychic space is organized, and thereby constituted, in society. The mnemic trace, the return of the repressed, the persistence of drives and affects, the nature of phantasy and representation: these are all part of the dialectical field of psychical and material reality. It is in seeking to capture the structure and form of this dialectic that social theory acknowledges a Freudian debt.

Psychoanalysis begins but does not end with Freud. Its subsequent development is extremely rich and diverse. Theoretical revisions, schools, and critiques have developed as strongly in psychoanalytic theory, if not more so, than in other traditions of thought. But despite conceptual innovations and discoveries, Freud's work remains the creative point of inspiration for clinicians and theorists alike. The major theorists in social and political theory who have engaged with psychoanalysis have similarly drawn on Freud. As such, while we will have occasion to consider the impact of more recent psychoanalytic research in subsequent discussion, this chapter is essentially concerned with elucidating the Freudian framework. In beginning with a review of Freud's work, however, there lurks a somewhat more ambitious aim. There are the foundations of a system of social theory to be *recovered* from Freudian psychoanalysis. This system cannot be discerned, however, merely through an appropriation of Freud's cultural and social writings, which has been the dominant approach of most sociologists in the English-speaking world.[1] The attempt to separate Freud's cultural studies from his analytic texts has sprung largely from the intellectual division in labour in the social sciences: from a psychologism that reduces social constellations to individual fantasy and experience (without questioning the nature of these categories themselves) and from a sociologism that liquidates the individual in a supra-individual sociology. This tendency towards reductionism finds its articulation in modes of social thought, in both Marxist and non-Marxist versions, which treat historical contexts as 'overtly social facts', and in conventional psychoanalytic criticism which proceeds as if it had no interest in the social world. But such crude distinctions between what is properly social and cultural and what is not is more than just some sort of conceptual error – it is a reinforcement of the experiential gap between the private and public, the psychological and social, the individual and history, through which modernity unfolds. It is my view that a more sensitive approach is required to overcome these traditional dualisms. Accordingly, in this chapter, I plan to situate Freudian psychoanalysis in an interdisciplinary texture, seeking to restore the contexts of its historical claims.

According to Freud, unconscious desire is the organizing principle of all human thought, action, and social relations. In order to appreciate fully the significance of this fundamental tenet of psychoanalysis, it is necessary to have some perspective on the theoretical principles and basic concepts of Freudian theory. While the account of Freud's work given here cannot but be partial and selective, my aim is to provide a detailed explication of the complex and intricate relations between subjectivity and the unconscious. I shall begin the chapter with a brief summary of Freud's theory of the nature of the unconscious. Here I will introduce many of the central concepts that will occupy our attention in subsequent discussions: Freud's models of the psyche, the concept of repression, and of representation and phantasy. After this overview, I shall try to show that, while demonstrating that a bar of repression is instituted with the formation of the human subject, Freud's work also emphasizes that the unconscious is a *constitutive* and *creative* feature of subjectivity. I shall trace the evolution of Freud's writings on the notion of the ego, locating his formulations within the broader problematic of self-identity and gender relations. Finally, I shall sketch the contours of Freud's view that the relation between the self and systems of domination are actually grounded in the dynamics of unconscious desire itself. It should be said at the outset that, in what follows, no attempt will be made to develop a critical appraisal of these tenets of psychoanalysis. The place for a critical analysis of psychoanalytic precepts for the purposes of social and political theory must be deferred until subsequent chapters. Rather, the overview of Freudian psychoanalysis provided here forms a backcloth for the critical examination of the social-theoretical contributions contained in this study.

The Unconscious: Representation, Drives, Affects

The discovery of the *mode* of unconscious psychic processes lies at the centre of Freud's most profound contribution to the analysis of human subjectivity. Of course many thinkers before Freud had recognized that there is more to psychic life than that which is readily available to consciousness. Philosophers such as Fichte, Schopenhauer and Nietzsche had all referred to an unconscious, though only in a general and unspecific manner: as natural will. And, as Freud so often stressed, it had been the romantic poets who first asserted the fundamental power of unconscious desire in their portraits of subjectivity. Rather, Freud's original and essential contribution is to be found in his specifications of a critical conception of the unconscious as *repressed*. Time and again, Freud makes plain that there is an unending dialectic of psychical conflict between repression and the surreptitious ways in which unconscious representations press toward expression. Largely by means of dissimulation and dispersal, this return of the repressed most subtly occurs in our everyday activities: in jokes, forgetting, parapraxes (the Freudian 'slip'). The unconscious is an important starting place, then, for a consideration of the import of the Freudian corpus for social theory, as it is this aspect of psychoanalysis that directly challenges the emphasis in Western thought on the power of reason and rationality, of reflective and conscious control over the self. In stressing the pervasiveness of unconscious processes, Freud effected a transition of major importance for the reflection of subjectivity: namely, in taking the individual subject to a moment in which forces exert a pressure without its knowledge. But while the psyche is forever thrown off-centre in relation to itself in Freud's theory, it is within the unconscious that we also find the essential well-springs of creativity, imagination and human agency. According to Freud, unconscious representations are symbolic wish-fulfilments, and as such constitute a realm of dynamic imaginary production. The following remarks are primarily concerned with elucidating this aspect of the *creativity of the psyche* in Freud's writings. To clarify my argument, I shall begin by considering Freud's concept of the unconscious and then proceed from this to his concern with the nature of psychical representation.

The unconscious, Freud wrote, is unaware of contradiction, time, or closure.[2] Indeed, it is blissfully and remorselessly untroubled by the demands of reality. Fully subversive of the world of reason and common sense, the unconscious is concerned only with the enactment of pleasure. 'The unconscious', as Freud remarks, 'is unable to do anything but wish'.[3] As we shall see, the forms by which this wishing is realized are many-sided. For the moment it is merely noted that even these opening comments on the unconscious are rather bad news for traditional sociological and philosophical thought, which imagines the individual subject to be in a state of informed and conscious control over the 'self'. As the realm of primary negation, the unconscious poses its own rather peculiar difficulties for individual and social analysis. In an essay written in 1911, Freud comments:

> The strongest characteristic of unconscious (repressed) processes, to which no investigator can become accustomed without the exercise of great self-discipline, is due to their entire disregard of reality-testing; they equate reality of thought with external reality, and wishes with their fulfilment ... [Thus] one must never allow oneself to be misled into applying the standards of reality to repressed psychical structures.[4]

This priority that Freud accords to psychical reality over the object-world has led to a popular misconception that the unconscious is a deeply hidden or mysterious place. The view that repressed psychical structures are to be found in a hidden area of the self, however, is defective. 'The unconscious', as Juliet Mitchell writes, 'is knowable and it is normal'.[5] Freud himself states this quite plainly in the essay cited above, 'Two principles of mental functioning'. The unconscious, he comments, contains thoughts and representations which are distinguished from consciousness by virtue of being transformed by the operations of the *primary processes*. The notion that unconscious thoughts and intentions are subjected to the workings of the 'primary processes', as contrasted with the 'secondary processes' of the conscious psyche, was first formulated by Freud in 1895, in his *Project for a Scientific Psychology*. In this early mapping of the psyche,

Freud holds that the primary processes run through the operations of the unconscious, in which energy is conceived as unbounded, flowing easily from one representation to another. By the free-floating condition of such energy, the psyche is able to invest representations with the fulfilment of unconscious desire. In effect, then, this hypothesized energy is the principal source from which pleasure is attained. Such unconscious satisfaction is in explicit contrast to the 'preconscious-conscious system', in which a bounded psychic energy is said to give rise to the workings of cognitive thinking. Stabilized through the 'postponement' of direct pleasure, the cognitive and reflective dimensions of consciousness increasingly develop in a systematic fashion with the surrender of the pleasure principle to the reality principle. According to Freud, this 'surrender' is itself a kind of decoy however. The primary processes only defer immediate pleasure in order to achieve a more stable and consistent type of pleasure. From this angle, unconscious desire is always at work, in search of fulfilment. A love or hate born and repressed in early childhood can remain as alive today as from the time it first originated. Thus Freud's crucial point is that, while the secondary processes of consciousness are vital to the constitution of the self, the pressure of the primary processes is always there, rising out of the unconscious.

I have said that the unconscious for Freud is extraneous to reality, but this now needs to be qualified somewhat. For if on one level the unconscious is fully resistant to reality, concerned only with the search for pleasure, this is so since at another level it is deeply entwined with the needs of the human body, the nature of external reality and actual social relations. Indeed, one of Freud's most subversive moves is to demonstrate that the individual subject only comes into being through an ambivalent repression – at once psychic and social – of its own libidinal drives, thoughts and feelings. In the Freudian vision, it is this repression of desire which is constitutive of the formation of the 'human subject', embedded within the dominant structures of social and political relations. Yet it is important to note that Freud's view is not simply a reworking of the traditionally conservative view that human society forbids the expression of individual impulses and desires in the name of collective order and harmony, as in the philosophy of Hobbes. From Freud's analytic perspective, psychical space is constituted through a splitting and repression which is the result of its own creation. In contrast to the classical view that self-identity is a transcendental datum, Freud's contention is that psychic reality is only slowly and rather precariously given structure and organization.

What is central to this constitution of the psyche for Freud is the radical disjunction between the instincts for self-preservation and the

emergence of sexual drives. (This disjunction is complicated termi-
nologically since Freud employed the German word *Trieb* to denote
drives, yet the editors of the English *Standard Edition* translate this as
'instinct' – thus propagating the sort of biological conception of motivation that Freud's theory of the drives actually opposes. Following
recent psychoanalytic commentary, *Trieb* is translated as 'drive'
throughout this study.) For Freud, what the birth of the 'premature'
human infant most decisively signals is the total dependence on our
caretakers, especially the mother, for the satisfaction of our biologically fixed needs. And it is the universal existence of nutritional and
physical need that leads him to posit an instinct for self-preservation.
Freud's radical insight, however, lies in the assertion that the formation of unconscious desire and sexuality is not determined by such
physical needs. Sexuality, on Freud's reckoning, is not there from the
beginning. It must be formed. Thus, the unconscious emerges out of,
yet is *severed* from, biological need. The exemplary psychoanalytic
case is the human infant sucking at its mother's breast. After the
biological need for milk is satisfied, Freud notes, the desire for
pleasure derived from sucking continues. The human infant halluci-
nates a phantasy of the pleasure derived from this original
satisfaction. This is said to form a basis for subsequent psychical
productions. As Freud develops this, 'The baby's obstinate persistence in sucking gives evidence at an early stage of a need for
satisfaction which, though it originates from and is instigated by the
taking of nourishment, nevertheless strives to obtain pleasure inde-
pendently of nourishment and for that reason may and should be
termed *sexual*.'[6] In deriving pleasure from the oral 'erotogenic zone',
Freud argues that a new libidinal relation with the *other* (which is
usually the biological mother) arises. Sexuality is born. The form that
this psycho-sexuality takes will be crucial to the subject's later
psychical productions and elaborations. Moreover, as we shall see,
such desires will repeatedly run up against social mediations, other
persons and objects.

     For Freud, what this gradual organization of libidinal drives refers
to are the 'dynamic' aspects of the unconscious. From an interplay of
forces, unconscious desire is born through separating out from bodily
needs toward more pleasurable goals. Veering away from the instincts
of self-preservation, the unconscious begins that repetition of the first
sensual pleasures experienced in early life, achieved through the
production of phantasy. But what, exactly, is the result of this 'veering
away' of desire in Freud's model of the psyche? What does it suggest,
in particular, about the contents of the psyche and, more generally,
how does this pertain to the question of the human subject? In order
to take up these questions, and to defend the notion that there is a

sector of the psyche that is radically distinct from conscious thought-processes, let us turn to examine the systematic arguments Freud sets out on these issues in his metapsychological papers.

The 'metapsychology' refers to Freud's account of basic mental processes. In his celebrated essay 'The unconscious', written in 1915, Freud begins an explanatory account of the unconscious by referring to those subjective or phenomenological experiences of psychic life that elude conscious intention and control.[7] In outlining this 'justification for the concept of the unconscious', Freud points to the large number of gaps in the field of consciousness, to the way the mind often resonates with ideas and thoughts that come from a place unknown. Referring to those contents which are not present in immediate consciousness, this is Freud's descriptive sense of the concept: the unconscious as adjective. The movement from a description of psychic acts that are only latent, temporarily unconscious, to a systematic use of the unconscious occurs when he considers clinical phenomena such as the symptoms of hysteria, neurotic disturbances and the transference: these being mental activities in which 'strong unconscious ideas' exert a determining influence. From these considerations, Freud divides his first topography of the psyche into the unconscious, preconscious and conscious. The preconscious realm, from a descriptive point of view, is actually unconscious; yet it is radically distinct from Freud's conception of *the* unconscious since its contents are not repressed. Like the more common-sense understanding of something unconscious, the preconscious system is a kind of vast storehouse of memories, any of which may be recalled at will. By contrast, unconscious thoughts for Freud are distinguished since they are 'cut off' or are 'buried' from consciousness. The most important (though often neglected) feature of Freud's topography, then, is that the unconscious is constructed not as 'another' consciousness but as a separate psychical system with its own distinct processes and mechanisms. That is to say, Freud's account of the unconscious posits representations that are prevented access to consciousness by forces that block their reception. The unconscious, Freud remarks, cannot be known directly. It is only discernible through its effects – through the distortions it inflicts on consciousness.

From this topographical division of the psyche, Freud constructs the following account of the individual subject's internal conflicts. Bluntly put, unconscious desire leads to the mental representation of a libidinal drive which, in turn, encounters the resistance of consciousness (the ego's defence mechanisms) when these wishes are registered as being too painful or incompatible with the demands of external reality. Charged with the memory of unpleasurable feeling, the result of our 'premature' insertion into the symbolic order, the subject seeks to bar such associations from entering consciousness. This operation, of course, is known as repression and it is crucial to Freud's account of desire. 'The repressed', as Freud remarks, 'is the prototype of the unconscious'.[8] The amount of repression that human beings are able to sustain depends on many factors, such as the subject's inner world, psychic creativity and – though only implicitly suggested by Freud – their place within the structure of social and economic relationships. One thing of which Freud is quite certain, however, is that human beings are only prepared to tolerate repression as long as deferred unconscious pleasure is granted the possibility of a more durable and lasting gratification. In deconstructing any strict opposition between the pleasure principle and the reality principle, Freud's central point is that too much repression leads inexorably towards neurosis and unhappiness. In probing the causes of much of the disillusionment and disenchantment of the modern era, as we shall see in subsequent chapters, this suggestive insight has been of immense significance for social and political theory.

According to Freud, 'the essence of repression lies in simply turning something away, and keeping it at a distance, from the conscious'.[9] Here Freud distinguishes between two types of repression. The first is 'primal repression', which operates prior to any rejection of unacceptable thoughts or ideas. It is in and through primary repression that drives find mental representation, a point we will shortly consider when examining the creativity of the psyche. Second, this primary repressed material forms an unconscious nucleus which acts as a force of attraction to further connected associations and representations.[10] This is what Freud terms 'repression proper', or 'after-pressure', in which new representations become linked with, and organized around, the originally repressed material. That is, materials currently available to consciousness will *undergo* repression because they trigger associations in the repressed unconscious. This second phase of repression is particularly important, as it suggests that the unconscious is not 'static' but is rather highly 'dynamic'. As an elusive and unlocatable force, unconscious thoughts are said to develop at an acutely menacing pace, motivating behaviour and social activity in largely overdetermined ways. Indeed, Freud's account of these phases of repression has been appropriated as an allegory for the entire structure of social practice. The concept of repression has been of crucial significance in social theory for analysing the subjective forms in which oppressive social practices are reproduced and sustained. In the critical theory of the Frankfurt School, as will be discussed in Chapters 2 and 3, repression designates both intrapsychic and social processes – the latter field contributing to what Herbert Marcuse has called 'surplus repression'. In contrast, Lacanian and post-structuralist theories understand by the process of repression a more universal subjection of the subject, constituted by the structure of language. These divergences, as I try to show in subsequent chapters, are matters of serious controversial dispute in modern social theory.

Repression, then, is the foundation of the theory of the unconscious. Yet while all repressed material is unconscious, unconscious processes are not coterminous with that which is repressed. The function of repression certainly consists in cutting off thoughts and feelings from consciousness, but it does not bar them from their psychical representatives. As Freud comments, 'the process of repression lies, not in putting an end to, in annihilating, the idea which represents a drive, but in preventing it from becoming conscious'.[11] In this connection, the primary unconscious is of particular significance. As indicated above, primal repression in Freud's theory is the constitutive bonding of a drive to a psychical representation, the point of fixation being established in the individual's prehistory. The unconscious in this sense can be said to exist as a condition of subjectivity; it is the basis from which consciousness emerges. Let us look at these points concerning the primary unconscious in a little more detail.

It is in phantasy and its related imaginary formations that Freud finds the essential 'mechanisms' which constitute the primary unconscious. The 'royal road' to observing these mechanisms is dreams, originally analysed by Freud in his magisterial book *The Interpretation of Dreams* in 1900. Dreams have a privileged place in Freud's corpus as they offer a particularly rich glimpse of the meaningful symbolic productions of the unconscious. According to Freud, one can discern in dreams the dynamics of desire since specific unconscious thoughts will search for a fulfilment which they have been unable to attain in waking life. Attaching to some aspect of the silt of our daily experience and social activity, the unconscious will bring its own distinct modes of functioning to bear upon certain (pre)conscious thoughts, in order to achieve imaginary satisfaction. This imaginary fulfilment attained in dreams arises not from some chance play of psychical life, but from a specifically elaborated relation between unconscious drives and representation. The nature of this relation, Freud comments, is governed by a force that is 'indestructible' – the earliest wishes and fixations arising from our childhood. As Freud formulates this expression of wishes realized in the unconscious: 'A dream is a (disguised) fulfilment of a (suppressed or repressed) wish.'[12] This entwinement of force and meaning, to paraphrase

Freud, necessitates a strategy of analysis that is free from the common-sense assumptions of day-to-day life. Dreams, and the unconscious more generally, must be analysed as a *work*, a production of meaning that follows complex and strange rules. The dream thoughts themselves, Freud insists, differ in no special way from waking life. The essence of the unconscious, rather, consists in the 'dream-work', which, as representational activity, 'is completely different [from waking thought] qualitatively and for that reason not immediately comparable with it. It does not think, calculate or judge in any way at all; it restricts itself to giving things a new form.'[13] Freud designates this work of transformation as a *distortion*, a violence done to conscious meaning. What is peculiar to the unconscious as a psychical system is that it violently deforms, disfigures, or disguises meaning into something unrecognizable.

Distortion, then, is a key force through which the unconscious transforms and produces psychical representation. Crucial to this distorting force are four key unconscious mechanisms: condensation (*Verdichtung*), displacement (*Verschiebung*), considerations of representation (*Rucksicht auf Darstellbarkeit*), and secondary revision (*Sekundare Bearbeitung*). It is through these mechanisms that the fluid pressures of the primary processes search for the fulfilment of unconscious desire, sometimes with meaning being compressed or reduced into a single thought, and sometimes dislocated onto what appears to be an unimportant or trivial thought. These unconscious techniques of displacing and condensing, Freud argues, indicate the existence of an 'overdetermination' of some thoughts and feelings by others. The unconscious elements of our subjective life are thus inseparable from certain 'compromise formations' – a set of overdeterminations which license idiosyncratic ways of relating to the self, to others and to society. The production of these overdetermined forms, however, crucially depends upon what Freud describes as the 'considerations of representation'. It is here that the profoundly imaginary dimensions of the unconscious are most emphasized by Freud. There is no doubt that for Freud the transformative work of the unconscious – distortion, condensation, displacement – can only take place through a delegation of the drive through representation (*Vorstellungsreprasentanz des Triebes*). What this means, essentially, is that in order to attain psychical expression the libidinal drives must pass through a representational process which lends itself to a *forming of images* as a *hallucinatory fulfilment*. We shall come back to this aspect of representation shortly. For our present purposes it is important to highlight that the work of representation produces a fulfilment of desire, regardless of whether this promotes certain amounts of conscious gratification on the one hand or suffering and punishment

on the other. For Freud, what characterizes unconscious representation is this combining of forms, meaning and pleasure. Whatever the
difficulties and trials of everyday life, there is something in the representations of the unconscious that find an eternal fulfilment – which
is the very point of interrelation between representation, affect and
the pleasure principle. It is thus possible to show, through a careful
reading of Freud's theory of representation, that a whole set of
contemporary ideological oppositions – between commerce and
pleasure, masculine and feminine, the central and marginal, the practical and aesthetic – are potentially open to the dislocation of the
unconscious.

To review the foregoing arguments. Freudian psychoanalysis
vividly demonstrates that the conscious knowledgability of human
actors is 'bounded' by repressed psychical structures, by the
'dynamic' unconscious. Freud shows the human subject, split and
fractured by unconscious desire, to be forever thrown off-center from
itself. In general, as we shall see, recent attempts to incorporate the
unconscious for a theory of the subject have stressed this aspect of
consciousness as repressed or deferred. Human experience and
autonomy are to a large extent underwritten by the determining
influence of repression. Not surprisingly, many theories tend to treat
subjectivity as a surface phenomenon, an entity whose real origins lie
elsewhere – such as the focus on the 'administered society' in critical
theory and 'language' in Lacanian and post-structuralist thought.
Against such determinism, however, we have seen that the primary
unconscious both initiates the primal repression and is constituted as
repression. From this angle, the unconscious is not repressed in the
simple, everyday sense of the term, but is rather a complex and
differentiated 'bonding' or 'sedimentation' of libidinal drives to
representations. In the notion of representation, I want to argue, we
have the key to understanding the constitutive and creative dimensions of psychical reality. It must be stressed, however, that due to
the nature of the primary processes, the most basic structures of
waking thought are powerless before unconscious representation.
The analysis of representation requires a shift in perspective that
critical social theory has generally failed to achieve. In the remainder
of this section, let us turn to consider Freud's account of representation in more detail.

As I have suggested, the term 'representation' in Freud's thought
designates the psychical expression of a drive. That is, drives can only
be 'represented' in the unconscious through something psychical.
Even at this stage, however, it is vitally important not to confuse the
nature of representation with an 'idea' of consciousness – which, as
we shall see, is an essential problem with the Lacanian emphasis on

'signifiers' at the level of the unconscious. For, on Freud's reckoning, an idea is itself a *product* of the work of representation. The nature of representation consists rather in an indeterminable *imaging* of the drives. Freud's analysis of dreams demonstrates this well. As Freud remarks, there is always a part of the dream

> which has to be left obscure; this is because we become aware during the work of interpretation that at that point there is a tangle of dream-thoughts which cannot be unravelled and which moreover adds nothing to our knowledge of the content of the dream. This is the dream's navel, the spot where it reaches down into the unknown. *The dream-thoughts to which we are led by inter-pretation have to, in an entirely universal manner, remain without any definite endings; they are bound to branch out in every direction into the intricate network of our world of thought.* It is at some point where this meshwork is particularly close that the dream-wish grows up, like a mushroom out of its mycelium.[14]

There are few passages in Freud which more clearly underscore the creativity of the psyche. According to Freud, there is always a part of the unconscious which resists symbolization, even though it strives to be articulated. It is from this 'core' of the unconscious that represen-tational forms emerge in an *undetermined manner* – 'without definite endings', they 'branch out in every direction' of the individual psyche. This is not to say that such a capacity unfolds within the parameters of psychic interiority alone. The psychical expression of the drives, as we shall see, are always constituted within more encompassing social and political influences. Yet, in forming itself, the unconscious for Freud undeniably *creates* in the fullest sense of the term. Indeed, it is this capacity for self-representation and inno-vation which makes possible any kind of social transformation and cultural renewal.

This description of psychical creation inevitably raises the question of the origins of representation, an issue which Freud himself never satisfactorily resolved. Fundamentally, Freud sees the representational process as 'the most general and the most striking' characteristic of the unconscious, through which 'a thought, and as a rule a thought of something that is wished, is objectified ... is repre-sented as a scene, or, as it seems to us, is experienced'.[15] Yet to understand the interconnections between the unconscious and repre-sentational forms, the comments I made previously about how biological needs intersect with psychical expression need to be expanded. As noted, Freud posits that drives become bound to certain representations in the course of the human infant's earliest experiences, organized around the economic interplay of pleasure/pain. The drive can only be manifested in the psyche, remarks Freud, by means of a 'delegation through representation'. He explains this in the metapsychological papers as follows:

> An instinct can never become an object of consciousness – only the idea that represents the instinct can. Even in the unconscious, moreover, an instinct cannot be represented otherwise than by an idea. If the instinct did not attach itself to an idea or manifest itself as an affective state, we could know nothing about it. When we nevertheless speak of an unconscious instinctual impulse or of a repressed instinctual impulse ... [w]e can only mean an instinctual impulse the ideational representative of which is unconscious.[16]

For Freud, then, there is no such thing as a drive in its pure state. Libidinal drives are mediated through the forming of images, by representational forms. The exact means through which the drive achieves representation in the psyche, however, is only implicitly theorized in this passage. The experience of an affect, whether of pleasure or pain, cannot account for the emergence of representation. Moreover, Freud's own attempts to derive phantasy from the memory traces of real events, or the collective prehistory of humankind, only displaces the imaginary dimensions of the unconscious, dimensions which the bulk of his work uncovers.

Now one approach among interpreters of Freud's writings has been to claim that such a problem can be dispelled once we grasp that psychical representations only emerge slowly across time and, through intersecting with the external world, develop into richer impressions of reality. But the problem with this gradualist standpoint, as several commentators have pointed out, is that it simply evades the question of the origins of psychical representation altogether. Rather than being a passive entity in which images are somehow 'deposited', it is asserted that psychical representation must be seen as having its own distinctive characteristics. However unfashionable the search for origins may have become in certain strands of contemporary theory, I think we can draw profitably upon the work of Cornelius Castoriadis to develop the elements of an account of the primary features of representation.[17] While recognizing that the psyche cannot produce everything out of itself, otherwise there would be no reason for the human subject to open itself to other persons and objects, Castoriadis claims it is meaningless to see psychic reality as simply a 'receptacle' of the external world. For there can be no social practice without a subject; and with subjects there comes psychic organization and experience. Instead, the question of representation for Castoriadis centres on the capacity of the psyche itself to *create* and *make* representations. Inherent in the Freudian problematic, he writes,

we can say that the first delegation of the drive in the psyche is the affect, in particular that of displeasure. But we can find nothing in an affect, whether of pleasure or unpleasure, that could account for the form or the content of a representation; at the most the affect could induce the 'finality' of the representative process. *It is therefore necessary to postulate (even if this is only implicitly) that the psyche is the capacity to produce an 'initial' representation, the capacity of putting into image or making an image.* This may appear self-evident. But this image-making must at the same time relate to a drive, at a time when nothing ensures this relation. This may well be the point of condensation and accumulation for all the mysteries of the 'bonding' between the soul and the body.[18]

In Castoriadis's view, then, the unconscious *is* the capacity to produce representation. The production of 'representational activity', which is central to the foundation of the conscious/unconscious dualism, is a primary dimension of human subjectivity. Indeed, as we will examine shortly, it is through representational activity that the individual subject becomes fully anchored within the institutionalized world – with the passing of the Oedipus complex.

To speak of the representational character of the psyche is certainly at odds with much current social and cultural theory. For the whole concept of representation, the idea that the signified automatically assigns a set of stable images or representations to individuals, has seriously come to grief since the advent of Saussurian linguistics. In this connection, it is important to underline the following points. The term 'representation', as used by Castoriadis, does not denote some organic bond between images and things, ideas and the object-world. Rather, the nature of representation for Castoriadis is anchored firmly in bodily reality; the psychical representative is the moment of creation *ex nihilo* between the thrust of the drive and the individual's unique mode of being. 'The individual', writes Castoriadis, 'is not just a first concatenation of representations – or, better, a first "total representation"; he is also, and, from our point of view, above all, a ceaseless emergence of representations and the unique mode in which this representational flux exists'.[19] Unconscious representation, then, is a finite-infinite 'flux'; it is indefinite in form, and is indifferent to the rules of ordinary logic.

What is important here, for our purposes in any case, is that such a characterization highlights that unconscious representation is a *creative* and *constitutive* feature of human experience. The nature of psychical reality, once it has elaborated certain representational forms so as to create a semantic content, does not just 'register' other persons and the object-world, but actually makes their *humanization* possible. In Castoriadis's view, this radical image-creating dimension of the unconscious is an active accomplishment of all human agents. The nature of the unconscious creates *ex nihilo* the figures and images that render the productive flow of the institutionalized world possible. This point is of crucial significance, I shall argue in subsequent chapters, for any critical assessment of the capabilities of human subjects to effect social praxis and agency, as well as to resist the incorporative tendencies of social domination.

We are now in a position to sum up the discussion on the unconscious and representation thus far. The key points are as follows:

1. While the satisfaction of certain vital needs is essential to the psychic development of the prematurely born infant, there is no causal connection between biological needs and the psychical expression of libidinal drives.
2. In Freud's eyes, the fundamental condition for a drive to attain psychical expression is by means of a 'delegation through representation'. This involves primary repression, the fixation and sedimentation of drives to representational forms. The primary unconscious thus exists as a condition of subjectivity, from which 'repression-proper' and consciousness emerge.
3. The primal representations of the unconscious are the affective anchor for the fulfilment of desire and, as a matter of definition, specifically resist being brought to consciousness.

In subsequent chapters, we shall examine the implications of these dimensions of the unconscious for the self and their interconnections with the contemporary social world.

Ego Formation, Narcissism and Sexual Identity

The Freudian discourse on the nature of the unconscious I have examined so far powerfully deconstructs traditional philosophical problems in which a unified subject is imagined to confront a stable object. In the same manner that unconscious desire splits and disperses the human subject, rendering identity non-identical with itself, so too the boundaries of the object-world are cast within an imaginary space. The unconscious as a primal condition of subjectivity denotes a fundamental lack of distinction between self and other. From this point of view, the emergence of consciousness, as we shall see, is a painful and difficult departure from the unconscious realm of libidinal plenitude. In examining the conflicts and struggles that take place inside us, Freud was led to construct a picture of the human subject that radically transcends the Cartesian understanding of the ego as a fixed, indivisible and permanent whole. By a reliance on the metaphor of place, positing psychical not anatomical localities, Freud's dialectical interweaving of consciousness and the unconscious ruptured the certainty on which Western metaphysics had been premised: the rational and knowledgeable subject, the Cartesian cogito, whose first truth, 'I think, therefore I am', had been shattered. Freud argues that consciousness is *discontinuous*, being overdetermined and dislocated by unconscious processes. On this view, the essence of being lies not in the cogito, but in the vicissitudes of desire. Yet this very 'discovery' of desire in the Freudian system is turned around with a vengeance upon the claims of philosophy: unconscious desire is not a deeper ground of subjectivity since, in many ways, desire has no 'essence'. As we have seen, there is no stable ground at the level of the unconscious. Broadly conceived, the unconscious is an incessant irruption of representational forms, drives and affects, which as meaning and force continually displace one another. And it is precisely from this concern with the representational activity of the unconscious that Freud will theorize the subject's development of a relation to the self, the body, others and culture itself.

It is clear that the psychical processes I have been describing thus far are somewhat removed from the emergence of a purposive social agent, of the constituted 'human subject'. For the individual that emerges from the pleasure-seeking, libidinal play of unconscious drives is not yet capable of taking up its place within the wider structure of familial, social and political relations. Clearly, in order to become a 'socialized' individual, it is necessary for the subject to develop a sense of self, consciousness and reflexivity. While the great bulk of Freud's writings is concerned with tracing out the twists and decoys of the unconscious domain, viewing reason as founded in desire, he nevertheless accords a central place to consciousness within the mapping of the psyche. In fact, Freud repeatedly emphasizes that the theory of the unconscious is only made plausible by positing the existence of a contending force that prevents the former from breaking through into the latter. Despite this insistence on the properties of consciousness, however, Freud's attempt to clarify the functions of this psychic agency gave rise to serious difficulties. For the more psychic 'localities' in which Freud found the implacable force of the unconscious, the more it became necessary to revise the place and scope of consciousness. Let us turn now to examine briefly these conceptual problems and revisions.

Broadly speaking, Freud's writings on ego formation encompass two main directions. His early conception of the ego stresses that consciousness is *primeval*. As an active agency, the ego is portrayed as having a shadowy existence from the beginning of life and is slowly separated out from the realm of the unconscious as a consequence of its perceptual linkage with the external world. Charged with the demands of specific 'reality functions', listed in the *Project for a Scientific Psychology* as comprising perception, calculation and judgement, the ego reconstitutes the pleasure principle in relation to its surroundings of reality, to which it has privileged access. As an agency of adaptation, then, the ego differentiates itself from the unconscious through its contact with external reality.[20] On this view, the ego is a kind of synthesizer of ideas, a calculator of internal and external demands. Situated on the frontiers of the preconscious-conscious system, the ego seeks to protect itself from unconscious wishes and conflicts of affect largely through defensive operations – by bringing into play denial, inversions and reversals of affect. Through these specialized defences, the ego seeks to balance some of the demands of the unconscious with the 'reality principle', which is experienced as a law of the outside world. As we will see in the next chapter, when examining the appropriation of this conception of the ego in the critical theory of the Frankfurt School, an important critique of modern social processes emerges from this account of the psyche. In mapping the ways by which society separates human subjects from the pleasure principle into the fixed and repressive confines of the reality principle, critical theory is able to demonstrate how unconscious forms of domination and social power restrict the self-development of human beings – a highly significant political concern.

While Freud maintains this linkage between the structure of the ego and reality-testing throughout his career, it is well known that in his later writings he isolates the mechanisms of narcissism and iden- tification as fundamental to ego formation. This dramatic shift in Freud's thinking about the problematic of the ego was signalled with the publication in 1914 of 'On narcissism: an introduction'. In this essay, Freud argues that the ego is not simply a defensive agency which is tied to the reality principle, but that it is enmeshed within a broader interplay of 'thing-love' and 'self-love'. A range of clinical phenomena, such as the transformation of sadism into masochism as well as voyeurism into exhibitionism, suggested to Freud that there is an originary psychical interchange between the self and other. That is to say, there is a stage in which the human infant does not distin- guish between its own body and the body of the mother, represented by the breast. The constitution of the ego is thus said to arise from a fundamental break-up of this monadic state. In Freud's words:

There is no doubt that, to begin with, the child does not distinguish between the breast and its own body; when the breast has to
be separated from the body and shifted to the '*outside*' because the
child so often finds it absent, it carries with it as an '*object*' a part
of the original narcissistic libidinal cathexis.[21]

The break-up of this monadic state is something from which the
subject never quite recovers, seeking in representations of the self and
others to recapture this originary libidinal plenitude. Yet, as Freud
insists, this split in relation to the self and the other is crucial to
psychical organization and the development of the self and self-
identity. As Freud comments on this *secondary* elaboration of
narcissism, 'There comes a time in the development of the individual
at which he unifies his sexual drives (which have hitherto been
engaged in auto-erotic activities) in order to obtain a love-object; and
he begins by taking his own body as his love-object, and only subsequently proceeds from this to the choice of some person other than
himself.'[22] The input of the concept of narcissism – of the shift from
an originary narcissistic state to its secondary elaborations – led Freud
to reconsider the nature of the ego. The crucial focus now centres on
how a sense of selfhood is consolidated or disrupted. The emphasis is
no longer on a painful intrusion of the external world which establishes
in one fell swoop a 'reality-ego', but rather on the self's desires and
connections with other persons. For what the phenomenon of narcissism shows is that the libidinal drives can round back upon the ego,
making it an object of investment in just the same manner as 'external'
objects. This, in itself, significantly complicates Freud's early model of
the psyche. For it indicates that what had previously been kept
separate in the discourse of psychoanalysis – the topography of mental
functioning and the theory of the drives – are actually deeply interwoven. In the formation of the individual subject, there is a deep
interfusion of the libidinal drives and the structure of the ego. The
process of this development unfolds through a subtle interplay
between libidinal investments in self-identity (ego-libido) and investments in the outside world (object-libido). 'The ego', Freud
comments, 'is to be regarded as a great reservoir of libido from which
libido is sent out to objects and which is always ready to absorb libido
flowing back from objects'.[23] For Freud, the more we come to invest
in external objects, paradoxically, the more libidinally impoverished
will be the ego – a process that culminates in the state of 'being in love'.
To enrich one object, then, means to detract from another. Indeed,
these antagonisms refer to what Jean Laplanche has called a 'libidinal
balance of accounts', from which the ego emerges and develops as a
fully blown 'love-object'.[24]

From the analysis of narcissism, then, Freud argues that the self develops along an imaginary plane rather than through the brute enforcement of a 'reality-ego'. On this view, the ego is essentially a structure which emerges through multiple identifications with other persons. Freud's notion that the emergence of the self arises from an identification with objects is given greater theoretical specificity in the essay 'Mourning and melancholia' and the dense topographical revisions of *The Ego and the Id* (1923). Freud contends that the loss of a loved person necessitates an introjection of the other into the structure of the ego itself. Through the mechanism of narcissistic identification, the lost love is installed within the structure of the self as an act of self-preservation. In this way, the emotional investment in the lost object is sustained in a manner which fits with the demands of reality. As Freud comments:

> Each single one of the memories and situations of expectancy which demonstrate the libido's attachment to the lost object is met by the verdict of reality that the object no longer exists; and the ego, confronted as it were with the question whether it shall share this fate, is persuaded by the sum of the narcissistic satisfaction it derives from being alive to sever its attachment to the object that has been abolished.[25]

Accordingly, Freud analyses the self-critical emotions of grief and melancholia as the painful process by which human beings internalize and thus overcome a lost object of love. For the painfulness of abandoning a lost love sparks an unconscious anger and ambivalence which is intended for the object itself yet is reversed upon the self, in violent blows of self-punishment. However, it is the synthetic aspects of the grieving process – the internalization and, hence, preservation of the object – that Freud highlights in conceptualizing self-development. The consolidatory features of object-loss for the subject are summarized by Freud as follows: 'When the ego assumes the features of the object, it is forcing itself, so to speak, upon the id's loss by saying: "Look, you can love me too – I am so like the object."'[26] The constitution of the self through loss, Freud suggests in his late writings, leads to the notion of a *bodily ego*. The ego is given representation since it identifies, through an interplay of projection and introjection, with the surfaces of the body. 'In seeing itself on the model of the body', as Richard Wollheim writes, 'the ego sees its activities on the model of bodily activity'.[27] This process, it should be noted, cannot be dismissed as biological reductionism. This is so since for Freud the body-ego concerns the psychical representation of the subject; it is 'a mental projection of the surface of the body'.

In Freud's view, this internalization of loss through the work of mourning is a process that is essential not only to the constitution of the self but to gender formation as well. These links between the pain of grief and the acquisition of gender identity become apparent once it is realized that the first, and psychically most significant, loss suffered by the infant is its mother (all infants are libidinally attached to the mother, who, as Freud comments, must 'be shifted to the outside'). This loss of the maternal body is in fact so significant that it becomes the founding moment of psychical differentiation, individuation, meaning and sexual difference. In all of these instances, the constitution of the self and self-identity depends crucially upon an unconscious sexuality that is not anatomically determined, but psychically constructed. In this process of internalizing the loss of the maternal body, the infant's relationship with its father is crucial for the achievement of both selfhood and sexual identity. Indeed, the structural *position* of the father *vis-à-vis* the child–mother dyad forms one of the most fundamental postulates of Freud's work, the Oedipus complex. For Freud, the Oedipus complex is the nodal point of sexual development, the transition from 'psychic bisexuality' into the symbolic world of what our culture has organized as 'modes of sexuality'.

The Oedipus complex has been interpreted by cultural critics as central to the instalment of a code of sexual domination and self-subjection. We shall analyse the impact of contemporary social developments upon processes of psychical differentiation and the self in subsequent chapters. For the moment, a résumé of Freud's arguments about the Oedipus complex needs to be given. Though Freud did not develop a systematic account of the Oedipus complex in any one work, a survey of his formulations indicates that several common threads are relevant here. Freud postulates masculine and feminine dispositions at the level of the unconscious – a bisexuality that is 'polymorphous', functioning through the modalities of aim, object and source. In the case of male sexuality (and Freud invariably takes the male child as the paradigm), the infant desires the mother and wishes to possess her, hates his father for his 'control' of the maternal body and as such phantasizes his death. Here the infant encounters the superior powers of the father – phallic authority and the threat of castration – and must learn to renounce the phantasy of sexual unity with the mother, repressing desire and hostility permanently into the unconscious. Fundamentally, this internalization of the prohibition of the tabooed object of desire 'resolves' the Oedipus complex by setting up an internal agency of guilt and self-regulation, the superego. The superego, as we shall see, operates to enforce the paternal function within the psyche itself: internal guilt replaces the fear of the father's phallic powers. Thus, as a reading of social and sexual reproduction, the child's resolution of the Oedipus complex designates the unconscious reproduction of patriarchal culture.

From the standpoint of a normative heterosexual frame of reference, the trajectories of Oedipal conflict for the young girl are a good deal more complex. This is a topic that will be addressed in greater detail in subsequent chapters, but at this stage several preliminary remarks need to be made about the classical view of the female Oedipus complex. Originally, and as still popularly perceived today, Freud had posited a symmetry in the Oedipal development of male and female children: boys, as noted, love their mother and consequently desire the death of their rival in affections for the maternal body, the father; girls want and desire their father and consequently come to be jealous of their mother. However, Freud was quick to see the limits of this view – most importantly, its failure to attend to the psychical processes through which the girl turns away from her mother towards the father as a love-object. In the essay 'Some psychical consequences of the anatomical distinction between the sexes' (1925), Freud highlights some of the problems of assuming that female Oedipal conflict is only a variation on the male model of development, thereby seeking to recast the issue of female sexuality. In general terms, Freud suggests that the Oedipus complex for the young girl works in a reverse fashion to that of the male child. Instead of instituting the repression of Oedipal desire, the castration complex actually *produces* incestuous desire. Discovering that she lacks a penis with which to actively pursue her desires – Freud's phallocentric supposition that there is a common 'masculine' sexuality – the young girl imagines herself to have been 'castrated' and, in consequence, turns away from her similarly 'castrated' mother. The girl's wish for a penis, however, is so strong that, in Freud's view, it is then deflected on to the desire to bear the father a child – the paternal identification that ushers in the jealousy of the mother. This has enormous psychical consequences for the girl. At this point, Freud comments, the girl can either establish a 'positive' feminine Oedipus complex (love of the father) or a 'negative' complex (the failure to give up the lost maternal object). Significantly, Freud remarks that the complexities of female sexuality come to the fore in this transition from the pre-Oedipal to the Oedipal phase. Yet while pointing to the nature of these sexual identifications, Freud never adequately traces out the implications of the girl's jealousy of the mother, nor the processes involved in the dissolution of the girl's Oedipus complex.

As recent feminist criticism highlights, the structural position of the father in breaking up the child–mother dyad not only institutes the principle of individuation but it involves a repudiation of the feminine position itself. As we shall see, this defensive repudiation of the feminine position has immense consequences for the structuring of sexual difference and the reproduction of asymmetrical gender relations of power and domination. As a theory of gender reproduction, Freud's assumption that sexuality is masculine has been criticized for propagating certain ideological assumptions about the sexes. In this connection, it is well known that Freud links the psychological terms 'masculinity' and 'femininity' with activity and passivity, without really questioning the ideological nature of this split. On the issue of the resolution of the girl's Oedipus complex, for example, Freud remarks that whether a 'positive' or 'negative' sexual identification is established depends on the constitutional nature of the girl's masculine and feminine 'dispositions'. At the same time, however, much of Freud's work suggests that the construction of these sexual identifications should not be confused with established gender roles. As Freud notes:

Sex is a biological fact which, although it is of extraordinary importance in mental life, is hard to grasp psychologically. We are accustomed to say that every human being displays both male and female instinctual impulses, needs and attributes; but though anatomy, it is true, can point out the characteristics of maleness and femaleness, psychology cannot. For psychology the contrast between the sexes fades away into one between activity and passivity, in which we far too readily identify activity with maleness and passivity with femaleness.[28]

In part, then, Freud's linkage of the drives with sexual identity is an attempt to uncover how patriarchal societies structure the nature of our unconscious sexuality. As Juliet Mitchell has argued, Freud's theory offers the groundwork for an analysis of how the unconscious becomes interwoven within identifications of Oedipal conflict, and thus the reproduction of our unequal sexual world.

In questioning the forms of contemporary sexual domination, as we shall see in Chapter 6, some of the most fundamental postulates of Freud's theory have been invoked, criticized and rethought by feminist theorists. In this respect, a number of questions come to the fore on the basis of the foregoing considerations. These include the following: what forms do 'activity' and 'passivity' take and how precisely do they structure psychical constructions of masculinity and femininity? How do we identify such psychical constructions, and how are they to be distinguished from internalizations of the social field? To what extent is the construction of unconscious sexuality itself an effect of a set of internalizations of the law (Juliet Mitchell's enquiry)? To what extent are the key postulates of psychoanalysis about sexuality phallogocentric (Hélène Cixous's question)? Why is femininity repudiated in both sexes in the construction of sexual difference? In contrast to a universal psychical process, might the repudiation of the feminine position itself be an effect of current gender arrangements (Luce Irigaray's contention)? And what sources of feminine sexuality are still available to human subjects, given the nature of this repudiation, to disrupt the current repressive organization of the self (Julia Kristeva's enquiry)? These questions form a guiding thread for the terms of reference of this study, and I shall confront the implications of these issues in subsequent chapters.

Repression and the Constitution of Social Life

The foregoing sections have attempted to show how the human subject, in its earliest stages of life, begins to sketch out the elements and boundaries of an inner world. This construction of the psyche, I have stressed, is arrived at principally through the operations of unconscious representation and narcissistic identification. In considering this pre-Oedipal or imaginary phase of development, I have sought to emphasize its 'dyadic' structure of relations. The small human infant lives in a very close proximity to another body, usually the biological mother of the child, which at this stage represents all of external reality. Not surprisingly, the imaginary identifications forged during this phase centre exclusively on this other person. At this point, the child has no experiential divisions between subject and object, itself and the outside world. Rather, there is a ceaseless merging of objects and part-objects which are experienced outside of any fixed, social boundaries of time and space. 'As far as we can tell', as Juliet Mitchell comments, 'neither animals nor pre-Oedipal human infants divide time into future, past and present. Time for them would seem to be nearer to spatial relationships: here, there; come, gone; horizontal, punctuated duration rather than an historical, vertical temporal perspective.'[29] For the child to move past this imaginary stage and into the network of social and cultural relations it is essential that it begins to recognize that 'objects' are not simply manipulable according to its own wishes. This passage into received social meanings, as previously noted, occurs with the shift into a 'triadic' phase which functions to *break* the dyadic unit of child and mother. The symbolic father intervenes in the child–mother dyad, registered in the painful negotiations of the Oedipus and castration complexes, and thereby severs the child from the imaginary plenitude of the maternal body. It is this paternal prohibition – symbolic castration – which at one stroke constitutes repressed desire and the social code.

Though the castration complex is connected in Freud's writings to a phylogenetic account of collective prehistory, it is unnecessary here to examine the very dubious sociological and anthropological speculations upon which it was based. The central point of interest is that for Freud it represents the *structuring event* which breaks up the monad of the psyche, thereby bringing the individual subject into the network of pre-existing social and cultural relations. This complex, as Laplanche and Pontalis argue, 'is not reducible to an actual situation – to the actual influence exerted by the parental couple over the child. Its efficacy derives from the fact that it brings into play a proscriptive agency (the prohibition against incest) which bars the way to naturally sought satisfaction and forms an indissoluble link between desire and law.'[30] From the beginnings of an awareness of sexual difference, the small infant's desire for the mother is disrupted by the law of paternal authority, which is based upon the punitive force of the castration threat. The child's response to this threat, involving very painful feelings of terror and guilt arising from fear of the father's aggression, results in the repression of desire.[31] Within this drama, the function of the father is principally *symbolic*: to bar the child's imaginary relation with the desired object. Severed from an imaginary unity with the mother's body, the child becomes aware of the impossibility of an interpersonal relationship which is not already structured by the sexual and cultural forms of power relations in society. It is from this unconscious reorganization of the psychical economy that the subject becomes 'socialized'.

There are many familiar criticisms of Freud's account of the castration complex, either in terms of its claim to universality, or because it is seen to unduly privilege the familial institution of patriarchy in the construction of identity.[32] There is some truth to such criticisms. But it is important to see, I think, that the social and political implications of the Oedipus and castration complexes carry implications that are universal in scope. For they reveal the unconscious processes by which other persons are recognized as independent and autonomous agents, the very institution of 'social reality'. Indeed, what Freud shows is the essential condition of the psyche's entry into society, the establishment of a symbolic order, of received social meanings and practices, of things allowed and forbidden. As the law prohibits the child's libidinal desires toward its mother's body, the subject is accordingly introduced to the wider familial and social structures from which it will always remain, in a sense, 'excluded'. This 'exclusion' is the very meaning of the castration complex. It is the *dissolution of the self as omnipotent*. In the Freudian scheme, then, the processes which bring social meanings into the psyche are not external forces such as 'imprinting' or 'conditioning'. Rather, through the introjection of Oedipal objects, structured within a specific set of social and ideological relations, the subject at once constructs *and* encounters social meanings and significations.

Thus, it is important to keep in mind the nature of the breathtaking problem with which Freud was grappling. In short, the question he posed was this: how is it that, in psychic terms, the small child comes to acquire the social code of human society? Freud's most detailed analytical response to this question is set out in his major work of the 1920s, *The Ego and the Id*. In this work, he makes a number of fundamental revisions to the topography of the psyche, mostly because he came to believe that the Oedipus and castration complexes showed that his earlier model was too simplistic. The new topology is based on the view that human beings begin life with all of the contents of the psyche in the unconscious, which only later becomes separated into specific agencies. This separation of consciousness and the unconscious fuse into three agencies or instances of personality: id, ego, superego. The id is the home of the unconscious, the source of all libidinal drives, fuelling the activities of the entire psyche. Yet, at the same time, very significant parts of the ego and the second new agency, the superego, are viewed as containing unconscious material. The 'heir to the Oedipus complex', the superego is the central psychic agency of social and cultural acquisition. As the depository of guilt feelings, moral prohibitions and sadistic self-punishments, this psychic agency is the 'voice of the father'. Thus, the second model of the psyche directly links the Oedipus complex to the formation of psychical agencies.

It would be a mistake, though, to simply equate the superego with some kind of internal conscience or morality. Rather than understanding the reproduction of culture as in some sense a learnt or inculcated process, Freud's work stresses that the formation of the child's 'ego ideals' occurs through processes which are largely *unconscious*. As a residue of the id's earliest object-choices, the individual's 'higher ideals' are formed through a primary identification with significant other persons. The psychic energy which has been invested in such other persons in the marking out of self-boundaries is diverted into an *unconscious moral code*. It is as if the process of early object-identification is internally tied to a splitting of the ego, in which the restrictions and inhibitions of one part of the ego become out of step with the other part. Indeed, the demands of this superego are so wildly irrational when compared to the essential aims of the reality-ego that Freud views it as the most powerful, structured, and tenacious of all the psychic agencies. That the demands of the superego are so arbitrarily cruel and harsh, however, arises not simply from the internalization of the commandments of external authority. For Freud, there is an essential contradiction that lies at the centre of the superego. This contradiction is expressed as a 'reaction-formation' to the demands of authority, which designates both an acceptance *and* rejection of the subject's earliest object-choices. Unlike the structure of the ego, then, the superego for Freud is more than just a residue of early object investments: 'Its relation to the ego is not exhausted by the precept: "You ought to be like this" (like your father). It also comprises the prohibition: "You must not be like this" (like your father) – that is, you may not do all that he does; some things are his prerogative.'[33] Formed under the sign of contradiction, the superego operates as both ideal and punishment, desire and prohibition, carrot and stick. Its distortions confront the subject as something incomprehensible, leaving it with injunctions that are incapable of being obeyed.

If contradiction and ambivalence are the essential marks of the superego, this is so because Freud finds an even deeper force of conflict within this psychic system. Commenting on its acutely high levels of sadism, Freud advances the view that the superego is coterminous with aggression and hatred. Arising from the castration threat, which is the source of all social taboos and cultural prohibitions, Freud links the need for self-punishment to a primary aggressiveness. Revising the theory of the drives around the dualism of Eros, builder of unities and the foundation of all cultural relations, and the death drive, source of our primary aggressiveness and hatred, the superego is now defined as the tension between the two drives, the product of their intersection. Freud sketches this interweaving of primary narcissism and aggressivity in 1930, in *Civilization and its Discontents*: 'Whether one has killed one's father or has abstained from doing so is not really the decisive thing. One is bound to feel guilty in either case, for the sense of guilt is an expression of the conflict due to ambivalence, of the eternal struggle between Eros and the drive of destruction or death.'[34] The role of primary aggressiveness in the generation of the superego, Freud remarks, contains two central dimensions. First, there is the aggression which the small infant feels threatened with due to the father's *symbolic power* of possession of the mother's body. The paternal prohibition is backed by a claim of violence, the castration threat. Second, in unconsciously learning this law of society and culture, there is the child's own aggression towards the father, later to be displaced onto all symbolic prohibitions. In Freud's own terms, then, the superego is said to contain all the elements of aggression and hatred that the human subject originally directed against the paternal threat of castration. The crucial difference is that this aggression is now 'owned' on the inside, it has been introjected, from which it then sadistically punishes the enfeebled ego.

All of this suggests that the superego, as embodiment of the law, exerts an astonishing degree of domination and repression over the strivings of the individual subject. But if this is the case from what has been said so far, it is even more so from another angle. According to Freud, the superego is such a powerful agency, not only because it is developed through the vicissitudes of sexuality and aggression, but because our relation with authority comprises the first important, and most lasting, identification. Since human beings are born 'prematurely', the first submission to authority arises as a result of the child's early dependence on parental figures. Indeed, the first subjective seeds of human autonomy are seen as being internally tied to parental dominance. And while it may be the case that sexuality later emerges as a liberation from such domination, driven by the separating out of need and desire, the individual's submission to authority is held to be so deep-seated that this drama with authority is destined to repeat itself. What is crucial for Freud is that authority is experienced and introjected largely in unconscious ways. Speaking of an *identification* with the unconscious operations of society, Freud insists that 'a child's super-ego is in fact constructed on the model not of its parents but of its parents' super-ego'.[35] It is this primary identification that Freud refers to as the 'individual's father of personal prehistory'.[36] Domination and submission thus precede the constitution of conscious rationality on Freud's account. 'By "nature"' as Philip Rieff argues, 'love is authoritarian; sexuality – like liberty – is a later achievement, always in danger of being over-whelmed by our deeper inclinations toward submissiveness and domination ... By showing that the tie to authority arises prior to rela-tions of desire, Freud ingeniously accounted for social compliance and the formation of moral ideas as well.'[37]

Through situating authority in direct relation to the constitution of the superego, Freud's tripartite model of the psyche provides a particularly rich account of the ways in which social relations of domination and exploitation are reproduced and sustained. In tracing the earliest processes of object-identification, fuelled by a need and desire for the law itself, the Freudian superego significantly complicates prevailing notions of how human beings are 'positioned' within the dominant political relations of modern societies. In one sense, it is as if the established social order were able to ensure its continued survival through implanting an 'internal police agent' within the psyche – a vision that, in many ways, parallels the Marxist notion of 'false consciousness'. Indeed, Freud himself often likened the structure of the psyche to such images of social control. 'For our mind', he wrote, 'is no peacefully self-contained unity. It is rather to be compared to a modern State in which a mob, eager for enjoyment and destruction, has to be held down forcibly by a prudent superior class.'[38] Yet this analogy with the State is far more complex in character than any form of political coercion that might be exerted upon human beings by an external power. For Freud, the superego, source of the law of society and cultural relations, is actually founded in unconscious desire itself. The law is, in effect, a product of a differentiation of the id. This is so because repressed desire came into being with the prohibition of the law. Severed from the object of imaginary plenitude, the prohibition of the law at one stroke constitutes repressed desire. The result of this is that Freud's work powerfully undercuts traditional philosophical notions that posit the possibility of a transcendental law or rational authority. Instead, the order of authority is shown to be constituted to its roots by the vicissitudes of desire. The law is fully prey to the cruel, sadistic excesses of the unconscious. According to this standpoint, then, the opposition between reason and unreason dissolves. As Rieff comments, 'morality, so far as it is internalized by libidinal coercion ("identification"), draws upon the natural resources of the id ... Implicitly Freud presumes that the decisions of conscience are invariably irrational; indeed conscience is defined as being – it is a powerful rhetorical affront – no less irrational than the instinctual id.'[39]

That the superego is so internally complex in formation carries a number of far-reaching social and political implications. As Freud's work uncovers, the identity of a subject is constituted only through the introjection *and* repression of the existing forms of social and sexual roles in society. The scattered elements which we have considered in Freud's account can be brought together to illuminate the intricate ways in which existing social relations and practices come to order the psyche into socialized form: parental-object identification; emergence of intense libidinal and aggressive impulses; modification and repression of guilty desires through the Oedipus complex; internalization of the parental prohibition and, thus, the law. These processes of the socialization of the psyche, as we will see, should not be regarded as exhaustive. In the strands of modern social theory that will be examined in subsequent chapters, a cluster of new social and cultural developments is identified as crucial to the structuring conditions of the modern psyche, including the crisis of the nuclear family and the impact of the mass media industries. Nonetheless, Freud's account remains important, I believe, for understanding the complex psychic processes in which subjectivity is formed within the existing structures of social and cultural relations.

One of the most strategic and subversive political insights of Freud's work is to show that the law is actually founded in desire itself. In radical contrast to the traditional sociological view that external authority is in some sense imprinted upon passive subjects, Freud reveals that the introjection of cultural prohibitions is a direct result of the earliest object-choices of the id. Since desire is born through an identification with authority figures, the law itself can be viewed as being dissimulated within the unconscious. Human subjects, on Freud's reckoning, desire limitation, constraint, law. It is this *dissimulatory dimension of the unconscious* which is of such crucial importance to the reproduction and maintenance of social power. The social order, the law is able to present itself with the mark of legitimacy and rationality, thereby concealing its more exploitative aspects, since it draws upon and incorporates the unconscious desires and passions of human beings. In the words of Terry Eagleton:

> If Freud is to be believed, late capitalist society sustains its rule not only by police forces and ideological apparatuses, but by raiding the resources of the death drive, the Oedipus complex and primary aggressivity. On this theory, it is because such regimes are able to tap into the very energies involved in the turbulent constitution of the human subject that they appear to have all the obdurate resistance to upheaval of a mountain range. The forces which sustain authority, in short, are compulsive and pathological ... Civilization reproduces itself by cornering the currents of the id in order to outflank it, flexing those drives back upon themselves through the relay of a portion of the ego in a repression every bit as intemperate as the life of the unconscious itself.[40]

The ways by which a social system is able to situate the desires of human beings in a manner which then excludes recognition of such psychic investments, operationalized through mechanisms of repression, are thus vital to the reproduction of social power and domination. It is as if the more repressive features of the contemporary social order, once having colonized the superego, depend upon a forgetting of the needs and passions of human subjects. Indeed, in Freud's view, this dissimulation of unconscious desire is a fundamental condition by which relations of power and domination are secured.

The dissimulation and concealment of unconscious desire within modern social processes has become a key issue in social theory. In exploring the links between the unconscious and human society, the exploitative power relations that are dissimulated through the complex domains of repression have become the central targets of social and political critique. The aims of such critiques have been to probe the necessity of this coercive unification and domination of self-identity, thereby seeking to open the possibility for a restructuring of ideologically inscribed subject positions and an enrichment of human social relationships. This directly relates to the vexed question, much debated in contemporary social theory, as to whether the realization of another form of society, with its attendant restructuring of social relationships, is actually possible. The perspectives offered on this issue in certain strands of contemporary theory are, as we shall see, somewhat varied – though the dominant impulse tends towards a certain political pessimism. The identifications forged with authority in early childhood are seen as being largely 'immanent' in social relations, such that it appears difficult to identify any features of our psychical structure that may refer *beyond* this introjection of the law. In the critical theory of the Frankfurt School, the possibilities for creative social action are acutely delimited since human autonomy, while involving an active element of resistance, is understood as being internally tied to the introjection of the repressive authority of the father in the Oedipus complex. The result of this, for a range of reasons, is said to be an ever-intensifying fragmentation of human experience, which in turn is incorporated into the overbearing demands of the social order. A similar, though perhaps more dramatic, threat to the possibilities of autonomous action hangs over the question of the subject in Lacanian and certain versions of post-structuralist thought. According to such viewpoints, the subject is radically divided through the destabilizing effects of language. Outstripped and decentred, the ego is 'subjected' to the pre-given structure of social and political relations, instantiated and symbolized by the 'Law of the Father'. All of this can be pictured, then, as a kind of demise of authentic subjecthood, leaving little room for creative agency and communal action.

The implicit determinism arising from this view of the superego would certainly appear to be rather bad news for those concerned with the fashioning of a radical political project. Indeed, any emergent cultural or political action would appear seriously compromised by the oppressiveness of a superego which binds us libidinally to the institution of social relations and their ideological dissimulation. As 'heir' to the Oedipus complex, the superego may well usher the individual subject into received social meanings and practices but it also places him or her repressively within the existing field of the dominant ideologies – of class, race, gender and the like – by which modern societies are reproduced. And it is because Freud views human subjects as identifying with such ideologies, as desiring the law in some sense, that there seems little room left for any *alternative* political project. 'Freudian analysis', as Russell Jacoby argues, 'is the steadfast penetration of the injured psyche. It takes so seriously the damage that it offers nothing for the immediate.'[41] Yet, from another angle, Freud's critical examination of the repressive features of psychical life are at the same time a *resistance* to the social processes that sustain and perpetuate them. At the very root of Freud's pessimism about humankind, as Theodor Adorno knew well, there is a revised conception of the possibilities for caring and creative human relationships. It is as if Freud believed that any theory concerned with the human transformative process must found its vision upon a full examination of the most painful and distressing aspects of human life.

Let me try to concretize this point a little by asking how the application of psychoanalytical theory affects existing conceptions of social transformation and the possibilities of an autonomous society. The restructuring and transformation of social relations, Freud writes in the *New Introductory Lectures*, must be situated in relation to the central modes of feeling, valuing, and caring which exist in any given society. Criticizing certain mechanistic accounts of social transformation, Freud argues that such viewpoints tend to ignore the complex ways in which the past comes to shape the present:

> It seems likely that what are known as materialist views of history sin in underestimating this factor. They brush it aside with the remark that human 'ideologies' are nothing other than the product and superstructure of their contemporary economic conditions. This is true, but very probably not the whole truth. Mankind never lives entirely in the present. The past ... lives on in the ideologies of the superego and yields only slowly to the influences of the present and to new changes; and so long as it operates through the superego it plays a powerful part in human life, independently of economic conditions.[42]

Once we have recognized this structuring role of human passion and desire, then it is possible to conceive of processes of social transformation in a new light. It is not simply a matter of starting from the premise that our existing systems of power and economy are unjust and should be changed: it is a matter of recognizing that our unconscious feelings and dispositions are already bound up with these systems, and seeking to allocate from this a space for their development and alteration toward more creative ends. Viewed in this light, the possibility of a desirable future is not taken to be discontinuous with present social arrangements. This is one of the most significant and enduring insights that Freudian psychoanalysis offers social critique. As we will see in this study, the recognition of these intimate links between desire and social power in certain strands of recent social theory has proved both theoretically fruitful and challenging.

Thus, in the political sphere, the Freudian account of the formation of the subject has a good deal to contribute to the deepening of our understanding of the numerous difficulties involved in processes of personal and social change. This is not simply a matter, though, of achieving a more comprehensive account of the structure and form of modern social processes – though this is undeniably a significant concern. Psychoanalytic theory, or so I want to propose, promotes not just a 'wider' look at social relations, but it is intimately bound up with the tracing of phenomena that may both extend and enrich our communal lives. For to analyse any 'bounded' form of social knowledge, such as unconscious processes, involves positing – even if only implicitly – a 'possible world' in which human beings might creatively act and reflect upon such repressed and distorted conditions. The possibility of another form of social organization in which internal deformations and pathologies become available for critical reflection, however, does not imply a full-blown ideal communicative situation – as proposed by Habermas. Habermas's rather implausible proposition that the values of autonomy and freedom demand a society in which 'interpreted needs' (that is, libidinal drives) become fully transparent to discursive and social action will be examined and criticized in Chapter 3. My point is rather that psychoanalytic theory can play a radical part in social critique since, in probing the deformed and crippled forms of repressed desire, it is intricately interwoven with deciphering the possibilities of an *alternative future*.

The power of Freudian psychoanalysis as a critical discourse, however, moves on an even deeper level than this. Freud's work, in short, is concerned not only with the vicissitudes of desire which *exist* in any given society, but also with the unconscious processes that work *against* domination and social power. The law of the superego locates human beings within the repressiveness of the social order, but it is also the source of their deepest resistances and struggles against it. There is a profound ambivalence of affect at the centre of the human psyche. This is so on Freud's reckoning since the earliest identification with authority, our love of the law, is matched by a 'reaction-formation' against parental dominance, our buried hatred of authority figures – the dialectic of domination and rebellion. What is important for our purposes is that such a perspective stresses that cultural production cannot be viewed as a uniform process which in some sense 'orders' the psyche. Freud's work highlights the active *state* of the subject in social analysis, the productive elements of psychic representation and identification. This is deeply significant, I shall argue in subsequent chapters, as it suggests that human subjects cannot be wholly 'incorporated' or 'subjected' to modern social processes. There is the theoretical insistence in Freud's writings that systems of domination, no matter how apparently 'total' in character, cannot contain or exhaust the individual subject's unique 'mode of being'. Indeed, modes of being – that is, psychical representations and resistances – are the very stuff of an alternative 'consciousness' and the source of all counter-discursive struggles within existing systems of domination and social power. Yet it is this 'doubleness' of psychic reality, that subjects are located within the symbolic order while always being potentially capable of alternative action, that many strands of modern social theory either pass over in silence or just blindly ignore. In contrast, the argument I shall develop in this study is that the *displacement* of the primacy of consciousness in Freudian psychoanalysis should not be made to be coextensive with a *dissolution* of human agency and autonomy. A radical theory of subjectivity demands a conception of the psyche which, while acknowledging the fractured and dispersed quality of unconscious desire, must nevertheless recognize the creative and critical dimensions of selfhood.

In this chapter, some of the major tenets of Freudian psychoanalysis have been described, selected for their relevance to the central concerns of this study. The chapter began with an overview of Freud's theory of the unconscious, stressing in particular the disguised, fragmented and overdetermined quality that constitutes repressed desire. The nature of the unconscious carries a number of important implications for the analysis of subjectivity and social relations: most significantly, that the conscious knowledgeability of human actors is 'bounded' by repressed psychical structures. Nevertheless, it was suggested that the bar of repression instituted with the formation of the human subject does not imply that subjectivity is *determined* by unconscious processes. Freud's work equally highlights that the unconscious is a *constitutive* and *creative* feature of human experience. This is particularly evident, it was argued, in the production of unconscious representation since Freud's work stresses that the individual subject creates thoughts and images in an undetermined manner against the trace of desire. In recent theoretical analyses, as we will see in subsequent chapters, this capacity has become a matter of controversial dispute, evident in debates on the fragmentation of the human subject, the manipulation of unconscious processes and the decomposition of cultural meanings characteristic of modernity.

This overview of the nature of the unconscious prepared the way for a discussion of Freud's writings on the notion of the ego. Stressing the ambiguities and complications of Freud's views on the ego, it was argued that there are two key derivations of the 'self' from his various formulations: first, the ego as a psychic phenomenon which has privileged access to external reality; and second, the ego itself as a libidinal object. In contrast to traditional sociological accounts which assume a pre-given, rational core of the self, it was argued that Freud's work is important since it is explicitly concerned with the *formation* of gendered subjectivity – of the ways in which subjecthood becomes constructed and organized within the contemporary sexual world. Finally, I sketched some of Freud's central claims associated with the entry of the human subject into the existing network of social and cultural relations. Through an enquiry into the specific conditions of the Oedipus complex, the castration threat and the emergence of the superego, I examined Freud's view that the social order is actually grounded in unconscious desire itself. It was suggested that, as concerns the development of a radical social theory, this implies more than just recognizing that subjects hold unconscious beliefs which mirror the broader meaning systems of existing social formations. Rather, Freud's work reveals that the dynamics of unconscious desire have an *internal connection* to the maintenance and reproduction of social power. Some preliminary remarks were then made as to the ambivalent and contradictory political implications of this standpoint.

In sum, then, I have examined a range of issues in Freudian psychoanalysis that focus on the nature of the unconscious, subjectivity, and the structure of social formations – issues that form a thematic for the whole of this work. It is to a detailed inquiry of how these themes have been developed and extended in certain strands of modern social theory that the remainder of this study will be concerned. In the next chapter, I will begin this examination by turning to that account of the unconscious and human society formulated in critical theory.

2 The Manipulation of Desire

Critical Theory and the Problem of Fragmentation

Of all the attempts in modern social theory to transcend the split between the individual and society, it is in the work of the first generation of critical theory – the so-called Frankfurt School of the *Institut für Socialforschung* – that the interconnections between the psychic and social fields are most explicitly proposed as an object of enquiry. Extending the insights of Weber and Lukács on social rationalization, critical theory sought to integrate the study of the individual psyche within the analysis of cultural forms – an area long neglected by traditional Marxism. To do this, Freudian theory was used to bridge the abyss between the sociological and psychological realms in order to interpret aspects of the social whole.[1] In tracing the relations between self and society, the writings of Herbert Marcuse and Theodor Adorno, the two most prominent critical theorists, have had a major impact on the concerns of contemporary social and political theory. Already dissatisfied with the work in this area of their former colleague Erich Fromm, from the early 1940s Marcuse and Adorno sought to map the points of connection between culture, society and the human psyche. That the psychic and social domains had become divided was suggestively underscored by Adorno, who argued that any such link offered by psychoanalysis could only be projected theoretically: 'The separation of sociology and psychology is both correct and false. False because it encourages the specialists to relinquish the attempt to know the totality which even the separation of the two demands; and correct insofar as it registers more intransigently the split that has actually taken place in reality than does the premature unification at the level of theory.'[2]

If our vantage point were the sociology of knowledge, a number of interrelated factors which precipitated this theoretical turn to psychoanalysis could be identified, such as the development of Stalinism in Russia, the rise of Fascism in Germany and Italy, and the absence of a revolutionary consciousness in the West.[3] My focus, however, concerns those relations between self and society developed in the work of Marcuse and Adorno. In particular, we need to ask the following connected questions: what view of subjectivity did psychoanalysis offer in this period? And what are the implications of this view for the identification of problems with which modern social theory should be concerned?

In this chapter I shall discuss several perspectives developed in the writings of Marcuse and Adorno concerning subjectivity, the fragmentation of the self, and the nature of modern social relations. By focusing on their contributions to this specific theme, I shall necessarily have to sketch in rather broad strokes many aspects of their sociological and philosophical analyses. Moreover, in what follows, I make no claim to deal with the astonishing range of critical studies published by these authors in areas such as aesthetics, music, and philosophy. Rather, I shall analyse a number of central themes which are common to their rethinking of the relations between self and society. Of course, it must be stressed that the work of Marcuse and Adorno cannot be understood in any real sense as a unified enterprise. Even though they acknowledge a mutual indebtedness in their studies on self-identity, Marcuse and Adorno never worked directly together and were generally concerned with rather different linkages between the psychic and social fields. But despite this, it is well established that there is something like a consensus in their theoretical orientations on the thesis of psychic fragmentation in the 'totally administered world'.[4] Accordingly, in this chapter I shall examine certain threads of consensus in their writings on the self and modern identity. I shall begin by outlining the main parameters of the thesis of psychic fragmentation and their theories about the intersections of the psychic and social domains. I will then present a critical assessment of Marcuse's and Adorno's reliance on Freud's early theory of the drives. I shall try to show that, while identifying several key aspects of the interweaving of the psychic and social realms, their rather traditional and mechanical reading of Freud has not worn well and is ultimately deficient for the theorization of human subjectivity. What has been of lasting importance in Marcuse's and Adorno's appropriation of psychoanalysis, however, is their incisive analysis of the fragmentation of the human subject in modernity. Following this, in probing the limitations of a monadic view of psychic internalization upon which their analysis of fragmentation is founded, I shall argue that the critique of domination developed by Marcuse and Adorno, whilst powerful, is based on a rather simplified and schematic interpretation of certain tendencies in modernity. I shall conclude by suggesting that these insights, concerning the tendencies towards psychic fragmentation, are nevertheless of considerable importance for the analysis of self-identity.

Marcuse and Adorno on Subjectivity and the Unconscious

A characteristic feature of Marcuse's and Adorno's analyses of contemporary society and self-identity is their employment of the early 'biological' Freud – what can be termed 'drive theory'. Rooted in the traditional Freudian vocabulary of an energetics of the mind, drive theory supposes that consciousness only gradually emerges from a differentiation with the unconscious as a result of the intrusion of external reality. As Marcuse puts it: 'the ego retains its birthmark as an 'outgrowth' of the id. In relation to the id, the processes of the ego remain secondary processes.'[5] The ego, in the antagonism ensuing in the shift from the pleasure principle to the reality principle, is seen as both the centre-point of consciousness and the opponent of unconscious drives. At first sight, this deployment of an instinctual conception of the ego might be viewed as both a startling and problematic conceptual move. This is especially so if seen against the backdrop of the linguistic turn in much recent social theory and Anglo-American philosophy. But whilst Marcuse's and Adorno's use of drive theory is certainly a main source of the theoretical limits of much of their work, it also accounts for the scope and richness of their social critique. In penetrating the internal landscape of political and social domination within the individual, drive theory provided an effective framework for the first generation of critical theorists to map the depth psychical consequences of social oppression in a manner unique to Marxism. It was for this reason that Marcuse and Adorno viewed the analytic revisions developed by the neo-Freudians, such as Hartmann, Horney and Sullivan, as a liberal attempt to rob psychoanalysis of its revolutionary potential. For the accounts of 'autonomous ego functions' provided by these ego-psychologists were said merely to perpetuate at a conceptual level the exaggerated illusions of autonomy and selfhood that mirrored the experiential nature of modernity.[6]

In connecting the central theoretical tenets of drive theory to an analysis of modern culture, a number of common preoccupations emerge in Marcuse's and Adorno's work. Among the most prominent are: the imbrication of historical and social factors in the structuring of the psyche; the subterranean points of connection between unconscious elements of self-identity and structures of domination; and the oppressive weight of technological reason upon modern social life. In what follows, I shall explore these themes in some detail. It is important initially to emphasize, however, that Marcuse's and Adorno's perspectives on these issues are substantially informed by the critique of consciousness developed in the *Dialectic of Enlightenment*, written during the 1940s by Adorno and his

Frankfurt colleague, Max Horkheimer. There are several psycho-analytic and sociological dimensions of this thesis, which is a speculative philosophy of history, that underpin Marcuse's and Adorno's writings on the self and contemporary society. The fundamental theme of the *Dialectic of Enlightenment* is that the humanization of the drives, resulting in the transformation from natural instinct to the conscious self, produces a form of control of the ego. But this level of conscious control is double-edged since it is established at the cost of a new inner division and sense of isolation and powerlessness. The Janus-face of this process reveals itself in the repression of inner nature as the price of learning to dominate external nature. Subjectivity and rationality are constituted by the drive for self-preservation, but the separation from nature this involves also places, indeed fixes, the subject as victim. This is expressed in the *Dialectic of Enlightenment* as follows: 'Man's domination over himself, which grounds his selfhood, is almost always the destruction of the subject in whose service it is undertaken; for the substance which is dominated, suppressed and dissolved through self-preservation is none other than that very life as a function of which the achievements of self-preservation are defined; it is, in fact, what is to be preserved.'[7]

Marcuse's Mapping of the Psychic and Social Fields

In Marcuse's work during the 1950s, there is a sustained attempt to reconceptualize this *dissolution* of the individual subject within the psychic and social fields of modernity. In his seminal work *Eros and Civilization*, Marcuse effects a systematic reconstruction of Freudian psychoanalysis into a progressive social-theoretical framework. Not surprisingly for someone who is both a Hegelian and a dialectical Marxist, he argues that Freud's theory of the human subject must be rethought in the light of contemporary social developments. According to Marcuse, the insidious rise of systems of technology and bureaucracy has led to a breakdown of the stable features of self-identity. This breakdown has generated the progressive subsumption and manipulation of human subjects under modern technologies of the 'administered society'. As a consequence, Marcuse contends, the traditional object of psychoanalysis – the individual dissected into id, ego, and superego – has become obsolescent. The 'bourgeois indi-vidual' has vanished. Throughout his career, however, Marcuse maintained that the principle of subjectivity cannot simply be discarded, as is the case in certain versions of post-structuralism. Instead, Marcuse tackles head-on the Freudian theory of instinctual drives, which have usually been viewed as implying the idea of a human nature and thus as inherently reactionary. The emphasis on an instinctual realm of the psyche, he argues, is in fact unequivocally positive. For whatever formations of repression come to predominate in society, the existence of the instinctual realm indicates that an alternative, personal core of selfhood always remains, timelessly residing in the unconscious. Hidden in psychoanalysis, Marcuse claims, there lies a true principle of identity.

In the opening chapters of *Eros and Civilization*, Marcuse traces the emergence of modern forms of self-identity through an analysis of some of Freud's most controversial claims. These include the oppositions between the pleasure principle and the reality principle, the life and death instincts, and the view that civilization necessarily entails a repressive transformation of the libidinal drives. A distinctive facet of Marcuse's analysis of these ideas is his retracing of them within a comprehensive sociological and historical perspective. The aim of this reconceptualization, he writes, is to develop a social theory capable of mapping 'the mechanisms of social and political control in the depth dimension of instinctual drives and satisfactions'.[8] To do this, he takes as fundamental to his analysis Freud's view that the human psyche is formed through contradiction; fractured through the painful split between the pleasure principle and the reality principle. As discussed in the last chapter, in Freud's early work the psyche is regulated by two principles of functioning which are fundamentally antagonistic: the pleasure principle (connected with processes of unconscious satisfaction) and the reality principle (connected with the impinging of the object world on psychic reality). Marcuse speaks of these principles as the foundation of both subjecthood and culture: 'The vicissitudes of the instincts are the vicissitudes of the mental apparatus of civilization. The animal drives become human instincts under the influence of external reality.'[9] Through these intersecting processes, then, the individual comes to be 'socialized'; formed as 'a conscious thinking *subject*, geared to a rationality which is imposed upon him from outside'.[10] In Freud's account, as we have charted, this surrender of the pleasure principle to the reality principle occurs in order to achieve a more durable and lasting kind of unconscious gratification. Marcuse, however, differs from Freud on this point. Taking the interplay of these principles to an extreme limit, Marcuse argues that contemporary social developments suggest there has been a 'transubstantiation' in the very notion of pleasure itself. Increasingly subjected to the crushing repressiveness of the current social order, unconscious gratification, as we will shortly examine, is now conceived as a by-product of the pathologies of social power and domination.

Marcuse presses this Freudian theory of the repressive transformation of libidinal drives into an historical account of ever-intensifying levels of social coercion. Positing the 'struggle with nature' as the basis of human material existence, the renunciation of unconscious desire is taken to be necessary for social and cultural development. The level of repression for the progress of civilization, however, is not fixed. The increasing complexity of social organization demands that psychological repression be continually reinforced *and* increased. For Marcuse, this is 'the history of repression'. The transmutation of 'animal drives' into the constituted 'human subject' represents a shift from primitive societies to modern culture:[11]

From	*To*
Immediate satisfaction	Delayed satisfaction
Pleasure	Restraint of pleasure
Play	Work
Receptiveness	Productiveness
Absence of repression	Security

Marcuse thus accepts the essentials of Freud's claim that the repression of unconscious drives has underpinned the existence of all historical forms of social organization. But he differs from Freud in rejecting the view that psychological repression is necessarily the fate of humankind *in toto*. Marcuse's fundamental move is to introduce the argument that Freud generalizes the structure of psychological repression from a specific form of the reality principle, the economic order of capitalism, and extends it to all types of social organization. The crucial problem, as he formulates it, is that Freud's perspective is reductive: it too easily strips social dimensions of their force in the formation of the psyche. In contrast to Freud's fixed and ahistorical account, Marcuse's contention is that the content of the reality principle is the product of several determinations – it is structured through ideological, political and economic axes. Yet to capture these determinations, Marcuse argues, it is not necessary to add a sociological account to Freudian theory since this reductive analysis already contains 'the elements of its opposite'. For Marcuse, Freud's theory of repression must instead be 'unfolded' and 'recaptured' through its own content.

While a certain amount of basic repression is necessary for the continuation of civilization, Marcuse postulates that processes of repression are always structured within the particular constitution of the social-historical world. Though the 'reality principle demands a considerable degree and scope of repressive control over the instincts', he argues, 'the specific historical institutions of the reality principle and the specific interests of domination introduce additional controls over and above those indispensable for civilized human association'.[12] In order more adequately to separate the specific forms of socio-historical domination from their biological underpinnings, Marcuse introduces two crucial neologisms: surplus-repression and the performance principle.[13] Surplus-repression refers to those specific forms of political and ideological domination that induce extra-libidinal renunciations. It comprises any restrictions placed upon the libidinal drives which re-groove basic repressions in the interests of domination. The performance principle refers to the specific cultural form of reality which is constituted by the economic order of capitalism. According to Marcuse, the central features of this domination include: the restrictions placed on sexuality by the monogamic-patriarchal nuclear family, the hierarchical division of labour experienced in late capitalist society, and the pathologies of mass commodified culture. It operates through the stratification of human subjects into competitive economic 'roles' and 'performances'. As a modality that engenders repression which is predominantly surplus, it is internally connected to the reproduction and maintenance of asymmetrical social relations of power. For Marcuse, it is this entwinement of surplus-repression and the performance principle which has led to the progressive loss of individual autonomy in modern society.

It will be clear by now that the main purpose of Marcuse's work is to reformulate the Freudian theory of repression in order more adequately to comprehend certain contemporary intersections between the psychical and social fields. Marcuse was not content, though, to analyse the points of connection between the social and psychic realms at such a high level of abstraction. Throughout a series of publications, he sought to connect his account of the increasing repressiveness of modern social processes with an analysis of specific cultural and political changes affecting identity formation. In Marcuse's view, Freudian psychoanalysis is again valuable to social theory, when historically contextualized, since it explores in detail the processes of identity formation during the liberal phase of capitalism. Crucial to this understanding of the constitution of the 'bourgeois individual', he argues, is the Oedipus complex. Through the dialectic of resistance and compliance to a feared outside authority figure (the father), the individual subject in the liberal epoch slowly forged a unity of the self and won a sense of human autonomy. It was through the processes of internalization and identification with the father that the subject came to reproduce the bourgeois relationship to authority. Measured in terms of the *Dialectic of Enlightenment*, however, this primary identification with authority is viewed by Marcuse as both enabling and repressive. It generates a degree of autonomy through constituting selfhood and yet perpetuates domination since it is based upon a prior acceptance of authority. But while autonomy may only be partial during the epoch of liberal capitalism, such a social order does provide the *possibilities* for authentic subjecthood and new social experience.

On Marcuse's account, however, today's social conditions are significantly different from those in which Freud analysed the formation of self-identity. The massive social and industrial transformations which have occurred this century, changes in systems of economy and technology as well as cultural production, have all resulted in a radical escalation in psychological repression. For Marcuse, the more the new technological society has advanced, the more repression has become surplus. In order to sustain the asymmetrical relations of power characteristic of the current social order, the immense productive capacities released from technology, modernism and monopoly capital have been turned back upon the subject with a vengeance. Repression is at once made self-regulative *and* self-intensifying. These developments are directly linked by Marcuse to changes in the role of the father in the context of individual development. The transition from market to monopoly capitalism, Marcuse argues, signals a major change in the function of the family in the reproduction of social and economic relationships. The position of the father, in particular, is thought to be rendered vulnerable through a wide variety of sources: his declining economic status (caused by recurring inflation and unemployment) means his image of power and strength as an authority figure is shattered. As a consequence, individuals are said to forge identifications less and less through Oedipal processes. Instead, they turn increasingly to a range of extra-familial authorities. This ties in directly with the intrusion into family relationships of a host of external forces of socialization. These include the mass media industries, the modern state and the pressures of commodified culture. For Marcuse, the modern subject tends to identify increasingly with the mechanical and rigid value-systems which these agencies promote. This is said to result in a disintegration of ego autonomy. Hence, the individual's psychological state is marked more and more by conventional and stereotyped modes of thinking and affect.

Only a few further elements in Marcuse's treatment of the structuring properties of modern self-identity deserve mention here. In a highly subtle treatment of the organisation of social life under capitalism, Marcuse argues that the erotogenic zones of the body undergo a profound psychic restructuring for the maintenance and reproduction of alienated labour. He contends that this can be discerned in the shift from sexuality as 'polymorphous-perverse' – without any temporal and spatial constraints on its expression – to the hierarchical and centralized organization of the libidinal drives in modern work relations. 'Originally the organism in its totality and in all its activities and relationships is a potential field for sexuality, dominated by the pleasure principle. And precisely for this reason it must be desexualized in order to carry out unpleasurable work, in order, in fact, to live in a context of unpleasurable work.'[14] This 'desexualization' is achieved through the channelling of libido into 'repressive desublimation': the harnessing of erotic energy to the performance principle. This occurs through the repressive distribution of time in modern societies. The structuring of the average working day, as well as the routinization and regimentation of daily life, contributes to the subjection of libidinal relationships in the interests of capitalist domination. But, equally important, are the spatial repressions placed on the libidinal drives. Not only is non-procreative sex restricted so as to release libidinal energy for alienated labour, but there is also a repressive centralization of the libido which mirrors the dominative rationality of liberal morality. In sum, there is a centralization of the various aims of the libidinal drives into one desired object (usually of the other sex), resulting in the dominance of genitality over all other libidinal forms of expression. Thus, Marcuse argues, modern sexuality only exists 'part-time'.[15] Through this repression the erotogenic zones of the libidinal drives, the body becomes 'free' for use as labour power. Such a restructuring of the psyche is held to cement the very dissimulation of administered domination, providing the foundation for a high degree of integration in modern industrial societies.

Adorno on Self-Identity and Narcissism

In a series of essays written in the 1940s and 1950s, Adorno also examines the points of connection between self-identity and human autonomy.[16] Defending the importance of Freud's work, Adorno argues that psychoanalysis explores in detail the classic processes of identity formation in the late nineteenth and early twentieth centuries. In contrast to Marcuse, he is not much concerned with the methodological linkages of the psychic and social fields. On philosophical grounds, Adorno refuses to articulate the conceptual foundations of such concepts. Rather, he employs psychoanalytic theory to understand recent changes in the psychical dynamics of modern social processes. As Martin Jay observes, 'what instead drew Adorno to the early Freud was the way in which his theory unflinchingly registered the traumas of contemporary existence. Telling the harsh truth was itself a kind of resistance to the acceptance of those traumas as inevitable.'[17] A central purpose of Adorno's appropriation of psychoanalytic theory is to juxtapose the stasis of nature with the dynamism of the social-historical world. Psychic processes must be rethought in the light of modern social conditions better to conceptualize the increasingly compulsive features of self-identity in the 'administered world'. For Adorno, the internal contours of self-identity demanded such deciphering since the compulsive drive for self-preservation has become all but invisible in modernity. He expresses this perpetuation of the subject's 'compulsive identity' in *Negative Dialectics* as follows: 'Since self-preservation has been precarious and difficult for eons, the power of its instrument, the ego drives, remains all but irresistible even after technology has virtually made self-preservation easy; that power surpasses the one of the object drives whose specialist, Freud, misconceived it.'[18]

According to Adorno, the nature of Freud's misconception concerns the ego. This is so, Adorno feels, since the ego is the representative of contradictory functions in Freud's metapsychology. As he puts it, 'the ego is supposed to be both, qua consciousness, the opposite of repression, and qua unconscious, the repressive agency itself.'[19] As the representative of both cognitive operations and the coordinator of libidinal impulses, then, there is an immanent contradiction at the centre of ego functions. In order to live and operate in society, the ego functions through cognitive testing and yet, because of the repressive and pathological dimensions of modern social processes, it must also effect unconscious prohibitions. Throughout the liberal phase of capitalism, these contradictions are forged through a resistance to, and internalization of, the authority of the father in the Oedipus complex. With the ushering in of the 'administered world of late capitalism', however, Adorno concurs with Marcuse that there has been an eclipse of the social conditions from which individuation develops. Internalization fails. As a consequence, what ego autonomy there was from the bourgeois humanist legacy is today increasingly undermined. The possibility for human subjects to experience caring emotional relationships and authentic sociality is shattered through the increasing weakness of the ego. 'Where the ego fails to develop its intrinsic potential for self-differentiation', Adorno writes, 'it will regress, especially toward what Freud called ego-libido, to which it is most closely related, or will at least mingle its conscious functions with unconscious ones. What actually wanted to get beyond the unconscious then re-enters the service of the unconscious and may thus even strengthen its force.'[20] Less and less an agency of critical self-reflection, the subject's own ego is taken as the central love-object for modern selfhood.

In Adorno's view, these developments influence the shape of subjectivity in two central ways: there is a chronic weakness of ego-identity and, subsequently, a dramatic rise in narcissism. The narcissistically weakened self, he affirms, becomes an increasingly prevalent character type in modern society since the requirements of late capitalism demand a reversal in self-awareness. In Adorno's view, the historical precursor to these developments can be seen in the rise of Fascist mass movements this century. In 'Freudian theory and the pattern of Fascist propaganda', written in 1951, Adorno argues that Freud's work on group psychology foresaw the rise of Fascist movements without sliding into the regressive crowd psychology of Le Bon and others. The psychological mechanisms uncovered by Freud's analyses of group processes are vitally significant, Adorno argues, since they draw attention to the ways in which individuals yield to political manipulation by external, social agencies. Following Freud, Adorno contends that, when in a large group, the individual tends to identify less with its own 'ego ideals' and more with impersonal 'group ideals'. This is said to discourage individual autonomy through the undoing of unconscious repressions, thereby releasing the powerful destructive energies necessary for the underpinning of any Fascist collectivity. The key mechanism for this release of violent and sadistic unconscious drives is identification. For it is through an identification with the Fascist leader that the follower is unconsciously able to introject desensitized and ruthless celebrations of brute power itself. This process of identification, which contains a strong narcissistic dimension, is capable of making 'the beloved object part of oneself'. According to Adorno, such narcissistic tendencies are becoming a crucial part of our most paranoid identifications in modern social processes as a whole. As he explains:

> this process has a psychological dimension, but it also indicates a growing tendency towards the abolition of psychological motivation in the old, liberalistic sense. Such motivation is systematically controlled and absorbed by social mechanisms which are directed from above ... The psychological 'impoverishment' of the subject that 'surrendered itself to the object,' ... anticipates almost with clairvoyance the postpsychological de-individualized social atoms which form the fascist collectivities.[21]

According to this view, the present-day weakness of the ego renders the unconscious liable to the formations of domination and social power itself. The libidinal drives, which were traditionally coordinated by the autonomy of the ego, become increasingly absorbed by destructive and alienating social forces, such as Fascism and the culture industry. Thus, there is a breakdown of the vital distinctions between consciousness and the unconscious.

An interplay of these main concepts – narcissism, identification and their interconnections in social processes – is further elaborated in Adorno's essay 'Sociology and psychology'.[22] Due to the increasingly instrumental and reified forms of modern social processes, writes Adorno, the ego must forgo self-awareness in the interests of self-preservation. By withdrawing into the unconscious, the ego is said to be increasingly rigidified through narcissistic illusions of self-containment. This taxing, and ultimate demise, of the ego is expressed by Adorno as follows:

> The social power-structure hardly needs the mediating agencies of ego and individuality any longer ... The truly contemporary types are those whose actions are motivated neither by an ego nor, strictly speaking, unconsciously, but mirror objective trends like an automaton. Together they enact a senseless ritual to the beat of a compulsively repetitive rhythm and become emotionally impoverished: with the destruction of the ego, narcissism, or its collective derivatives, is heightened.[23]

In Adorno's view, then, narcissism comes to replace internalization. Fathers, as representatives of bourgeois authority, are no longer dominating figures worthy of identification and emulation. As David Held comments, for Adorno the individual subject in the contemporary epoch no longer wants 'to become like his father but, rather, like the image projected by the culture industry (or by fascist demagogues, as in Nazi Germany)'.[24] The decline of the ego thus leads to a profound modification of the nature of unconscious drives. In short, the unconscious becomes exposed towards what were characteristic ego goals.[25]

Adorno thus concludes this investigation into modern selfhood by advancing the provocative thesis that social mediations become fully pressed into the service of the unconscious. According to this standpoint, psychic reality unfolds through the direct manipulation of unconscious drives and impulses by social agencies. Libidinal relationships are today mobilized, structured and sustained through the organized domination of the culture industry. Unconscious gratification, increasingly centred around destructive impulses, is directly manipulated through phenomena of repetitive cultural production. Purposeless diversions and the encouragement of empty pursuits are valorized by the communications media, through the dissemination of advertising, films and pop music. As Adorno puts this, a 'brutal standardizing society arrests all differentiation, and to this end it exploits the primitive core of the unconscious. Both conspire to annihilate the mediating ego; the triumphant archaic impulses, the victory of id over ego, harmonize with the triumph of society over the individual.'[26] Passively handed to the fully rationalized world, powerless to act in anything but the most paralysed manner to every social stimulus and demand, the psychic structure of the individual subject regresses to the planned obsolescence on which the social structure is predicated. The adaptation of the unconscious, Adorno affirms, becomes an invisible 'inner continuation' of a society fully structured through instrumental and technological reason.

At this stage, it might be useful to try to bring together the main threads of the arguments considered so far. We can distinguish four central aspects (no doubt more could be found) of Marcuse's and Adorno's interpretation of modern processes of repression and fragmentation.

1. *A theory of selfhood based upon internalization*: In the liberal epoch of market capitalism, self-identity is understood as being forged through the internalization of paternal authority. Connecting Freud's account of the Oedipus complex to the themes of the *Dialectic of Enlightenment*, Marcuse and Adorno argue that this process of identity formation is double-edged. The dialectic of resistance and submission to paternal authority in the process of individuation both constitutes and painfully splits the human subject. The forging of self-identity is thus internally tied to the social-historical process of internalizing authority.

2. *The eclipse of internalization*: With the ushering in of the 'administered world of late capitalism', Marcuse and Adorno contend that the social and political role of the family in identity formation is defused and undermined. The process of individuation, through internalization, is 'eclipsed'. Replacing the relative degree of individual autonomy once generated through the internalization of paternal authority, the rationalized world of commodified culture and depersonalized social relations generates a failure in ego development. As Marcuse argues, the modern subject's 'ego has shrunk to such a degree that the multiform antagonistic processes between id, ego and superego cannot unfold themselves in their classic form'.[27]

3. *The manipulation of the unconscious*: According to Marcuse and Adorno, the movement from the liberal phase of capitalism to the 'totally administered society' eliminates the requirements for an ego that is relatively adaptive and has a measure of autonomy. The result of this is the emergence of new social forms of repression. Discovering a hidden form of the drive for self-preservation, the ego is said to have withdrawn into the unconscious. As such,

the relations between consciousness and the unconscious are fully betrayed by incoherence and fragmentation. It is true that a display of individuality and spontaneity is retained – as is witnessed in the so-called 'liberation' of sexuality in modern times. But even this 'private space', Marcuse remarks, is just another commodity sphere in which the images and products of sexuality can be disseminated, thereby heightening the curse of 'repressive desublimation'.[28] Thus, the manipulation of unconscious processes by the 'totally administered society' produces what Adorno evocatively terms the 'boundlessly elastic, subjectless subject.'[29]

4. *The repression of consciousness*: In the liberal epoch, when internalization reigned supreme, the formation of the self revealed its Janus-face in the repression of libidinal drives as the price of self-control. What is said to distinguish modernity from previous forms of social existence, however, is that it is now the ego that comes into a state of conflict and is, ultimately, rendered obsolete. This fourth point is already implied by the other three. The increasing isolation of the modern subject in situations of powerlessness serves to constrain feeling and action, thereby subverting awareness and perception. Consciousness and the capacity for critical self-reflection become repressed. Drawing on the work of Franz Alexander, Marcuse speaks of an 'automization' and 'corporalization' of the psyche. As he explains this, the 'defence consists chiefly in a strengthening of controls not so much over the instincts as over consciousness, which, if left free, might recognize the work of repression in the bigger and better satisfaction of needs'.[30] Accordingly, subjecthood is granted a certain degree of autonomy for the purpose of self-preservation, but not enough to threaten the content and form of the social structure. With the repression of cognition, as well as human desire, the modern subject enters a historical context of unprecedented fragmentation.

Repression, Domination and the Social Order

The work of Marcuse and Adorno offers one of the most challenging descriptions of the interrelations between subjectivity and the unconscious on the one hand, and the effects of social and political organization on the other, wrought by recent historical developments. Throughout their analyses, the nature of the unconscious is intimately related to social and historical features of modern life. The matrix of problems arising from modernity, as it is posed here, hinges on the observed connections between increasingly evident social changes – economic and political but also changes of media in cultural production – and the overwhelming repression of the modern subject. As we have seen, Marcuse and Adorno locate the origins of the fragmentation of the subject in the drive to self-preservation. In the liberal phase of the economic order of capitalism, the forging of self-identity reveals its Janus-face in the repression of unconscious drives as the price of self-control and a measure of autonomy. In repressing its own libidinal drives in the name of autonomy, the drive to self-preservation inflicts a permanent damage on the self. This damage *is* the formation of selfhood brutally shot through with inner division, isolation and repetitive compulsion. This ambivalently emancipatory and repressive forging of the ego for Marcuse and Adorno, as we have charted, is most clearly discernible in the dialectic of struggle and submission in the Oedipus complex. Introjecting the dominative reason of the father in order to win a sense of selfhood, the emergence of autonomy is understood as internally tied to the prior submission to a repressive authority. The shift into the 'administered world' of late capitalism, however, signals the complete breakdown of the subject's already fragile sense of self-identity. According to Marcuse and Adorno, the previous antagonisms between the pleasure principle and the reality principle, the individual and society, are all but obliterated. Instead, a new and more powerful form of ideological incorporation arises. The individual subject today is incorporated within the dominant cultural values of society by the manipulation of unconscious processes.

At the outset, it is important to stress that this conceptual structure provides a critical perspective on self-identity and modern social processes. Marcuse's and Adorno's work offers detailed accounts of the interrelations between consciousness and the unconscious. On this view, the simultaneously emancipatory and repressive forging of consciousness is internally connected to a similar structure of antagonism in the unconscious. This fundamentally ambivalent conscious/unconscious dualism is, paradoxically, the social foundation of both creativity and oppression, empathy and violence, autonomy and heteronomy. The general features of this view of the internal complexity of self-identity is of signal importance when contrasted to much present-day social and cultural theory which either rejects or is silent about such crucial concepts as identity, subjectivity and the psyche. For even when Marcuse and Adorno announce the 'obsolescence of the subject' their analyses still hold firm to the principle of subjectivity. Similarly, their stress on self-identity as comprising both consciousness and the unconscious makes plain the central limitations of current postmodernist debates on the psyche. For, in their more naturalistic versions, such accounts have tended to hypothesize a split between a repressive order of consciousness and the emancipatory disorder of the libidinal drives. The result of this view, as represented in Gilles Deleuze and Félix Guattari's theory of 'desiring machines', is a naive espousal of human liberation through the free play of libidinal drives.[31] For Marcuse and Adorno, however, such a one-sided privileging of the unconscious is merely symptomatic of the very crisis of modernity, epitomized in the fragmentation of the subject. Reconciliation is to be found neither in the destruction of consciousness (in which there would be no subject left to enjoy any newly founded sensibility) nor by a reversion to a more 'natural' harmony, but by the transformation of society itself.

Yet it is also worth noting that Marcuse's and Adorno's project is ambivalent in political terms. On the one hand, it is a radical critique of the subterranean connections between the rise of modern institutions and the repression of the individual subject. The increasing normalization and alienation of modern social processes is shown to be deeply interfused with the subjection of the individual to mechanical passivity and conformity. Repression of the self is the converse side of a destructive and pathological social order which forces human subjects into an empty, narcissistic concern with the ego. On the other hand, the view that the drive to self-preservation is marked by a compulsion that hardens into a ever-intensifying repression of the self leads to a dangerous neglect of the complexities of social modernization. Marcuse's and Adorno's notion of identity is so focused on compulsive unconscious drives that it fails adequately to take into account the different modalities of political and ideological forces which impinge upon everyday life. Not all systems of economy and bureaucracy are equally repressive of self-identity. Yet it is doubtful that their account of self-identity has the conceptual means of separating the features of the social system which can provide a gain in autonomous expression from those which reproduce repression and domination. It is in this context that some commentators have argued that Marcuse and Adorno tend to ignore the vital political differences between the principles of liberal democracy and Fascism.

These political ambivalences, I suggest, have their basis in deeper conceptual problems. What is perhaps most difficult to accept in Marcuse's and Adorno's analyses is their specific use of the notion of repression to explicate the general contours of social development. If repression is the result of the drive to self-preservation *in toto*, as Marcuse and Adorno claim, then self-identity can only be viewed as inherently compulsive and destructive. Yet there are reasons for believing that this view simplifies the highly complex psychic processes involved in the repression of the libidinal drives. Psychical life, as Freud shows, often has a compulsive aspect to it. But to claim that this is unequivocally the main dynamic of modern self-identity seems to me a highly dubious argument. If Marcuse's and Adorno's standpoint is wrong, as I believe it to be, it is necessary to retrace the processes by which repression becomes deeply locked into culture and societal reproduction. My argument, broadly speaking, is that repression is constituted not through a monadic drive to self-preservation, but through a complex and intricate process in which unconscious drives intersect in our relations with others.

In offering some critical reflections on the work of Marcuse and Adorno, my aim is to identify certain tensions and difficulties in their conceptualization of the links between the psychic and social realms. In the following paragraphs I cannot attempt to elaborate my arguments in the full detail that they require. Instead, I shall, for the sake of clarity, focus my critical comments by briefly listing three problems or aporias in Marcuse's and Adorno's arguments: theses which are particularly questionable and problematic. They are (1) that repression is constituted by the drive to self-preservation; (2) that the process of repression involves a 'subjugation' of the libidinal drives, of 'inner nature'; and (3) that the increasing complexity of societal modernization necessarily demands increased psychological repression. In criticizing these viewpoints, I shall suggest that it is necessary to break with such presuppositions in a radical way. I shall elaborate upon what sort of perspectives might replace these in later discussions, particularly in the concluding chapter.

The first aporia, then, is Marcuse's and Adorno's compression of the complex and intricate processes of repression into the single mechanism of the 'drive for self-preservation'. This view, as we have charted, appears in various formulations. But, essentially, it involves the following claim. The drive to self-preservation arises, and is necessary, to release the self from its bondage to nature. This drive shifts the individual subject from the pleasure principle, an order of gratification and fulfilment, into the repressive confines of the reality principle, a culturally specific order of domination and exploitation. Moreover, once established, the drive to self-preservation becomes both self-regulative and increasingly opaque to everyday consciousness. Derived from Freud's early model of the psyche, the self-preservative instincts are theoretically brought in to account for the 'transmutation' from 'animal instincts' to the fully constituted 'human subject'. However, the use of the drive for self-preservation in this connection is a hazardous one. It has a peculiarly shadowy status in Freud's writings and, after the revisions necessitated with the introduction of narcissism, it was later subsumed within the general notion of the life drives. While Freud certainly referred to the bodily functions necessary for the preservation of the subject generically, he failed ever to trace out whether such functions are actually libidinal drives or biological instincts.

However, in later psychoanalytic doctrine there has been a broad consensus that the self-preservative functions are part of the biological structure of the body and not of the libidinal drives.[32] On this view, the instincts for self-preservation – the biological requirements for warmth, nourishment, shelter and so on – do not play a determining role in the dynamics of repression. As Laplanche and Pontalis comment, it is important to stress

> the artificiality of attempts to establish a strict parallelism, genetically speaking, between the self-preservative functions and the sexual instincts, on the grounds that both are equally subject to begin with to the pleasure principle, before gradually coming under the dominion of the reality principle. In fact the self-preservative functions ought instead to be assigned to the side of the reality principle from the start, and the sexual instincts to the side of the pleasure principle.[33]

As we will examine in Chapter 4, this viewpoint is derived from Jacques Lacan who makes an analytical distinction between 'need', 'demand' and 'desire' to transcend the elision in Freud's writings of biological needs and unconscious drives. From this viewpoint, a clear terminological distinction emerges between libidinal drives, which because of their plasticity are treated as desires, and the functions of self-preservation, which due to their instinctual rigidity are treated as biological needs.[34] On this view, it is within the former domain, unconscious desire, that the dynamics of repression are structured.

These psychoanalytical interpretations suggest there are serious shortcomings in Marcuse's and Adorno's view that the phenomenon of repression, produced today at levels of crippling proportion, is the result of a 'drive to self-preservation'. Indeed, Marcuse's opening claim in *Eros and Civilization* that self-identity is at once forged *and* repressed when 'animal drives become human instincts under the influence of external reality' begins to look faintly absurd. For it seeks to compress the complex processes through which the libidinal drives and object-world interfuse through the specification of a single sovereign mechanism. My comments, however, should not be taken to imply that the needs of self-preservation are entirely unconnected with the formation of repressed desire. As discussed in the last chapter, the emergence of unconscious desire is originally inseparable from the satisfaction of biological needs. Yet, as Freud tirelessly repeats, the specific configurations of repressed desire only develop through separating out from the satisfaction of these needs. Repressed desire emerges through, yet is radically *severed* from, the needs of self-preservation. As regards social development, such processes of unconscious pleasure and gratification similarly separate out from the satisfaction of these transhistorical, fixed needs. Indeed, it is in this separating out of the unconscious, in and through which cultural production is structured, that the mysterious connections between repression and cultural domination, desire and law, are located. Against Marcuse and Adorno, it can be argued that repression is not organized into set practices of compulsion and repetition. Repressed desire swerves onto many *different* paths of social and historical development. These may include the possibilities for friendship, love or the forging of new communal identities. Alternatively, they may be drawn toward practices of exploitation characteristic of the contemporary capitalist order, the possibility of nuclear war, or the obliteration of cultural minorities. But my point, for reasons I shall later try to identify, is that paths of repressed desire develop through our concrete implication with others. It does not operate, as Marcuse and Adorno suggest, through an already fully-fashioned compulsive drive to self-preservation.

This latter view that repression is constituted through our concrete interaction with others leads directly to the second aporia of Marcuse's and Adorno's work: their tendency to imagine that repression involves a 'subjugation' of pre-formed libidinal drives. Baldly stated, it is supposed that there is a 'subjugation' or 'transformation' of originally spontaneous libidinal drives into the repressive confines of self-control and calculation. Modern social processes, in short, are seen as placing obstructions upon the expression and attainment of libidinal gratification. It is certainly the case, as I argued in Chapter 1, that the forging of self-identity depends upon a repression and mastery of unconscious drives. But it is quite mistaken to conceptualize self-identity as arising from a monadic 'subjugation' of an original spontaneous desire. The view that there is a personal and timeless core of subjugated desire is inadequate, since its conception of repression is too simple. It is not the case that individuals have some fully-formed core of selfhood which is not already part of the everyday contexts that define their immersion in the social world. What is missing in this understanding of repression is any focus on the place of *human relationships*, of the connections between self and other.

Anthony Wilden has persuasively argued that the use in critical theory of an 'orthodox' Freudian model of the instincts actually suppresses their conceptual focus on the problems of alienated human relationships.[35] The central problem is that such a focus on the instinctual realm of the psyche leads to a neglect of the place of other persons in understanding phases of repression at both the individual and social levels. The difficulties of a monadic view of repression are described by Wilden in the following way:

whatever the biological instincts (needs) require of the biological individual, the human drives (desire) are the new products of organization as such, and at another level. They are discontinuous with what went before or below; the drives are social by their very nature. They come to us, not from ourselves, but from our relation to the Other; they are not the simple continuous transformation or repression or subjugation of something else in us or in our past.[36]

Characterized this way, the libidinal drives are not something that are already formed and which, subsequently, undergo the pressure of repression. As Freud's later writings make plain, repressed desire is an outcome of specific processes of identification and interaction *between* human beings. Desire and repression are constituted at one stroke through a mutual process of human expression, structured within specific social contexts. This theme connects to wider issues about the nature of self-identity, which I will consider in greater detail in the next section.

Finally, the third aporia concerns Marcuse's and Adorno's conception that social and cultural development has been associated with intensified levels of psychological repression. For them, repression is a specifically historical notion which is the key to interpreting processes of societal modernization. The transition from traditional societies to modern culture has entailed the inculcation of increasingly repressive prohibitions. And this heightened degree of psychological repression is directly contrasted to the 'playfulness' and 'spontaneous expression' of emotion in less complex societies. Several commentators, however, have argued that Marcuse's and Adorno's appeal to the notion of a 'spontaneous self', which exists prior to the inception of social development, is nostalgic and regressive.[37] This criticism is surely right. But it is necessary to question the contours of their claims further since its implications for this study are vitally significant. That there are major differences in the quantity of libidinal repression between traditional forms of social organization and modern culture is a highly dubious hypothesis. Sociological and anthropological research refutes the idea that there is any distinct correlation between psychological repression and the level of material and economic complexity in different societies.[38] On the contrary, as regards the repression of emotion and desire, the existence of firmly entrenched moral prohibitions and other renunciations can be said to have characterized the daily life of many early forms of social existence. This should not be taken to imply, however, that the character of subjecthood and modern personal relations have not been significantly transformed by the major institutional transitions brought into existence by modernity. The accelerating changes in the social world in the twentieth century have intimately interlocked with the nature of selfhood and the unconscious. But, as I shall argue in the concluding chapter, such transformations have equally accompanied attempts by subjects to create new forms of personal relations and authentic sociality. It is not the case, then, that human social development can be reduced to a linear dynamic of an intensified, tortured psychological repression.

It is necessary to resist the view that repression is a historically cumulative process. The separation of self-identity from unconscious drives by the 'barrier of repression' is fundamental to all societies, notwithstanding the vast cross-cultural differences in forms of libidinal expression. The existence of the barrier of repression within all types of social systems, however, does not mean that we cannot generalize about the repressiveness of given social arrangements. For this is surely what is so attractive to social theory about Marcuse's and Adorno's conceptual approach. But, characteristically, the standard that tends to be offered in their work for assessing cultural domination is an implicit focus on the *quantity* of repression – the amount of libidinal gratification which is denied the individual by society. The relation between societal modernization and repression is rarely explicitly considered in terms of the *quality* of human social relationships that a given social order makes possible. Yet this is clearly not because either Marcuse or Adorno were insensitive to the destructive and oppressive effects that modern social processes inscribe upon the self. On the contrary, their work represents an urgent plea against such subjective deformations. But in analysing processes of dominative rationality and social power through a monadic conception of the psyche, the subtlety of their cultural criticism is certainly limited by the crudity of their understanding of the nature of repression.

Of course, it might be argued that Marcuse's account of 'surplus repression' is precisely such an integration of these unconscious elements of selfhood within intersubjective, political and ideological dimensions of social life. But even the notion of a 'surplus' accumulation of denied gratification is still inadequate, since its account of the connections between repression and society is too simple. Marcuse is correct, I believe, in conceptualizing processes of repression within the asymmetrical relations of power of contemporary social processes. But the way in which these processes are traced out too drastically reduces the space – at once psychic and social – of individual subjects. To claim that basic libidinal renunciations are re-grooved by 'surplus repression' as a result of monogamous sexuality and commodified culture – entities which are presented in his analyses as external, social forces – results in the paradoxical situation of a reductionist sociologism that Marcuse sought to escape from in the first place. The problem, as Jean Laplanche comments, is that Marcuse fails to specify in what manner basic repression might be said to be reconstituted as 'surplus-repression'.[39] Marcuse's notion is certainly a model of socialized repression, but not one in which there is a connecting track between the conscious and unconscious formations of representation on the one side and the increasing control of these states of representation by social and institutional relations on the other. Again, as Wilden argues:

> The morphogenic restructuring which produced society is simply not in itself a sociological process, but the way Marcuse seeks to make a distinction between the phylogenetic-biological level and the sociological level implies that it is, because he assumes precisely what has to be proved: that man (which he calls 'the animal man') is possible outside the social conditions which seem to be, not simply his environment, but actually the very condition of his being.[40]

Against Marcuse, the relations of domination and exploitation that become deeply layered within unconscious elements of self-identity are not simply pressed in from the social and ideological field. The relation between social processes and repression has to be understood instead as a psychically creative process of production. While human subjects are positioned within social, political and ideological relations, it must be acknowledged that such positions are necessarily also invested with psychic energy – which, in turn, 'feeds back' into the social world. It is only within this dual process that specific sites of cultural renewal and struggle become intelligible. I shall develop the implications of this point in greater detail in subsequent chapters.

Self-Identity, Repression and Social Relations

The deficiencies in Marcuse's and Adorno's account of repression are connected to a fundamental assumption about the nature of self-identity. This is the assumption that the constitution of self-identity occurs against the backdrop of a monadic and uniform introjection of the law of social and cultural relations. Repressive subjecthood is traced as the result of the internalization of the authority of the father. A reliance on this monadic theory of identity formation is directly responsible, I believe, for some of the main problems of Marcuse's and Adorno's view of subjectivity. It also connects, as I shall try to show in the next section, with problems in their account of contemporary culture. One major line of criticism on these issues, developed by post-modernist critics, has been to deconstruct the very goals of 'individuation' and 'autonomy' embedded in such a standpoint. From this perspective, a standard response is to seek to demonstrate that such metaphysical notions act in complicity with the dominant Western modes of understanding, thereby only reproducing modernist illusions that serve to structure the very crisis of modernity itself. In what follows, I want to take a different approach. Rather, I shall argue that the theory of internalization and repressive selfhood developed by Marcuse and Adorno is ultimately incoherent since it fails to comprehend the processes – at once psychic and social – in which self-identity is constituted. To do this, it is necessary to retrace certain assumptions which underpin Marcuse's and Adorno's account of internalization – the traces of which, in the present epoch, are said to contain the last vestiges of resistance against social domination.

A number of issues concerning the plausibility of Marcuse's and Adorno's account of the formation of self-identity can be raised. First, there is much to be made of the oft-repeated charge that their account of the process of internalization is unduly restrictive. It will be recalled that this account of internalization posits a one-shot emergence of individuation through the resolution and acceptance of the authority of the father in the Oedipus complex. Through an iden-tification with paternal authority, the subject is said eventually to win a sense of autonomy and develop a social identity. In doing so, however, the ego itself becomes an intrapsychic agent of authority and domination. The internalization of parental authority is set up as an 'inner compulsion' of subjecthood. In Marcuse's and Adorno's view, then, a fateful impasse arises since individuation leads to its own internal destruction. Accordingly, the specific aspects of self-identity where resistance might be thought to exist, in critical self-reflection, rationality, and so on, are already internally tied to the acceptance of repressive authority. In turn, this thesis is used as a benchmark to assess the political structures of modern societies. The formation of self-identity and rationality is seen as being unavoidably tied to the repressive forces of political domination and oppression through which the social order is reproduced and sustained.

There are many problems, however, with the general theoretical assumptions which inform this account of the process of internaliza-tion. Approaches such as Marcuse's and Adorno's, with their assumption that self-identity is an internalized continuation of repres-sive authority, fail to explore what is most in need of explanation: the active psychic processes enmeshed in the construction of subjectivity and selfhood. As discussed in the previous chapter, Freud's writings demonstrate that there is a rich diversity of ways in which human subjects (always uniquely) pass through the Oedipus complex. The labyrinth of emotional identifications forged within this phase of development cannot be reduced to a single mechanism by which social authority is inculcated. Yet, Marcuse and Adorno fail to accord variations between self and others any substantive considera-tion. Their interpretation of the Oedipus complex, paradoxically, tends to mirror the more rigid and pathological aspects of the very social processes that they are concerned to probe and criticize. It is an interpretation which privileges rationality over emotion, law over creativity. However, the assumption that these psychological mech-anisms are fully contaminated by the prior acceptance of a repressive authority cannot logically be sustained. The theoretical aim of Freud's account of the Oedipus complex, as Julia Kristeva argues, 'was not, as he has been too easily accused of, to respect the paternal law of taboos that sketch our social interplay ... [but rather] to sort out the types of representations of which a subject is capable'.[41] Psychoanalysis does not claim that repressive subjectivity is the fated outcome of all Oedipal struggles. Rather, such distortions and pathologies are but *one* possible outcome of human interactions.

The central deficiency of Marcuse's and Adorno's account of internalization, then, is that it treats human subjectivity as a uniform *object* of an internalized social compulsion. This viewpoint, as we have charted, is based upon the assumption that the subject is closed off in a separate, asocial world until, through the monadic internal-ization of paternal authority, a repressive self-identity is forged. However, this assumption is only possible if one ignores the point that processes of identity formation are embedded within specific social contexts of intersubjective relations. For, as Jessica Benjamin argues, the function of paternal authority in the Oedipus complex cannot be reduced to a 'model' of power which is simply introjected by the individual subject.[42] Rather, an intersubjective focus high-lights that the father can just as easily be a *partner* in forging emotional understanding and empathy. Indeed, it is through the development of interactive identifications that individual autonomy arises. Instead of concentrating solely on the limits that social orga-nization places upon subjectivity, then, Benjamin suggests we should concentrate also on the gains in emotional expression that Oedipal interactions generate. Or, to repeat the Freudian formulation discussed in the previous chapter, the constitution of self-identity should be traced as the complicated interplay of independence and dependence, autonomy and heteronomy.

Second, notwithstanding these problems, there is confusion about the nature of the symbolic in Marcuse's and Adorno's work. Here I refer specifically to the symbolic role of the father in the formation of self-identity. As we have seen, Marcuse and Adorno view the decline of the father's social prestige as inevitably bringing with it a disintegration of moral conscience and individual autonomy in the current social order. In psychoanalytical theory, however, the function of paternal authority in the Oedipus complex is principally *symbolic*: to bar the small child's desire toward the mother through introducing the structuring law of social relations, the prohibition of incest. This function, it should be emphasized, is symbolic in character and mediates external reality (the *real* father) in complex ways. That is to say, there is no direct correlation between the actual father (that is, his social and economic status) and his symbolic role in breaking up the child–mother dyad. For example, clinical evidence suggests that a 'weak father' (defined as having low self-esteem, autonomy and social status) can actually 'produce' children with excessively strong and sadistic superegos.[43] The general point here is that, by reducing the Oedipus complex to the actual influence of the parents over the subject, Marcuse and Adorno altogether lose sight of the symbolic character of psychical identification. As such, this is a poor theoretical basis upon which to project such massive cultural transitions in identity formation.

Third, in fixing the internalization process so fundamentally around the Oedipus complex, Marcuse and Adorno neglect the important psychic processes of the subject's pre-Oedipal development. In doing so, it is clear that much about the psychical paths toward individual autonomy is screened from view. As Melanie Klein's analytic work with children demonstrates, the first three to four months of life, prior to the mother's construction as a whole person, are crucial to a subject's later imaginary space and capacity for rational autonomy.[44] Indeed, the progressive valorization of objects, from a persecutory stage of splitting to a state in which ambivalence can be tolerated, depends on this pre-Oedipal constitution of the ego. Such a standpoint also theorizes in a more thoroughgoing fashion the influence of maternal authority as well as the psychic differences in female child development. The failure of Marcuse and Adorno to consider pre-Oedipal processes in any substantive detail is a major deficiency in their account of subjectivity.

Subjectivity, Fragmentation and Cultural Modernity

In this final section, I shall make several critical remarks about the implications of Marcuse's and Adorno's work for the interpretation of contemporary culture. A central argument developed by Marcuse and Adorno is that, with the emergence of late capitalism, there are increasing psychic tendencies towards conformity, acceptance and passivity. From this standpoint, as I have emphasized, the more society becomes integrated through instrumental reason and technical rationality, the more severe is the repression of subjectivity. That the conflictual and antagonistic processes of modernity inscribe and reform the psyche in such a one-sided and homogeneous fashion, however, seems a rather simplistic and dubious line of argument. Consider, for example, Marcuse's discussion of the temporal restructuring of the psyche generated by contemporary work practices in late capitalism. Marcuse suggests that work processes in modern industrial societies are entirely structured by the organizational principles of social and bureaucratic domination. As he develops this, it is the routinization and regimentation of the daily labour schedule, the strict adherence to 'clock-time', that gears psychic reality towards a measurable, homogenous and linear experience of work. Through the repression of libidinal drives and individual spontaneity, modern systems of domination are able to implant a 'happy consciousness' that is practically unopposed by society. But there can be little doubt that Marcuse's analyses of these processes, which are only pointed to in the most general way, are oversimplified and excessively deterministic. Such an analysis leaves no room for the autonomous action of acting subjects, which forms the starting-point for the progressive unfolding of social contradictions. Because the burdens of suffering in the workplace are seen as the result of a technical rationality and formalized repression writ large, the actual experiences people have of labour processes and institutional organizations are written off as mere 'delusions of autonomy'.[45] This gives the impression that the connections between social power and the structure of modern work practices affect everyone in an equal manner. It thus completely ignores the intricate ways in which repressive work practices and industrial relations are produced, sustained and experienced by individuals in various social settings.

These points connect to deeper theoretical difficulties in the work of Marcuse and Adorno. Whatever the fragmentary and dispersed character of modern self-identity, an image of cultural modernity is actually projected by them of an increasingly homogenous and unified social system – of a 'totally administered society'. The reproduction of the political order is viewed as a complex process of 'social incorporation' to the dominant cultural values and institutional arrangements of society. This incorporation is traced as the result of several factors: the manipulation of unconscious processes, the repression of cognition, and the disintegration of individual autonomy. Yet the picture of a 'totally administered society' is surely a misleading one in many ways. The social and economic conditions of the advanced capitalist societies over the last fifty or so years have been far more conflictual and antagonistic than Marcuse's and Adorno's analyses recognize. This is symptomatic of the failure in the first generation of critical theory to accord any real weight to the structural differentiations of late capitalist society, or of the proliferation of social divisions between its members.[46] This neglect is highly significant since it screens out the performative consequences of specific strategies of political contestation and cultural resistance: of the *conflictual* reproduction of widely differentiated systems of power and forms of oppression and exploitation. The increasing importance of social movements in modern social life perhaps provides something of a baseline here. The struggles of countercultural groups – such as the ecological, peace and feminist movements, as well as the more traditional solidarities of labour associations – all provide a glimpse of the multidimensional and contested political character of the modern world. Seeking to secure and advance the rights of political and economic equality, these associations represent a crucial site of collective action against social power and domination. As a mode of political engagement in modern social life, social movements highlight that the creative and active dimensions of human subjectivity have not been entirely repressed. Clearly, Marcuse's and Adorno's theory of an intensifying dull conformity, however much it then captured the Cold War mood in American society, is palpably unable to come to grips with these aspects of contemporary social processes.

The foregoing comments on the theory of a 'totally administered society' highlight that Marcuse's and Adorno's analyses are based upon a consensual model of social reproduction. My critical remarks, however, are not intended to suggest that Marcuse and Adorno were themselves ignorant of the objective fragmentations of contemporary capitalist societies. On the contrary, many of their observations demonstrate a keen awareness of these processes. But it is because of the *fractured* character of self-identity, of the split between consciousness and the unconscious, that Marcuse and Adorno project an inverse level of social incorporation for modern subjects to dominant institutional arrangements. There is a good deal of recent social research, however, which suggests that the reproduction of the social order is dependent not so much upon a consensus of collective values, but rather upon cultural fragmentations and tensions.[47] On this view, dominative relations of cultural production are structured not through a prior ideological incorporation (whether conscious or unconscious), but through the very propagation of social antagonisms and divisions. Such antagonisms, precisely because of their fragmented character, are unable to pose any real threat to systems of power within the present system. Rejecting the view that social reproduction operates via a unification of the social field, John B. Thompson comments:

oppositional attitudes do not necessarily generate a coherent alter-native view which would provide a basis for political action. Hostility and scepticism are often interfused with traditional and conservative values and are commonly tempered by a sense of resignation ... The reproduction of the social order may depend less upon a consensus with regard to dominant values or norms than upon a *lack of consensus* at the very point where oppositional attitudes could be translated into political action.[48]

This argument can be pressed further on issues of psychical struc-ture. The social divisions and antagonisms that these studies point to are certainly a consequence of human social activity. But it is impor-tant to see that these fragmentations and tensions of the ideological field actually 'feed back' into the emotions and desires of individual subjects. Marcuse's and Adorno's contention that it is the fractured quality of self-identity, the split between consciousness and the unconscious, which provides the basis for an *inverse* level of social incorporation, is inadequate. Contemporary social divisions, it can plausibly be argued, are actually *ramified* by unconscious axes – axes which are at once creative productions and yet which already bear the weight of ideology upon them. Unconscious mechanisms of displacement, condensation, symbolic representation and reversals of affect significantly deepen and re-groove fundamental social conflicts centred around class, gender, and race.[49] The general point is that such divisions and tensions do not operate solely on a socio-logical plane, but they become inscribed deeply in subjective-unconscious experience. If this is so, this gives an even greater plausibility to the viewpoint that the current social order is reproduced and sustained more through dissensus than through a unification of the ideological field.

To be sure, there is a major controversy in much current cultural theory about the alleged ubiquity of psychic fragmentation and narcissism. On the one hand, clinical evidence highlights a dramatic increase in the number of individuals experiencing pathological narcissism.[50] This evidence suggests that the nature of such psychic disorders concerns fragmentation anxieties about the unity and intactness of the self. Unable to form relationships with any real emotional commitment, it is said that such personalities often prove socially adaptive by masking such anxieties through grandiose, narcissistic illusions of self-containment. These narcissistic 'illusions' characteristically centre around the pursuit of material success and power. The work of Kernberg and Kohut, two leading psychoanalytic writers on disturbed narcissism, indicates that underneath the narcissist's veneer of social adaptation lie intense feelings of separation and isolation.[51] These feelings can become so intense that they surge into disintegration anxieties and fears of self-annihilation. Other writers have reached much the same conclusion, but connect these feelings of powerlessness more directly to the cultural forms of modern social life. In a major essay on the links between narcissism as a pathogenetic entity and as a sociological trend, Joel Kovel comments that as a result of these modern fragmentations

> the individual suffers from a kind of emptiness. Experience seems drained and lifeless, without real texture. It is not that things are not perceived sharply – for usually the narcissistic character is if anything hypersensitive – and it is not that correct functioning is impossible – for quite often, the world being what it is, the individual functions at quite a high level. It is rather that, in the zone of felt experience between perception and action, a kind of cold hollowness transpires.[52]

In teasing out the sociological implications of this, Kovel argues that there are a multiplicity of narcissistic forms in modern personal relations. Moreover, he suggests that narcissism plays a substantial psychic role in the fortunes of late capitalist society. These themes also connect directly to the more popularized writings of Christopher Lasch, who uses such evidence of psychic fragmentation to posit a 'culture of narcissism'.[53] In Lasch's view, modernity signifies the penetration of fragmentation and commodification into the very tissue of the psyche and human social relationships.

On the other hand, the work of an array of authors, such as Jürgen Habermas, Jessica Benjamin and Anthony Giddens, suggests that the fabric of modern personal relations has not been normalized and fragmented in this way.[54] While there is by no means a consensus of opinion among these authors, there is the theoretical insistence in their work that the transition to modern forms of personal relations contain the *possibility* of new modalities of self-actualization and individual autonomy. Alert to the repressive, narcissistic and instrumental aspects of modern social life, these writers, in divergent ways, also stress the gains in freedom and expressive possibilities which flow from mutual interaction. Accordingly, for these commentators, modernity exhibits a series of ambivalent tendencies for the future of human social relationships. What this suggests is that it is possible to acknowledge the psychic costs caused by capitalist development, without concluding that subjective fragmentation is the inevitable fate of humankind. For Habermas, it is this totalizing critique of cultural reification by Marcuse and Adorno which most blurs the contours of self-identity in modernity. As he remarks, the critical theorists

> detach the concept of reification not only from the special historical context of the rise of the capitalist economic system but from the dimension of interhuman relations altogether; and they generalize it temporally (over the entire history of the human species) and substantively (the same logic of domination is imputed to both cognition in the service of self-preservation and the repression of instinctual nature). This double generalization of the concept of reification leads to a concept of instrumental reason that shifts the primordial history of subjectivity and the self-formative process of ego-identity into an encompassing historic-philosophical perspective.[55]

It is not my purpose here to insist on the priority of either of these competing interpretations of modern identity, nor to seek to attempt some sort of reconciliation between them. Like all terrains of subjectivity, the situation is assuredly more subtle and complex. I do not think it justifiable, however, to see the phenomena that Marcuse and Adorno analyse as showing the power of capitalist modernity to empty out the human subject of all personal identity and feeling, as draining whatever was left of ego substance and psychic interiority. Though the thesis of psychic fragmentation has undeniably served to discredit the influence of liberal notions of a self-autonomous subject, it would appear that there are a number of obscurities that attend any attempt to assess the concretization of this doctrine in contemporary social processes. It may well be that, at present, it is not possible, or even desirable, to separate the gains from the losses here. That is, whatever the actual impact of the fragmentation of subjectivity, it is extraordinarily difficult to work out whether these changes merely reflect the lived experience of modernity or whether it suggests the development of new, alternative processes of subjectivity. But a more plausible interpretation might be that contemporary social development in some sense intersects with a subjectivity torn with psychical ambivalences – between unity and fragmentation, hope and despair.

This chapter has explored several key intersections between the psychic and social realms developed in the work of Marcuse and

Adorno. I began by describing the specific ways in which their work employs Freudian psychoanalysis to analyse the relationships between subjectivity, the unconscious and modern social processes. I argued that their work provides important insights on the intricate ways in which self-identity and the unconscious are constructed within contemporary systems of domination and social power. On the other hand, I argued that their rather biological reading of Freudian psychoanalysis leads to a significant neglect of the formative impact of psychic phenomena on social processes. Rejecting the viewpoint that selfhood is formed only via the repressive introjection of parental authority, I argued that a theory of identity-construction must situate the individual psyche within actual contexts of intersubjective development. In more recent psychoanalytic and social theories of the subject, as we will examine in the work of Habermas as well as Lacanian and post-structuralist thought, such a focus on the intersubjective sphere has become central to current debates on individuality and the possibilities of personal and social transformation.

Nevertheless, I suggested that Marcuse's and Adorno's work is important due to their detailed investigation of the psychic relation between the fragmentation of consciousness and the unconscious. In their view, the more destructive and alienating aspects of modernity are firmly fixed within the workings of the unconscious. Thus, the emergence of phenomena such as narcissism and psychic fragmentation are viewed as an ideological smoothing-out of any potential political resistance in a social order that has become wholly incorporative, indeed 'totalitarian'. However, as we have seen, alternative social-theoretical readings of the impact of modern social processes on the psyche contradict this vision: they suggest that the transvaluation of cultural values may provide a source for new forms of autonomy and ideological consciousness.

In conclusion I should emphasize that, while criticizing many assumptions of Marcuse's and Adorno's work, it has not been my purpose to suggest that their work may be dismissed out of hand. On the contrary, their work offers many valuable ideas that I shall refer to in the subsequent chapters on the intersections between subjectivity, the unconscious and modern social processes. My argument rather has been that their writings in this area do not contain a theoretically adequate formulation of such a theory.

3 Repression and Social Transformation

Critical Theory Beyond the Politics of Domination

In this chapter, elaborating upon the theme of the repression of the self, I shall trace some implications of critical theory for social and emancipatory critique. At issue here are the links between the self and autonomy. By raising questions about the most desirable and just political organization, critical theory aims to disclose new possibilities of meaning beyond the purely repressive and ideological. Critical theory seeks to uncover, in brief, liberatory human desires and aspirations which have been rendered retrogressive by modern social conditions. In what follows, I want to examine this tracing of repressed desire and gratification as elaborated by Herbert Marcuse and Jürgen Habermas. In the first section of the chapter, I begin by outlining Marcuse's account of the possibilities for transcending social domination – what he terms the emergence of 'libidinal rationality'. In the second section, I shall raise some conceptual problems in this account of the relations between individual and collective autonomy. This will then clear the way, in the final sections, for an examination and critical assessment of Habermas's theory of communicative action as an attempt to theorize the movement of emancipation.

Marcuse and the Politics of Libidinal Rationality

In Marcuse's account of the fragmentation and destructive tendencies of the modern subject, as we saw in the previous chapter, a bleak picture of contemporary society is painted. The paradox of late capitalist society is that the very social conditions which permit a reinstatement of autonomy cannot be comprehended by its fragmented and alienated subjects. Given the fixed horizons of this picture of modernity, then, it is particularly surprising to discover a supremely optimistic strand in Marcuse's writings on the possibilities for the transfiguration of human social relationships. Marcuse founds this optimism upon certain immanent institutional possibilities of the current social order. The possibilities for change contained in the social system, however, do not converge upon any single, revolutionary agent. As early as his work *Reason and Revolution* (1941), Marcuse argues that 'neither the Hegelian nor the Marxian idea of Reason have come closer to realization; neither the development of the Spirit nor that of the Revolution took the form envisaged by dialectical theory'.[1] Quite to the contrary, the vast transformations in the dynamics of identity formation, the disappearance of class struggle, and the assimilation of aggression to the values of the culture industry suggest that there can be no privileged agents in the transfiguration of social life. Yet, in his theoretical critique, Marcuse still holds firmly to Marxian principles of connecting interpretation and practice. On the political level, Marcuse argues that social critique with a utopian intent must relate human needs and individual desires to the immanent possibilities of current social processes.

The repressive social conditions which Marcuse mourns – the totalitarianism of a system of domination and administration, the fragmentation of the subject, the manipulation of the unconscious, the loss of individual autonomy – are to be redeemed by a condition which he terms 'libidinal rationality'. As a kind of sublime realm of utopian possibilities, Marcuse speaks of this condition as 'a new *rationality of gratification* in which reason and happiness converge'.[2] This realm is said to provide the basis from which a new reality principle can be developed and radical social reconstruction effected. The condition of libidinal rationality, in brief, will lead to a reconciliation between external nature, society and the individual subject. In contrast to the repression and domination of the current social order, libidinal rationality is a world of individual gratification and fulfilment. Marcuse describes this social transfiguration in the following way:

[Liberation] involves a radical transformation of the needs and aspirations themselves, cultural as well as material ... Moral and aesthetic needs become basic, vital needs, and drive toward new relationships between the sexes, between the generations, between men and women and nature. Freedom is understood as rooted in these needs, which are sensuous, ethical, and rational in one.[3]

On Marcuse's reckoning, the avenues for desired social change are in fact already present in contemporary society. The vital constituent for this transformation is the industrial-technological advancements which have been generated by late capitalist society itself. Marcuse argues that technological progress in Western industrial societies has reached a stage that makes the goal of overcoming scarcity, surplus-repression and alienated labour meaningful. The material affluence of the contemporary period renders alienated labour unnecessary and the 'performance principle' of late capitalism obsolescent. It is as if, paradoxically, technological reason itself is the collective historical carrier of the process of social transformation. In sum, Marcuse is adamant that the very technological reason which created surplus-repression and stunted human capacities in the first place has now developed to the point where these afflictions can be fully eliminated. The political implications of this standpoint, it might be noted, are ambivalent. On one hand, the faith invested in the technological advances of capitalism is clearly immense – the exploitations of the Third World which render economic advances possible are entirely ignored. Yet, on the other hand, in recasting the relations between the existing social order and emancipation in this manner, Marcuse is able to hold firmly to the Marxian view that history will be transformed by its most contaminated institutions. In Marcuse's work, the contradictory nature of late capitalist society provides both the basis for social critique and emancipatory politics. While he laments the mechanistic and destructive quality of industrial capitalism, he also claims that technological reason bears the stamp of its own collapse, in ways which help to transform the social order.

Under these new social conditions, Marcuse contends, Freud's equation of civilization with repression can be rejected. The immanent tendencies of concrete social relations and modern institutions suggests that a *non-repressive* social order is a possibility. However, Marcuse cautions, if this foregoing analysis is correct, it is vital that social theory and philosophy begin the preliminary task of seeking to reawaken the utopian impulse. For the cultural traces of freedom and autonomy, deemed so essential to the emergent social order, have been brutally supressed and all but obliterated by the 'performance principle' of the economic order of capitalism. The one-dimensional society has only developed by denying its own past and collective aspirations. Utopian meanings must be rediscovered, Marcuse argues, since today they are no longer confined to the realm of fantasy. Rather, utopian-orientated thought can actually help the emergent, desirable future to be realized.

For Marcuse, a central pathway beyond the current 'performance principle' is opened up by the pure and unrepressed realm of phantasy. Likened to a personal core of inner selfhood, phantasy is at once a kind of negation of the repressiveness of the social world and somehow also prefigures new possibilities for that world. Indeed,

Marcuse speaks of phantasy as providing a privileged glimpse of the individual subject's needs and desires prior to the brutal distortions and pathologies which are inscribed by modern social processes. Marcuse sketches the importance of the unconscious for the project of self-actualization in the following way:

> According to Freud's conception the equation of freedom and happiness tabooed by the conscious is upheld by the unconscious. Its truth, although repelled by consciousness, continues to haunt the mind; it preserves the memory of past stages of individual development at which integral gratification is obtained. And the past continues to claim the future: it generates the wish that the paradise be re-created on the basis of the achievements of civilization ... The rediscovered past yields critical standards which are tabooed by the present ... The *recherche du temps perdu* becomes the vehicle of future liberation.[4]

Lodged uneasily between the pleasure and reality-ego, phantasy for Marcuse retains the psychic tendencies of imaginary plenitude and gratification originally known at birth. In this sense, phantasy is not simply a 'replay' of times past and lost, but is actually the *precondition* of human happiness and of any refashioned subjectivity. In phantasy, there is a temporary reconciliation between the pleasure and reality principles. And it is from this reconciliation, however partial and brief it may be, that Marcuse envisages a new rationality of gratification.

But what does it mean to claim that phantasy is prefigurative of a new attitude to reality? It means, essentially, that in this pure and unrepressed state of libidinal satisfaction a genuinely free and autonomous subjectivity can become a possibility. Phantasy emerges as the messenger of a new subjecthood. At the same time Marcuse is deeply aware that, as the psychic realm which underlies the possibility of freedom, such a condition is not just bound to spring into existence. Indeed, it may well never exist. The repressions and irrationalities of modernity may have suppressed these unconscious dynamics irreversibly. But, Marcuse argues, there is something in the nature of the unconscious which suggests that this has not been the case. While currently denied satisfaction by the 'performance principle', phantasy itself cannot be *eternally* denied: 'Imagination envisions the reconciliation of the individual with the whole, of desire with realization, of happiness with reason. While this harmony has been removed into utopia by the established reality principle, phantasy insists that it must and can become real, that behind the illusion lies knowledge.'[5] In short, subjectivity can be released from repression by phantasy. Moreover, Marcuse hints that we are rapidly approaching a turning-point in history where the release of phantasy can for the first time create a new reality principle. The connections between the collapse of technological reason and the creative release of phantasy will together curb the destructive antagonisms which have caused so much suffering and pain in the Western world.

Marcuse's valorization of phantasy is connected with the assumption that the individual body needs to be resexualized for the creation of harmonious social relations. In contrast to the repressive insistence on procreational genitality under the 'performance principle', Marcuse claims that the release of phantasy will lead to the development of a sensual Eros. This liberation, in brief, will involve the activation of pregenital impulses which will extend to all parts of the body. Drawing upon the work of Friedrich Schiller, Marcuse claims that this transfiguration of the human body will directly help to produce a 'senuous order' in which spontaneous cooperation, play and intimacy can be forged. The new reality principle arising from the transformative power of phantasy, however, does not involve some kind of 'release' of sexuality – as in Wilhelm Reich's programme of 'sexual revolution'. Enthusiastic though he is for the transformation of desire, the new sensuous order for Marcuse signifies a transfiguration of Eros and the very notion of sexuality: 'In contrast, the free development of transformed libido within transformed institutions, while eroticizing previously tabooed zones, time and relations, would *minimize* the manifestations of *mere* sexuality by integrating them into a far larger order, including the order of work. In this context, sexuality tends to its own sublimation.'[6] Once desire is for the first time allowed full expression, it can become transformative of the conflict between the life and death drives, Eros and Thanatos. Eros would redeem aggressive and destructive drives into the service of life itself. In this sense, Marcuse looks to Freud's death drive as a source of hope: as that which aims at peace, quiescence and the absence of pain. 'Death would cease to be an instinctual goal. It remains a fact, perhaps even an ultimate necessity – but a necessity against which the unrepressed energy of mankind will protest, against which it will wage its greatest struggle. In this struggle, reason and instinct could unite.'[7] Freed from the destructive forces of surplus-repression, the preconditions of libidinal rationality will allow people to die with dignity.

If this sounds somewhat fantastic, which in a certain sense it is *meant* to be, it is important to stress again that the philosophical basis of Marcuse's doctrine cannot be regarded as social escapism. In connecting the subjective desires of individuals to institutionally immanent possibilities, Marcuse defends this political project by asserting that these ideals have become increasingly realistic in modern times. The relation between human wants and current material resources have reached the point where we can imagine a fundamental social transformation to the good society. As Marcuse remarks, in such conditions 'the pertinent question is whether a state of civilization can be reasonably envisaged in which human needs are fulfilled in such a manner and to such an extent that surplus-repression can be eliminated'.[8] And while it may be difficult to know exactly how such a state as 'libidinal rationality' may ever come about, Marcuse argues that social critique must seek to further these possibilities of a fulfilling and satisfying life for everyone.

Desire and the Repression/Expression Model

As we have seen, Marcuse claims that the very social conditions of late capitalism are producing the possibilities for the creation of a communal life without domination, exploitation, or repression. Extrapolating from the social tendencies of the advanced industrial societies, Marcuse argues that the interconnection between systems of technology, high levels of social wealth, and the development of new needs and values makes meaningful the project of a qualitatively different, more liberating society. In tracing the linkage between systems of economy and technology on the one hand, and the trans-valuation of sensibility and culture on the other, the sphere of the affective is directly connected to concrete social relations in Marcuse's work. Hence, his description of the alternative society as a 'concrete utopia'. Yet many critical appraisals of Marcuse's work, such as that developed by Leszek Kolakowski, dismiss his writings on social transformation for their 'naive utopianism' and neglect of institutional developments from which social change might be realized.[9] Throughout his career, Marcuse sought to combat such pejorative critiques of the liberational character of utopian meanings. In 'Philosophy and critical theory', he writes that radical social critique

> always derives its goals only from present tendencies of the social process. Therefore it has no fear of the utopia that the new order is denounced as being. When truth cannot be realized within the established social order, it always appears to the latter as utopia. This transcendence speaks not against, but for, its truth. The utopian element was long the only progressive element in philosophy, as in the constructions of the best states and the highest pleasure, of perfect happiness and perpetual peace.[10]

In response to the charge that his political doctrine supports only the most narrowly abstract conception of social transformation, Marcuse repeatedly argued that he was concerned with the tendencies towards change that contemporary society is *already* expressing, albeit in a hidden and distorted way. As the foundation of a new political realism, then, Marcuse's revolutionary project focuses on the objective possibilities of modern culture and of the repressed desires of individuals. And it is from this perspective, it seems to me, that we should locate the importance of Marcuse's mapping of the emancipatory possibilities that are dissimulated within capitalist social relations.

To raise the issue of dissimulation is to return once again to the complex and intricate connections between the imagination or phantasy and the nature of the social order. Marcuse's key argument is that phantasy is of crucial significance to the utopian impulse since it represents that sector of the unconscious which resists dissimulation within repressive social conditions. The 'truth value' of phantasy, Marcuse writes, 'lies in the specific function of memory to preserve promises and potentialities which are betrayed and even outlawed by the mature, civilized individual, but which had once been fulfilled in his dim past and which are never entirely forgotten'.[11] As an embodiment of pure libidinal gratification, then, phantasy offers an escape from the prison-house of subjectivity. The function of phantasy is to uphold the 'tabooed images of freedom'; since it 'speaks the language of the pleasure principle' it represents a psychic state that one day may become a social possibility. It is because we have known a period of imaginary plenitude, prior to the instantiation of received social meanings in the Oedipus complex, that the individual psyche seeks a return to this pure state of libidinal gratification. The central claim, in short, is that phantasy contains repressed desires which in a non-repressive society would be permitted gratification. Marcuse's argument that unconscious phantasy embodies a potentially liberative capacity, an insistance on the negation and transcendence of the current social order, is an important contribution to the theorization of an emancipated subjectivity. Notwithstanding the role that the imaginary has been accorded in contemporary theory, from Lacan to Kristeva, Marcuse's linkage of phantasy and social transformation remains important. In particular, his claim that the prospects for the realization of liberation and human autonomy are to be found in the immanent tendencies of phantasy processes needs to be appraised critically.

The fulfilment of phantasy for Marcuse involves the creation of 'libidinal rationality', a realm of experience in which reason becomes affective and produces a 'sensuous order'. On this view, reason does not repress libidinal drives but actually promotes their expression and gratification. The entwinement of the cognitive and affective, law and desire, makes possible the development of creative communal relationships based on mutual affection, love and happiness. According to Marcuse, a newly defined aesthetic-erotic rationality must implant itself squarely within the affective foundations of subjectivity. This viewpoint, it should be stressed, is a significant qualification of traditional philosophical paradigms, such as the German rationalist heritage, which promotes reason as the sole basis upon which social change is to be effected. Marcuse entirely rejects the rationalist dichotomy which views reason as the ground of bourgeois Enlightenment and desire as disruptive and disorderly. Yet if Marcuse is sceptical of the rationalist heritage, he is equally aware of the dangers of privileging the emancipatory potential of desire itself. Unlike certain postmodern celebrations of the untamed and liberational character of libidinal desire, as in the work of Gilles Deleuze and Félix Guattari, Marcuse argues that libidinal gratification cannot develop outside of the symbolic dimensions of cultural life. In short, then, Marcuse is not advocating any kind of 'free play' of libidinal desire. Rather he is suggesting that a new reality principle, instead of repressing desire, could produce a libidinal order in which unconscious drives could be fulfilled. It is through the interfusion of reason and passion, law and desire, the cognitive and affective, that the current repressive social order may be transcended. And, as we have seen, the formation of a 'libidinal rationality' is to be brought into effect through the creative release of phantasy processes.

The question which I now want to raise is whether, in the social and political spheres, the full realization of the truth content of phantasy can actually produce the sort of radical changes in concrete social relations which Marcuse envisages. For *why* should the complete fulfilment of collective phantasmatic processes necessarily lead to a more autonomous and democratic society than that which is already currently evidenced by their partial and fragmentary expression? Surely the more politically troubling effects of phantasy, however much released from repression, cannot be expected to dissipate. Consider, for example, the specific social conditions of the oppression and repression of women. Notwithstanding the sensuous and harmonious quality that Marcuse attributes to the imaginary, it must be asked how the full expression of men's unconscious phantasies might in any way overcome the problem of the massive asymmetries of power between the sexes? How far can the release of libidinal phantasy eradicate the inequalities and exploitations involved in ties of domestic labour and oppressive sex roles? These and other parallel problems are nowhere satisfactorily dealt with by Marcuse. Indeed, his analyses tend to ignore the point that phantasy processes *have* been deeply engrained historically in the vast exploitations, brutalities and violent tensions of sexual relations. These deep connections between phantasy and the reproduction of gender inequalities suggest that attempts to move to an altered form of human social relationships will come up against severe resistance. Yet Marcuse's programme fails to reflect on the specific social and political *content* of phantasy processes. It offers little practical insight into the ways in which phantasy may be mediated by social and political phenomena for more creative cultural purposes.

In one sense, this obscurity of Marcuse's political doctrine springs from the ambiguities of the notion of emancipation itself. Exactly how it is that phantasy and the object-world, desire and law, will come together is, from the vantage point of the current social order, theoretically impossible to specify. Marcuse was deeply aware of this. Hence, his repeated assertions that social theory should not legislate on specific details of political reform. Yet, in another sense, the obscurity of Marcuse's political approach goes to the crux of the deficiencies of his theoretical elaboration of the connections between phantasy and social transformation. For, as we have seen, Marcuse's analysis is based on the division between the current repressive social order, in which the 'truth content' of phantasy is suppressed, and the realization of a new social order, in which the reconstruction of subjecthood requires the full expression of phantasy. But how can such a sharp distinction be drawn between alienated and creative phantasy without emptying the notion of all practical content? How is it possible to distinguish, that is, between phantasy that is 'blocked', 'suppressed' or 'outside' of the current social order and phantasy that is capable of constitutively transforming social and political relations? As I suggested in Chapter 1, phantasy is best seen as a complicated interplay of two psychic tendencies. On the one hand, phantasy is an essential well-spring of the creative imagination, a realm suggestive of possible futures. On the other hand, phantasy is the productive underpinning of all existing human social relationships, providing the essential images and representations in which modern institutional life is rooted. Of these two tendencies, it seems to me, Marcuse adopts only the former, thereby detaching phantasy from its organizing role in contemporary social relations. And it is this neglect which leads him to advance the provocative, though ultimately flawed, view that phantasy is denied gratification by the current social system.

J. Laplanche and J.B. Pontalis, in their seminal essay 'Phantasy and the origins of sexuality', provide a useful corrective to the sort of realist conception of phantasy proposed by Marcuse.[12] In tracing the problematic of the origin of phantasy, Laplanche and Pontalis stress that unconscious processes of phantasy are a constitutive and productive feature of the 'psychic space' of the human subject.

According to this viewpoint, phantasy is not something that is 'blocked' or 'prevented' from achieving expression, but is rather already intricately interwoven in the forging of self-identity. 'Phantasy', as Laplanche and Pontalis argue, 'is not the object of desire, but its setting. In phantasy the subject does not pursue the object or its sign: he appears caught up himself in the sequence of images. He forms no representation of the desired object, but is himself represented as participating in the scene.'[13] Phantasy is not only the disguise of a repressed desire, it is an unconscious *fulfilment* of that desire. From this angle, the view that phantasy might be denied gratification, as a truth which is prevented expression, appears simply as a realist residue. This is significant since it suggests that Marcuse is mistaken to conceptualize phantasy exclusively in terms of an unconscious force which, in some sense, is severed from the 'object of desire' (in this case an expressive and aesthetic subjectivity). By characterizing phantasy in this way, Marcuse fails to grasp the role of these unconscious processes as already constituting what is real.

In criticizing Marcuse's approach I do not wish to suggest that his account of phantasy can be dismissed out of hand. On the contrary, I believe that he is correct to stress that unconscious processes are an essential medium for the imagination of emancipation and autonomy. Indeed, as Fredric Jameson has convincingly argued, Marcuse's work highlights that phantasy serves as a creative mediator between the oppositions of the individual and society, the psychological and the political, from which the utopian imagination derives its deepest source of inspiration.[14] My objection, however, is that Marcuse is wrong to view phantasy as an unequivocally positive phenomenon which, if released from repression, is *ipso facto* transformative of human social relationships. If phantasy is a positive phenomenon, as a creative mediator for the utopian impulse, it also has features which are primarily negative in character. As we have seen, phantasy is a productive representational source through which concrete social relations and institutional arrangements are sustained. And since phantasy is deeply rooted in social life, it is also bound up with existing power systems of domination and oppression. Phantasy processes bear the marks of these ideological conditions in quite distinct ways and, thus, it is inadequate to see it as a realm of experience which is outside of the law of social and cultural relations. Rather, as I have argued, it is vital that the content of phantasy processes be connected to the social and political conditions in which they are enmeshed.

These contradictions reflect broader political dilemmas. The dual character of phantasy, reproducing at once positive and negative features of social life, arises because of the imbrication of repressed desire and the law. Repressed desire, as explored in Chapter 1, occurs as a result of a legal prohibition laid down during the Oedipus complex. By severing the small infant from the body of the mother, as we have charted, the intrusion of a third force – the father – instantiates repressed desire in one stroke. As a consequence, human needs, affects, desires and phantasies are internally connected with social relations of power. Yet, if this is so, Marcuse's doctrine that phantasy can completely release us from the authority and domination of the social order would appear defeated. The interfusion of repressed desire and power highlights that there can be no simple privileging of the libidinal drives as a point of resistance against the law of social and cultural relations. This point can also be considered from another angle. If subjective experience can never escape the reach of the law, even within the deep levels of the unconscious, this is so since desire is not only internally connected to authority but is, in a sense, a product of its numerous manifestations. That is to say, the vast range of existing power systems of modern social and institutional life play a determining role in the constitution of repressed desire. Yet, if this is the case, Marcuse's entire emancipatory project is close to being rendered politically empty. For it implies that the unconscious core of selfhood, upon which Marcuse places such stress, is no more than a simple by-product of social power and domination.

A useful way of exploring the implications of this issue is through a comparison of Marcuse's political doctrine with the later work of Michel Foucault. Like Marcuse, the central aim of Foucault's work is to chart the increasing rationalization and homogenization of society in the contemporary epoch. Foucault is primarily concerned to develop a method for mapping the networks of power relations which have evolved historically. The point of such a structural-historical study of configurations of power is to trace possible localized strategies of resistance to social practices that are politically oppressive. In his late writings, this theme of the normalization of social life is explicitly connected to an analysis of modern forms of regulated sexuality and coercive self-identity. And it is in probing this institutionalization of inner passion and impulse that we can locate certain affinities, I think, between Foucault's and Marcuse's discussion of sexuality and its possible transformation. In Marcuse's account of self-transformation, as we have seen, the development of genuine emotional relationships is said to result from the transition from 'repressive desublimation' to an order of 'libidinal rationality'. This vision of an order of rationality which is placed within the bonds of libidinal impulse and mutual affection certainly has loose affinities with Foucault's notion of an 'erotics of perpetual reversal', in which any point of transgression resists the possibility of closure. In less obtuse terms, Foucault's argument that 'we must not think that by saying yes to sex, one says no to power' in many ways parallels Marcuse's trenchant criticisms of the 'sexual liberation' and 'permissive society' of the 1960s. In both Foucault and Marcuse, then, the political focus shifts from the notion of liberation through sexuality – the major proponent here being Wilhelm Reich – towards the idea of a transformation of sexuality itself.

Despite these similarities, though, Foucault's analyses of the intricate relations between modern forms of power and the forging of coercive self-identity are entirely different in theoretical orientation from Marcuse's work. Whereas Marcuse takes Freud's theory of phantasy as a basis from which to recoup the creative and erotic core of subjectivity, Foucault's work develops Nietzsche's method of genealogy. On this view, self-identity is an effect or function of power itself. Subjectivity is not simply connected or tied to relations of authority and knowledge, but is rather seen as constituted to its roots by the operations of power. Foucault's elaboration of these connections between subjectivity and power are instructive for exploring some of the major theoretical difficulties of Marcuse's work. For in contrast to Marcuse's account of the current social system as entirely repressive of subjectivity, Foucault holds the opposing view that the modern self is actually *defined* through its immersion in power relations. According to Foucault, it is quite mistaken to speak of the possibility of a society which is outside the boundaries of power relations. He specifically contrasts his position to Marcuse's, in an interview, on these links between power and repression:

> I would also distinguish myself from para-Marxists like Marcuse who give the notion of repression an exaggerated role – because power would be a fragile thing if its only function were to repress, if it worked only through the mode of censorship, exclusion, blockage and repression, in the manner of a great Superego, exercising itself in only a negative way. If, on the contrary, power is strong this is because, as we are beginning to realise, it produces effects at the level of desire ... The fact that power is so deeply rooted and the difficulty of eluding its embrace are effects of all these connections. That is why the notion of repression which mechanisms of power are generally reduced to strikes me as very inadequate and possibly dangerous.[15]

In the light of these comments, it is perhaps not surprising that Foucault demonstrates a persistent concern throughout the 1970s with the generative social consequences of power. 'We must cease once and for all', he argues, 'to describe the effects of power in negative terms: it "excludes", it "represses", it "censors", it "abstracts", it "masks", it "conceals". In fact power produces; it produces realities; it produces domains of objects and rituals of truth.'[16] Forms of human experience and systems of meaning can proceed, then, only via the operations of power. At the root of power for Foucault there is, in short, a certain productivity.

The viewpoint that power has as its focus the constitution *and* administration of the individual subject is taken up explicitly in Foucault's late writings. In *The History of Sexuality* he argues that modern technologies of power increasingly take the world of inner passion and impulse as their object.[17] Sexuality is not, in Foucault's view, a natural phenomenon which is subsequently subject to the power mechanism of repression. Instead, he makes a great deal of the concept of a 'deployment of sexuality' which is organized through a system of discourses and practices. He argues that technological discourses permeate the control of individual sexuality and pleasure in modern society. In claiming this, Foucault tackles head on the repression/expression model. He contends that social criticism must break from the 'repressive hypothesis', the view that desire is an exterior domain to which power is applied. The character of sexuality, according to Foucault, derives not from the 'repression of desire' but from an internal organization by disciplinary power. Debunking the assumption that the workings of power are exerted upon a pre-existing desire, Foucault writes:

> One should not think that desire is repressed, for the simple reason that the law is what constitutes desire and the lack upon which it is predicated. Where there is desire, the power-relation is already present: an illusion, then, to denounce this relation for a repression exerted after the event; but vanity as well, to go questing after a desire that is beyond the reach of power.[18]

From this standpoint the idea of some inner core of selfhood, of a rebellious desire to authority, is part of the same historical network organized by power as that for which 'repression' is denounced. For Foucault, the irony of a liberation from repression is that this very notion is actually part of the 'deployment of sexuality' and thus of our servitude to such discourses.

Foucault's proposal that all existing forms of desire are actually created by social power is not intended as a normative assessment of the nature of modern sexuality. To be sure, he does not deny that certain historical periods, as with the puritanism of the Victorian epoch, have placed high moral and cultural restrictions upon sexual life. However, he does argue that a general economy of the forms of desire should not be concerned to assess whether power is more tolerant than repressive. In Foucault's work, the fundamental focus is on the *paths* of discursive production that modern technologies of power have brought into effect. This can be achieved, he argues, only by examining the ways in which power has established 'sex' as the central discourse which structures everyday life. Yet, because Foucault has no positive theory of desire or of the acting self, the factors leading to the normalization and control of inner impulse and passion can only be traced as a result of the manipulation of the body. The body, regarded by Foucault essentially as a kind of biological machine, is seen as being coercively unified through the articulation and implementation of sexual discourses. The manufacturing of discourses on 'sex' and 'desire', he comments, gives rise to the illusion 'that there exists something other than bodies, organs, somatic localizations, functions, anatomo-physiological systems, sensations, and pleasures'.[19] Rejecting the 'principle of subjectivity', Foucault concludes that power and sexuality, in its various manifestations and formations, are coextensive. There is no originary desire prior to power relations; just the ever-expanding rationalized system of social control which submits bodies to an intensification of pleasures through the order of sexual domination. As a consequence, Foucault rejects the idea of a culture or politics 'beyond power'. Rather, the idea of political transformation must be retraced as the demand for a *proliferation* of discourses of power and sexuality. Only by transcending the binary oppositions of the repression/expression model of desire can we ever become freed of the current impasse of power relations.

Here we might return to Marcuse. In one sense, Foucault is surely right to criticize the repression/expression model and Marcuse's particular elaboration of it. The interfusion of power and desire highlights that Marcuse is mistaken to suppose that an intrinsically creative desire is prevented expression merely because of the oppressive effects of power. If social power constitutes the desire it is meant to control, then it is clearly implausible to locate that desire as the emancipatory opposite of repression. The central problem here concerns the concept of power. As the foregoing discussion suggests, Marcuse is wrong to view power as inherently oppressive. If, as Foucault claims, it is also a positive phenomenon, power cannot be seen as simply the obstacle to emancipation and autonomy; rather it is their essential medium. This should not, of course, lead us to neglect the constraining effects of power – an issue I shall return to shortly. But a concern also with the generative effects of power does highlight the major aporias of Marcuse's political doctrine. When, like Marcuse, one levels down the complexity of societal moderniza- tion to processes of the fragmentation of the self, of the manipulation of the unconscious, of a uniform 'surplus-repression', then one is hardly able to confront the persistent sociological and political ques- tions about the ways in which human beings and their social praxis can transform actual social and power relations in modern society. And it is because Marcuse sees power as a category which is inher- ently repressive that his account of emancipation is forced to cling to a residual naturalism: to the view that a private core of selfhood, the primary processes in themselves, can potentially liberate human subjects from the current repressive social order. What is required is a more comprehensive analysis of human needs and libidinal desires on the one hand, and their embeddedness within specific social and historical contexts on the other. The possible ways in which individ- uals and collectivities might reflect on human needs and desires cannot be left to the narrowly abstract – it requires analysis.

This having been said, I do not wish to imply that Foucault's work provides a more sophisticated account of the interconnections between human needs and social power. In the brief foregoing excursus on Foucault, I have outlined his view of the connections between power and desire in order to illuminate certain conceptual shortcomings in Marcuse's position. I am not interested here in developing a critical appraisal of Foucault's arguments – a task that has been well accomplished elsewhere.[20] However, one or two points should be made. If Marcuse places an exclusive emphasis on the utopian potentials of 'libidinal rationality', of the power of the primary processes in themselves, then Foucault's arguments express an equally one-sided selectivity, narrowing down modern formations of power to a Nietzschean impression in which these processes appear as prior to subjectivity, meaning and truth. Foucault's insis- tence on the productivity of power leads to a serious neglect of the constraining properties of power upon subjectivity. That systems of power are repressive as well as enabling, that they are oppressive as well as generative, tends to be written out of Foucault's excessively positive account of power. Equally one-sided is Foucault's claim that modes of subjectivity, systems of meaning and domains of reality are only objectified through the operations of power. The shortcomings of this standpoint, from a psychoanalytic angle in any case, are clear. Foucault's work misses the point that the social and ideological field can only be 'objectified' for a subject with a *pre-existing psychic reality and capacity for subjective response*.[21] In contrast to the reductionist view that the self is a standardized epiphenomenon of social discourse, I suggest that human subjects bring to the social field a

range of psychical operations – derived from the primary unconscious – which are of signal importance to the conceptualization of
being and action.

Habermas on the Colonization of the Self and the Life-World

An attempt to overcome the conceptual limitations of the first generation of critical theory, which retains a suggestive perspective on
social and cultural domination, is to be found in the contemporary
writings of Jürgen Habermas. A social theorist associated with the
work of the Frankfurt School, Habermas has proposed a complex
and detailed account of the connections between reason and subjectivity that differs in many respects from the first generation of critical
theory. While Habermas, like the early critical theorists, retains many
of the links between social power and the forging of repressive self-
identity, he refuses to accept that processes of fragmentation, loss of
individual autonomy, and the manipulation of the unconscious
provide an adequate characterization of the cultural framework of
late capitalist societies. According to Habermas, this fatalistic vision
of reason as self-mutilating in critical theory arises because of a
specific theoretical assumption: namely, that technological rationality
applies writ large in all spheres of social action.[22] In contrast,
Habermas argues, societies develop not only through technological
modes of action but also through symbolic interaction, or what he
now calls 'communicative action'. As Habermas expresses this opposition, while the control of the external world is dependent upon
forms of instrumental rationalization, the world of communicative
action is organized through the *intersubjective* transmission of cultural
and historical traditions. For Habermas, the importance of this separation is that it permits us to see that there are cognitive, moral, and
expressive dimensions of modern social life. The expansion of
science, morality and art in modern culture, in Habermas's view,
suggests that rationality can be divided into 'three worlds': our
relation to the external world, our social relations with others, and an
aesthetic-expressive dimension which we bring to our own 'inner
nature'.

This insistence on the differentiation of the cognitive, moral, and
expressive spheres of cultural rationalization permits Habermas to
develop a highly subtle analysis of social development. In recent
writings, Habermas has sought to connect this schema of rationality to
an analysis of the communicative basis of interpersonal relations.[23] In
what he argues is an epistemological break from the philosophy of the
subject, the theory of communicative action posits a distinctly different focus from traditional philosophy, which takes a self-identical

subject to confront a stable object-world. Instead, Habermas's communicative framework begins from the symbolically structured 'life-world', in which subjectivity is constituted through reflexive linguistic interaction. The continuity of the life-world is understood to be dependent upon the coordination of a range of action orientations that involve both moral and practical agencies. However, the analysis of the communicative foundations of the life-world is not the only methodological basis for the explication of social interaction. The reproduction of social life, in Habermas's view, involves conditions other than those of communicative rationality. Drawing on and refashioning the systems theory of Talcott Parsons, through the writings of Luhmann, Habermas argues that communicative action is necessarily structured into the 'functional conditions of systems reproduction' – to those impersonal forms of collective regulation in society. In any complex modern society, there will be a vast range of administrative and bureaucratic structures which coordinate the functioning of society; what Habermas calls 'systems integration'. The social and cultural effects of systems integration are ambivalent. On the one hand, systems integration, the institutionalization of technical knowledge, and the growth of anonymous economic and bureaucratic structures, provides the foundation for all existing life-forms in society. On the other hand, with its instrumentalizing logic, it can pose serious threats to social integration and the consensual foundations of modern culture. Indeed, as we shall see, Habermas believes this is exactly what has occurred in the present age.

It follows from this analytical separation that one must distinguish the rationalization of economic and administrative systems from the distortions of the communicative foundations of the life-world. As differentiated spheres of the social world, Habermas argues that the rationalization of systems on the one hand, and that of the life-world on the other, follow entirely different logics. The thrust behind this distinction is vital to Habermas's political project: it allows him to break from the standpoint in the first generation of critical theory that technological rationalization is *internally* tied to the repressive coercion of self-identity. This viewpoint, he argues, is fundamentally mistaken in that it conflates all social structures and processes into the immediacy of the life-world. According to Habermas, the uncoupling of 'system' from the 'life-world' is *not* a sign of cultural domination, but is intrinsic to modernity. Modern societies, in short, are dualistic in character. On one side, there are system domains, specializing in the material reproduction of capitalism and the modern bureaucratic state. On the other side, there is the modern life-world, specializing in symbolic reproduction, that is, the nature of the self, socialization and cultural transmission. Accordingly,

Habermas stresses, any account of the normative potential of rationality must recognize that the system-mechanisms of modernized societies will not dissipate. The collective regulation of society, which necessarily entails the coordination of economic and administrative structures, is an essential part of modern social processes. Such ineliminable aspects of modernity must be carefully distinguished, however, from those conditions in which the rationalized logic of systems reproduction penetrates deeply into everyday communicative practice. In Habermas's view, the spheres of systems and communicative rationalization intersect to produce specific social and cultural crises. And it is this reorganization and control of the life-world by the instrumentalizing logic of systems integration which is properly the site of cultural domination and reification.

From this more differentiated account of rationalization, Habermas is able to return to the traditional concerns of critical theory: analysing the distorted and pathological aspects of the modern era. Like Marcuse and Adorno, Habermas agrees that modern culture has become increasingly subjected to administrative and bureaucratic control. As the modern state becomes increasingly centralized and systematized, so too the communicative and consensual foundations of the life-world have been subjected to rationalization. In fact, systems integration in modernity has become rationalized to such an extent that Habermas speaks of an 'inner colonization of the life-world'. He summarizes this destruction of the resources of cultural tradition as follows:

> The analysis of processes of modernization begins from the general assumption that a progressively rationalized life-world is both uncoupled from and made dependent on formally organized action domains, such as the economy and state administration, which are always becoming more complex. This dependence, stemming from the mediazation of the life-world through system imperatives, assumes the social-pathological form of an *inner colonisation* in so far as critical disequilibria in material reproduction (that is, steering crises accessible to system-theoretical analysis) can be avoided only at the cost of disturbances in the symbolic reproduction of the life-world (i.e., of 'subjectively' experienced, identity-threatening crises or pathologies).[24]

In modernized societies, then, functional rationalization has reached the point where it threatens the very foundations of cultural transmission, socialization and the formation of self-identity upon which it depends for its own legitimation. Having gone beyond their facilitating roles, the economic and administrative systems of the institutional order are today producing 'pathological' effects via the rationalized penetration of the life-world. However, the distinction between 'system' and 'life-world' allows Habermas to claim that processes of rationalization are not as total in character as they might first appear. There is a deep resistance, he contends, at the core of subjectivity. The pathological effects of such cultural rationalization will often be defended against by the life-world. The rise of new social movements, such as ecological and anti-nuclear associations, highlights for Habermas the existence of such tendencies.

For our purposes, Habermas's account of the ways in which rationalization imposes itself upon the self and self-identity is particularly important. For the penetration of a bureaucratizing logic into the very tissue of subjectivity, in both cognitive and affective terms, is the principal means in which systems integration threatens and destroys the cultural foundations of communicative action. According to Habermas, the spread of organizational rationality into the 'aesthetic-expressive' realm of selfhood is only achieved at the expense of a *repression* of 'inner nature'. Such a repression results in the distancing of our *linguistic access* to inner selfhood. In short, the more pathological effects of administrative logic prevent us from being able to reflect critically upon and understand the motivations and drives of our actions. It is as if the very soul of subjecthood becomes detached from the public discourses of critical reason, leaving the individual subject in a state of psychological crisis. For Habermas, the Freudian unconscious is a pivotal concept for analysing this internal repression of the subject's needs and desires from public and political life. Taking Alfred Lorenzer's work on psychoanalytic linguistics as a point of departure, Habermas seeks to conceptualize distorted unconscious elements of motivation through recourse to linguistic pathologies.[25] According to Habermas, unconscious drives result from the distortions of language in general, and from communication in particular:

> The libidinal and aggressive instinctual forces, the prehistorical forces of evolution, permeate the species subject and determine its history. But the biological scheme of the philosophy of history is only a silhouette of a theological model; the two are equally precritical. The conception of the instincts as the prime mover of history and of civilization as the result of their struggle forgets that we have only derived the concept of impulse privately from language deformation and behavioural pathology. At the human level we never encounter any needs that are not already interpreted linguistically and symbolically affixed to potential actions.[26]

In identifying the libidinal drives with processes of language deformation, Habermas reconstructs the conscious/unconscious dualism as
an embodiment of 'systematically distorted communication'. In this
communications reading of Freud, consciousness contains the
discourses of the public sphere, while the unconscious contains those
needs and desires that are prevented or denied access to communicative action. Repressed desire is formed through a process that
Habermas, following Lorenzer, calls 'desymbolization'. This process
essentially involves the splitting off of needs, desires, and meanings
from daily interactive communication. Rendered inaccessible to life-
forms, the trace of these desires gains only a 'private linguistic
significance' for the individual subject. Habermas explains this
conceptualization of the unconscious in his essay 'On systematically
distorted communication'. There he argues that the unconscious
contains:

> those parts of the self that are isolated from the ego and whose
> representatives become accessible in connection with the
> processes of repression and projection. The 'id' is expressed indir-
> ectly by the symptoms which close the gap which develops in
> everyday language when desymbolization takes place; direct
> representation of the 'id' is found in the illusory paleo-symbolic
> elements dragged into the language by projection and denial.[27]

Moreover, he contends that Freud's metapsychology 'reflects fundamental experiences typical of a systematically distorted
communication. The dimensions established by id and super-ego for
the personality structure correspond to the dimensions of deformation of the intersubjectivty of mutual understanding in informal
communication.'[28] According to this standpoint, the unconscious is
a deformed and distorted realm of selfhood: 'it is reified, for the ego,
into a neuter, an id (it)'. Yet, paradoxically, it is this privatized realm
of language which returns to distort or cripple our public discourses.
   Notwithstanding the proliferation of these internal distortions,
Habermas rejects the standpoint, developed in critical theory, that the
unconscious has been subjected to manipulation by social forces. On
the contrary: the *depersonalization of the superego*, which was mourned
by Marcuse and Adorno, is seen by Habermas as a mark of moral
progress. It suggests that ego development is not as dependent on the
elements of cultural tradition and paternalism as it once was. In developing this view, Habermas relies on the contributions of ego-
psychology to the analysis of personality development.[29] He argues
that the identification of 'primary autonomous ego functions' in ego-
psychology – such as the capacity for judgement and reflexivity – are

of fundamental significance for understanding the ways in which autonomy is built up through developmental levels of social interaction. Conjoining these autonomous ego functions with the developmental psychology of Piaget and Kohlberg, Habermas argues that these reconstructive studies indicate that there has been an *advancement* in moral and rational autonomy. His analysis of these materials is complex, and I shall not attempt to summarize it here.[30] But, essentially, what he is claiming is that new modes of socialization and the development of new cultural values suggest there is an increasing shift towards 'post-conventional' forms of morality. The moral orientation of these forms of subjectivity connect to Kohlberg's account of certain universalistic ethical discourses which concern the protection of public rights and entitlements. The existence of such moral orientations, Habermas argues, is a prerequisite for any reconquest of the life-world through communicative action. For what a radical politics must seek to *reverse*, in Habermas's view, is the extremely unbalanced relationship between systems of functional rationality and their increasing penetration of the communal basis of modern life-forms. What must be undone, in brief, is that colonization of moral-practical and aesthetic-expressive realms which has led to the increasingly rationalized character of everyday life. Thus, the emergence of post-conventional socialization and morality is seen as a potential communicative foundation upon which this reconquest can proceed.

To claim that the communicative foundations of the 'life-world' anticipate in some sense the possibility of emancipatory democratic and participatory processes might seem naively utopian. To anyone living in the modernized societies of today, in which aggression and hatred have been progressively systematized into the growing global possibility of nuclear self-destruction, the analysis offered by Habermas probably does seem excessively rationalistic and out of date. Habermas has been particularly concerned, however, to defend the theory of communicative action against such charges of rationalism and formalism. In an essay on the cultural tradition of early critical theory, Habermas specifically discusses the issue of happiness as it affects his own understanding of emancipation and moral progress.[31] The question which he considers is the following: 'Could an emancipated humanity one day confront itself in the expanded scope of discursive will-formation and nevertheless still be deprived of the terms in which it is able to interpret the good life?'[32] Habermas's response to this question is, in short, to affirm the correctness of early critical theory's linking of emancipation with happiness. In this respect, he comments that communicative rationality is not a sufficient condition for individual and collective autonomy. Accordingly, Habermas argues that the perspectives on moral autonomy developed by Kohlberg and others must be supplemented with a focus on the emotional domain. To do this, Habermas seeks to refashion Freud's account of unconscious drives and motivations into his programme of communicative ethics. From this standpoint, unconscious drives are rendered as 'drive potentials' or 'need interpretations' which become inserted into the 'communicative structure of action'. By allowing 'need interpretations' access to moral discourse, Habermas believes that it is possible to reconcile the demands of rationality and happiness. He contrasts this incorporation of human needs and emotions with traditional moral theory in the following way:

> need interpretations are no longer assumed as given, but are drawn into the discursive formation of will. Internal nature is thereby moved into a utopian perspective; that is, at this stage internal nature may no longer be merely examined within an interpretative framework fixed by cultural tradition in a naturelike way ... Inner nature is rendered communicatively fluid and transparent to the extent that needs can, through aesthetic forms of expression, be kept articulable or be released from their paleosymbolic pre-linguisticality.[33]

The development of collective autonomy, then, demands a sensitivity towards human needs. Freedom demands a fluidity, a 'working-through' as it were, of the unconscious forces that so deeply structure the affective form of human social relationships. 'Ego identity', Habermas comments, 'means a freedom that limits itself in the intention of reconciling – if not of identifying – worthiness with happiness'.[34]

Finally, we can represent Habermas's account of the links between the unconscious and autonomy in summary form as follows:

1. From the standpoint of communications theory, the unconscious is characterized as a result of the desymbolization of public communication. The repressions engendered produce a privatization of language which distorts public communication. As the depository of distorting influences within the psyche, the unconscious is viewed by Habermas as a defective element of human subjectivity.
2. Developing the contention that psychic reality is a prime example of 'systematically distorted communication', Habermas seeks to link the 'distortions' of the unconscious to the social phenomena that produce heteronomy and alienation, such as ideology and power.
3. Connecting the psychoanalytic goal of the lifting of repression to the tasks of ideology-critique, Habermas contends that the

process of emancipation entails the elimination of unconscious determinants in human activity to secure the self-reflective movement toward autonomy and free communication. At the collective level, this demands the organization of social relations in such a way that 'interpreted needs' become accessible to the 'communicative structure of action'.

Desire and Communicative Action: Evaluation and Critique

Given the mixing of reason and desire which lies at the centre of this imaginative proposal for the attainment of individual and collective autonomy, we must seek to clarify Habermas's understanding of these entities and of their possible crossroads. Habermas's writings have been subjected to a great deal of critical debate in the social sciences over the last ten years or so.[35] In this final section, I shall focus my critical remarks on two major themes in Habermas's conceptualization of the self and the self-transformation of society. The first is that of Habermas's conceptualization of the unconscious and repressed desire. In offering a critical appraisal of the standpoint that the unconscious is a deformed or alienated aspect of our subjecthood, I shall argue that there are a number of serious misinterpretations concerning the nature of the unconscious in Habermas's work. The second theme concerns Habermas's linkage of 'need interpretations' to the goal of the emancipated society. By critically examining the claim that 'need interpretations' can be inserted into the 'communicative structure of action', I shall try to show that this formalistic concept of autonomy cannot accommodate human needs and desires in anything but the most abstract manner.

A useful way perhaps of beginning to address these issues is by briefly comparing Habermas's work with that of the first generation of critical theory. As we have seen in Chapter 2, a basic dilemma is posited in critical theory between unconscious drives on the one hand, and their repressive organization through the forging of consciousness on the other. In critical theory, a comprehensive account is developed of the ways in which human needs and desires are manipulated by social processes that are beyond the conscious control of the individual subject. The intensification of these processes of manipulation, however, gives rise to a number of important political problems. Since subjectivity is seen as constituted by a drive to self-preservation that actually mutilates reason and consciousness, the only possible escape route from repression must lie within the dynamics of unconscious desire itself – as posited in the work of Marcuse. In this sense, and notwithstanding his more subtle diagnosis of self-identity, Marcuse's work parallels certain tendencies in postmodernism which view desire as the radical *other* of coercive reason and social modernization. In contrast, Habermas's account of communicative action rejects the viewpoint that the unconscious should be privileged as *the* other, or even as a major source of opposition, to Enlightenment reason. Seeking to correct the deficiencies of a monadic conception of the self in critical theory, Habermas draws from alternative perspectives on socialization to argue that there has been progress in rational and moral autonomy; and that there are a variety of identity patterns in contemporary society. In particular, Habermas takes from ego-psychology an analysis of primary autonomous ego functions which evolve through contexts of inter-subjective involvement. The conceptual tracing of these involvements is said to lead either to autonomy or to psychopathologies and unconscious blockages – to those silences, gaps and displacements of social interaction. For Habermas, the task of critical theory is to trace out such distortions, especially their links with power and ideology. The issue which I now want to raise is whether Habermas's concern with the possible autonomy of the ego is not achieved at the expense of altogether losing the dynamic unconscious in social relations. That is, does Habermas's conceptual focus manage to deal adequately with those problems identified by critical theory: the internal connections between the unconscious and social power and domination; the repression of emotion and, most significantly, the question of happiness as it affects whole social formations?

There has been an emerging consensus among commentators that Habermas's reading of Freudian psychoanalysis in terms of communications theory is seriously flawed. The conceptualization of the unconscious as little more than an oppressive and distorted force which works upon the individual subject involves some serious misunderstandings about the character of unconscious processes. For it involves the assumption that the unconscious is principally negative in character, without allowing any room for the more positive and creative aspects of this realm of the psyche. Such a reinterpretation of Freudian psychoanalysis no doubt has its conceptual basis in Habermas's linguistic approach to problems of subjectivity and the field of the intersubjective. Habermas's viewpoint, as we have seen, proceeds upon the basis that unconscious elements of selfhood arise from the systematic distortions of human social relationships; relations which, he feels, are principally governed by language and communication. The very vicissitudes of unconscious desire of which we are made, then, are traced as a result of the distortions of public communication. This communicative reading is pushed so far that Habermas speaks of the dark recesses of unconscious drives as containing a 'paleosymbolic linguisticality'. On this view, all human needs and desires are *potentially* open to linguistic articulation. This provides the possibility of an authentically fluid and unrepressed relation to our inner nature.

Yet, as several commentators have been quick to point out, this assimilation of the unconscious to the category of the linguistic is highly questionable in several respects. Joel Whitebook, in a particularly insightful appraisal of Habermas, claims that such a 'linguisticalization' of the unconscious has the ultimate effect of destroying the main insights of Freudian psychoanalysis.[36] The fundamental problem, according to Whitebook, is that Freud's *pre-linguistic* realm of the unconscious cannot be contained within Habermas's 'linguistic idealism'. Unconscious processes of condensation, displacement, representation and reversals of affect, processes which exist prior to the mastery of language, are of an entirely different order to the communicative utopia posited by Habermas. As Whitebook argues, this

> communicatively conceived methodological program causes Habermas to violate a cardinal tenet of Freudian psychoanalysis, namely, the reality and independence of the body as formulated in the theory of the drives Habermas must privatively derive the drives from the distortions of communication ... rather than grant them an independent status in their own right.[37]

And again:

> He tries to assimilate as much of inner nature as possible to the category of the linguistic by constructing it as protolinguistic. This would have the effect of blunting the categorial distinction between the linguistic and nonlinguistic within humans. Habermas wants to argue that, as inner nature is susceptible to socialization, i.e. 'linguisticalization', it must in some sense already be protolinguistic; thus, he must deny the existence of the unconscious as a 'non-linguistic substratum'.[38]

For Whitebook, Habermas's linguistic approach has the effect of cancelling out the vital interplay between the conscious realm of language and unconscious drives, reason and desire, the cognitive and affective. Habermas's excessively rationalistic account of the conscious/unconscious dualism fails to capture, in short, Freud's fundamental emphasis on an 'inner foreign territory' of the self.

Much of Habermas's communications reading of Freud that we have looked at does tend to view the unconscious as a 'reflection' or 'expression' of the structures of public language. On this view, the unconscious is a kind of internal 'reproduction' by the individual subject of the external deformations and pathologies of social communication. The unconscious for Habermas enacts the split-off elements of public communication; it embodies the distorted aspects of critical reason. Such a conceptualization of the unconscious, however, can only be maintained as long as one ignores the point that between libidinal desire and the reproduction of language a creative process of transformation has intervened. This process, as explored in the discussion of Freud in Chapter 1, centres on the capacity of the unconscious to create and form representations. As a pre-linguistic realm of subjectivity, it is this constitutive process of image-production which renders social relations and the institution-alized world possible. As Freud's analyses of dreams show, a dream is not simply an expression of the unconscious. Rather, it is a creative process of *production*. The 'dream-work', as an unconscious transfor-mation, takes aspects of conscious experience (the day's residues) and reorganizes it through phantasy. Similarly, everyday life is also structured through certain unconscious mechanisms – condensation, displacement, distortion. Thus the unconscious, *pace* Habermas, does not consist of a recording or registration of the relations between society and inner nature. It consists primarily, as Freud's account of the dream enables us to see, in creating the psychical conditions in which representations about these relations come to be established and systematized. It is in this sense that Whitebook is correct, in my opinion, in charging Habermas with a failure to accord the primary processes any independence in his model of commun-icative action. For though unconscious desire can only happen because we are caught up in linguistic, social, and cultural codes, this does not imply that the former can be reduced to the latter.

These misinterpretations of the nature of the unconscious lead directly to the excessive rationalism and formalism of Habermas's ideal of human autonomy and freedom. In the model of commun-icative ethics, the crippled and distorted aspects of our public discourses, buried in the unconscious, are to be redeemed through critical self-reflection. The presence of such irrational forces must be mastered and brought to rational control in the life of the individual subject. For Habermas, the 'paleosymbolic linguisticality' of even the most disturbing and resistant blockages indicates that inner nature and the unconscious are potentially capable of linguistic articulation and transfiguration. Accordingly, Freud's fundamental maxim of psychoanalytic therapy, 'Where id was, there ego shall be', is given a literal reading. Connecting Freud's formula to the theory of 'distorted communication', Habermas interprets this to mean: where unconscious distortions once controlled the life of the individual, the conscious self must come to be. Autonomy, in short, consists in making the unconscious conscious. Communication for Habermas is in principle open to everything but the limits of rationality. And it is from this program of the rational mastery of unconscious drives that Habermas projects the possibility for a reflexive radical democracy.

One way of understanding Habermas's interpretation of Freud's statement would be as an attempt to extend the Enlightenment commitment of curbing subjective irrationalities to the entire field of public life. Just as Freud saw psychoanalytic practice as a way of uncovering paralysing forces of our selfhood, so Habermas's communicative ethics interprets the links between autonomy and the unconscious as a matter of overcoming the irrational dross of our distorted discourses and of thereby attaining the possibility of an ideal community of free communication. But stating this affinity between Habermas and Freud in such general terms also reveals how deep are the differences in their respective approaches. While Freud's work undoubtedly displays a profound commitment to reason and critical self-reflection, its exploration of the unconscious can also be seen as an urgent plea for the re-evaluation of these very concepts and of our estimation of human capacities. It is in this sense, as I argued earlier, that Freud's corpus demonstrates just how tyrannically repressive reason has become in modern society. Russell Keat, in *The Politics of Social Theory*, contends that Habermas adopts the principle of rational self-actualization from Freud in only the most *narrow sense*, and thereby generalizes it to the entire discourse of psychoanalysis.[39] According to Keat, in placing only rational limits upon self-reflection, Habermas neglects Freud's fundamental point that the unconscious is indestructible. That the unconscious knows nothing of the demands of rationality, logic, or time means it can only be brought to a limited, and always shifting, level of conscious control. Yet, as Keat points out, 'Habermas's conception of the goal of psychoanalysis involves a quite different interpretation. Having (mis)understood the concept [of the unconscious] as the alienated ego, he presents in effect a literal and unqualified reading of Freud's dictum, so that the abolition of the id is seen as a possible and desirable outcome.'[40] The solution to the distorting enclosure of the unconscious, then, consists in attempting to do away with it altogether. The more the split-off aspects of public communication are redeemed through critical self-reflection, the more the unconscious will simply wither away. This point can also be made in another way. Since Habermas tends to equate the unconscious *in toto* with repression, the *recovery* of discourses which have been driven out of the public sphere will thereby nullify the power of the unconscious. What is lost from sight in this model, however, is the very specificity of the primary unconscious – that is, condensation, displacement and symbolic representation. These conceptual lacunae fuse together to produce significant political ambivalences in Habermas's conception of decolonization and his model of emancipation. In this connection, the problematical aspects of Habermas's understanding of the self and the unconscious work to undermine his broader social and political analysis. In order to demonstrate this, let me return briefly to Habermas's emancipatory critique.

In Habermas's concept of communicative action, as we have seen, a universal-ethical process of intersubjective involvement is posited as a basis from which abstract and general norms can be defined and worked out as part of a rational consensus. It is within this universalistic moral orientation that the public sphere can attempt to reassert its control over autonomized economic and bureaucratic systems, legislating on vital issues of human rights and entitlements. And it is against this backdrop of an ideal communicative forum, in which people have full and equal rights to participation, that the possibility of a radical political democracy might begin to take shape. Habermas criticizes the ethical theories from which he is drawing, however, since he believes that they cannot account for the inner motivational resources which actually permit the realization of public discourses in line with such moral principles. They cannot account, in brief, for the psychological elements which drive the human actions through which such rights are articulated and defined. To overcome these problems, Habermas argues that 'universalizable need interpretations' must become fully accessible to the structure of moral discourse. 'Drive potentials', the concrete needs and desires of human subjects, must become communicatively fluid. In this sense, Habermas rejoins the spirit of the first generation of critical theory by stressing that an emancipated society and fulfilled selfhood demand one another.

This linking of the social field and individuality, reason and desire, justice and happiness makes plain the inadequacies of recent criticisms that Habermas's project wholly ignores those aesthetic values which are central to an expressive subjectivity. Developed largely in postmodern quarters, by writers such as Lyotard, Huyssen and others, it is alleged that Habermas's work displays something of a perverse preoccupation with the formal properties of rationality – remaining insensitive to the manifold complexities of aesthetic experience.[41] In a reply to these criticisms, Habermas has argued:

Nothing makes me more nervous than the imputation – repeated in a number of different versions and in the most peculiar contexts

– that because the theory of communicative action focuses on the social facticity of recognized validity-claims, it proposes, or at least suggests, a rationalistic utopian society. I do not regard the fully transparent society as an ideal, nor do I wish to suggest any other ideal.[42]

Against such objections, a central emphasis of Habermas's work is on the concrete entwinement of human rationality and the expressive resources of subjectivity. Both aspects are necessarily demanded by the emancipatory potentials of modern culture. Indeed, as Habermas has argued, the one-sided celebration of the values of the aesthetic and untamed desire as a means of opposing societal modernization in postmodernism can be turned against itself. It can be argued that, without a concern for the rational articulation of human and political rights as well as for the democratic forums which permit self-determination, there is little prospect for the realization of expressive subjectivity.

The problem, then, with Habermas's conception of emancipation is not so much in linking rationality to practical social activity. Rather it concerns the implicit assumptions which inform Habermas's conceptualization of collective autonomy. That is to say, there are problems in Habermas's account of the *conditions* necessary to permit human subjects to engage in augumentation free from the exercise of force. In one sense, the model of communicative rationality Habermas develops is certainly in keeping with Enlightenment notions of autonomy. For Habermas, human subjects can best contribute to society and politics through public debate and opinion formation, drawing on their capacities for speech and consent in the dynamics of dialogue. As we have seen, however, Habermas recognizes that purely cognitive and rationalist features of communication are inadequate for the social development of autonomy. Consequently, he makes room in his model of communicative rationality for human feelings, needs and desires. This domain of affectivity, however, is severely curbed by the formal conditions of rational consensus that he sets. Habermas presupposes that desire and feeling are available to critical self-reflection only if they are fully defined in linguistic interaction. The inner, affective sources of human motivation, in short, must become the subject of discussion. In the communicative ethics model, it is within the *process* of discursive argumentation that human needs and desires will become the object of rational transformation. Those inner needs and emotions that are discursively articulated are rendered true and those which cannot be verbalized are implicitly rendered false. However, what this perspective fails to take into consideration is the *bar of repression* by which systems of distorted communication are reproduced and sustained. It misses the psychoanalytic point that certain deep, affect-ive features of human experience specifically resist being drawn into the realm of discourse. It also misses the way in which human needs, desires and aspirations are concealed in social discourse, through mechanisms of displacement, condensation, reversal of affect and negation. Implicitly, then, this model softens these disruptive aspects of the broader affective and unconscious dimensions of meaning. While claiming to incorporate affectivity, as Iris Marion Young comments, Habermas reintroduces 'the unity of the speaking subject that knows himself or herself and seeks faithfully to represent his or her feelings'.[43] Reason once again repressively triumphs over desire.

A range of problems inevitably arise from this. In the first place, if repressed desire is deeply inscribed in social discourse as a 'deforma-tion', then how might human beings come to understand the internal contradictions that generate their social activity? If it is through free communicative practice, does this mean that a rational consensus would be faithful to the emotions and desires of human subjects? What precisely would constitute a successful 'incorporation' or 'decolonization' within signifying practices of desire? And, if it recog-nized that unconscious desire is in some sense actually constitutive of social practices, then how might this affect our understanding of human autonomy?

The importance of these issues becomes clear if we consider the links between the capacity to engage in social discourse and public debate and certain contemporary ideological biases which repress, privatize and displace particular interests from the dialogic process. Nancy Fraser, in a persuasive critique of Habermas's work, argues that male dominance and female subordination are a basic element of the current gender system which profoundly delimits equal sexual access to the medium of public debate.[44] Fraser charges Habermas's model with a gender-blindness in theorizing the conditions for free communicative practice, claiming that it represses any consideration of women's institutional incapacity to bring certain issues, thoughts and feelings to light. As an example of women's incapacity to enter public discourse, Fraser points to the many legal jurisdictions in which marital rape is not sanctioned as a crime. If, in the legal domain, women are unable to refuse sexual relations, Fraser enquires, how can they possibly bring their deeper needs, aspirations, and desires to a dialogic process which renders their interests invalid? If women's relationship to collective autonomy is already systemat-ically distorted in this way – 'when a woman says "no" she means "yes"' – then surely the crucial matter of women's participation in political debate is also likely to be consistently misunderstood and devalued? The key problem, in Fraser's view, is that Habermas's model closes down consideration of the relation between the public sphere of political speech and the institutional repression of interests precisely at the point in which the most pressing problems arise. This dissonance between the ideological character of sexual relations and Habermas's model sheds further light on struggles for social and political autonomy. Habermas's theory of communicative action, I think, is based upon a delimitation of the everyday aims and interests, at once cognitive and affective, through which human subjects actually question and uncover those ideological forces which entrap them within relations of domination and power. For it is surely a little too convenient to imagine that ideological struggle might ever take place through a form of communication untainted by the desires, needs, passions and phantasies which human beings bring to all communicative interaction. Perhaps the crucial point in this respect is that uncomprehended needs, as well as desires and affects, certainly play a key role in the movement of emancipation, but this is so only through a creative engagement with, and nurturing of, these imaginary dimensions of experience. In short, it is not a matter of bringing internal pathologies and deformations to light in the hope of exhausting their influence, but rather of giving *expression* to our inner nature. The social conditions in which an expressive subjectivity can be universally developed requires not the elimination of uncomprehended needs and phantasies, but the cultivation of an emotionally responsive cultural framework in which human particularities, identities and desires are essential to collective autonomy.

In a detailed appraisal of the philosophical foundations of critical theory, Seyla Benhabib has formulated very clearly the difficulties which stem from this neglect of human needs and desires in Habermas's line of argumentation.[45] Benhabib argues that the universalistic moral theories upon which Habermas draws, from Kant to Kohlberg, disregard the realm of 'inner nature' in favour of those *public* actions and discourses which have been the traditional fare of normative political theory. She sees embedded in this opposition between public and private life the dominant, repressive splitting of reason and desire, rationality and affectivity, masculinity and femininity. And while Habermas's introduction of the concept of 'need interpretations' within communicative ethics goes some distance toward correcting this bias of the Western philosophical tradition, Benhabib argues that it is still locked within the standpoint of what she terms the 'generalized other' – a view focused entirely on male values, rights, and entitlements. The moral categories which accompany these values, she argues, have no adequate way of thematizing individual particularities, needs and emotions which human subjects necessarily bring from the life-world when they enter into forms of communication. It cannot conceptualize, in short, the 'concrete other'. As this is formulated:

> the standpoint of the 'concrete other' cannot be accommodated within [Habermas's] rather ego-centred notion of self-actualiza-tion ... the 'concrete other,' by contrast, requires us to view each and every rational being as an individual with a concrete history, identity, and affective-emotional constitution. In assuming this standpoint, we abstract from what constitutes our commonality and seek to understand the distinctiveness of the other. We seek to comprehend the needs of the other, their motivations, what they search for, and what they desire.[46]

According to Benhabib, then, Habermas's model of collective autonomy would appear too formalistic and rationalistic to question adequately what forms happiness and fulfilment might take at the level of a whole society.

It would be idle at this stage to pretend to understand the precise implications of these recent criticisms of academic thought for any image of collective autonomy or of immanent utopian possibilities. But what they do clearly suggest is the bankruptcy of any social-theoretical account of utopian possibilities that does not ground its perspective upon a concern for individual particularities, human needs and desires. And it is in this sense, I suggest, that Habermas's valuable concern with these aspects of human experience is revealed as simply not concrete enough. The implications of repressed desire, and of its various techniques of re-grooving social and political rela-tions, cannot be left to the narrowly abstract, concerned only with the reabsorption of unconscious drives within the field of intersub-jective relations. For, as I have argued thus far, the central modes of feeling, perceiving and desiring which make up any social formation are internally connected to the maintenance and reproduction of social power. Accordingly, these modes of affectivity cannot be expected simply to wither away – however politically troubling some forms of desire may be. Affective experience, desires, phantasies, needs and human aspirations need to be treated with full seriousness by social theory; particularly in the positing of alternative social frameworks which take as their overriding concern the nature of human capacities, qualities, and values. But it should be stressed that desire and emotion, even as deeply buried in the unconscious, are not an alternative to moral considerations: they are those considera-tions taken in full seriousness. And it is from this angle, I believe, that we can locate one of Habermas's most urgent political messages: the goals of freedom and autonomy are deluded in their own terms if they do not equally promote the abolition of surplus-repression and the domination of subjectivity.

In this chapter I have analysed two central perspectives on the possibilities for social transformation offered in modern critical theory. First I traced the development of Marcuse's account of 'libidinal rationality' and of the transfiguration in social life that this realm is said to encompass. I then argued that, notwithstanding its linkage of unconscious desire and the utopian imagination, there are serious difficulties in Marcuse's work. These difficulties, I suggested, are particularly evident in Marcuse's one-sided evaluation of the emancipatory potential of phantasy, as well as his narrow construction of the connections between social power and repression. The second part of this chapter has focused on the philosophical and sociological departures from the first generation of critical theory initiated by Jürgen Habermas. I have examined his conceptual tracing of the crisis tendencies and potentials of modern culture, with particular emphasis on the implications this carries for the self and self-identity. I have developed certain criticisms of Habermas's work by focusing on a specific problem: the links between repressed desire and autonomy. My aim was to show that, in developing an approach to the self and the self-transformation of society, centred exclusively within a linguistic framework, Habermas actually loses sight of the dynamics of repressed desire. This results in a perspective on individual and collective autonomy that is unable to accommodate individual particularities, needs, and desires in anything but the most formalistic and abstract manner.

The question still remains open, though, whether the complex links between unconscious desire, power and autonomy might not be pursued from another angle; and it is to this that we will now turn.

4 The Language of Desire

Lacan and the Specular Structure of the Self

The previous chapters examining contemporary critical theory have traced several attempts to introduce a more explicitly social and political dimension for analysing the self in modern culture. In the work of Marcuse and Adorno, several major developments are identified – the fragmentation of the subject, the manipulation of the unconscious, the ever-intensifying levels of repression – which signal the demise of individual autonomy in the present epoch. Similarly, Habermas's reworking of these themes within communications theory paints a picture of the 'colonization' of consciousness by bureaucratic and administrative structures. What is treated as symptomatic of the decay of the self in contemporary critical theory, however, is approached from a radically different angle in the work of the French psychoanalyst Jacques Lacan. Perhaps more than any other single thinker associated with post-structuralism, Lacan's infamous 'return to Freud' addresses the problems of the lures, traps and deceptions of selfhood. In a major debt to structural linguistics, as we shall see, Lacan contends that the self, rather than being drained by distorting social pressures, actually exists by virtue of the alienation of desire itself. In exploring these alienating and non-cultural features of desire, Lacan advances the following central claims: that the self is a misrecognized object of the imaginary; that primary narcissism is fundamental to the structuration of subjectivity; that the other (person) is unknowable to the self; and that the unconscious is an effect of linguistic difference.

In order to approach Lacan's theory of the human subject it is necessary at the outset to stress the centrality of the concepts of the imaginary, symbolic and real orders. The narcissistic phantasies that Lacan attributes to the human subject are originally evolved from the pre-Oedipal imaginary stage, but continue to exert a profound influence over all subsequent self and other relations. This imagination of which Lacan speaks is distinctively different from the conception of the imaginary which I develop in this book. Unlike the constitutive

110

imaginary which derives from the primary unconscious, outlined in the Introduction and Chapter 1, Lacan's imaginary exists *before* the unconscious is brought into existence. The imaginary order in Lacan's writings is rather a world of distorted illusions. It comprises images and delusions that are constituted through a reflecting surface, a mirror. For Lacan, what serves to break up this imaginary hall of mirrors, and thereby prevents human subjects from psychosis, is the symbolic order. The symbolic in Lacan's work is that plane of received social meanings, differentiation, individuation. Language plays a key role in the subject's separation from the imaginary into the symbolic order. The process of symbolization which language facilitates represses the imaginary traps of specular images, and thereby for Lacan constitutes the *structure* of the unconscious. Language and repression are thus twin boundary posts which bring the subject into being as an 'I', separated from that which is 'Not-I'. This entry into social relations and meanings, however, is not as clear cut as it may at first look. For not only is Lacan's subject of language forever destined to be outstripped by the imaginary, by the narcissistic illusions of the ego, but it is also continually decentred by the disruptive effects of the real order. The real order for Lacan is that aspect of reality which resists both mirror-play and attempts at symbolization. It is that domain beyond representation, linked to desire and the death drive. (The Lacanian order of the real will be discussed more fully in Chapter 5.)

One of the principal concerns of this chapter is to explore Lacan's reconceptualization of Freudian psychoanalysis, and to reflect critically upon some of the theoretical assumptions upon which it is based. I cannot attempt to provide a general introduction to the work of Lacan in this chapter. Rather, in what follows I wish to adopt a more selective and critical procedure.[1] Therefore I will bracket Lacan's stress on the coexistence of the imaginary and symbolic orders in psychical life, and undertake to assess some of his key claims concerning each of these domains of the psyche. I shall begin by presenting the central premises of Lacan's account of specular identity and the imaginary order. I shall then examine Lacan's concept of the symbolic order, tracing his reconceptualization of the unconscious in terms of structuralist and post-structuralist theories of meaning. The latter half of the chapter is then critical in character, and I examine the impasses of Lacan's theory of the specular self, arguing that, by treating 'lack' as an ontological given, Lacan's writings inevitably raise certain issues about psychical reality which indicate the incoherencies and mistakes in his approach to subjectivity and self-identity. I then discuss certain problems in Lacan's reformulation of the conscious/unconscious dualism as a linguistic relation. In making these critical observations, I shall attempt to give some indication throughout of how these difficulties might be overcome.

Lacan's Mirror Stage: The Misrecognition of Self

Throughout the first phase of his career, from his first paper to the International Psychoanalytic Association in 1936 through to the mid–1950s, Lacan elaborates a complex account of the constitution of human subjectivity. The central focus of these early writings concerns those primordial points of ego formation that Lacan names the 'imaginary order'. The imaginary for Lacan is that aspect of psychical organization which is formed in and through pre-Oedipal experience. It is a realm of being in which the division between subject and object does not exist. In fact Lacan claims that from this imaginary merging of self and other it is possible to redramatize the genesis of the ego. Concerning this emergence of the self, Lacan contends that narcissistic identifications enable the formation of selfhood, that a primordial alienation characterizes the subjective process, and that 'lack' structures all self–other relations.

The main philosophical themes in Lacan's writings are to be found not so much in his interpretation of Freud, but in his discussion of Hegel and the dialectic of intersubjectivity – in an analysis which is avowedly indebted to Alexandre Kojève's reading of Hegel's *Phenomenology of Spirit* (1807).[2] The general import of the Hegelian-Kojévian account of self-consciousness, Lacan claims, is its stress on the constitutive place of the other (person) in the formation of the self. In this respect, Lacan often cites Hegel as support for the view that the self can only grasp itself through its reflection in, and recognition by, the other person. It is to this aspect of the *Phenomenology*, the fissures and ruptures through which consciousness passes in order to achieve recognition, that Lacan's account of subjectivity is particularly indebted. Throughout his *Ecrits*, Lacan often returns to Hegel's discussion of the master–slave dialectic and to the oscillations of mutual reaction in which both strive for recognition of desire and self-consciousness. However, Lacan will have no truck with the Hegelian postulate of the self-realization of 'spirit' (*Geist*); with the idea of human reciprocity through mutual recognition and conscious understanding. Indeed, he strongly criticizes Hegel's privileging of conscious agency.[3] Rather than finding any points of connection between human recognition and the emergence of self-identity, Lacan follows Kojéve's interpretation that the first experiential moment of intersubjectivity is one of rupture and disunity. According to this view, physical need leads human subjects into a fundamental dependence upon external objects. This outward search for satisfaction, however, leads to a sensory awareness of lacking those objects upon which a secure sense of selfhood depends. At the level of intersubjective relations, the connections between self and other are thus understood to be inherently unstable. The other (person) is at once a prerequisite for the development of a sense of self as well as being a haunting reminder of that 'lack' and 'otherness' which is at the heart of subjectivity.

Lacan's appropriation of Hegelian themes serves as the theoretical basis with which to question the biologism of Freud's models of the psyche. Rejecting the scientism and essentialism of Freud's doctrines concerning the monadic psychic organism, Lacan puts a new emphasis on intersubjectivity as the vehicle for the movement of desire. On this view, it is not inner nature or instincts that traverse desire, but rather the contradictions and disruptions inherent to the self and its sense of otherness. An adequate account of human subjectivity and its objects of desire, Lacan emphasizes, must move beyond the biological reductionism of psychology to confront the problem of the relations between self and other at the level of language. The important point about the other as a condition of subjectivity, Lacan argues, is that it installs itself at that point where conscious thought and action are continually disrupted by the sweeping power of desire itself. In particular, the fluid space between self and other is said to guarantee the individual subject's life-long oscillation between meaning and non-meaning, unity and dispersal.

This, then, is the route by which Lacan seeks to trace out the primordial points of self-identification. Lacan's writings of the formation of subjectivity draw from, yet radically refashion, Freud's theory of the ego – particularly his work on narcissism, mourning and melancholia. As discussed in Chapter 1, Freud's concept of the ego encompasses two broad directions. According to the first approach, to be found as early as the *Project for a Scientific Psychology* onwards, the ego is located as the privileged system of consciousness and perception. It is the direct representative; it harnesses the demands of external reality. Its diverse functions cover the processes of rational thought and perception, as well as defending against instinctual demands. Alternatively, Freud's second approach, introducing a set of overlaying themes with the publication in 1914 of 'On narcissism', emphasizes that a unified ego is not present at birth, but is only developed through processes of identification. On this view, the ego is itself an object of libidinal investment, which is later displaced onto the object world, only to be continually recalled and recathected (the duality of ego- and object-libido). Outlining this later view of the self, Freud notes that the 'ego is a precipitate of the abandoned object-cathexes, it contains the history of these object choices'.[4] Of these themes in Freud's writings, Lacan rejects the former biologically grounded theory of the ego. Throughout his career, Lacan repeatedly challenged mainstream psychoanalytic notions that the ego is a product of biological and evolutionary forces. For it was the adoption and extension of this aspect of Freud's work in Anglo-American ego-psychology – which constructs consciousness as an agency of adaptability, integration and synthesis – which Lacan particularly reviled. For Lacan, the key limitation of such an approach is that a potential unity and completeness is attributed to psychical life which is, in fact, lacking. He argues that it is as if the psychoanalytic movement, notwithstanding its founding insights into the split and fractured quality of unconscious desire, had been compelled to reintroduce a totalization of the (would-be) autonomy of the self. In contrast to these tendencies, Lacan seeks to redevelop Freud's insights into the unstable and shifting movements of identification, mapping the way in which the ego is formed through miscognition. Conjoining Freud's theory of identification to the Hegelian-Kojévian account of 'otherness', Lacan seeks to explicate the underlying structure through which the ego functions to entangle subjectivity within the fissures and conflicts of desire.

In 'The mirror stage as formative of the function of the I' (1949), Lacan contends that somewhere between the age of six and eighteen months the human infant apprehends a sense of bodily unity through the recognition of its *image* in a 'mirror'. As a metaphorical and structural concept, the 'mirror' for Lacan serves to anchor the human subject within the specular movements it sees reflected, thereby constituting the 'I' or ego in its primordial form. This is held to be in direct contrast to the lack of coordination and fragmentation of bodily functions that the infant has known during its first months of life. It is important to stress here that these imaginary identifications of which Lacan speaks are not connected to the responses or interactions of other persons, as is the case with D.W. Winnicott's account of the mother's mirroring.[5] For one thing, the imaginary can only be constituted for Lacan through a reflecting *surface*. The self as presented in the mirror is a reflected object, at once outside and other. Second, Lacan's ego (*moi*) comes into being as an object that is alone, cut off and alienated. As Lacan describes the infant's fascination with its reflected image:

> unable as yet to walk, or even to stand up, and held tightly as he is by some support, human or artificial ... he nevertheless overcomes in a flutter of jubilant activity, the obstruction of his support and, fixing his attitude in a slightly leaning-forward

position, in order to hold it in his gaze, brings back an instantaneous aspect of the image.[6]

Notice that, even in this early characterization of subjectivity, Lacan filters out any suggestion that the self arises from a deeper internal or psychic disposition. Instead, what is underscored is that the infant, who still lacks physical coordination and biological mastery, is confronted with a *reflected* image that both constitutes and organizes its vision of the world. Yet this image is profoundly 'imaginary' for Lacan since the gratifying reflection of self-unity in the mirror is actually in direct contrast to the fragmentary state of the subject's body. Thus the jubilation and narcissism which the infant derives from its reflected image cannot be viewed in a positive light. For the split between the subject's real body and its specular image means that the ego is painfully cut off from others; others who might possibly have acted as an emotional basis for the development of mutuality and intersubjectivity. The mirror stage thus requires the subject to relinquish any such hope of mutual dependency and experience. 'Lacan's account of the "specular" moment', as Malcolm Bowie writes, 'provides the ego with its creation myth and its Fall'.[7] The Lacanian self is thus located from the beginning within a damaging *imaginary* space, inserted into a radical split between an illusory sense of selfhood and something profoundly other.

In contrast to Freud's view, then, that the ego is a direct outcrop of the unconscious, and which subsequently becomes aligned with the demands of reality, Lacan situates the formation of the 'I' in a line of fiction. This is a very significant point, and it is one that is often ignored in Anglo-American considerations of Lacan. In more detail, the split that the subject experiences between its exterior form as a 'mirage of coherence' on the one hand, and its inner sense of turbulence and asymmetry on the other hand, lead it into an alienating misrecognition of its own truth (*meconnaissance*). The capture of the 'I' by the reflection in the mirror is, in short, inseparable from a *misrecognition* of the gap between the fragmented subject and its unified image of itself. This process of misrecognition, Lacan claims, 'situates the agency of the ego, before its social determination, in a fictional direction, which will always remain irreducible for the individual alone, or rather, which will only rejoin the coming-into-being of the subject asymptotically, whatever the success of the dialectical syntheses by which he must resolve his discordance with his own reality'.[8] Lacan's human subject is thus formed in the fissure of a radical split. In a moment which precedes and is radically distinct from the subject's entry into language and the symbolic, which, as we shall see, is an intervention of further alienation, the imaginary identifications of the mirror phase are constituted as a relationship of *otherness*. In the very formation of the imaginary, the human subject becomes other than itself. And it is, moreover, continually threatened by its own otherness. As a mirage of unity and coherence, then, the imaginary order is the basis upon which human beings construct a *misrecognized* centre of self.

In his later writings on the imaginary order, Lacan advances the view that the heterogeneous elements of human desire, upon which the mirror phase confers a primordial misrecognition of unity, are sketched out during the first six months of human life. During this *pre-mirror* period, the human body is experienced as a series of fragmented needs, organs and part-objects. Lacking any defined centre of self, objects pass continually into the subject and desire slides around its incapacity to capture or nail down an object. These earliest experiences of fragmentation centre around objects that, paradoxically, can only exist as *lacking objects* – what Lacan calls *objet petit a*. It is important to distinguish here what Lacan means by the *objet a* from those first objects referred to in object-relations theory and Kleinian psychoanalysis. Unlike these latter perspectives which attribute a pre-given subjective capacity to endow certain objects (breast, penis, faeces) with meaning, Lacan's *objet a* refers to objects that play a *constituting* role in the structuration of the psyche. The *objet a* refers to the introjection of certain primordial images and signs which always *escape* the knowledge of the subject. These objects refer to any part of the body whatsoever (gaze, lips, voice, imaginary phallus) that *fails* to be mirrored or symbolized. Structured by the inescapable lack and destitution of the real order, the crucial point for Lacan is that such zones of the body always escape the imaginary and symbolic capacities of the subject. 'These objects', writes Lacan, 'have one common feature in my elaboration of them – they have no specular images, or in other words alterity ... It is what enables them to be the 'stuffing,' or rather the lining, though not in any sense the reverse, of the very subject that one takes to be the subject of consciousness.'[9]

The idea that 'lacking' objects generate imaginary identifications, referents and the self might appear somewhat far-fetched. Yet Lacan's theoretical reasons for introducing the notion of the *objet a* are clear. If, as Lacan claims, the imaginary always inflects the other person as a mirror, then the question arises as to how people construct particular unities, meanings, identities. That is to say, the question arises as to how the imaginary plays a role in the formation of the subject's ego ideals. The difficulty with Lacan's early looping of self and other through mirror identifications is that it makes the imaginary operate in a rather unspecific manner. Thus, the introduction of the *objet a* at the heart of subjectivity allows for a more complex and differentiated account of the specific unconscious mutations and relays that affect desire. In short, the *objet a* provides a perspective on the foundations of psychical reality. It operates through different modes of the 'real of desire' which thereby structures subjective experience. Through an in-mixing of body, desire and signifiers the *objet a* inscribes a particular subjective style and *causes* certain imaginary phantasies that 'cover over' or 'suture' that gap which is taken by Lacan to be at the centre of human subjectivity. Accordingly, it is because the human subject first experiences its body *as* fragmentation, lack, and loss that it is forever prevented from establishing itself as 'complete' or 'whole'. For Lacan, this is the fundamental trajectory that desire will follow in all human social relationships. 'The mirror stage', he notes, 'is a drama whose internal thrust is precipitated from insufficiency to anticipation ... [and] the armour of an alienating identity ... will mark with its rigid structure the subject's entire mental development'.[10]

Lacan sets out these relationships of otherness in the structuration of the psyche in his so-called L-schema graph (see Figure 4.1). This graph illustrates Lacan's thesis of the alienation of the subject's desire, connecting it to the dialectic of intersubjective relations. In particular, it focuses on the oscillating intersections between the 'imaginary order', of the desired object and the ego, and the 'symbolic order', the place of the subject and the Other, designated by Lacan as language or the unconscious.

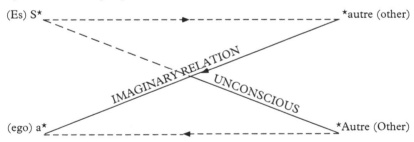

Figure 4.1 The L-schema.

Note: The effect of subjectivity in the L-schema is located entirely within the place of the Other. *S* denotes the unconscious subject of speech (as the space of the subject of desire). The *Other (A)* is the impact of language itself. The lower case *a* and *other* designate the ego and imaginary object of desire respectively.

To review, we have examined Lacan's account of the formation of the ego, regarded as being brought into existence through fragile and fractured processes known as the 'mirror stage'. For Lacan, both the ego and the apprehension of self-identity are imaginary in the sense of the misrecognition which reflection generates. Instead of locating any capabilities for critical self-reflection within the ego, Lacan claims that the narcissistic illusions of the self only lead to an infinite regress. Our capability for truth and knowledge, rather, lies at the level of the 'subject of the unconscious' – as we shall now see in examining Lacan's account of the symbolic order. I want to note here, however, an important divergence between the Freudian and Lacanian accounts of the human subject on the basis of the foregoing considerations. In psychoanalytical theory, identification is the psychical basis from which the ego is constituted, and which thereby structures social relations between self and other. In Freud's account, the capacity for psychical identification arises from the primary unconscious, with social identifications only emerging with the repression of the Oedipus complex. In Lacan's theory, however, primary identification with the self is shifted to another moment, the mirror phase. This identification arises not from the unconscious – there is no unconscious for Lacan prior to language – but rather through imaginary reflections. Such a revision of Freud, I shall argue later, carries serious consequences for understanding the relations between the conscious and the unconscious and, ultimately, displaces some of the most vital discoveries of Freud's work.

Language, Symbolic Order and the Unconscious: The Impact of Structuralism

Broadly speaking, the central focus of Lacan's mature writings concerns the various negativities – those lacks, gaps and fissures – which structure the 'subject of the unconscious'. Throughout the mid to late 1950s Lacan's work shifts from a concern with the ego and the imaginary towards elaborating a theory of the unconscious within the parameters of a new register termed the 'symbolic order'. The main emphasis of this phase of Lacan's work is to demonstrate the degree to which the specular lures and illusions of the ego are ineluctably decentred and fractured by unconscious networks of symbolic and linguistic associations. The key papers in which Lacan outlines this conceptualization of language and the unconscious are 'The function and field of speech and language in psychoanalysis' (1953) and 'The agency of the letter in the unconscious or reason since Freud' (1957). In characterizing the unconscious as an organized system of discontinuities and displacements, Lacan's theoretical emphases depart significantly from Freud's topographical picture of the psyche. Insisting that the unconscious is a logical structure of differential elements, Lacan says there is no 'instinctual' or 'archaic' unconscious which works to 'break through' the repressions of society. As he remarks: 'the unconscious is not ambiguity of behaviour, nor future knowledge which knows itself already by not knowing itself, but lacuna, *coupure*, rupture, which inscribes itself in certain lack'.[11]

In Lacan's reconceptualization of the Freudian unconscious, a crucial link is forged between this endless return of 'lack' at the heart of psychical life and the order of language and symbolization. The entry into language as such, Lacan argues, constitutes individuation, identity and the rules of intersubjectivity. But this acquisition of the rudiments of symbolization, logic and differentiation also entails a massive cost – registered in the splitting and repression of subjectivity itself. Lacan argues this time and again through reference to what is termed the *need–demand–desire* triad of childhood. According to this model, the shift from that narcissistically enclosed space of the imaginary into the symbolic order of language comes about through absence and loss. Words come to 'stand in' for the loss of imaginary desires and loves, as the small child seeks to overcome 'lack' through symbolic expression. According to Lacan, however, these specific acts of symbolization can never cancel out that fundamental and irreducible 'lack' which *is* the subject. For example, when the small child first articulates certain basic needs to other persons, most usually the mother, it finds that these demands always go beyond anything that the other might possibly offer in reply. 'The demand for love', as Benvenuto and Kennedy argue in Lacanian vein, 'goes *beyond* the objects that satisfy need'.[12] The opening up of the unconscious through language thereby functions, paradoxically, as a site for the 'impossibility' of desire. It is through the *splitting* of need and demand – a gap which is constituted by language – that unconscious desire is born. 'Desire', as Lacan puts it, 'begins to take shape in the margin in which demand becomes separated from need'.[13]

Lacan claims repeatedly that the weight he accords to language in the formation of the unconscious is a faithful return to the spirit of Freud's corpus. It is well known that Freud analysed lapses, gaps and errors in linguistic production – both speech and writing – as symptomatic of unconscious meanings and emotions. Indeed, the child's mastery of language for Freud seems only to occur by a repression of the disruptive, primary processes of the unconscious. Language at once conceals and reveals the deep forces of unconscious desire. In this respect, it is not surprising perhaps that Lacan retraces Freud's theory of the unconscious principally from *The Interpretation of Dreams*, *The Psychopathology of Everyday Life*, and *Jokes and their Relation to the Unconscious* – texts in which Freud is particularly sensitive to linguistic mediation. That Freud himself had not elaborated a detailed theory of the interworking between language and the unconscious is, in Lacan's view, the result of historical chance. In the linguistic sciences, comparative philology was the dominant approach during Freud's life-time – an approach that provided little, if any, insights into the complex links between the structure of language and the psychical world. The advent of modern linguistics, however, provides psychoanalysis with the conceptual means to return to Freud's alleged aim of linking the unconscious and language. Indeed, it is to furnish Lacan with the necessary theoretical armour to develop his main intuition that a theory of the unconscious should be reconceptualized around linguistic concepts.

The implications of these links between language and the unconscious must be underscored before proceeding further. Since language had always been a crucial medium for psychoanalytic therapy – the 'talking cure', as it is called – it might be thought that Lacan is simply restating the argument that unconscious conflicts and blockages structure an individual's (defensive) speech patterns. However, Lacan will have little truck with the notion that the unconscious determines the structure of human language. Rather, throughout his writings, it is made plain that he views language as *constitutive* of the unconscious, and not the other way round. As he remarks:

> The analysable symptom ... is supported by a structure which is identical to the structure of language. And by that I do not mean a structure to be situated in some sort of so-called generalized semiology ... but the structure of language as it manifests itself in the languages which I might call positive, those which are actually spoken by the mass of human beings.[14]

In Lacan's work, then, language is conceptualized as an organized system. It is a pre-existing structure which integrates the psyche into the systemic nature of that order. And it is for this reason, as we will now see, that the methodological principles of structuralism – from Saussure on the arbitrary nature of the sign to Lévi-Strauss on the elementary form of symbolic systems – come to exert considerable sway over Lacan's later works.

In reconceptualizing the unconscious as co-terminous with language, Lacan forges an account of the human subject which draws from Saussure's concept of the arbitrary nature of the linguistic sign. Although there has been considerable debate about the extent to which Lacan's formulations adhere to, and depart from, Saussure's theory, their linkage can in fact be quite easily stated. According to Saussure's formulation, outlined in his *Course in General Linguistics*, language is a system of signs – signs being the conjunction between a thought-realm (a signified) and a sound-realm (a signifier).[15] Language is thus conceived as the site in which meaning circulates, generated by the internal play of differences. On this view, the connection between words and external objects or events is arbitrarily fixed since meaning is established through a difference from other meanings. Words as such do not 'mean' their objects. One important consequence of this Saussurean formulation is that meaning can be given no secure footing – it is established through convention rather than any intrinsic connection between words and objects.

Lacan accepts the key tenets of this Saussurean formulation of meaning, but argues that it is necessary to rethink even this 'arbitrary' symmetry between signifier and signified. In 'The agency of the letter in the unconscious', Lacan inverts Saussure's formula for the linguistic sign, advancing the view that the signifier has primacy over the signified in the creation of meaning. In his discussion of the internal play of the differences of language, and the unconscious states which might accompany them, Lacan emphasizes the unrealizable character of the Saussurean endeavour – that is, searching for the arbitrary production of the signified, or the concept. According to Lacan, the signified can never truly be pinned down or fixed since it is constantly slipping out of view, such is the productivity of the signifier in shaping meaning. The reason for this has to do with the elusive and repressed quality of desire itself. For Lacan, what exists within any internal play of linguistic differences – that 'spacing' between words – is the 'subject of the unconscious', or the 'otherness' of language. Whereas for Saussure the sign arises from the reciprocity of signifier and signified, for Lacan unconscious desire is a realm where even this arbitrary relation fails. Instead, signifier and signified are placed in radical opposition; there is a 'cut' (*coupure*) at the very root of the Saussurean sign. And it is this 'cut' or 'rupture', itself a result of the unconscious, which accounts for what Lacan calls the 'incessant sliding of the signifier under the *signified*'. Unconscious desire in Lacanian terms, then, just is this endless movement and slippage of the subject from signifier to signifier.

According to this standpoint, the tie between language, the unconscious and the process of signification can be specified as follows. In highlighting the supremacy of the signifier over the signified, Lacan's contention is that the structure of unconscious discourse is to be located in the signifying chain itself. As a signifier, the unconscious is regarded as having only an arbitrary relation to the human subject, as a signified. The radical discontinuity and vacillation of the unconscious as signifier prevents any straightforward determination of meaning. As such, an irremovable bar is inserted between signifier and signified. And given this chronic semantic instability, this frantic sliding of each signified under the signifier, the human subject is conceived as a structure subjected to the supremacy of language. The unconscious, Lacan argues, represents 'the sum of the effects of the parole on a subject, at the level where the subject constitutes itself from the effects of the signifier'.[16] The implications of this are considerable. Since the unconscious is 'a barrier resisting signification', there can be no simple shift from thought to meaning. Rather, it is the structure of the signifying chain itself which is the proper object of study.

It will be apparent by now that Lacan regards this 'entry' into language as constitutive of the fundamental splits and divisions that plague the psychical life of the human subject. Just like the primal repression of desire in the Oedipus complex that Freud describes, there is a shift for Lacan from the full, imaginary plenitude of the mirror phase into that emptiness which is constituted by the crippling 'otherness' of language. This 'otherness', itself a result of the endless process of difference marked by the signifying chain, is so dividing that it is experienced as castration. 'Castration for Lacan is not only sexual', as Jane Gallop argues, 'it is also linguistic. We are inevitably bereft of any masterful understanding of language; and can only signify ourselves in a symbolic system that we do not command, that, rather, commands us.'[17] In entering language, then, desire becomes fully prey to the signifier.

To understand how we are subjected to language in this way, Lacan draws on the work of the linguist Roman Jakobson. Lacan repeats Jakobson's key thesis that, underlying any signifying chain, there exist two poles of language organization: metaphor and metonymy. But Lacan takes the matter further by contending that these poles of language are formally equivalent to the processes that Freud discovered as being fundamental to unconscious functioning – connecting metaphor with condensation, metonymy with displacement. Moreover, Lacan specifies their respective functions as signifiers by linking metaphor to the discourse of the human subject, and metonymy as its relation to an object. In metaphor, for example, Lacan suggests the place of the subject is determined by replacing one word for another. That is to say, the bar which separates the signifier and signified is momentarily re-established. This forging of meaning is what Lacan calls 'points de caption', literally the 'buttons' or 'nodal points' at which signifiers and signifieds become interwoven. Yet because the human subject is constantly fading into the unconscious, such meanings quickly evaporate as a result of the formal intrusion of metonymic sequencing caused by other signifiers.

In contrast, the process of metonymy, defined as the slippage from signifier to signifier, never succeeds in transcending the bar which separates the imaginary ego from the 'subject of the unconscious'. Hence the desired object is *always* excluded by language. 'The chain of metonymic significations, associations, and substitutions, which represent the desire of the other', as Judith Butler argues, 'is simultaneously a displacement of that desire, so that the effort to know desire is always deflected from its course'.[18] For Lacan, then, the entry into language fully excommunicates the subject from the plenitude of desire which it experienced in the imaginary order. As he remarks, 'the S and s of the Saussurian algorithm are not on the same level, and man only deludes himself when he believes his true place is on their axis, which is nowhere'.[19]

Malcolm Bowie has argued that questions about the chronological priority between the unconscious and language begin to dissolve once the structuring force of the Lacanian symbolic is conceptualized.[20] In acquiring language, the individual subject is inserted into a symbolic order which organizes unconscious desire within the systemic pressures of that structure. In this respect, the unconscious is governed by the same rules as all other symbolic systems. And it is this conception of the symbol which paves the way for Lacan's incorporation of Lévi-Strauss's structural anthropology. Drawing upon Lévi-Strauss's conception of the unconscious as a symbolic system of underlying relations which order social life, Lacan argues that the rules of matrimonial exchange are founded by a preferential order of kinship which is constitutive of the social system:

The marriage tie is governed by an order of preference whose law concerning the kinship names is, like language, imperative for the group in its forms, but unconscious in its structure ... The primordial Law is therefore that which in regulating marriage ties superimposes the kingdom of culture on that of a nature abandoned to the law of mating ... This law, then, is revealed clearly enough as identical with an order of language. For without kinship nominations, no power is capable of instituting the order of preferences and taboos that bind and weave the yarn of lineage through succeeding generations.[21]

This primordial law to which Lacan refers is, of course, the Oedipus complex, now rewritten in linguistic terms. What Lacan calls *nom-du-père* (Name-of-the-Father) designates the break-up of the small infant's imaginary unity with its mother through a disturbance of outside processes, including language and wider familial and social networks. Broadly speaking, Lacan is not arguing that each individual father forbids the mother–infant unity, but that there is a 'paternal metaphor' which intrudes to refer the infant to what is outside, to what has the force of the law – namely, language.

In identifying these organizing mechanisms of the unconscious, Lacan advances a strong conception of the *determination* of the human subject by the symbolic order. In *Ecrits*, he characterizes this social determination as follows: 'Symbols in fact envelop the life of man in a network so total that they join together, before he comes into the world, those who are going to engender him "by flesh and blood"; so total that they will bring to his birth ... the shape of his destiny.'[22] Or, more succinctly, that the symbolic order 'cannot be conceived of as constituted by man, but as constituting him'.[23] Such a treatment of the structuring properties of subjectivity bears a close affinity of course with Lévi-Strauss's infamous contention that structuralism 'claims to show, not how men think in myths, but how myths operate in men's minds without their being aware of the fact'.[24] But Lacan's adoption of the methodological principles of structuralism was neither uniform nor uncritical. Indeed, as early as the mid–1950s, throughout a series of articles, he had already forged a powerful critique of the objectivist claims of structuralism.[25] Against Lévi-Strauss's conception of the unconscious as a 'category of collective thought', Lacan argues 'it isn't a matter of positing a communal soul somewhere ... The symbolic function has absolutely nothing to do with a para-animal formation, a totality which would make of the whole of humanity a kind of large animal – for in the end, that's what the collective unconscious is.'[26] Rather, Lacan's repeated stress on unconscious desire, and appreciation of the intricacies of human recognition, always prevented him from participating in the structuralist attempt to bracket the subject from social analysis. Thus in order to conceptualize the trajectories of the symbolic order upon subjectivity – without reducing the individual to a mere epiphenomenon – Lacan introduces the term 'the Other'.

Of all Lacan's ideas, the term 'the Other' is perhaps the most elusive and ambiguous. Yet it plays a crucial role in Lacan's account of the structuration of the psyche. As Bowie notes: 'Lacan's term "the Other" refuses to yield a single sense; in each of its incarnations it is that which introduces "lack" and "gap" into the operations of the subject and which, in doing so, incapacitates the subject for selfhood, or inwardness, or apperception, or plenitude.'[27] Despite its multitude of meanings, though, there is broad agreement that 'the Other' designates that which is *beyond* subjective intention – hence the unconscious/language. As Lacan remarks: 'the presence of the unconscious, being situated in the place of the Other, is to be sought for in every discourse, in its enunciation'.[28] Or, as he states aphoristically: 'The unconscious is the discourse of the Other.' As such, there is a fundamental separation in Lacan's work between 'the Other' (language/the unconscious) and the 'other' (person) of imaginary identifications. That is to say, Lacan contends that, in all intersubjective involvement, the individual subject searches for a confirming image or reflection of his or her own self-identity through the other person. But given the specular lures and traps of the imaginary order, as previously discussed, the identifications forged through such involvements are said to result in fundamental subjective misrecognitions. With the introduction of the symbolic order, however, Lacan argues that mutual recognition is absolutely unobtainable since the Other introduces an uncertainty, and interminable shifting, into language. As Lacan formulates this tragic ontology: 'Language is constituted in such a way as to found us in the Other, while radically preventing us from understanding him.'[29]

Subjectivity as Lack: Castoriadis and Related Critiques

We have seen that for Lacan the infant's earliest construction of the self is at once narcissistically mediated and an alienating process. The Lacanian subject, by identifying with itself as a reflected image in the mirror, introjects an object that is both part of the self and something profoundly other. Yet Lacan's specular theory of the self, I want to argue, is unable to account for the psychical production of imaginary identifications with objects. Lacan's position is untenable since it casts the specular image itself as the foundation of the imaginary, and thereby erases the primary capacity of the psyche to make representations, identifications, affects. In order to expand upon this argument, in this section I shall (1) analyse the central ambiguities in Lacan's theory of the specular self and indicate the key points that need clarification; (2) discuss some contributions to contemporary debates on the status of the Lacanian subject, particularly as regards the concept of the *objet a*; and (3) assess the theoretical difficulties of treating 'lack' as a baseline of psychical reality.

There are major unresolvable difficulties in conceptualizing the self from a Lacanian standpoint once the following problems are raised: why does the human subject become 'captivated' by her or his specular image? Is it something about the nature of the self or is it something about narcissistic reflection? And what, in any case, are the identificatory processes which allow the subject to apprehend the specular movements before her or him? From a Lacanian angle, it is clear that it is the reflection itself, the specular counterpart of the subject, through which the ego is formed. 'The position of the imaged "I"', as Julia Kristeva argues in Lacanian vein, 'introduces the position of the object, itself separated and signifiable.'[30] The reflection of the human image provides the basis from which the ego develops a world of objects. Lacan, moreover, emphasizes throughout his work that the specular image inflects the imaginary. In his words, 'Man starts from nothing at all ... and he learns by *a mechanism of neutral recording which constitutes a reflection of the world* that we call, like Freud, conscious or not. Man becomes aware of this reflection from the point of view of the other; he is an other for himself.'[31] In Lacan's theorization of the imaginary, then, it is not the subject which puts images into representation. Images appear behind, or always beyond, individuals. However, there are immense difficulties with this privileging of the specular object in the formation of the imaginary. How does the psyche, for one thing, 'record' this 'reflection of the world'? How exactly does the self, in psychical terms, construct or register itself as an 'other'? The basic deficiency here can be simply stated: Lacan does not account for what mediates between the reflected mirror image on the one hand, and the production of such representational forms on the other hand. Indeed, Freud's pivotal theorization that the psyche submits the drive to a 'delegation by representation' is entirely bracketed in Lacan's work. (The issue of representation is discussed more fully below.)

In perhaps one of the most graphic critiques of the antinomies of specular logic, Cornelius Castoriadis argues that Lacan's 'mirror stage' is one further interpretation in Western thought that erroneously characterizes psychic formations as a 'response' to, or 'reflection' of, an externally given moment.[32] Lacan's theory is strongly criticized by Castoriadis for its assumption that the imaginary is only constituted when the self is *reflected* as an object. Rejecting the standpoint that the imaginary is born from a specular image which is somehow 'already there', Castoriadis rather contends that the production of images and forms actually *is* the work of the imaginary. In his words:

> The imaginary does not come from the image in the mirror or from the gaze of the other. Instead, the 'mirror' itself and its possibility, and the other as mirror, are the works of the imaginary, which is creation *ex nihilo*. Those who speak of the 'imaginary', understanding by this the 'specular', the reflection of the 'fictive', do no more than repeat, usually without realizing it, the affirmation which has for all time chained them to the underground of the famous cave: it is necessary that this world be an image *of* something.[33]

For Castoriadis, the argument that the ego is constituted through a misrecognition of its reflected image fundamentally ignores the point that it is the psyche which *invests* the 'mirror' with desire. The problem with Lacan's position is that surely for an individual to begin to recognize its reflected image in the 'mirror' it must *already* possess the imaginary capacities for identification and representation, or what Freud named psychical reality. In the end, Castoriadis argues, Lacan's theory palpably cannot account for the psychical processes by which mirror images are *created* and *formed*. That is to say, Lacan's account of specular identity fails to address how it comes about that the other as mirror is perceived as real – how the reflected object is rendered intelligible to the subject.

Castoriadis has further argued that Lacan's theory places the imaginary within a universal, self-enclosed space of deception and illusion.[34] To the extent that Lacan's imaginary is a mere specular surface, entwined in a depressing ontology of repetition, death and narcissism, human subjects are forever condemned to a pre-existing frozen world, to the purely determinate realm of the self-same. Despite the immense complexity and diversity of imaginary forms, the self for Lacan is simply always and everywhere the result of misrecognition. Exactly how such a universal structure of miscognition fits with the wider libratory assumptions of psychoanalysis, however, is not easy to understand. 'If the true being of the subject is dis-being', Castoriadis enquires, 'what difference does it make if he dis-is in one way rather than another? If "truth" is altogether on the side of the unconscious, and if all "knowledge" is mere deception, what importance can the subject's words have, and how can those of the analyst be anything but deceptive?'[35] The problem here is that Lacan's account of the imaginary quite plainly leads to an infinite regress. If all knowledge and selfhood is rendered a function of imaginary deception, how can the subject ever hope to achieve self-alteration or insight? And what of the validity of Lacan's theory itself? How can Lacan's claims about the alienating entanglements of self and other escape the distortions of the imaginary realm?

Lacan's theory can offer no solution to this quandary. This is so since Lacan makes it clear, throughout his writings, that his stress on the misrecognition inherent in the imaginary is a totalization. As we have seen, he presents a history of the subject in which there is an inevitable progression from the misrecognition of the ego in its primordial form to the narcissistic structure of individuality, to the traps of intersubjectivity, to the alienation of language. The specific constitution of individuality and the imaginary world is thus transferred into a general ontology of narcissism that has no clear limits. Narcissism, and the extent to which it contributes to pathological forms of self-isolation, is not something that can be potentially transfigured or worked through. Any such concern with the capacity for critical self-reflection, and thus an alteration of the psychical economy of the self, is repressed at this level of Lacan's work. At the same time, there is no sense that structures of narcissism intersect in and produce different forms of self-identity. Unlike the focus of psychoanalytic theorists such as Heinz Kohut, Otto Kernberg and others who distinguish between certain self-enhancing forms of narcissism and its more pathological contours, Lacan's narcissistic human subject is simply one of general fact.[36] Hence in Lacanian terms all individuals, in modern social conditions, live an imaginary, narcissistic position of misrecognized selfhood. Yet what is perhaps most ironic about this narrowing down of the existing modes of self-constitution is that, while Lacan explicitly eschews the 'sociologizing of the ego', he actually ends up in a related position. The imaginary foundations of human subjectivity in Lacan's theory must always inflect the other (person) as a mirror. Lacan thus elaborates a view of the social field as uniformly and homogenously affected by the imaginary structure of narcissism and misrecognition.

These considerations lead directly to the nature of the imaginary itself, and to the function of this order in psychical life. The concept of the imaginary in Lacan's theory, as we have seen, is closely allied to the notion of 'lack'. In subsequent writings on the structure of language, Lacan stresses that 'lack' and its symbols – most importantly, the mark of the phallus – are central to psychical differentiation. The phallus, and the 'lack' it inscribes, is understood to tear the subject away from the imaginary world of free-floating signifiers and to refer her or him to received social meanings. As I have indicated, however, the concept of 'lack' also has a more fundamental place in Lacan's work. On the plane of the imaginary, 'lack' exists prior to castration or the Name-of-the-Father; indeed, it is for Lacan an ontological given. From this angle, then, 'lack' is at the very heart of human subjectivity, the imaginary being an 'effect' of 'covering over' of this constitutive absence. The imaginary misrecognition of the ego thus refers to that process by which human subjects come to secure a degree of self-cohesion and regularity, thereby distancing themselves from that painful 'lack' which undercuts all subjective experience. For Lacan, this constitutive 'lack' interacts with the constitution of the *objet petit a*. As we have seen, the *objet a* is presumed by Lacan to be always already in existence; it is an unconscious object that cannot be mirrored or symbolized. Inscribed within a fundamental lack, these objects of desire form an inmixing of body, phantasy and signifiers.

The concept of the *objet petit a* has been much debated in contemporary theory, with many Lacanians asserting that the structural positioning of these objects provides a route out of the aporias of specular selfhood discussed in the foregoing paragraphs. Emerging from an interplay of 'lack' and desire, yet elaborated prior to the mirror stage, it has been argued that Lacan's *objet petit a* offers a non-reflexive theory of the constitution of the subject. On this view, such unconscious objects are indissolubly bound up with the subject's earliest identifications. In order to consider the implications of this viewpoint, I shall give a brief overview here of a recent theoretical exchange on this issue. The interventions considered come from Manfred Frank and Peter Dews.[37] Each of these interventions is interesting, I believe, since they address in a sophisticated theoretical manner some of the key issues concerning Lacan's ideas about the nature of 'lack'. After outlining these respective standpoints, I will try to indicate how our thinking on these issues might be further advanced.

According to Manfred Frank, the split between the specular 'I' and the 'subject of the unconscious' is one that Lacan's theory cannot ultimately conceptualize. Frank finds Lacan's elaboration of subjectivity deeply problematical on two grounds: first, because, like Castoriadis, he argues that the mirror stage can make no sense of how the specular self is actually identified by the psyche – however much systematic misrecognition is inherent to this process. Second, Frank finds misrecognition in any event an inadequate ground for asserting the primacy of the 'subject of the unconscious'. As we have seen, the self-entanglements of the imaginary order are for Lacan a function of the misapprehension of desire. Desire causes the subject to misperceive and misinterpret itself. Yet there are logical problems, Frank insists, with such a formulation. Frank argues that the state of misrecognition, no matter how delusory, is nonetheless still a subjective *recognition*. In Frank's words:

It is very difficult to understand in the case of Lacan what criterion will make it possible in his point of view for the specular I (*moi*) to identify with itself at all. To be sure, Lacan tells us that the specular I (*moi*) is imaginary. But even imaginations have a Being, and this (even if relative) Being has to be clarified in a theory that discusses them. This is particularly true for Lacan's notion of the imaginary I (*moi*), since it justifies the recourse to the 'true subject' on the basis of the mere relativity of the mode of Being of the *moi*.[38]

By reducing the imaginary to the flatness of the specular object, the psychic dimensions of subjective response are repressed. As Frank points out, such an approach contains no criterion of identification which would allow human subjects to (mis)identify with the self as an object. Lacan's theory, in brief, fails to explain why an individual subject should find another person to mirror back a particular set of meanings for the self.

It is precisely this question of the *individuality* of the subject in Lacan's work which prompts Peter Dews to take issue with Frank's remarks.[39] According to Dews, Lacan himself was aware of the sorts of problems which have been subsequently raised by Frank and it was in order to resolve them that he developed the notion of the *objet petit a* – the object of desire in unconscious phantasy. As discussed at the beginning of this chapter, the *objet a* represents that *lost* part of the self which the 'subject of the unconscious' forever tries to recapture through phantasies of wholeness. It is, in effect, the essential lack which structures the desire of the human subject. In Lacan's theory, a part of the body must be separated from the subject in order to avoid complete absorption into the symbolic order, into the radical 'otherness' of language. These objects are constituted through an introjection of fragmented images, sounds, textures. The presence of the *objet a*, of an unconscious part of the subject as signifier, is thus said to guarantee the existence and individuality of the subject. It is a repressed signifier to which the subject can always *cling* when threatened with the radical 'otherness' of language.

For Dews, this constitution of the *objet a* is vitally significant since it occurs prior to the mirror phase in the life of the infant and is accordingly *non-specularizable*. The *objet a*, in brief, is necessarily unconscious. Dews develops the implications of this by comparing the relation between the ego and its other with the relation between the 'subject of the unconscious' to the *objet a*:

> For Lacan, both these relations are imaginary, in the sense that they imply a delusory immediacy, an overlooking of the gap between subject and object, but in all other respects they are radically opposed. The imaginary other, as the support of the ego, is characterized by an arbitrariness and reduplicability, whereas the object *a* is a 'paradoxical, unique, specified object' ... the object *a* is 'non-specularizable' – it cannot appear in the mirror. But, although it cannot be reflected, made an object of consciousness, it is that which the subject is in search of in every self-representation. The object *a* therefore provides the criterion of identification which Frank argues is required in order to explain why the subject *recognizes* itself in a particular image or sequence of images: it defines the particularity of this sequence for any subject.[40]

In Dews's interpretation, then, these unconscious objects of phantasy are already presupposed in any process of imaginary mirroring. As that which is constitutively unconscious, the *objet a* structures the centre-point of our unique individuality. It is the reason why we are driven to hunt for particular (lost) meanings and signifiers.

Once again, however, it can be argued that Lacan's conceptualization of the subject opens itself to criticism. By ranking these unconscious objects as compensations for an ontological 'lack', Lacan takes up a reactionary position on psychical reality, rendering the imaginary merely a derivative realm. For the consequence of this drastic homogenizing of different modes of self-constitution and the investment of phantasy objects is to rationalize the imaginary as nothing more than a reflex of the object itself. In *The Four Fundamental Concepts of Psychoanalysis*, Lacan claims that the '*objet a* is something from which the subject has separated itself, in the form of an organ. It functions as the symbol of a lack, that is to say of the phallus, not as such, but insofar as it is lacking.'[41] Despite this proclamation that the earliest pre-identifications operate as a reordering of 'lack', Lacan fails to consider the implausibility of this formulation. (A central difficulty in Lacan's entire discourse is his use of tautologous statements, as in the assertion that 'lack' structures desire, to validate his theory of the subject.) To parody this Lacanian standpoint somewhat: how can an object that is lacking be implanted at the roots of subjective life? How exactly does the *objet a*, to the extent that it is lacking, reorder a fundamental 'lack' for the subject? And how, in any case, can a lacking object induce the imaginary to forge certain images and representational forms? Surely this cannot derive from the lacking object itself, whether specularized or repressed, since this would do away with the notion of psychical reality entirely. The problem here is that Lacan's formulation seeks to pin down an external event which sets off the reordering of the self – outlined variously as the mirror stage, the *objet a*, or, indeed, structure itself. Yet the terms of this approach are all wrong: lack, absence, object-loss, and the 'mirror' are not pre-given phenomena. Rather, they can only come into existence for the subject *through* the unconscious imaginary.

The issues involved here require deeper consideration if they are to be satisfactorily elucidated. It is necessary to insist, as was stressed earlier in this study, that questions concerning the nature of psychical representation have no intrinsic connection with 'lack'. It is fundamentally wrong to attempt to derive the features of psychical reality from the nature of the object itself, whether lacking or not. There are two key considerations in this respect which need to be clarified. First, to claim that the imaginary is formed through 'lack' ignores the point that, for an object to be constituted as lacking in the first place, it must have been originally invested by desire, the unconscious, psychical reality. That is to say, 'lack' can only be experienced to the extent that there is a relation between representational forms, drives, and affects. Second, and this follows from the first point, the lacking object must therefore have originally been a centre-point of experience and concern for the infant. To note the observations of Castoriadis again:

> How can we speak of an object that is lacking if the psyche has not first posited this object as desirable? ... If there is to be a lack for the psyche, the psyche must be that which makes something be – representation – and the psyche may make something exist as 'lacking' ... It is when Freud speaks of the breast as 'hallucinated' by the infant that we are relatively close to the psychical imagination, to the radical imagination – not when one speaks of the 'specular', which is no more than a derivative of the vulgar ontology of 'reflection'.[42]

This analysis of the constitution of object-loss by Castoriadis is very useful here since it serves to underscore the creative involvement of the psyche in the organization of the self and its objects. Emphasizing that the imaginary is the creative means through which individuals come to experience object-loss, Castoriadis's comments suggest that 'lack' is simply one aspect of the nature of the object – although undeniably a fundamental one.

The central point to note at this stage is that the creativity of the psyche enters into an involvement with objects that are both present *and* absent. The first privileged object in psychoanalytic discourse, the breast, is at once created and plentiful on the one hand, and missing and absent (or always potentially absent) on the other. The discovery of this is forged, not through a pre-given 'lack', but through the psychical articulations of phantasy, representations, drives, affects. 'Articulation' here, in contrast to Lacan, should not be understood as implanted by an external structure, but as a set of distinct and original psychical creations – as when Freud refers to the active 'hallucination' of the breast.

By placing 'lack' prior to the operations of desire, Lacan is able to situate the superficially radical appeal of his work at the level of enquiring why the ideals of our innermost needs and wishes are persistently unrealizable. However, the manner in which this link is conceptualized, as I have indicated, is particularly questionable. If we regard desire as being prior to lack, and if we reject Lacan's distinction between specular misrecognition and the 'subject of the unconscious', we reach a different conception of human subjectivity and unconscious experience. This would be a conception which stresses the affirmative character of psychical productions and representational forms – as implied by Freud's claim that all unconscious phenomena are not so much wish-fulfilments as *fulfilled wishes*. This is an issue I shall pursue further in the concluding chapter.

Rethinking the Symbolic: Critical Observations

I have argued above that the imaginary comprises a good deal more than just specular images, illusions, traps. As a psychic mode of elaborating self and objects, the imaginary is a constitutive feature of human subjectivity. It is the creation of a certain relation of the individual subject to itself, forged through phantasy, drive and affects. Such an imaginary elaboration of the self is at the same time the origin of certain representational forms which are crucial to the entire structuration of subjectivity within society. The prime difference between this standpoint and Lacan's theory, as indicated previously, hinges on the status of the unconscious. At the origins of subjectivity, I have argued, lies the primary unconscious. In Lacan's theory, however, there is no unconscious until the instantiation of the symbolic order.

Despite these divergences, Lacan's writings on the symbolic order are of enduring interest since they deal (in excess of Freud's formulations) with the constitution of social reality for the psyche. Lacan's reformulation of the Oedipal drama in terms of the human subject's accession to language, individuation, differentiation and social signification raises important questions about the nature of this transformation. For Lacan, there is nothing at the level of the psyche which suggests such a transformation into the socio-symbolic order is pre-given. The interface between subjectivity and the social field can only come into existence in Lacan's view through the instantiation of the signifying order itself, conceived in post-structuralist terms as the differential elements of language. As we have seen, this entry into linguistic differences *is* the unconscious in Lacan's theory. 'There is nothing', writes Lacan, 'in the unconscious which accords with the body'.[43] Rather, Lacan's notion of the unconscious/symbolic is on the 'outside', structured in and through the effects of language. There are, however, severe problems with this deterministic account of the subjection of persons to the symbolic order. In what follows I shall focus on two interrelated difficulties. The first concerns the nature of the unconscious; the second, the constitution of the symbolic.

The Nature of the Unconscious

Lacan's statement that the 'unconscious is structured like a language' has been enthusiastically greeted by some, rejected by others (especially in Anglo-American psychoanalysis).[44] For those who applaud this reinterpretation of the psychoanalytical canon in terms of language, Lacan's theory is seen as a valuable attempt to formalize the overwhelmingly complex rules and mechanisms that structure human desire. As Fredric Jameson explains this, Lacan's 'linguistic materials are not intended, it seems to me, to be substituted for the sexual ones; rather we must understand the Lacanian notion of the Symbolic Order as an attempt to create mediations between libidinal analysis and the linguistic categories, to provide, in other words, a transcoding scheme that allows us to speak of both within a common conceptual framework'.[45] On the other hand, many commentators have strongly criticized Lacan's reconceptualization of the unconscious as being naturally tied to language. On the whole, the key objection to Lacan's theory is the Freudian point that the unconscious is resistant to ordered syntax. In so far as Lacanians have responded to this sort of criticism, it is usually argued that the unconscious for Lacan is not dependent on a well-ordered language, but is rather embedded in a potentially endless world of linguistic slippage and difference. I do not intend to trace out here the nuances of these debates. Rather, I shall focus on certain aspects of them which relate directly to those themes developed thus far in this study.

In conceiving the conscious/unconscious dualism as a linguistic relation, I want to argue, an 'absent core' emerges in Lacan's doctrine: as previously suggested, this concerns the nature of representation. So far as representation in the broadest sense is concerned, we have seen in Chapter 1 that for Freud this process is 'the most important and the most striking' aspect of the unconscious. This is so because the libidinal drives cannot be manifested in a pure state; they cannot be known directly. The drives, rather, consist in a ceaseless forming of images. Now, since Lacan treats the libidinal drives as an incoherent fiction, his account of the nature of psychic representation is, in my view, inadequate. In Lacan's work, the centrality which Freud accords to the 'considerations of representation' are lifted to the secondary processes of language, as a complex set of differences. Representation, that unconscious production of images and forms, is seen by Lacan as an *effect* of the signifier; it is its 'means of staging'. 'The subtle process that the dream is seen to use to represent these logical articulations', Lacan comments, 'once more confirm[s] that the dream-work follows the law of the signifier'.[46] Let us look at Lacan's statement here in a little more detail. What, exactly, are the 'logical articulations' which are being produced at the level of the unconscious? From what has been said about unconscious processes in the foregoing chapters, it should be clear that there is nothing within this psychic strata that could be labelled a 'logical articulation'. Indeed, the characteristic features of the primary processes – described by Freud as the complete absence of temporal distribution, negation, and reality connections – are indifferent to the basic structures of logic. The unconscious, in short, is fully resistant to the rigid structures of conscious organization and waking language. Moreover, in what manner can it be said that unconscious representation follows 'the law of the signifier'? What is this universal linguistic law? Perhaps individual representations are no more than substitutable elements (as Lacan suggests), generic entities of metaphor and metonymy, scripts or texts that always 'stand for' something else? Perhaps the broad organization of representational forms follows a prefabricated 'code' or 'algebra' of signifiers, fixed and structured by the desire for a missing object? These explanations, however, do not sound convincing. Why would individuals ever experience (and actually construct) different significatory forms, dreaming variously of fire, money or death, or forging dispositions for masochism or fetishism, if there were a pre-given, formal structure of unconscious representation? Furthermore, if the unconscious is really on the 'outside', structured in and through linguistic laws, surely this must lead to the obliteration of psychical reality. That is to say, there is an implicit absorption here of the psyche into the social, or, more accurately, structure itself.

Jean-François Lyotard has convincingly argued that the unconscious is not only irreducible to language, but that it is entirely different from it in scope.[47] Lyotard rejects the application of structural linguistics to unconscious processes, focusing rather on Freud's argument that unconscious image-production is a transformative work that itself consists in the imaginary fulfilment of desire. In this respect, Lyotard radically questions Lacan's argument about the colonizing power of the signifier at the level of the unconscious. To do this, he specifically draws attention to Freud's account of the dream-work, which transforms the raw materials of 'dream thoughts' into 'dream contents'. 'The dream-work', Freud wrote, 'is not simply more careless, more irrational, more forgetful and more incomplete than waking thought; it is completely different from it qualitatively and for that reason not immediately comparable with it. *It does not think, calculate or judge in any way at all; it restricts itself to giving things a new form.*'[48] Following Freud on this point, Lyotard claims 'the unconscious does not think'.[49] What Lyotard means by this is not that the unconscious is not a site of human signification, but rather that it should not be seen as simply a reflection or reproduction of discourse, the translation of waking thought into another language. For Lyotard, rather, the unconscious is a productive *transformation* of discourse. In describing the nature of this transformation, Lyotard speaks of an object 'forged in depth', 'imaged', 'disfigured', 'permeated by spatial dimensions' – a congeries of terms that suggests the unconscious is a field which resists discursive articulation. As he remarks, 'the dream-work is not a language; it is the effect on language of the force exerted by the figural (as image or as form)'.[50] The spatial dimension of the unconscious as a signifying matrix is particularly important in Lyotard's view since this aspect of psychical life is fundamentally absent from linguistics. In his words, the unconscious

> cannot fail to have recourse to a spatial dimension which is precisely excluded from the linguistic system. To erase a fragment from one place on the page (remove it from a particular point in the chain) and put it elsewhere (where space will have to be made for it) demands that the extract move above the text. This movement takes place, therefore, in depth ... It is this that constitutes a kind of murder: desire, with its dimension of depth, disfigures the table of the Law. And simultaneously, by the same token, it is illegible, hence hidden. Its concealment demands the depth which discourse excludes.[51]

On this standpoint, the distorting pressure of unconscious desire is far more extensive than what any semantic instability – Lacan's 'slippage of the signifier' – would suggest. Rather, the effects of unconscious desire disrupt and disfigure language. It is a process that produces what Freud called 'a *disguised* fulfilment of a repressed wish'.

It is from this angle that Lyotard contends that the fundamental aspects of the primary processes – distortion, condensation, displacement, considerations of representability and secondary revision – function in an entirely different manner from the operations of waking language. His discussion of displacement and condensation in this respect is very illuminating. According to Lyotard, condensation is a compression of multiple thoughts into a particular set of images, operating as an overdetermination of the energy of the primary processes. In contrast to Lacan's reformulation of condensation as the endless metaphorical slippage of desire, Lyotard argues it is best conceived as a process in which desire is *realized* by being 'crushed' into spatially reduced objects. The process of displacement in Lyotard's view is also fundamentally non-linguistic in character. Because desire searches for surreptitious ways of finding satisfaction, Lyotard argues (with Freud) that unconscious meaning becomes dislocated onto what might at first sight appear to be insignificant ideas or images. These connections are only understood as insignificant, though, until one sees that they represent a crossing point in which unconscious desire finds satisfaction. To illustrate that displacement operates through *spatial* forms, Lyotard refers to the example of a poster advertising a film about the Russian Revolution, entitled *Revolution d'Octobre*.[52] In the advertisement, the letters are 'crushed' in such a way that they appear as a banner that is blowing in the wind. Lyotard contends that the process of displacement consists in this 'zoning' or 'freezing' of certain letters so that some become graphically visible and others masked from view. For instance, he remarks that that this poster might be seen as *Revons d'or* ('let's dream of gold'). By reinforcing certain parts of the text as a dense image in this way, then, displacement operates as a preparatory work for processes of condensation and over-determination.

There is much that is informative in Lyotard's account of the unconscious (and the critique of Lacan it develops), but it needs to be recast substantially. This is especially the case if we are to discern the complex dialectical links between unconscious representation, subjectivity and the social field. It should first of all be noted that the unconscious does not operate only as a transformation of the secondary structures of waking language, as much of Lyotard's work implies.[53] Rather the representational forms of the unconscious actually make possible the condition of language, as well as the reconnection of repressed memories to speech, as is the case with psychoanalysis as a therapeutic method. This accordingly implies that the representational capacity of the unconscious exists 'in itself' and operates as a creative interface between human subjectivity and society. Let us consider this point in a little more detail by returning to Freud's discussion of the unconscious and representation.

In his later writings, Freud discusses in some detail the question of the absence of rational thought processes in the unconscious in the metapsychological paper 'The unconscious'. In outlining the topographical distinctions between the unconscious and the preconscious-conscious system, Freud makes it exceedingly clear that he regards the former as a *non-linguistic* domain. Central to this distinction is Freud's discussion of 'word-presentations' (*Wortvorstellungen*) and 'thing-presentations' (*Sachvorstellungen*). In outlining these 'presentations', Freud argues that 'thing-presentations' are 'unconscious thought processes' which consist in the mobilization of desire, and which culminate in condensations and displacements. This mute realm of desire, he contends, intersects with the secondary structures of language only through a psychic investment in 'word-presentations'. In a particularly clear summary of this process, however, he insists that these domains of the psyche remain phenomenologically differentiated. Given the importance of this differentiation for the purposes of this study, it is worth quoting Freud here at some length:

> We now seem to know all at once what the difference is between a conscious and an unconscious presentation. The two are not, as

we supposed, different registrations of the same content in different psychical localities, nor yet different functional states of cathexis in the same locality; but the conscious presentation comprises the presentation of the thing plus the presentation of the word belonging to it, while the unconscious presentation is the presentation of the thing alone. The system Ucs. contains the thing-cathexes of the objects, the first and true object-cathexes; the system Pcs. comes about by this thing-presentation being hyper-cathected through being linked with the word-presentations corresponding to it. It is these hypercathexes, we may suppose, that bring about a higher psychical organization and make it possible for the primary processes to be succeeded by the secondary processes which is dominant in the Pcs. Now, too, we are in a position to state precisely what it is that repression denies to the rejected presentation in the transference neuroses: what it denies to the presentation is translation into words which shall remain attached to the object. A presentation which is not put into words, or a psychical act which is not hypercathected, remains thereafter in the Ucs. in a state of repression.[54]

Here we might return to Lacan. The upshot of the foregoing discussion concerning the representational nature of the unconscious is as follows: when Lacan states that the 'unconscious is structured like a language' he is clearly not taking his cue from Freud. Rather Lacan's employment and radicalization of Saussurean terms seeks to constitute the theorist as a formalizer of the signifying fabric of the 'language of desire'. In treating language as coterminous with the unconscious, Lacan offers a set of impersonal rules which govern the field of human passion. Yet it does not follow that, because the outward expression of desire is often mediated through discourse, the unconscious is itself a 'language'. In this respect, Freud's characteristically interesting discussions about slips of the tongue, as well as other linguistic infractions, can be seen as an attempt to go beyond the threshold of language to that non-discursive realm of representation and affect. In fact, as Freud emphasized, the reason for the analysts' explorations in words is to discover the key characteristics of the representational psychodynamics of human subjects – tracing the multiform ways of relating to the self, to others, to love and to society.

The foregoing paragraphs indicate that the unconscious should not be understood as the differences embedded in a linguistic structure, but as a meaningful organization of representational forms, drives and affects. As Freud's writings suggest, 'representation' here is not just an empty intersection between the self and external objects, but an energetics of practice whereby individuals organize a set of experiences as representational activity. As the *other side of language*, then, the unconscious is a creative means whereby human subjects establish an interpersonal space between self and other. This representational capacity, to repeat, is creative in the fullest sense of the term, and ought not be reduced to the deterministic logic of 'structure'. On an analytical plane, it is the principal means through which persons reflect upon phantasies, and is central to the process of achieving autonomy. The relationship between unconscious representation and autonomy is an issue I shall discuss in more detail in the concluding chapter of this study. At this juncture, however, the foregoing considerations lead us directly to question certain assumptions in Lacan's account of the symbolic order.

Society and Symbolic Forms

Accompanying Lacan's reconceptualization of the conscious/ unconscious dualism as a linguistic relation, as we have observed, there is a fundamental stress on the ordering power of the symbolic. The symbolic for Lacan impacts upon the small infant's world of imaginary plenitude and narcissistic enclosure to refer her or him to received social meanings. Language, the symbolic, the law: these are, in Lacan's theory, the mechanisms through which individuals are forced to confront the outer world. In the work of Lacan, however, the individual subject is understood as essentially passive in relation to the symbolic order. Since the imaginary is accorded little creative status, the symbolic is largely seen by Lacan as a force that orders the psyche into socialized form – in this case an order which determines the psychical reactions of people in the face of social institutions. In this final section, I want to express disagreement with these deterministic assumptions of Lacan's work, stressing the ways in which this focus obliterates the creativity of the psyche and the space of the social field.[55]

However much Lacan emphasizes that desire only exists as 'lack', there can be little doubt that, at the level of the symbolic order, this 'lack' becomes fully interwoven and structured by an intersubjective order of speech. There are several features about this *structuring* of desire which are relevant here. First, human subjects are always alienated in Lacan's theory since language is conceived as a system of differences extrinsic to human gratification and passion. The insertion of the subject into the symbolic order smashes the imaginary plenitude of the reflecting mirror, with an immutable gap opening between signifier and signified as desire 'sinks' or 'fades' into that system of linguistic differences which, for Lacan, *is* the unconscious. As Lacan describes this *primacy of the symbolic*: 'The effect of speech is the cause introduced into the subject. Through this effect, he is not the cause of himself; he carries within him the worm of the cause that cleaves him ... [The subject] could not signify anything unless it be for another signifier: to which then the subject who is listening is reduced.'[56] Second, this insistence on the symbolic determination of desire and subjectivity is considered by Lacan to be founded by the prohibitive law, the Name-of-the-Father. This law, as we have seen, is understood to act in a universal fashion. 'It is in the *Name-of-the-Father*', writes Lacan, 'that we must recognize the support of the symbolic function which, from the dawn of history, has identified his person with the figure of the law.'[57]

Although Lacan's work suggestively underlines the point that there must be a third figure to break up the imaginary dyad of child and mother, his elusive references to the law and the structure of language no sooner raises issues about social context than it closes them off from consideration. Consider some of the following difficulties. If language as such and the Name-of-the-Father are the foundational bases of alienation, then this surely suggests that a homogenous amalgam of social and political forces informs the structure of desire. Yet is it necessarily the case that the in-mixing of language, the law and the function of the father always operate in such a uniform way in instituting psychical differentiation? Are they always so rigid and repressive? The problem with Lacan's undifferentiated account of the law and symbolic, it becomes clear, is that it flattens out the important, contradictory ways in which these forces are the outcome of specific political and social relations. Unlike the focus of critical theory which reconnects the psyche to society and politics, as we have seen in Chapters 2 and 3, Lacan's generalized law eludes an understanding of the social and political forces which differentiate such diverse practices as the language of modern family relations, the language of Auschwitz, the language of the nuclear arms race, and the like. These forces of the social cannot be abstracted as they impact upon psychical reality into a universal structure of language. To do so is to destroy the political and historical constitution of language, and specifically the manner in which it frames human subjectivity and desire. While Lacan himself might have rejected such a universalist interpretation of his theory, it is surely clear that his failure to ground the psyche in social and historical contexts leaves open this type of criticism.

As an illustration of this, let us look briefly at Lacan's discussion of Edgar Allen Poe's 'The Purloined Letter'.[58] His seminar on Poe's narrative is illuminating for our purposes as it clearly suggests that the universal primacy of language and the symbolic is one of the main emphases of Lacan's theory. The key point here is the following one: in contrast to the opinion of the police officers in the story that their power rests upon a wielding of force, Lacan argues that it actually derives from the symbolic ordering of language. In Lacan's view:

Every legitimate power always rests, as does any kind of power, on the symbol. And the police, like all powers, also rest on the symbol. In troubled times, as you have found, you would let yourselves be arrested like sheep if some guy has said *Police* to you and shown you a card, otherwise you would have started beating him up as soon as he laid a hand on you.[59]

But is self-identity really subject to the fate of the symbolic in the manner that Lacan suggests? Given the strength and ambivalence of affect associated with the unconscious, there is clearly something awry about Lacan's view. Characterized this way, the unconscious only embodies those aspects of our submission to authority. It gives little space to our unconscious feelings of hatred and anger towards authority figures. Yet what a person feels capable of saying in a specific social context surely depends on these types of factors. The entwinement of desire and social power is crucial to whether individuals accept or resist the symbolic codes with which they are confronted. However influential symbols of authority might be, the hierarchical organization of power in society certainly does not go unresisted. In the end, then, Lacan is little interested in the representational forms or the affective grounds from which social meanings come to be challenged, or of the capacity of human subjects to resist social domination. Rather, his concept of the symbolic focuses on those mechanisms of the structural ordering of the self and self-identity.

These deterministic emphases in Lacan's theory, I want to argue, lead to a misleading view of the connections between the imaginary and symbolic capacities of human subjects and the more encompassing influences of the social field. A satisfactory theoretical account of these interrelations must focus on the complex interplay by which the symbolic significations of society shape, yet are actively reshaped by, psychical life. That is to say, it can be said (with Lacan) that it is necessary to focus on the symbolic ordering of the psyche, but it is also necessary to focus on those points of support which the psyche lends to the social domain. While it is not possible to consider in detail all of the factors that enter into this dialectical interplay here, it is necessary to outline the following points. An adequate account of the psyche in relation to the social field must recognise that (1) on a broad level, human subjects are never passively fabricated by the symbolic forms of society, but actively receive such significations and creatively reconstitute them in the light of their representational activity; and (2) that the reception of symbolic significations does not simply operate against a universal backdrop of linguistic differences, but rather occurs within social relations which are asymmetrical with regard to the distribution of power. Let us finally consider these points in a little more detail.

All psychical experience of the social world is mediated – the process of which Freud termed 'sublimation'. Broadly speaking, the nature of sublimation consists in the transition of libidinal investment from an 'interior', imaginary fulfilment to an 'exterior', socio-symbolic activity – such as painting, music, talking, and so on. It concerns, in short, the enigma of culture itself considered from a psychical angle. Although Freud never fully developed the concept of sublimation, he left a valuable outline of this process in the *Introductory Lectures on Psycho-analysis*. Sublimation, he argued, 'consists in the sexual trend abandoning its aim of obtaining a component or a reproductive pleasure and taking on another which is related genetically to the abandoned one but is itself no longer sexual and must be described as *social*'.[60] And elsewhere Freud contends that sublimation arises from a displacement of unbound energy which intersects with the social field through a change in the object or goals of the libidinal drives.[61] This view of the links between the imaginary and the socio-symbolic field alerts us, I believe, to many of the shortcomings of Lacan's account of the symbolic. For it suggests that the transition from imaginary omnipotence to the symbolic plane of social significations arises, not through a supra-individual superego or uniform 'law', but rather through the psychical investment in social conditions (which are external) deriving from the representational capacity of the psyche – each of which is irreducible to the other.

To be sure, the theoretical complexities here are immense. How does the psyche come to be enmeshed within social significations that are at first external to it? What creates the interface between psychical reality and the appropriation of social objects? The analysis of 'transitional objects' worked out by D.W. Winnicott provides a useful starting point for analysing these issues, focusing as it does on the connections between the creativity of the psyche, symbolization and culture.[62] 'Transitional objects', in Winnicott's theory, refer to the active 'discovery' or 'bridging' of a potential space between self and other, inner reality and outer world. The child's use and control of a transitional object, such as a toy or blanket, signals for Winnicott the intervention of a symbolic plane as well as the 'coming into being' of the infant into an intersubjective reality. This finding of external reality necessarily involves the discovery of other individuals and things. As Winnicott puts this: 'The [transitional] object is a symbol of the baby and the mother (or part of the mother). The use of an object symbolizes the union of two now separate things, baby and mother, at the point of time of the initiation of their separateness.'[63] Typically, this process involves a repression of the mother as an erotic object. These repressions lead the child to recognize that the mother has an independent existence, outside and beyond the self. As Winnicott makes clear, though, unconscious feelings from the earliest days of life exert a profound influence over these symbolic elaborations of the relations between self and other. On this view, the imaginary, unconscious features of psychic life do not prevent but actively structure the transitional space of symbolization. The symbolic is not, as with Lacan, an alienating structure 'imposed' upon the self through language. It is rather, as Winnicott emphasizes, an enabling medium through which a shared reality is experienced.

The investment of imaginary, unconscious forms in symbolization and culture rests on the alteration of the psychical monad and the creative involvement of the self. This involves an essential transformation in the aim of the libidinal drives and their entwining in the object-world. The infant, as Winnicott puts it, 'creates an object but the object would not have been created as such if it had not already been there'.[64] This imaginary investment in shared symbolic forms is important since it highlights that the human subject is not merely an 'effect' of the signifier, but actively engages with and transforms the social field. From this angle, subjectivity cannot be determined by the socio-symbolic order; it is rather formed through it as *indeterminable*. This interlacing of the unconscious imaginary, symbolic forms and external reality is an ongoing process for the individual. As Winnicott argues, 'it is assumed here that the task of reality acceptance is never completed, that no human being is free from the strain of relating inner and outer reality'.[65]

Winnicott's notion of 'transitional objects' indicates that it is through a creative involvement with others and the object-world that the self becomes enmeshed within socio-symbolic forms. These symbolic forms are not externally imposed upon the subject, but nor are they merely at the disposal of the imaginary. Rather, through the representational nature of the imaginary, they are appropriated and reconstituted as part of a shared reality. To the extent that the imaginary and symbolic interlace in this way, it is vital for critical social theory to recognize that human subjects are constituted and reconstituted in different political and ideological configurations in relation to culturally specific symbolic forms. In this theoretical context, language intersects with the self and desire, not as a 'universal' structure of differences, but as a social and historical phenomenon infused within broader networks of power. Language and the unconscious are not coterminous. To speak a language is a *sublimated activity*; an activity which situates the self within everyday social life as well as within culturally specific ideological conflict. This demands the recognition that the imaginary organization of the self is shaped by, yet reshapes, socio-symbolic institutions and practices. In the concluding chapter, I shall sketch out my own account of how these imaginary dimensions of the self are essentially linked to asymmetrical relations of power and force.

In this chapter, in the course of examining the views of Lacan, I have essentially set out two main arguments. First, that neither Lacan's elaboration of the imaginary nor that of 'lack' can offer an adequate criterion for understanding how self-identity and the self are rendered intelligible to the human subject. In contrast to Lacan's 'derived' imaginary, I have tried to show that 'mirror misrecognitions' and 'lack' can only come into being for the subject *through* the primary unconscious. Second, that in treating the origins of subjectivity and the imaginary in this way, Lacan is consequently left with an excessively deterministic account of the symbolic. In this respect, I have set out a number of critical observations concerning his application of structural linguistics to the unconscious, as well as his account of the ordering power of the symbolic order.

These criticisms carry a number of far-reaching implications for assessing the relevance of Lacan's work for a theory of social reproduction, cultural domination and ideology. In the ten or so post-structuralist years since Lacan's doctrines have made a major impact upon social theory in the English-speaking world, many attempts have been made from a Lacanian angle to question how subjectivity and social relations of power and domination intertwine. It is this issue which provides a convenient transition to the next chapter.

5 Psychoanalysis, Ideology and Modern Societies

Post-Lacanian Social Theory

In recent decades, the theory and analysis of ideology has been dramatically transformed by the impact of modern psychoanalytic thought. The strength of this impact is due partly to the attention psychoanalysis has generated concerning the complex and problematic links between ideology and unconscious desire. Alert to the shortcomings of the traditional rationalist view of ideologies as conscious, well articulated sets of beliefs and thoughts, many authors have sought to widen the concept of ideology toward a broader focus on the ways it constitutes the affective, unconscious dimensions of lived experience. They have, in differing theoretical ways, sought to analyse the reproduction of modern ideologies of nationalism, class, race and sexism within the context of our more primary attachments, drives, fantasies and desires. In general terms, this attention to the internal, unconscious structuring of ideological forms has not sought to displace sociological, economic and political analyses of such phenomena. On the contrary, this broadening of the concept of ideology has tended to stress that it is only in conjunction with such approaches that the complex ideological tissues of subjectivity can be adequately conceptualized. However, if, as Freud argued, all rationality is internally framed within desire, it would seem clear that the distortions and deformations traditionally associated with ideology are not just an automatic effect of objective social structures. Seen in this light, rather, the forces which Freud discovered at work within psychical life – mechanisms such as repression, disavowal, introjection and sublimation – are also central in the regulation and stabilization of ideological conflict. In short, ideological forms resemble what Freud called the 'psychopathology of everyday life', the complex ways in which the affective dynamics of pleasure and unhappiness are invested in the social field.

The reconceptualization of Freudian psychoanalysis developed by Lacan in the light of structuralist and post-structuralist theories of language, the fate of which I have traced in the previous chapter, has exercised a vast influence upon some of these reworkings of the concept of ideology. At first glance, this influence might seem surprising. Lacan's emphasis on the inescapability of alienation within the signifier, his characterization of desire as 'lack' structured through the symbolic order, his reconceptualization of the unconscious within a universal and ahistoric structure of language: these and other related aspects of his theory would seem to forestall, rather than promote, critical social enquiry. However, the cultural and political consequences of Lacan's work, as it has been developed and extended in contemporary social theory, are not so clear cut. Many authors have argued for the importance of Lacan's ideas to the development of a theory of ideology; to the analysis of cultural and political domination; and, as we shall see in the next chapter, to feminist theories of gender relations. To a significant extent, Lacanian theory has been employed to challenge the humanistic model of ideology as 'distorted consciousness', to question the idea that we might ever perceive the social world in an undistorted way, and to highlight that our current notions of knowledge and truth are inadequate. Stressing that the human subject develops as a configuration of the imaginary, the symbolic and the real orders – which are structured in and by ideology – much Lacanian and post-Lacanian work has sought to deconstruct, as well as rethink, the possibilities for political emancipation and autonomy.

In this chapter I want to examine several post-Lacanian contributions to the theory and analysis of ideology. My aim will be to trace the ways in which Lacanian concepts have been used to examine certain key characteristics of ideological forms, and to reflect critically upon some of the broader theoretical assumptions which inform these efforts to reconfigure the subject and society. In order to appraise the relevance of post-Lacanian positions for social theory, the work of Louis Althusser, Ernesto Laclau and Chantal Mouffe, and Slovoj Žižek has been selected for consideration. I begin by examining the influential work by Althusser on the imaginary foundations of ideology. Providing one of the first systematic accounts of the imaginary as an indispensable medium for the constitution of human subjects, Althusser's work is a valuable contribution to reassessing the role of ideology in social and political life. As I try to show, however, Althusser's employment of Lacanian psychoanalysis for the theory of ideology is flawed in several important respects. In this connection, the work of Laclau and Mouffe, and Žižek, are significant attempts to situate Lacanian concepts within a more sophisticated framework of the social and political fields. As such, I consider the contributions and limitations of their respective work later in this chapter. There I try to show that their work, while important and provocative in many respects, does not ultimately provide an adequate framework for analysing the complex relationships between subjectivity, the imaginary forms of ideology, and modern social processes. In particular, I shall argue that there is one major shortcoming which these broadly post-structuralist accounts share: a failure to deal with the complex ways by which imaginary forms, in particular unconscious desire and fulfilment, are sustained within asymmetric power relations.

Althusser on Ideology and Imaginary Misrecognition

The French Marxist social theorist Louis Althusser was among the first post-structuralist thinkers to argue for the importance of psychoanalytic ideas for the development of a theory of ideology.[1] Highlighting the shortcomings of rationalist accounts of ideology as conscious, well articulated sets of ideas, Althusser attempts to trace the more symbolic dimensions of ideology. In his view, these dimensions cannot be attributed to some kind of 'human essence' or to subjectivity itself. Indeed, it is precisely such humanist notions of the centred and unitary subject, who mysteriously posits its own desires and passions, that Althusser wishes to discredit. In order to develop a theory of ideology which embraces this problematic of decentred subjectivity, then, he argues it is necessary to supplement structural Marxism with a reading of Lacanian psychoanalysis. Althusser's thinking and most important contributions to these issues are outlined in his seminal essays 'Ideology and ideological state apparatuses' and 'Freud and Lacan', and it is to a consideration of these essays that I shall now turn.[2]

Althusser's theory of ideology seeks to break from the dominant tendency in Marxist thought – derived from various comments in Marx's *The German Ideology* – that treat ideology as some kind of 'reflection' of the real structures of society. In Althusser's eyes, to understand the ideological field as a reflex of the economic 'base' of society is to render it a mere epiphenomenon. The view that social practices are real, while the ideas and beliefs which sustain them are simply false illusions, mistakenly assumes that ideology is imaginary in only a passive sense, as a weak copy of the structures of our social practice. For Althusser, if this opposition is deconstructed we can begin to see that imaginary forms are actually constitutive of our social practice; they are deeply inscribed in their very texture. He thus contends that it is necessary to redefine ideology as a constitutive *region* of the social world, as a material practice with definite effects on the day-to-day conduct of social agents.

In breaking from the imaginary/real opposition of traditional Marxism, where the former stands as a sort of ethereal medium which veils real political and economic structures, Althusser outlines a conception of the relation between ideology and the imaginary of considerable complexity. It is clear that for Althusser ideological discourse is not to be found in the actual representations of social and political conditions themselves. On the contrary, he asserts that the imaginary is embodied in the relations to the real that are organized and sustained through ideology. Ideology is the *imaginary relation* of individuals to their real conditions of social existence. This imaginary dimension of ideology, which as we will see is developed from Lacanian psychoanalysis, is not understood as some kind of private space internal to individuals. Rather, Althusser emphasizes that the imaginary dimensions of ideology exist on the 'outside', but are continually woven through us as an effect of subjective positioning. He defines this process as follows:

> All ideology represents in its necessarily imaginary distortion is not the existing relations of production (and the other relations that derive from them), but above all the (imaginary) relationship of individuals to the relations of production and the relations that derive from them. What is represented in ideology is therefore not the system of real relations which govern the existence of individuals, but the imaginary relation of these individuals to the real relations in which they live.[3]

On this view, then, ideology is the social cement of human society. It positions human subjects at a place where ideological meanings are constituted, and thereby structures the real organization of social relations. It establishes, in sum, the deeply pervasive and unconscious modes by which subjects come to 'live out' their real relation to society.

At the heart of these systematic effects which are attributed to the imaginary lies Althusser's rigorous distinction between ideology and science. Unlike the subject of ideology who is always inscribed within the domain of the imaginary, science for Althusser is not an enterprise entrapped within the distortions of misrepresentation. Focused as it is upon the construction of a 'theoretical object' purely internal to itself, science is defined as subjectless and open-ended: 'the author, insofar as he writes the lines of a discourse which claims to be scientific, is completely absent as a "subject" from "his" scientific discourse (for all scientific discourse is by definition a subject-less discourse, there is no

"Subject of science" except in the ideology of science)'.[4] On this view, the purpose of scientific discourse is not to attempt the dissolution of distorted knowledge embedded in ideology, since (as we shall see) ideology is not actually any form of knowledge at all. Rather, a scientific problematic is, for Althusser, focused upon the autonomous horizon of epistemological discourse; a horizon that can produce new forms of knowledge and, in turn, react back upon ideology. It is from this extraordinary privilege granted to science that Althusser's Marxist discourse claims to lay bare the functioning of society as a 'centre-less' entity, comprising different levels of 'regions' and 'structures' which constitute social life. In a similar fashion, Althusser views human subjectivity as necessarily decentred and unstable; an entity which can only be integrated as a purposive social agent through the imaginary effects of misrecognition. As the realm of this misrecognition, then, what ideology grants is not so much a form of cognitive knowledge, but rather a symbolic, unconscious consistency which brings subjectivity into existence as purposeful and meaningful. To designate this ideological operation Althusser borrows the Freudian term 'overdetermination'. Thus the human subject, for Althusser, just *is* that overdetermined product of the social – which, when stripped of its ideological distortions by science, is revealed as purely contingent, incomplete, open-ended. The political implications of this incomplete character of the social are clear from the standpoint of Marxist theory: that individuals come to misrecognize the processes of their self-constitution, mistakenly viewing themselves as coherent and self-generating subjects, is fundamental for any radical decoding of the ways in which human beings unknowingly submit to the dominant ideologies of late capitalist society.

Since ideology for Althusser is essentially a non-cognitive realm, the misrecognition of which he speaks is less a matter of our knowledge of the world than it is a failure to understand the nature of our selfhood. That is to say, the misrecognition essential to ideology is fundamentally a *self-misrecognition*. Althusser describes these systematic distortions inherent in the forging of self-identity by recourse to Lacan's theory of the 'mirror stage'.[5] Designating the existence of a 'duplicate mirror-structure of ideology', Althusser claims that an individual's relation to society in many ways parallels that closed, narcissistic encircled space of the Lacanian imaginary order. Like the small child before a reflected mirror-image, jubilantly imagining itself to possess a unity and completeness that in reality it lacks, the subject of ideology similarly misrecognizes itself. What the mirror of ideological discourse essentially does is to implant a network of social meanings at the heart of subjective life. Hence, the individual is structured through ideological discourse to recognize himself or herself as a 'subject' – an identity constructed upon social influences such as class, race and nationalism. Ideology thus constructs an imaginary map of the self within society.

What all of this amounts to, in short, are the complex ways in which individuals come to have an unconscious, psychical invest-ment in their lived relation to social conditions. According to Althusser, it is only because human subjects come to feel (at an ima-ginary level) centred within ideology that purposive social life is rendered possible at all. But how, exactly, are these imaginary processes of psychic life incorporated into the dominant ideologies of society and politics? In what manner do imaginary misrecognitions affect, and in what ways are they affected by, historically and polit-ically situated social relations? Althusser's treatment of this issue is contradictory, and at times certainly confusing. Essentially, however, he argues that imaginary misrecognitions are constituted in symbolic form through a process which is termed 'interpellation'. It is through ideology, Althusser claims, that society 'interpellates' or 'hails' the individual as a 'subject', simultaneously conferring an identity *and* subjecting the individual to that social position. Such social posi-tioning is reproduced and sustained by institutions he calls 'ideological state apparatuses' – which range all the way from the government, mass media communications, trade unions and political parties, down to schools, the church and the family. It is through our day-to-day involvements with these social institutions, Althusser argues, that the terrain of class struggle occurs. Interpellating subjects to *different positions* in social relations of production, the exploitative symbolic encodings of ideology ensure that subjects misrecognize their social position as a matter of their own free initi-ative. This can be demonstrated, Althusser claims, by considering the internal contradictions of the liberal ideology of individualism:

> In the ideology of freedom, the bourgeoisie lives in a direct fashion its relation to its condition of existence: that is to say, its real relation (the law of the liberal capitalist economy), but incorpor-ated in an imaginary relation (all men are free, including free workers). Its ideology consists in this word-play about freedom, which betrays just as much the bourgeois will to mystify those it exploits (free!) in order to keep them in harness, by bondage to freedom, as the need of the bourgeoisie to live its class domination as the freedom of the exploited.[6]

In Althusser's eyes, then, subjects come to live out their *imaginary relation* to the real conditions of existence through *symbolic forms* which are reproduced and sustained by late capitalist society.

In a move characteristic of much post-structuralist thought, Althusser argues that the decisive level of social analysis in the individual's submission to the prevailing social order is language. Following Lacan, he argues that this is so because the imaginary unity which the child experiences with its mother is *broken* from the outside with the entry of a third determinant – the symbolic order of language. Were this not to happen, the result would be the eventual ruin of all ideological mirrors and the subject would fall into psychosis. As a symbolic system which ensures the continuation of imaginary significations, then, language is that component of contemporary society which most forcefully discloses the constitution of the individual's political subjection. As Althusser writes in 'Freud and Lacan', it is 'within the law of language in which is established and presented all human order, i.e. every human role'.[7] While Althusser interestingly fails to acknowledge the importance of the socio-symbolic order for the formation of the gendered self, he does stress its critical value for linking the imaginary effects of subjectivization to the submission of a 'super-Subject', the law. In fact, so closely are these processes intertwined that for Althusser 'individuals are always-already subjects'. In sum, then, it is through imaginary misrecognition, language and the symbolic order that subjects are positioned within the pre-given structure of social and economic roles which form the very basis of politics and society.

It is important to notice that, in making ideology coterminous with lived experience, certain tensions inhere in Althusser's theory, tensions which he, Althusser, tried to reconcile. On the one hand, much of the boldness of Althusser's work stems from his break with traditional theories that view ideology as a realm of distorted knowledge or illusion. By focusing on the imaginary constitution of ideology, Althusser shows that such psychical mechanisms are an indispensable feature of the tissue of our daily life. On the other hand, by treating all lived experience as ideological, it becomes increasingly difficult (if not impossible) to determine whether some forms of life do more violence than others within the wider contexts of society. Such a broad definition of ideology appears to delimit the important critical concern with relations of domination and asymmetries of power between individuals and groups of individuals. Althusser's response to this dilemma is, in short, to affirm the importance of both conceptions of ideology. He insists that ideology is an enabling medium for the constitution of social life, providing the very imaginary terrain in which social struggle is fought. Like the unconscious which structures it, he argues, 'ideology is eternal'.[8] Yet he also emphasizes that the content of these imaginary significations cannot be above suspicion. For Althusser what is symbolized or inscribed within ideology, in class societies of the modern West at least, is the very existence of asymmetrical relations of domination and power. And it is in this sense, he claims, that the self-misrecognition which occurs in the 'mirror' of ideological discourse actually works to sustain the dominant power interests of modern societies. Whether Althusser is successful in reconciling these enabling and constraining features of ideology, however, we must now turn to consider.

Social Reproduction and the Imaginary

The Althusserian theory of ideology is a significant attempt to rethink the relations between the imaginary order and the constitution of the socio-historical world. Ideology, and its imaginary dimension, is no longer conceived as a false reflection or distortion of reason. It is an inherent and indispensable feature for the reproduction of everyday social life. Formulated in contrast to the reductionist tendencies of traditional Marxist thought, Althusser's account of ideology powerfully demonstrates how the imaginary and institutional life interweave in social and political practice. These considerations are especially pertinent, Althusser argues, for any assessment of what post-class societies might look like. In orthodox Marxism, since psychic life is usually rendered an epiphenomenon of the economic domain, the entwinement of desire and social power carry no particular significance for the revolutionary project. Forms of repression and domination that are deeply lodged in the unconscious can simply be expected to dissipate with the socialist transformation of the means of production. Althusser's thesis, however, profoundly questions such assumptions. Ideology, as deeply interfused with the unconscious imaginary, is projected as a necessary medium of all future societies. According to Althusser, the imaginary order does not simply replicate the field of the economic ideologically, but possesses an autonomy that in many ways negates that context. Through an appropriation of psychoanalysis, developed through the spectacles of Lacan, Althusser's theory highlights that processes of social change are never the simple unfolding of 'objective contradictions'. Rather, political and ideological turmoil is bound up in the most intimate ways with the unconscious economy of human subjects. Social upheaval *is* an imaginary crisis of human relationships.

Viewed from this angle, Althusser's account of ideology has made important contributions to understanding the imaginary order in relation to a *critical* view of the reproduction of modern societies. There have been many severe criticisms, however, of Althusser's work; particularly of his strict separation of ideology from the domain of science. There is no point in rehearsing these objections here, especially since Althusser's separation of ideology and science finds few advocates nowadays. Such shortcomings usually concern, above all, Althusser's refusal to recognize that scientific knowledge is itself embedded in historical and social contexts. And while Althusser certainly sought to escape from the polarity of ideology as 'false' and science as 'true', there can be little doubt that his standpoint grants an extraordinary privilege to science as an undistorted realm which investigates the beclouded minds of pre-scientific subjects. Instead of retracing these territories, I want to focus on certain problems in Althusser's work that pertain to the more fruitful area for critical enquiry of social reproduction and the imaginary constitution of human subjects. In this respect, there are at least three serious diffi-culties which delimit the critical value of Althusser's work. They are (1) his characterization of the Lacanian orders of the 'imaginary' and 'symbolic', and the fate of individuals within them; (2) his account of the nature and role of imaginary 'positioning' in ideological forma-tions; and (3) his monolithic conception of the impact of class upon ideological forms in modern societies.

(1) Althusser's account, as we have seen, posits an intimate connection between the Lacanian imaginary order and the human subject's ideological integration into society. Individuals exist only in and through the imaginary register of misrecognition. This imaginary dimension of ideology serves a dual purpose. It at once confers a coherent sense of self-identity, reflected in the 'mirror' of ideological discourse, and also masks the subject's true decentred and frag-mented state of being. Accordingly, ideology for Althusser is not a wholly negative phenomenon. It is an indispensable medium which allows human social life to come into existence as purposeful and meaningful. No doubt there is some plausibility to Althusser's account of these centring and unifying aspects of ideology and the imaginary order. It is no doubt the case that, in order to become centred on the world, individuals must feel to some degree a sense of self-coherence and orientation. In this respect, the 'imaginary' dimension of human experience plays a vital role in ordering the vast array of bodily drives and capacities into a relatively organized form.

There are major deficiencies, however, in Althusser's theory. To begin with, whatever the narcissistic illusions of the ego, it is surely implausible to suggest that subjects are as passively centred and unified within ideological formations as Althusser does. In psycho-analytic terms, what is missing from Althusser's picture of unified selfhood are those destabilizing effects which result from a psyche that is internally split and fractured; a psyche that is forever located within that unstable desire which *is* the unconscious. At issue here is

Althusser's interpretation of Lacanian psychoanalysis. What Althusser understands to be the 'subject of ideology' is, in effect, the Lacanian *ego* – that register of imaginary misrecognition which is constituted in a 'mirror'. In Lacanian theory, however, the concept of human subjectivity is a good deal more complex, comprising the three orders of the imaginary, the symbolic and the real. The imaginary dimension of human experience, then, upon which Althusser places such stress, is only one side of the Lacanian subject. Along with those illusory entities which constitute for Lacan the imaginary, there are the accompanying orders of the symbolic, which structures our perception of social reality and the real, which is that core of desire resistant to both mirror-play and symbolization. For Lacan, as we have seen in Chapter 4, each of these orders is traversed (to varying degrees) by the displacements, gaps and fissures of language. The implications of this misreading of Lacanian theory are clear: it renders Althusser's account of subjectivity a good deal more unified and coherent than the Lacanian orders of the imaginary, symbolic and real would grant licence.

In order to develop this point, consider the case of the imaginary order. In describing the imaginary dimension of ideology exclusively as one of centring, unity, and cohesion, Althusser screens from analysis those treacherously fragmenting experiences that are equally central to this domain. For it is precisely because the human subject is not *really* as integrated as its mirror 'image' suggests that it is forever plagued by a profound sense of otherness and despair. As we have seen, the experiential sense of turbulence and asymmetry that Lacan ascribes to the imaginary order centres on this fundamental split between unity and contradiction, self and other. This structuration of anxiety, or what in Lacanian terms is called otherness, means that there is always a contradictory space within the ideological sphere. Yet in marking out the imaginary field of ideology as a full-blooded support for later symbolic forms, Althusser unjustifiably severs this element of contradiction from social and political life. The same problem can be seen in Althusser's treatment of the symbolic order. Put simply, the symbolic for Althusser 'interpellates' individuals as subjects, enforcing a stable set of ideological signifiers that are deemed to be essential for social reproduction. Like some omnipotent superego, ideology operates to subject individuals to predetermined social positions, in which all identifications are formed in accordance with a totalizing, symbolic presence. Once again, however, it is not hard to see that the contradictory and ambiguous nature of Lacan's symbolic order has been jettisoned by this reading. For Lacan, the symbolic order encompasses the whole field of language (the Other), conceived in post-structuralist terms as a differential system of elements. And while Lacan's view of this order is to be redefined and reconsidered throughout his career, a basic tension remains within the symbolic as a structured universe of received social meanings on the one hand, and of the elusive nature of the signifying network itself on the other. However, this latter dimension of the symbolic, that shifting terrain in which signifiers miss their mark, is passed over in relative silence by Althusser. Instead, Althusser's subject of ideology is caught within the symbolic order as a self-reproducing object of domination.

In the political domain, these theoretical deficiencies become manifest if we turn to consider the way in which ideological meanings are structured and reproduced in modern societies. Althusser's rendering of Lacanian theory suggests that, at an unconscious level, ideology operates to 'cement' together individuals within a social formation. He contends that there exist different sets of core values and beliefs which are attached to specific positions within the polity, the economy and society. And it is precisely the function of ideology to adapt individuals – via 'interpellation' – to such role requirements, whether as capitalist, worker, priest, house-worker, or whatever. Although existing evidence about ideological consciousness is not definitive (and for fairly obvious reasons), it is far from indicating that anything like an imaginary connection exists between an individual's social position and their deeper dispositions, beliefs and desires.[9] The difficulty with Althusser's approach is that it exaggerates and generalizes the extent to which individuals inculcate existing modes of socialization. It seriously downplays the existence of, and possibilities for, *dis*-identification with dominant forms of ideological discourse. For in contrast to assuming an imaginary connection between specific social roles and ideology, as John B. Thompson argues, 'the reproduction of the social order can be an unintentional outcome of the *rejection* of the values and norms propagated by the official agencies of ... socialization'.[10] To parody Althusser's case a little: in the case of someone who is unemployed, a trade unionist, a Tory, as well as sexist, is social analysis really just a matter of decoding an original 'hailing' into ideology? More specifically, how do human subjects renegotiate, and often manage to hold, conflictive ideologies? The central political difficulty here is that Althusser's theory of ideology commits individuals to an endless repetition of fixed subject-positions. As such, it is forced to pass over the important, contradictory ways in which self-identity is renegotiated within ideological struggle.

From the foregoing considerations, then, it can be seen that Althusser's theoretical approach to social reproduction and the imaginary has a distinctly reductionist flavour. By severing the psychic

forces of contradiction and fragmentation from the 'unity' forged in
the imaginary order, as well disregarding their complex interplay with
the socio-symbolic order of modern societies, Althusser offers a
theory of ideology which is, at best, only a partial account of the
vastly differing *modes* of subjectivity in modern societies. Individuals
are never simply the sum total of imaginary supports of a social
order. The disruptive, fracturing effects of unconscious desire, as
Freud and Lacan after him affirm, suggest that a subject's relation to
the socio-symbolic order is a good deal more unstable and internally
contradictory than Althusser allows. In sum, then, Althusser's model
assumes exactly what needs to be examined: how it is that the dispersion and displacement of unconscious desire both situate and
fragment subject-positions, and how these imaginary forms operate
to reproduce, sustain, or challenge relations of domination.

(2) The second deficiency of Althusser's model concerns the
actual status of the imaginary itself in his account of the 'positioning'
of human subjects in social and political relations. As we have seen,
Althusser's theory of ideology posits that individuals are constituted
as subjects in an 'imaginary relation' to the real structure of social
relations. It sees, rightly, that ideological effects occur in and through
human beings at the level of those deep affective, unconscious
images which we carry both of ourselves and others. But if its
strength is to recognize the constitutive role of imaginary significations within ideological discourse, its weakness rests with its inability
to capture those processes by which this imaginary domain is formed.
For Althusser, the individual subject can only 'recognize' itself by
misrecognizing its relation to the real structures of society. This
Lacanian-based formulation, however, encounters a number of
logical problems. How does the individual come to recognize itself,
to identify and live within an ideological formation? How, exactly,
does it cash in on this conferring of 'ideological identity'? The
problem with Althusser's account, as with Lacan's theory of the
specular ego, is that surely for an individual to begin to recognize
itself within ideology it must *already* have some sense of subjecthood.
That is to say, the misrecognition which Althusser takes to be fundamental to ideology is nonetheless still a recognition. For how else
might an ideological discourse be *rendered intelligible* unless an individual already possessed the subjective capacities for response and
recognition; in short, a psychical reality. Althusser's awareness of the
difficulties of trying to derive identity from the logic of self-reflection
is registered by his claim that individuals are 'always-already'
subjects. Ironically, though, such a view only further displaces the
profoundly imaginary dimensions of the unconscious from the social
field.

These issues connect to deeper theoretical problems in Althusser's account of the unconscious imaginary. Like the small child captivated by its self-image in the Lacanian mirror, ideology for Althusser enforces its imaginary encodings into a passive and inert human body. That is to say, an individual does not receive an ideological discourse in Althusser's view unless he or she is actually constituted by the processes of its production. But the central weakness of this position is that it eliminates any concern with the complex mechanisms by which ideology is actually received and made sense of by human beings. The imaginary only operates as a kind of empty receptacle, a psychic structure into which ideology is implanted in a uniform and universal way. Consequently, Althusser's position is unable to specify, at the level of imaginary significations, whether differing forms of self-constitution reproduce or challenge ideological meanings. Ideology is simply universal, at once constitutive and oppressive of subjectivity. The issue of how forms of domination and exploitation are generated and change across time at the psychological and cultural level becomes almost impossible to identify from this perspective. In the end, then, Althusser's social theory becomes a logical extension of the Lacanian claim that the imaginary operates as a universal mirror of misrecognition – at once permitting and deforming human social relationships.

This point can also be made another way. For Althusser, individuals are treated essentially as effects of, or as 'constituted by', social processes. In psychoanalytic terms, however, such a view offers only a very partial account of the complex modalities of self-constitution and the unconscious imaginary. It represses the psychoanalytic insight that the structural complex through which ideology is formed arises from a subject's desire and sexuality as much as it does upon 'external' social conditions. This repression primarily relates to Freud's theory of identification. According to Freud, in order to take up any cultural value or meaning a subject must necessarily 'identify' with it. This capacity for identification, as we have seen in Chapter 1, is closely connected to Freud's discussion of the representational process – that unconscious architecture of images which always provides the possibility for a redefinition of meaning. At issue, then, is not so much Althusser's reading of Lacanian theory but the very assumptions which inform this account of the imaginary. It is because Althusser passes over in silence the question of identification that he is unable to elaborate the ways in which individuals respond to ideological discourse. By neglecting the vast plenitude of unconscious forces as they intersect with the social and political field, Althusser's theory of ideology fails to attend to the rich imaginary forms by which subjects make sense of 'interpellation'.

(3) The third difficulty of Althusser's work concerns his rather monolithic, pessimistic conception of modern societies as self-reproducing objects of class domination. This problem emerges most forcefully in his account of the ideological state apparatuses. To begin with, Althusser argues that this very broad range of institutions – the government, schools and the family – are the principal sites in which ideological struggle and conflict occur. But, later in the same essay, he rides roughshod over this by contending that, 'in the last instance', these institutions are the mechanisms through which the dominant ideological relations of capitalism are reproduced and sustained. In effect, then, these institutions are seen as merely functional domains by which human beings are subjected to their specific positions within the social division of labour, or located within the relations of domination and subordination between classes and class factions. It has long been recognized that Althusser's notorious economism here drives him to portray the development of modern societies, and their social relations, as being fully structured and integrated around the economic 'base' of society. That such an account of the structuring of the ideological field is too economistic is today surely clear. But what I want to focus briefly on here is a different, though related, deficiency: namely, the way in which Althusser fails to explore, and indeed short-circuits, the influence of psychic processes on social structures, such as the economy, and the degree to which these structures mediate the psyche.

While Althusser's theory of ideology offers a useful Lacanian psychoanalytic view of the speaking subject as formed within language, it avoids making the connection between these unconscious, affective dimensions of ideology and the multiplicity of concrete social relations. Instead, it abstracts the multiform ways in which unconscious desire and social practices intertwine, and projects the former into the control of a totalized domain of economic or class relations. In doing so it thereby flattens out complex psychical processes of major importance for the analysis of ideology into an approach that is class-reductionist. In levelling this criticism I do not want to claim that an institution like the family, for example, does not play a substantive role in ordering the unconscious drives and phantasies of subjects into a form conducive to the social division of labour and the world of monopoly capitalism. However, to view the family solely as a medium for the reproduction of dominant class relations does obscure the contradictory ways in which unconscious states shape, and are shaped by, social relations. Treated this way, it simply evades any consideration of the important emotional values and relations that are fostered within familial relations. Furthermore, it results in a lack of attention to the concrete ways in which desire and power interfuse in other equally important relations of domination, such as gender, race and ethnicity. In sum, then, it is certainly important to be alert to the complex ways in which repressed desire and sexuality intersect with structural features of class relations, but a satisfactory psychoanalytic social theory should not treat this phenomenon as the origin of asymmetric relations of power.

In the foregoing pages I have examined some of the central claims and assumptions of Althusser's theory of ideology. In focusing on the human subject as a problem of ideology, Althusser's work uncovers many of the key mechanisms through which the affective, unconscious features of self-identity are constituted. I have tried to show that one of his most suggestive insights in this regard is to highlight the imaginary dimensions of ideology as an indispensable medium of human subjectivity. However, I have also argued that, in many respects, it is now widely agreed that Althusser's theory of ideology contains serious limitations: it contains several important misinterpretations of Lacanian psychoanalysis; only a very partial account of the nature of the imaginary order of psychic life (deriving from its reliance on Lacan's work); and a position on social reproduction and relations of domination that is class-reductionist in character. Whatever these limits of Althusser's work, however, there have been some important recent attempts to articulate more precisely what Lacanian theory has to contribute to the analysis of the links between subjectivity and the ideological-political field. Given the challenging and innovatory character of much of this contemporary work, the remainder of this chapter will be given over to examining these trends, focusing particularly on the post-Lacanian social theories of Laclau and Mouffe (1985), and the work of Žižek (1989).

Post-Marxism through the Lacanian Real: Laclau and Mouffe

In *Hegemony and Socialist Strategy*, Ernesto Laclau and Chantal Mouffe offer the outlines of a post-Marxist social theory that aims to rethink the nature of political domination, as well as trace the possibilities for a radical democratic politics in the late modern age.[11] In linking many post-structuralist themes to a revised Gramscian theory of hegemony, the main thrust of their work is to break with objectivistic theories of the social; that is, theories which connect objectivities to either universalizing forms, a self-identical subject, or the control of the social. Such theoretical closure in their view, evident in both liberal and Marxist discourses, fails to comprehend that social phenomena cannot be assigned an 'objective' logic, have no teleology, and certainly offer no guarantees for the future. In developing a non-essentialist social theory, by contrast, the work of Laclau and Mouffe seeks to come to grips with the demise of traditional grounds for political emancipation (the displacing of traditional working-class politics by new social movements, the incorporation of potentially oppositional political forms into the mass culture of commodified society, as well as the relations of domination and inequality structured in societies which have claimed to be socialist in some sense). To do this, Laclau and Mouffe draw from a diverse range of philosophical traditions in their analyses of political hegemony – from classical political theory to hermeneutics; from phenomenology to post-structuralism. There is, however, one consistent theoretical thread which implicitly informs their position on the social as incomplete, decentred, unstable: Lacanian psychoanalysis. Indeed, it has become increasingly clear that certain Lacanian concepts are crucial for understanding their preoccupation with the social as being *structured upon a central impossibility*, that traumatic fissure designated by Lacan as the real order. In this respect, I want now to examine key Lacanian themes in the work of Laclau and Mouffe in some detail.

In focusing upon the relations between subjectivity and hegemony in politics, Laclau and Mouffe begin by tracing the application of Althusserian epistemology to critical enquiry. In their view, Althusser's deployment of the psychoanalytic concept of over-determination radically opened the field of *contingent* practices for theoretical reflection. In demonstrating that subjectivity can only emerge against the backdrop of a symbolic fusion of elements, Althusser shows that social meanings can never be ultimately fixed. 'Althusser's statement that everything existing in the social is over-determined', they argue, 'is the assertion that the social constitutes itself as a symbolic order. The symbolic – i.e., overdetermined – character of social relations therefore implies that they lack an ultimate literality which would reduce them to necessary moments of an immanent law.'[12] For Laclau and Mouffe, however, Althusser was unable to theorize adequately the open and plural dimensions of identity because of the implicit economism in his work. By ultimately fixing identity 'in the last instance' to the mode of production, Althusser's model collapsed overdetermination into economic determination. Yet it is precisely this potentially open and contingent character of overdetermination, they argue, that must be recovered in order better to grasp the social field.

For Laclau and Mouffe, to pursue this contingent character of symbolic overdetermination requires recasting the position of identity in modern social theory. In contrast to the classical model of subjectivity as a pre-given, substantial entity, they propose that individual and collective identities are constituted through non-essential relational elements of social discourse. That is to say, identities are formed through a *discursive construction* of the various, differential elements of a given symbolic order. In a move common to much of post-structuralism, Laclau and Mouffe configure the social as a discourse which is always in a certain state of contingency and movement. On this view, the social and political interests of human subjects are not pre-packaged. The problems that the working class have encountered in forming itself this century as a historical subject (with its attendant splits and fragmentations in alliances), they argue, bears witness to this point. Any 'subject-position' that is constituted in modern politics cannot pretend to stand on the solid ground of rationality or on universal claims of human interests. Rather, collective identities are always open to dispersion and fragmentation of their positionality. This is so since they are structured by an overdetermination of some discourses by others. But if Laclau and Mouffe are post-structuralist in this way, they are also to some degree aware of the limits of a deconstructive understanding of identity as sheer difference, multiplicity, indeterminancy. In their view, the post-structuralist claim that subject-positions are always fully dispersed is just as regressively essentialist as the Althusserian tendency to reduce overdetermination back into the very ideology of identity. For Laclau and Mouffe, such a focus only severs subjects from any social terrain or context in which discursive identities are formed and established, however precariously. To this end, they propose that the discursive construction of elements within discourse must be understood as occurring within an *articulatory* context.[13] Daily life is the reproduction and transformation of multidimensional 'articulations', and it is through such processes that subject-positions are constituted and, from a political angle, hegemonized.

Laclau and Mouffe's insistence on a moment of articulation might seem at first glance to contradict their previous emphasis on identity as discontinuous, multiple, dispersed. For what can possibly create or sustain the identity of any ideological form if nothing positive inheres within subjectivity? The answer to this, in their view, demands discriminating adequately between the impossibility of an ultimate fixity of meaning on the one hand, and the necessity for certain partial fixations in order to arrest the flow of differences of language on the other hand. This filtering of differences into meaning is, they claim, the hegemonic medium of the ideological-political field. Following Lacan, they argue that structures of meaning are constituted through 'nodal points' (*points de capiton*) in which signifiers and signifieds are temporarily sewn together. These

overdetermined points operate to fix the multitude of 'floating signifiers' which circulate in the ideological field, and thereby structure a
surplus signification through their articulation in relation to other
elements of language. On this view, then, ideological struggle *is* the
attempt to fuse, and subsequently control, free-floating signifiers into
structured networks of meaning. For example, consider the political
appropriation in recent times of certain key signifiers relating to
'freedom' in social life. The expansion of neo-conservative defini-
tions of 'democracy' in both Europe and the US during the 1980s
was, to a large extent, discursively established by redefining existing
perceptions about egalitarian democracy, such as the Welfare State,
as a threat to the autonomy and private rights of individuals. In
response, a good deal of attention has been devoted by the political
Left to deepen the current discourses relating to individualism,
stressing the vital links between individual freedom and equality of
rights. For Laclau and Mouffe, however, the crucial analytical point
here is that these discursive, ideological spaces are always potentially
subject to transformation. And this is so because what is at stake in
all political struggle is whether certain meanings can be made to stick
within discourse, or whether such meanings merely fade back into
the unconscious, the latter being understood in Lacanian terms as
that spacing of differences within the symbolic order.

On this view, then, all social practice is defined according to its
mode of articulation. Political and ideological forms are configured
as relations among discursive elements that are always open to transformations of their identity. For Laclau and Mouffe, ideological
struggle is not about the expression of pre-existing interests; rather,
it consists of the ever new articulation of identities and differences.
Stressing this open, plural and contingent character of the social,
Laclau and Mouffe situate the concept of 'articulation' as follows:

if we accept the non-complete character of all discursive fixation
and, at the same time, affirm the relational character of every
identity, the ambiguous character of the signifier, its non-fixation
to any signified, can only exist insofar as there is a proliferation of
signifieds. It is not the poverty of signifieds but, on the contrary,
polysemy that disarticulates a discursive structure. This is what
establishes the overdetermined, symbolic dimension of every
social identity. Society never manages to be identical to itself, as
every nodal point is constituted within an intertextuality that over-
flows it.[14]

A useful example of what Laclau and Mouffe mean by this arbitrary
character of discursive fixation is shown by the current multiplicity of

positions within the ecological movement. In the counter-struggles of ecological movements, whether a subject constructs a discursive subject-position as a socialist ecologist, a conservative ecologist, or some type of apolitical 'green', largely depends upon how that position is marked by metaphoric signifiers from other elements of the ideological field. In the case of a conservative or reactionary ecologist, for instance, the reversal of environmental damage might be discursively linked to an authoritarian, anti-democratic state that would seek to reassert control over the management of natural resources. The point that must not be overlooked, argue Laclau and Mouffe, is that such discursive articulations are always 'radically contingent'; they result entirely from symbolic condensation and not from some internal or objective necessity of social positions. This 'radical contingency' of the relation between signifier and articulation is, the authors claim, vital for understanding the limit of the social. They define this limit as resting upon a lack of foundation of the symbolic order; a lack of foundation which prevents symbolic condensation from ever becoming *integrated* into the social. Unlike the Althusserian position, then, which accords priority to symbolic interpellation over the openness of ideological struggle, Laclau and Mouffe attribute a contingency to the symbolic order which is somehow always inscribed within its own internal form. The question of what defines this contingency of symbolic identities is, as we shall now see, resolved by appeal to the Lacanian real – to that domain that subsists outside symbolization.

That any discursive articulation is always radically contingent, and not the result of internal needs or interests, leads to the central argument advanced in *Hegemony and Socialist Strategy*: that 'society' as such does not exist. 'The social', they write, '*is* articulation insofar as "society" is impossible'.[15] In making this claim Laclau and Mouffe do not intend, absurdly, to deny the existence of subjective experience, human social relationships, nor the fact that the organization of society at a symbolic level has real effects. Rather, their notion of articulation opposes any *absolute* fixing of the term 'society' as self-enclosed, necessary, natural. Drawn from the Lacanian proposition 'Woman doesn't exist', Laclau and Mouffe are insistent that the social also lacks ultimate foundation, structure, unity. Just as Lacanian theory understands gender-identity to denote an imaginary field of images which are illusory fantasies to which the split and fractured human subject aspires, so too can the social field be unmasked as existing upon a central impossibility which then obscures this lack of ground. This impossibility, while intangible in form, can be simply stated: the socio-symbolic reality is structured around a traumatic fissure (the real order) which cannot itself be symbolized. In

Lacanian theory, as noted in Chapter 4, the real order is that elusive realm of desire situated at the furthest reaches of the Other, functioning as an impossibility which marks and blocks our deepest wishes for self-unity. The real order then is both prior to mirror-play (the imaginary) and resistant to symbolization (the symbolic). The socio-symbolic order can never actually represent the real; and, moreover, the real only becomes available to interpretation through its effects.[16] To comprehend the impact of the real order upon the social field, Laclau and Mouffe try to show that it is impossible to achieve a closure of subject-positions. Any symbolic position that is established in society can never become fixed since the latter is structured upon the traumatic field of the real; at once a sustaining presence of the symbolic order and also a limit to the achievement of any absolute categories. From this angle, then, the real is that which defines the limit of the social, ensuring that every attempt at symbolization at once succeeds and fails. These internal limits of the Lacanian real are incorporated into the work of Laclau and Mouffe through the concept of 'antagonism'. In the same way that the Lacanian real intrudes upon and distorts desire, the existence of a fundamental antagonism in the social field disrupts intersubjective relations. In fact such disruptions, extended in Lacanian vein by Laclau and Mouffe, force upon the self the existence of an unobtainable Other. Furthermore, having rejected the category of the non-discursive, these antagonistic splits between self and Other are understood to be entirely internal to the discourses which condition them.

What lies behind this notion of antagonism is, of course, a Lacanian conception of the subject as lacking, insufficient, decentred. The aim of modern politics and ideology, argue Laclau and Mouffe, is to repress everything that suggests this lack. Relations of domination and asymmetries of power are characterized as hegemonic attempts to 'fill in' this insufficiency of the subject. Modes of subjectivatization permit human beings to escape from this painful, traumatic experience which exists at the boundary of the real. To conceptualize this, Laclau and Mouffe link hegemonic practices to the Lacanian category of 'suture'; that *filling-in* of the lack of the subject. In a somewhat cursory footnote to a category that implicitly informs much of their criticism, Laclau and Mouffe comment: 'It is this double movement that we will attempt to stress in our extension of the concept of suture to the field of politics. Hegemonic practices are suturing insofar as their field of operation is determined by the openness of the social, by the ultimately unfixed character of every signifier. This original lack is precisely what the hegemonic practices try to fill in.'[17] What this argument effectively does, then, is to reconceive the imaginary dimensions of ideology as that which fills out the void of the subject. Whether one is in the grip of some piece of male chauvinist doctrine, religious fundamentalism or revolutionary nationalism, these are all antagonistic *mis*-recognitions formed in the hegemonic realm of ideology. To subvert these suturing, hegemonic discourses, the task of modern criticism is to find a way to undo such ideological fantasies and to return the subject to her or his true, repressed insufficiency.

This invalidation of the term 'society' as an object of discourse, argue Laclau and Mouffe, should not lead radicals to political resignation or despair. For it is the very contingency of the social, those open and indeterminate dimensions of subjectivity, which permits the space for both hegemonic practices and their political opposition. Towards the end of *Hegemony and Socialist Strategy*, the authors specifically consider the prospects for radical democracy in the late twentieth century. While being understandably cautious, they argue that a new era of politics is emerging, one that brings to a close the classic ideal of a single revolutionary agent. To this end, they point to new social movements – free speech and democratic movements; peace, ecological and feminist movements and the like – as representing a growing tendency of diversity, fluidity, and plurality within modern societies. They describe this multiplicity of social antagonisms as being driven, and continually displaced, by the 'egalitarian imaginary'. As they point out, however, the political forms of the imaginary cut both ways, in reactionary and progressive directions. In response to this dilemma, they urge that a truly radical and plural democracy might best be formed by deepening the terms of democratic-egalitarian political discourse. The democratic tendency in politics should be affirmed through an articulation of diverse struggles for equality. In their words:

there is no radical and plural democracy without renouncing the discourse of the universal and its implicit assumption of a privileged point of access to 'the truth', which can be reached only by a number of subjects. In political terms this means that just as there are no surfaces which are privileged *a priori* for the emergence of antagonism, nor are there discursive regions which the programme of a radical democracy should exclude *a priori* as possible spheres of struggle. Juridical institutions, the educational system, labour relations, the discourses of the resistance of marginal populations construct original and irreducible forms of social protest, and thereby contribute all the discursive complexity and richness on which the programme of a radical democracy should be founded.[18]

Beyond Interpellation and the Social Fantasy: Žižek

With the work of Laclau and Mouffe certain concepts of Lacanian psychoanalytic theory are critically developed and expanded to forge a complex account of the relations between subjectivity and the social field. Viewed as decentred and desubjectivized, the social-ideological field is conceived as a locus of partial fixations of meaning; a hegemonic screening of social antagonisms; and an imaginary covering of that fundamental lack of the split, desiring subject. Many of these same directions are taken in the recent work of the Slovenian social theorist Slavoj Žižek. A leading member of the Slovenian Lacanian school, Žižek has for some time been redefining the complex interplay between subjectivity and the imaginary dimensions of ideology. He has most explicitly addressed the question of the subject as a problem of ideology in *The Sublime Object of Ideology*.[19] This work can be seen as a systematic effort to deepen the status of the human subject once the social field is conceptualized as being complicated by the Lacanian real and the notion of social antagonism. Indeed, Žižek often specifically links his approach with the work of Laclau and Mouffe. Yet unlike their tendency to collapse all of subjectivity into discourse, Žižek explicitly draws connections between certain deep structures of psychical life on the one hand, and social contexts on the other.

At several points in his work, Žižek poses the question of the human subject by contrasting certain versions of post-structuralism with Lacanian theory. In this respect, it is interesting to note that Žižek, like Laclau and Mouffe, argues against the post-structuralist perspective that meaning derives from a play of absolute differences internal to language. The problem with this totalization of difference, Žižek argues, is that it has no conceptual means of tracing linguistic effects back to the self-identity of speaking subjects. Individuals are only understood to experience the social world through the effects of 'subjectivization', which, in more sociological terms, can be described as a 'thick' process of socialization. In post-structuralist thought, the human subject is reduced to an effect of a pre-subjective process, analysed variously as the text (Derrida), power (Foucault), or desire (Deleuze and Guattari). And it is this pre-subjective process which is viewed as constituting individuals to their roots as 'subjects' of the social-historical world. Žižek criticizes these standpoints for their failure to recognize that modes of subjectivization can only traverse the subject to the extent that there are internal dimensions of human life. In short, individuals must have some capacity for subjective response and identification in order to be situated within varying subject-positions. It is at this point that Žižek highlights the differences between the post-structuralist notion of 'subject-positions' and the Lacanian account of the split and decentred subject. For Žižek, this difference hinges on that lack, insufficiency and loss which fundamentally marks the desire of the human subject. In Lacan's theory, as discussed in Chapter 4, the first object of the imaginary order is only perceived as existing once it becomes lost to the human subject. This impossibility of recovering the longed-for object is then further distorted when the subject enters the domain of symbolic representation, as the subject dissolves into those differences of language which, for Lacan, *is* the unconscious. In Žižek's view, this *subject of lack* is that boundary which exists prior to any mode of subjectivization. It is the 'empty place' of individuality which different modes of subjectivization attempt to repress and fill out. 'The *subject*', as he observes, 'is therefore to be strictly opposed to the effect of *subjectivization*: what the subjectivization masks is not a pre- or trans-subjective process of writing but a lack in the structure, a lack which is the subject'.[20]

As we have seen, it is from this Lacanian notion of the subject as lacking that Laclau and Mouffe boldly posit the social as that para- doxical limit in which symbolization is doomed to failure. The paradox is that the full realization of any individual or collective identity is always internally thwarted through the disruptive effects of social antagonism. Žižek fully endorses this position. In his view, however, Laclau and Mouffe do not develop fully the implications that the theory of social antagonism carries for human subjectivity. While aware of the disruptive potential of the real for society, Laclau and Mouffe tend to repress these constitutive aspects of unconscious desire, and thereby run the risk of implying that social antagonisms are simply the outcome of conflictive 'subject-positions'. In order to extend this position, then, Žižek argues another step must be taken, one which more precisely distinguishes the constitutive antagonism from the ideological field of antagonistic subject-positions. That is to say, Žižek tries to show how the real order itself inherently disrupts subjectivity as well as all social relations. To illustrate the force of this constitutive antagonism he refers to class and sexual ideologies in modern society. In these ideological antagonisms, he argues, human subjects attempt to forge a social relationship which is 'impossible'. This impossibility, according to the Laclau–Mouffe position, is not a result of objective contradictions nor oppositions, but an outcome of a fundamental split structuring these relations. This split is a form of ideological misrecognition, such that subjects believe that once capi- talist or patriarchal oppression is destroyed a new form of social organization can be established that will permit the full realization of their self-identity. The radicalization of human potentials in such ideologies is tied to the destruction of the external enemy, in this case either the 'capitalist' or 'male chauvinist'. And it is this ideological interpellation – that it is the *other* which prevents individual subjects from realizing their true human capacities – which gives social antagonisms such as class and gender their enduring force. According to Žižek, however, while these ideologies are undeniably alienating, critical discourse must realize that the constitutive antagonism arises from the lack of the subject itself. On this view, it is the subject who is marked by a pure antagonism – alienated through self-blockage, insufficiency, internal traumatism – which is then displaced onto the symbolic field. In the fundamental antagonism, Žižek contends, 'it is not the external enemy who is preventing me from achieving identity with myself, but every identity is already in itself blocked, marked by an impossibility, and the external enemy is simply the small piece, the rest of reality upon which we "project" or "externalize" this intrinsic, immanent impossibility'.[21] Whatever the radical contingency of discursive positions in modern politics and society, then, the failure of every symbolic representation is correlative to the internal impossibility of desire itself.

How is this notion of a constitutive antagonism to be understood in relationship to ideology? It is not Žižek's intention to treat the notion of antagonism simply as an instrument for mapping the emergence of ideological meanings. On the contrary, he stresses that antagonism is a concept of considerable complexity. Unlike Althusser's account of the subject's interpellation into received social meanings, for example, the notion of antagonism specifically encompasses non-meaning and that dimension of desire which is pre-ideological – in Žižek's view, one of the main factors which neutralizes and destabilizes ideological meanings in terms of their hegemonic implications for society. Yet, according to Žižek, the Althusserian theory of ideology is not wholly empty; its focus on the imaginary foundation of self-constitution and misrecognition is of enduring importance. However the central limitation of Althusser's account of interpellation, Žižek contends, is that it seeks to grasp the effects of ideology entirely along imaginary and symbolic planes, and thus misses out the Lacanian order of the real. This omission is crucial, he argues, since it is this dimension beyond symbolic representation which functions as the cause of desire and thus accounts for the subject's *identifications* with ideological meanings. In respect of developing a theory of ideology, Žižek argues that there must be an identification with interpellations, an investment of psychic energy, which drives the actions of human subjects in social reproduction. In describing the real as that dimension 'beyond interpellation', Žižek contends that ideology involves both integration and dissolution, meaning and non-meaning. In his words:

Althusser speaks only of the process of ideological interpellation through which the symbolic machine of ideology is 'internalized' into the ideological experience of Meaning and Truth; but ... this 'internalization', by structural necessity, never fully succeeds ... there is always a residue, a leftover, a stain of traumatic irrationality and senselessness sticking to it, and that *this leftover, far from hindering the full submission of the subject to the ideological command, is the very condition of it*: it is precisely this non-integrated surplus of senseless traumatism which confers on the Law its unconditional authority.[22]

It is this disruptive potential of the real, in Žižek's view, which prevents his account of ideology from degenerating into pure socialization theory. Human beings receive and identify ideological discourses in complex and often conflictive ways. The reception of ideology, however, is in all cases traversed by the unconscious, the real of desire. 'Beyond interpellation', Žižek writes, 'is the square of desire, fantasy, lack in the Other and drive pulsating around some unbearable surplus-enjoyment'.[23]

From this Lacanian vantage point, we can now see why an ideological formation can never be closed on itself, structured entirely within discursive/symbolic supports, but is at its core always radically decentred, lacking, and insufficient. But what, exactly, does this mean for a theory of ideology? There are several important consequences of this view. First, the counterpart to the notion of the subject of lack is a conception of ideology as social fantasy, as an attempt to 'suture' this lack. On this view, the function of ideology is to provide men and women with a fantasized scenario of the possibility of their own social condition. Ideology, in short, provides an idealized vision of a 'society' which in reality cannot exist. 'Fantasy', writes Žižek, 'is basically a scenario filling out the empty space of a fundamental impossibility, a screen masking a void'.[24] Second, subverting this realm of social fantasy should consequently be a social and political aim; such deconstruction is a fundamental task of the criticism of ideology. Social criticism ought to theorize the subject's lack of plenitude, unearthing that antagonism which ideological fantasy masks – a method of ideology critique which Žižek calls 'going through the social fantasy'.

One example of the displacing of a fundamental antagonism which runs through a good deal of Žižek's work is the case of anti-Semitism. Žižek's discussion of this phenomenon seeks to illustrate that the figure of the Jew has functioned as a symptom of modernity's own fundamental antagonism. Anti-Semitism, he argues, is constituted through a symbolic overdetermination of floating signifiers onto the figure of the Jew. Structured by unconscious displacement, the fundamental antagonism of the social is reconfigured around the supposed threat of the Jew, thereby masking the impossibility of 'society' itself. This displacement of antagonism onto Jews is then further libidinally condensed. In Žižek's view, these condensations operate variously as economic antagonisms (Jews as profiteering parasites), political antagonisms (Jews having a secret plot for world domination), sexual antagonisms (Jewish sexual desire as being animalistic or corrupt), and so forth. Indeed Žižek points out that totalitarian ideologies, as in Nazi Germany, displace and condense the antagonistic character of the social so far that the Jews were projected as a kind of inverted image of the Aryans themselves; as a race seeking world domination, and which therefore 'needed' to be exterminated.

The figure of the Jew is thus important to Žižek as a special case of that suturing of antagonism which occurs in the ideological sphere. Jews are defined as something Other in modernity and are thereby constructed as the destructive force within an otherwise harmonious society. This argument is extended in Žižek's more recent consideration of the re-emergence of anti-Semitism in Eastern Europe in the 1990s. Here Žižek argues that the hatred of the Jews which has arisen in the nationalist populism of Eastern European states is experienced by subjects as an imaginary 'theft of enjoyment'. On Žižek's reckoning, this imagined theft of pleasure is painful and unbearable precisely for the reason that it acts as a reminder of the 'impossibility' of one's own enjoyment. 'The real "secret" of the Jew', Žižek argues, 'is our own antagonism'.[25] The hatred of the other is thus a hatred of the self, the inversion of which is an essential trick of all racist ideologies. The figure of the Jew is therefore a particular embodiment of a fundamental antagonism, a failed sense of selfhood, a compensation for that imagined theft which leaves subjects insufficient and lacking. 'Society', Žižek concludes, 'is not prevented from achieving its full identity because of Jews: it is prevented by its own antagonistic nature, by its own immanent blockage, and it "projects" this internal negativity into the figure of the Jew'.[26]

Post-Lacanian Criticism and its Limits

The social theories of Laclau and Mouffe, and Žižek are complex theoretical attempts to situate the problem of decentred subjectivity into an account of the political field as thoroughly multidimensional, contingent, discontinuous. Both theories, following Lacan, are profoundly critical of philosophical traditions that see social and political identities as deriving from objective interests, needs, or desires. Their position, by contrast, locates the emergence of identity as a contingent process of linguistic articulation. A discursive process of political hegemony at once creates social and cultural identities and, in so doing, covers over that insufficiency which is understood to lie at the heart of subjectivity. In reconfiguring these dimensions of self-identity in modern social theory, these theories offer a powerful treatment of the issue of postmodern politics. Viewed in the context of the social struggles of the 1980s and 1990s, with the emergence of diverse forms of opposition, their preoccupation with the radical contingency of social interests, subjective needs and desires, deserves attention. However, a close examination of these theoretical standpoints shows them to be highly problematic, and ultimately inadequate, for analysing the intimate links between subjectivity and the social. The critical comments which follow do not pretend to cover all of the deficiencies of these respective approaches. Rather, for the sake of clarity, I shall focus on those problems which are especially pertinent to our concern with the subject, society and ideological forms. There are three central issues which arise from these theories which I shall discuss under the following headings: (1) The imaginary and problems of agency; (2) discourse and the nature of human needs and desires; and (3) post-Lacanian theory and the critique of ideology.

The Imaginary and Problems of Agency

There are a number of substantial problems with the position that self-identity, and the affective dimensions of unconscious experience, are constituted as effects of linguistic articulation – understood in poststructuralist terms as a differential system of relations. Laclau and Mouffe, as we have seen, endorse the view that human subjects are 'constructed' through processes of hegemonic articulation. And while there is a significant ambivalence in their work as to whether hegemonic processes actually produce the identity of social agents entirely, or whether they just act to modify their construction within language, Laclau and Mouffe insist that the shifting and discontinuous elements of discourse ensure that subjectivity is inherently conflictual and unstable. The difficulty with this position, however, is that it precludes any substantial concern with the creativity of the psyche. Selfhood, the unconscious, and the imaginary are all understood as simply the product of linguistic location. On this view, an individual can only take his or her place in the world as a subject through entrance to, and subsequent positioning by, discourse. Yet there is a fundamental tension between the strong statement just made, that hegemonic articulations construct social identities, and the actual existence of a *pre-existing psychical reality*. In the work of Laclau and Mouffe, these elements of the psyche are simply moved into a register of the universals of language. The unconscious in their account (as for Lacan) is understood as a disembodied structure; it is reduced to a series of signifiers and signs that are determined by the operations of discourse. In expounding Lacan's specifically linguistic account of the unconscious, their position undercuts the creative capacity of the individual as a subject of representation. The imaginary representations created through the unconscious, which are located within the intensities of desire and phantasy, are thus lost from view. So too are the complex forms by which they affect and are affected by social relations.

In contrast to this exclusive focus on discourse, we have seen in previous chapters that the Freudian account of the unconscious provides a view of the complexity and productivity of the imaginary that structuralist theories lack. The theory of the unconscious imaginary, I want to argue, describes and requires an active subject that is capable of producing representations, drives, affects. Such a presymbolic capacity is taken as central to human subjectivity, development, and change; and thus to social life more generally. Of course, this emphasis on the fundamentally constitutive nature of the imaginary, which is at the source of all human creativity, would be rejected by Laclau and Mouffe since they are implicitly arguing against its existence as *real*. From their Lacanian vantage point, it is simply mistaken to think we could ever reach a domain outside of the symbolic. But, as I have argued with respect to Lacan's work, to understand the presymbolic as an order 'beyond' is quite needless. The fact that imaginary, affective experience is usually given expression through linguistic mediation does not mean that the former ought to be projected into the latter. Treated this way, everything we are and do becomes equated with language as such. Accordingly, as in the case of Laclau and Mouffe, it soon appears that there can be no subjectivity outside of discourse. Yet it is surely a little too convenient to imagine that the complex interplay of needs, desires and affects that infuse our social life are merely the product of discursive articulation.

Žižek paints a more nuanced picture of the relations between discourse and the unconscious, the cognitive and affective, law and desire. His stress on the subject *prior* to modes of subjectivization is important. It highlights that the unstable relations between the subject and the social are not only the result of a dispersion of the signifying process. Rather, the instability of the social is understood to be fully anchored within the mutations of desire itself. But since for Žižek (as with Lacan) desire is always traced as a 'lack', a void which exists prior to subjectivization, human subjects are always ultimately rooted in a universal and ahistoric integration within the law. In this vision of politics, individuals are constituted as subjects through a desire which is always already 'the last support for ideology'. However, there are problems with these determinist assumptions of Žižek's work. Why does this pre-discursive 'lack' necessarily provide the final support for received social meanings, or the law? How does this void of the real congeal into social structures? How do different types of social relations interact, conflict, and reinforce one another if their specific psychical underpinning operates in such a uniform way? The difficulty here is clear. Following Lacan, Žižek vastly narrows down the multiplicity of human possibilities that Freud discovered as flowing from unconscious desire; mechanisms such as sublimation, disavowal, substitution and splitting. In their place, Žižek offers a unidimensional measure – that 'lack' inscribed through the real – which paradoxically sustains the symbolic order while also condemning it to failure. Yet what if subjects actively resist incorporation into oppressive social relations? What if they reject a certain ideological discourse and overturn it for a new one? It is undeniable, of course, that human beings need to take up some general identification with received social meanings, otherwise they risk falling into psychosis. But if this is Žižek's argument, then it is pitched at such a general level that its critical value in social and political terms is rendered fruitless. The whole model is a good deal too cohesive, despite its continual emphasis on lack and insufficiency, passing over the more positive, contradictory ways in which subjects come to *dis*-identify with ideological and social formations.

These difficulties link to deeper theoretical problems with a Lacanian approach to subjectivity, the imaginary, and issues pertaining to human agency. As discussed in Chapter 4, the Lacanian subject is forever marked by a profound sense of 'lack'. This lack, which of itself constitutes subjectivity, is located within two main sources: imaginary desire, which is understood to swerve away and always miss its mark, and the universal structures of language, which is that process in which human needs are put into discursive form. The positions of Laclau and Mouffe, and Žižek endorse this Lacanian view that the subject is the 'empty point of a universal structure', an entity that is continually alienated through putting human needs into signifying form. Consequently, they treat the other side of language, that pre-discursive realm which is the imaginary, in an entirely negative sense. The imaginary, like the ideological fantasy, is that which seeks to 'cover over' or 'fill in' the fundamental lack of the subject, that immutable gap between self and

Other. However, this argument, while accurate in Lacanian terms, depends upon the prior assumption that the self is dominated by an unobtainable Other, and that social reality is always inherently antagonistic. Yet there is no valid reason to believe that this is the case. To do so only leads to the positing of an inevitable human condition which is the no-exit of lack and antagonism. Consequently, the analyses offered by Laclau and Mouffe, and Žižek, begin and end in the same place, in the closed imaginary system which no sooner fills in an antagonistic lack than it is revealed as breaking through our discontinuity from the Other. The difficulty with this view is that it assumes precisely what ought to be proven: that the agency and creativity which informs different modes of subjectivity has been flattened into a morbidly restrictive selfhood which can find no crossable boundaries between self and other.

These incoherencies indicate that there might be more fruitful and coherent ways of understanding the imaginary foundations of human subjectivity. I suggest that the unconscious imaginary is an irreducible capacity to create the representational forms and affects that deeply structure our modes of self-constitution, as well as our interpersonal relations. What I want to emphasize in this respect is that 'lack' – what Freud called 'the loss of the object' – can therefore only exist through the imaginary investment of desire. The Lacanian assumption, repeated by Laclau and Mouffe, and Žižek, that the imaginary is grounded in ontological 'lack' is mistaken. It ought rather to be the other way round. 'Lack', and the distortions of intersubjectivity it promotes, can only exist through the imaginary, desire, invented subjectivities. To hold otherwise, as in Lacan's theory, renders the imaginary derivative and selfhood no more than a mask. It is crucial for critical social theory to recognize that the imaginary foundations of human social relations, as well as their embedding in ideologies of asymmetric power and force, are created and defined by social agents in their daily social and political lives. From this angle, as Freud so often stressed, the interweaving of the imaginary and social reality arises when subjects come to recognize the *other person's subjectivity*; an emotional recognition that the other has needs, demands, and desires which are separate from the self. The upshot of this view is that the creation of imaginary forms and fantasies in which our social and cultural worlds are embedded are not necessarily marked by an internal impossibility of self and other. This is not to claim that such a tendency is not a part of intersubjective relations. But it is to assert that the existence of an unobtainable Other is only one specific mode of self-constitution; a mode of selfhood in which certain affects toward the *other as subject* have become split-off and depersonalized, resulting in a failure to recognize the other's subjectivity.

A useful way of focusing upon these problems, especially as they pertain to social and political analysis, is by recalling Žižek's account of the phenomenon of anti-Semitism. As we have seen, Žižek's central argument is that anti-Semitism is a fundamental displacement of social antagonism; it is a prime instance of how ideology 'sutures' the antagonistic split between the self and the unobtainable Other. On this view, the link established between the figure of Jew and racist ideologies is that the former works to mask the antagonistic fissure which prevents the latter from fully constituting itself; it provides a screen against that self-blockage which is intrinsic to subjectivity. However, the incoherence of this position is that, in using the immutable category of 'antagonism' as a measure of domination, it conceals the very contradictions it seeks to explain. By assuming the universal and ahistoric existence of antagonism, this viewpoint eliminates what should be a key question about contemporary modes of domination: how is it that certain imaginary forms can result in a *destruction* of the other (person) as a subject? Instead of this, however, subjects are rendered as little more than passive containers through which an antagonistic split expresses itself. Moreover, the actual content and values of such imaginary forms as they are elaborated within ideologies are ignored; ideologies of racism simply express, interact, and reinforce a primordial impossibility between self and other.

In contrast, it can be plausibly argued that anti-Semitism, and ideologies of racism more generally, result from specific sado-masochistic organizations of desire; imaginary forms in which hatred, aggression and idealization can render the existence of concrete emotional ties impossible.[27] In this case, the failure to accept the difference and independence of others as the very institution of social reality can lead individuals to seek imaginary fulfilments through submissions to authority and the displacing of aggressiveness onto outgroups. But the formation of these unconscious states of anger and hate are located within a failure to recognize the other as subject. The postulation of a fundamental antagonism cannot capture how the imaginary can destroy the subjectivity of the other, or of how such processes become self-regulating. By conceptualizing all imaginary forms as simply filling out an antagonistic lack, Žižek's position runs the risk of elaborating an account which merely bypasses the most pressing problems.

To review these points, the positions of Laclau and Mouffe, and Žižek, severely limit psychical life to only one particular mode of subjectivity – a discordance or estrangement between self and others. Their accounts displace the focus of analysis from the intertwining of desire and relations of power to the supposedly universal and ahistoric effects of language. Consequently, the imaginary, and its expression within ideological forms, is simply understood as a defence, a symptom, a 'suturing' of a subjecthood that is morbid and dark.

Discourse and Human Needs/Desires

The link established between social articulation on the one hand, and the fashioning of human interests, needs, and desires on the other is one of the most provocative aspects of the work of Laclau and Mouffe, and Žižek. As we have seen, this link is understood as one that is discursively constructed for particular ends (that 'filling in' of the subject of lack) and is a process which is 'radically contingent'. The priority accorded to this *contingency* of discourse is intended by Laclau and Mouffe, and Žižek, as a corrective to the traditional Marxist viewpoint that ideological interests always derive from one's objective economic location in society. Their anti-essentialist doctrine is intended among other things to refute such a classical model of representation; a model in which language and conceptual thought is understood to merely 'reflect' a pre-structured world of objects. From the vantage point of post-Marxism, it is simply a fallacy to assume that there are any interests which are external to our discourses. Rather, the relations between the social, political and economic fields are ones that human beings *construct*; they are carved into social and cultural shape *through* discourse. But while this argument may be a valuable corrective to certain reductionistic forms of social thought, it does contain important logical difficulties. To begin with, the position that social interests are entirely fashioned through a contingent process of discourse would appear to doom politics and ideology to a self-referential impasse. Social interests and ideological beliefs no longer have any referential or normative grounding, but are simply a matter of what a certain contingency of discourse defines them as being – which entirely leaves open the question of what it *is* exactly that is being fashioned into shape. In this respect, Terry Eagleton has argued that post-Marxism is based on a conceptual confusion between the *signified* (the differing ways interests can be defined through discourse) and the *referent* (the socio-economic situation which pre-exists discourse and yet is continually transformed through it).[28] The problem with the view that discourse entirely legislates the real conditions of politics and ideology into being is that it cannot specify the concrete ways in which the former transforms the actual material conditions of our social practices and institutions. It simply cannot provide a cogent account of the motivations and reasons which human beings bring to ideological conflict and political strategy. Human beings are deemed to take up political and ideological identities only to the extent that they have been constructed and transformed by certain contingent, hegemonic processes. But there is something clearly awry about this position 'Why', as Eagleton questions, 'should someone become a socialist, feminist or anti-racist, if these political interests are in no sense a response to the way society is?'[29]

These difficulties become clearer if we consider the relations between social interests and the repressed needs, aspirations, and desires of human subjects. Just as Laclau and Mouffe, and Žižek, view the contingency of discourse as untainted by material conditions, so too they do not hesitate to disconnect the discursive realm from the affective dimensions of human subjectivity. In order to understand the assumptions which frame this case, it is important to see that Laclau and Mouffe, and Žižek, entirely reject the standpoint that subjective interests are commensurate with biological needs. In their interpretation, to see the self as a stable organization of needs, needs which just magically assign individuals certain ideological interests and beliefs, is to commit the mistake of essentialism. In contrast, they argue, subjects can have no interests or aspirations which are not constructed through language. In order to conceptualize how language structures human needs and interests, then, Laclau and Mouffe, and Žižek, develop the Lacanian case that desire is both radically severed from biological need and inscribed within the instability of the signifier. Hence the argument which characterizes their whole discussion: any forging of human desires and ideological interests must simply be 'radically contingent'. But, as with the case of tracing our material interests, there are serious limitations in this view. While it is undeniable that unconscious desire always swerves away from the satisfaction of biological need, it is surely implausible to suggest that the symbolic forms through which desire finds expression are completely unconnected to what we materially are; entirely unconnected to the needs and limits of the body itself. In portraying human aspirations as merely the product of arbitrary discursive constructions, this case becomes just as regressive as the view that desire is somehow a natural expression of pre-constituted needs. Whatever the complex process through which unconscious desire separates out from biological need, the fact of the matter is that human needs are related to the possible routes of symbolic expression. The case of the women's movement is a clear example. Against reductionistic modes of thought which view ideological interests as being internally shaped, it is undeniable that the situation of being female does not automatically lead women to adopt a feminist political perspective. However, to claim that the links between women and feminism are merely 'radically contingent', involving no previously repressed needs and aspirations of human subjects, is surely mistaken. Feminist practices and modes of expression reflect a range of interests, such as the need for recognition, independence, and autonomy, which have been systematically distorted and crippled by the patriarchal sexual and social order of modern societies. In this respect, the language of feminism can be seen as the political attempt to reconnect certain repressed interests, needs, and desires to the symbolic positioning of women.

It would, of course, be dangerous to press these linkages too far. As Freud stressed, desire cannot be the satisfaction of biological need precisely since it functions at the level of representation. Indeed, the whole discourse of psychoanalysis is centred upon the insight that desire does not have the type of uniform relationship to objects that biological needs have. In short, needs can be satisfied through real objects (as with the breathing of air); whereas desire finds satisfactions through *signs* or *mental representations*. The constructive side of the work of Laclau and Mouffe, and Žižek, then, consists precisely in stressing the point that ideological interests and desires are by no means automatically structured by an internal necessity. But the limitation of their position is that it pushes too far in this direction, severing the vital links by which the mediation of human needs and desires into symbolic form reveals fundamental aspects of human subjectivity.[30] It is because human beings are born 'prematurely', and subsequently need the emotional care and relatedness of others, that a vital nexus arises between what we materially are and the ideological space in which repressed desires find symbolic representation. And it is surely for this reason that certain 'constructions' of interest, such as the ongoing desire for new modes of subjectivity, autonomy and freedom, take hold of political discourse, because they articulate repressed needs, aspirations and desires of human subjects. That previously non-discursive human desires may enter into communicative form does not mean that the former are some reified objectivity, entirely independent of discourse. Any attempt to critically reflect on human needs and desires will always involve linguistic mediation, as the practice of psychoanalysis testifies. But this does not mean that the libidinal, unconscious dimensions of the self, which affect and are affected by social relations, ought to be wholly subsumed within the category of discourse.

Post-Lacanian Theory and the Critique of Ideology

These inadequacies of the work of Laclau and Mouffe, and Žižek, their neglect of the agency of the self and subsequent conflation of human needs and desires into the category of discourse, gives rise to intractable problems for an account of the critique of ideology. What is at issue here is whether the Lacanian categories which inform the work of Laclau and Mouffe, and Žižek, are compatible with their broader political view of the need to deepen the democratic and egalitarian components of liberalism. In this respect, their limiting assumption that the human subject is always constrained by self-blockage, or the unobtainable Other, makes it extremely difficult to understand how human relationships or social activity might ever be able to institute these political values of freedom and autonomy. In other words, because their only model of society is one that is marked by a fundamental blockage (antagonism), it is not at all clear how human beings could form relationships other than the repressive ones that now preoccupy them.

From a political angle, of course, neither Laclau and Mouffe nor Žižek want to end up in this impasse. It is for this reason, perhaps, that Žižek has sought to link the work of Laclau and Mouffe to what he calls an 'Ethic of the Real'. As we have seen, this ethic requires that critical social enquiry goes through the social fantasy of modern individuality – that imaginary 'filling' which *is* ideology – and penetrates to the other side, to the impossible form of the Real. In this respect, the other side of ideology would be the indeterminancy of desire; Žižek speaks of an ethical requirement to 'come to terms' with the fact that society 'doesn't work', with that lack which is the subject; with the Real. However there are difficulties with this view that desire, even in its indeterminate form, can be liberatory of ideology. The main difficulty here is as follows: this position treats the real order as a universal and natural boundary in the political realm which can be appealed to as a means of undermining the symbolic and social order of modern societies. But why should the Real provide a position outside of ideology, from which ideology can be analysed free of imaginary conditions? In particular, why should an implosion of the Real into symbolic networks of meaning be treated as *ipso facto* 'revolutionary'. The central problem here is that such an approach pays too little attention to the imaginary content of ideology, its embedding in specific socio-symbolic conditions, and the political content in which such meanings are overturned and rejected. The dismantling of modern individuality itself is scarcely a radical endeavour if it is disconnected from the fashioning of new forms of subjectivity.

By idealizing 'lack' as the authenticity of the subject, the basis for any significant reconfiguration of social and cultural values is effectively undercut. The political and moral assumptions of this Lacanian model – that the law is omnipotent, the self narcissistic and derivative, intersubjectivity and communication illusory, social relations oppressive or, better, terroristic – leaves little room for any real vision of individual and collective autonomy. Instead, the Real of desire is projected as the uniform basis for assessing and evaluating social and political goals. At best, mature social relationships can hope to confront that fundamental lack or antagonism which is built into itself; and thereby rid itself of those distorting, imaginary ideologies in which it finds itself embedded. Yet it is highly doubtful, in my view, whether such a confrontation might be at all liberatory. As a critique of ideology, this position palpably fails to extend its own claims of understanding and critical reflection to human subjects themselves. Laclau and Mouffe, and Žižek, ultimately work themselves into a theoretical cul-de-sac by failing to develop a cogent account of the reflexive appropriation of human interests, needs and desires in modern culture. Self cognition, ego autonomy, and critical reflection and judgement, far from being redundant, are vital to politics and cultural association. Ideology is certainly always interwoven with the imaginary investments of subjects. But if an account of such processes is to have any critical value, it must recognize that the possibility of *disinvesting* from particular ideological forms can also only occur through the imaginary reorganization of the self and its related objects. Such disinvestments, because of the intensity of desire and affect, are likely to be protracted and painful experiences. But they can surely only proceed from a careful reconsideration of self-identity, developed *through* the creation of new imaginary relations between self and others. As such, a theory which seeks to interpret the manifold ways human beings resist, and continually reshape, social experience and institutions needs to account for these mechanisms of psychical life. In sum, a critical social theory, while conceptualizing subjectivity as internally divided by desire and the barrier of repression, must nevertheless recognize that subjects are capable of critical self-reflection and acting creatively and imaginatively upon human experience.

What are the implications of this enquiry into post-Lacanian accounts of ideological forms for critical social theory? By way of concluding this chapter, let me bring together some of the central ideas of the foregoing discussion. I have presented the work of Althusser, Laclau and Mouffe, and Žižek as complex and detailed attempts to link the psychical mechanisms of subjectivity with the reproduction of ideology and cultural forms. From a Lacanian understanding of the human subject as fundamentally split and fragmented, these approaches reveal ideology as providing an imaginary foundation to all human social relationships. The imaginary foundations of ideology are understood as at once a necessary medium for the production of subjects and the central basis of all self distortions, misrecognitions, traps. Such a focus, as developed and extended by Laclau and Mouffe, and Žižek, raises problems which are of considerable importance for critical enquiry – problems, for example, of meaning and its embedding in asymmetric relations of power, of the link between imaginary misrecognition and the constitution of the socio-symbolic world, of the relationship between individual and collective interests and the critique of ideology. I have tried to show, however, that on all of these points there are serious difficulties with these theoretical approaches. Many of these difficulties, I have suggested, have their roots in certain incoherencies and impasses of Lacanian theory itself.

Throughout the chapter I have emphasized one problem which is common to all three post-Lacanian approaches: their tendency to imagine that one particular *mode of subjectivity*, namely the constitution of an immutable gap between self and others, is intrinsic to the nature of the unconscious imaginary itself. Against this view, I have argued that to study ideological forms is not to analyse an imaginary 'covering' or 'papering' of a deeper, ontological lack, but is rather concerned with exploring the ways in which imaginary creations engender self-constitutions that are autonomous/enabling or alienating/repressive. The unconscious imaginary should not be seen as just some derivative realm, an attempt to 'suture' an original lack in the subject. Rather, the unconscious imaginary is the capacity to *create and transform something*; it is inseparable from phantasy, representation and affect. It is therefore pointless to search for a wider baseline, such as the Lacanian category of lack, from which ideology and cultural forms can be derived. Rather, the notion of the subject must be situated within a general social theory that recognizes this constitutive aspect of the unconscious imaginary, and of its related connection within social and cultural organization.

6 Sexual Division, Gender-Identity and Symbolic Order

Feminist Politics and Post-Lacanian Theory

In *The Second Sex* Simone de Beauvoir powerfully argues that women are denied an expressive subjectivity under patriarchy. According to de Beauvoir, this is because 'woman is determined and differentiated in relation to man and not to herself: she is the inessentiality, he is the Absolute, she is the Other'[1] Reconceptualizing this cancellation of femininity in psychoanalytical terms, Jacques Lacan argues that 'Woman does not exist'. In Lacan's theory, sexual 'masquerade' is the very definition of femininity; it offers an illusory unity to which split and fractured human subjects, both male and female, aspire. Lacanian psychoanalysis has had an immense and provocative impact upon modern feminist thought. Yet the core premises of Lacanian theory have proven to be something of a double bind for feminist concerns with gender-identity, female sexuality, and women's oppression. On the one hand, it has been a valuable theoretical resource for analysing all forms of patriarchal or sexist power. Lacanian and post-Lacanian feminist critics have challenged biological accounts of gender – which have so often been employed to justify and perpetuate sexist practices – and have demonstrated that gender-identity and sexual division are products of the symbolic order. On the other hand, the recurring problem for feminist theory when set within Lacanian parameters is that all dimensions of human subjectivity, including the capacity for critical reflection and political resistance, become trapped within patriarchal law. The construction of gender through language becomes coextensive with the subject's submission to the law, thereby imprisoning women and men within phallocentric discourse. One significant consequence of this has been the marked anxiety in feminist discourse in respect of developing plausible accounts of alternative gender relations.

Of the existing appropriations of Lacanian psychoanalysis by feminist theorists, there are three main approaches which have received sustained attention within modern social thought. In this chapter I shall outline the theoretical contours of these developments in Lacanian and post-Lacanian psychoanalytic feminism, and also consider some of the wider cultural and political implications that these approaches carry for problems of gender-identity and social analysis. Though there are many that might have been examined, I shall focus only on certain leading contributions to each of these respective approaches in Lacanian-influenced feminist theory. These approaches are defined as follows: (1) Sexual division and gender-identity as understood within the Lacanian framework of the symbolic order. This approach is particularly influential in British and American feminist contexts and here I examine the work of Juliet Mitchell. (2) Post-Lacanian theory which questions the centrality of the symbolic and attempts to valorize women's radical sexual difference from men. This approach is particularly influential in French radical feminism and here I review the contributions of Hélène Cixous and Luce Irigaray. (3) Post-Lacanian theory which focuses on the subversive aspects of feminine sexuality outside of gender categories. Here I examine the work of the French social theorist Julia Kristeva.

In the Name of Freud and Lacan: Mitchell's Account of Sexual Difference

The publication in 1974 of Juliet Mitchell's *Psychoanalysis and Feminism* represented a pathbreaking development in feminist social theory in the English-speaking world.[2] This widely read book argued strongly for the importance of psychoanalysis to feminist concerns with gender-identity and women's oppression, developed a powerful critique of the biologism inherent in then influential feminist psychologies, and introduced the name of Lacan to many English-speaking people. Mitchell's key political claim is that the unconscious acquisition of patriarchal law under capitalism is central to human experience in general and to women's condition and suffering within society in particular. In her view these affective, unconscious dimensions of women's oppression are important since they have been ignored in the feminist intellectual tradition. She contends that the urgent theoretical feminist task is to explore how subjectivity and sexual division are engendered within social relations in order to eventually destabilize and undo patriarchy. In Mitchell's analysis of femininity, sexual politics and the family, a Lacanian-based feminism is forged to stress certain basic premises: the centrality of the unconscious in the way individuals are positioned within asymmetrical power relations *as men and women*; the separation between biological sex and the construction of sexuality and sexual difference; and the consequent interlinking of sexuality and other forms of ideology for the replication of late capitalist society.

That the account of sexual difference offered by Freud and Lacan should be read as an *analysis* of the psychic roots of patriarchal social relations, and not as a justification for patriarchy, is perhaps the main contribution of Mitchell's early work to feminism. On this view, Freud's account of the central 'marks of womanhood' – masochism, penis-envy, jealousy, a weak superego – are understood as a consequence of women's subjection to patriarchal law, and not as innate psychological attributes. When reassessed in terms of contemporary feminist theory, however, Mitchell's work is often criticized for its failure to specify adequately the complex links between the unconscious and the reproduction of asymmetrical gender relations. Most critiques of *Psychoanalysis and Feminism* point out that, while drawing on Lacanian theory, it fails to develop an account of language as embedded in social context, and ultimately relies on a discredited Marxist account of ideology in appealing to women to actively struggle against patriarchy. Notwithstanding these criticisms, however, Mitchell's ongoing enquiry into how patriarchy structures the deep, affective dimensions of subjectivity is important. Her later work has continued to influence the trajectories of contemporary psychoanalytic feminism. Central to this influence has been her stress on the Lacanian concept of the symbolic in the formation of gender-identity. In an important introductory essay to a collection of Lacan's writings, 'Freud and Lacan: psychoanalytic theories of sexual difference', Mitchell situates the concept of the symbolic in relation to sexual difference, feminine sexuality and femininity.[3] In what follows here I shall (1) outline Mitchell's defence of Lacan's rereading of Freud in respect of sexual difference; (2) briefly discuss Mitchell's view of the theories of Freud and Lacan as compared to other psychoanalytical doctrines on feminine sexuality; and (3) assess the social and political implications of Mitchell's position for the analysis of gender relations.

Mitchell situates the importance of Lacan's account of sexual difference in direct relation to Freud. Like sexuality itself in Freud's perspective, femininity is understood by Lacan to be nothing outside of the various locations where it is constructed. Sexuality and subjectivity, intertwined in the unconscious, are constituted with the entry into the symbolic order; that is, into language and received social meanings. By making the construction of sexuality the condition of subjecthood, Mitchell argues, Lacan underlines Freud's crucial point that the unconscious is never pre-given, but is rather constituted. This necessarily shifting and uncertain constitution of the unconscious carries quite radical implications for analysing sexual identity. On this point Mitchell quotes Freud: 'In conformity with its peculiar nature, psychoanalysis does not try to describe what a woman is – that would be a task it could scarcely perform – but sets about enquiring *how she comes into being*.'[4] In similar fashion, she argues, Lacan's work is not concerned with explaining sexual dispositions and adaptations but with exploring how fragile structures of human sexuality and subjectivity are constructed and brought into existence. Before considering Mitchell's Lacanian-based account of sexual division, however, it is necessary to briefly retrace Freud's account of female sexuality and to indicate the nature of the debates it has generated within psychoanalytical theory. For, as we shall see, Mitchell's key argument is that the critical value of Lacan's work lies precisely in its radical reformulation of Freud's position and of demonstrating the incoherencies of certain alternative theories.

As we have seen in Chapter 1, the triangular relationship between child and parents in the Oedipus complex is for Freud the central determining instance of the socialization of the psyche. The process of oedipalization is the point at which the warring desires and anguished fragmentation of the small infant become organized within the structure of social relations. It signals the transition from the free reign of polymorphous desire to the reality principle – to the constitution of the individual as a human subject. At the heart of this complex is the *instantiation of sexual division*. Several features of Freud's theory are relevant here. In Freud's early writings, the particular forms through which the Oedipus complex are 'resolved' depends upon a simple set of human relationships. Prior to sexual difference, it is said there is an active, masculine sexuality for children of both sexes – 'the little girl is a little man'. In striving for satisfaction, the child at this stage pursues both active and passive sexual aims through a primary attachment to the mother, mediated through fantasies about bodily zones. Biological sex difference remains irrelevant for the child until the onset of the phallic phase, in which sexual difference becomes centered around the presence or absence of the penis. For the phallic phase, Freud originally assumed the existence of the child's heterosexual attraction to the parent of the opposite sex which, through the threat of castration, undergoes severe repression. In the case of boys, this depends upon the phantasy of the father's threat of castration; in the case of girls, castration is imagined as having already been inflicted.

In Freud's theory the developmental trajectories of female oedipalization, which is our central concern here, are especially fraught with difficulty. Instead of instituting the repression of incestuous desire, as in the case of boys, the castration complex for girls actually *produces* incestuous desire and the Oedipus complex. The girl's response to the discovery of genital difference leads her to imagine that castration has already taken place, upon both herself and her similarly 'castrated' mother. Here Freud introduces a major twist in his argument about female sexuality. Since this imagined castration calls into question the girl's former masculine sexuality – she realizes that she lacks the penis to pursue her active, libidinal desires – a radical transformation develops in regard to her sexuality and gender-identity. Indeed, Freud describes the impact of this reconfiguration of desire as monumental: it is that which inflicts a severe 'narcissistic wound' and leads women to 'fall victim to envy for the penis'. Rejecting the mother in fury and hatred for the loss of that object with which to pursue her masculine sexuality, the girl seeks to seduce her father. As Freud comments:

> [The] girl's libido slips into a new position along the line – there is no other way of putting it – of the equation 'penis-child'. She gives up her wish for a penis and puts in place of it a wish for a child and *with that purpose in view* she takes her father as a love object. Her mother becomes the object of her jealousy. The girl has turned into a little woman.[5]

Realizing that she cannot have her father exclusively, the girl is said to turn back unconsciously toward the mother, effecting an identification with her feminine gender position. In Freud's view, these changes in female 'object-love', from the mother to the father and subsequent feminine identification, are far from predetermined emotional paths and can have severe psychical consequences for women. However, Freud himself did not formulate an adequate explanation of how the girl's Oedipus complex dissolves, nor of how she achieves identification with the devalued maternal position.

The several components of Freud's account of sexual difference just described have been an area of ongoing theoretical dispute and contestation, both inside and outside of psychoanalytical quarters. The notions of a primary masculine sexuality, a phallic phase, a universal castration complex, and that which it implies about women's sexuality, penis envy, have been sharply criticized for their misogynist and androcentric assumptions. Freud's view that female sexuality arises from a failed masculinity has been discussed extensively in much of the general literature as a theoretical replication of the sexism prevalent in male-dominated society. Within the psychoanalytical movement itself, Freud's theories set in train a series of complex debates on the topic of female sexuality. Psychoanalysts including Ernest Jones, Karen Horney and Melanie Klein sought to revise Freud's central focus on the phallic phase as constitutive of sexuality, and also of the view that femininity emerges as a response to penis envy. They argued, in diverse theoretical ways, for an understanding of the psycho-sexuality of women and men that is 'different but equal'. The characteristic feature of these revisions centred upon the castration complex, which many believed was a concept derogatory to women, and the subsequent reinterpretation of it as a wider, gender-neutral *separation anxiety*. On this view, castration fears are understood as referring back to prior losses (of the womb, the mother, faeces). The small child, whether male or female, is understood as experiencing these losses as castrations. Both sexes fear castration in a parallel manner, yet are viewed as responding to these threats in different ways. To explain this Jones posits a 'primary femininity', Horney speaks of 'the biological principle of heterosexual attraction', and Klein theorizes a primordial feminine sexuality (the girl's unconscious vaginal knowledge) which subsequently is structured through the identification and introjection of objects.[6] In these revisionist theories, then, sexuality is understood as constitutionally based. Gender-identity arises from a biological predisposition, primary genital awareness, and in theories such as Klein's, through subsequent object identification.

According to Mitchell, however, these revisionist accounts of feminine sexuality altogether lose the radical focus of Freud's stress on the *construction* of sexuality and subjectivity – issues which are of central importance for feminist theory. The key problem, Mitchell argues, is the following: in viewing gender-identity as an outcome of internal bodily experiences, or as a biological predisposition for the parent of the opposite sex, these accounts assume a *pre-existing* sexual division between males and females. By describing gender-identity as corresponding to an innate masculinity and femininity these approaches reduce the complex psychical construction of sexuality to clear-cut, biological differences. Sexual difference is not something which is *created* by a particular social code or law; it is rooted in primary biological sex. Accordingly, sexual division is simply given – male and female gender-identity always-already exist – and the possibility for restructuring the relations between the sexes vanishes. For Mitchell the implications of this theoretical move are clear: by viewing phallic castration as merely one among other castrations for a subject that is already constructed, and not as something vital to that construction, these accounts are palpably unable to explain what distinguishes the two sexes. Consequently, psychoanalysis is reduced to essentialism, and the symbolic and socio-historical dimensions of the construction of subjectivity and sexuality are lost from view.

The strength of Freud's position in contrast, Mitchell argues, is that castration is understood to *institute* the humanization of the small infant in its sexual difference. Castration, the prohibition of the father against the child–mother dyad, embodies the law which structures the human social order. This prohibition, which intrudes from the outside into the child's world, confers the mark of sexual distinction and thereafter makes identification, individuation and meaning possible. This is the significance, Mitchell claims, of Freud's interest in the notion of cultural inheritance – of some external event in the prehistory of human beings which structures the relations between subject and society. The centrality of this structuring event in psychical life, Mitchell argues, led Freud to recognize the mistakes of his early view that the Oedipus complex simply dissolves naturally, as the developmental outcome of heterosexuality. Rather, as Freud later argued, identification only arises *because* of castration. It is castration which makes identification with a perceived gendered parent possible in the first place. But the formation of such gender identifications are always unstable and precarious. Sexual identification with the 'appropriate' parent is not pre-ordained; and it is in this context that Mitchell cites Freud's case-study of Dora, as an example of a woman who had constructed a masculine sexual identification.

It is these radical aspects of Freud's work – the castration complex, sexual difference as the result of a division and the concept of a structuring historical law – which Mitchell feels are fruitfully extended in the work of Lacan. In Lacan's theory, the subject's entry into human culture and sexual division occurs at the level of the symbolic order. As discussed in Chapter 4, the symbolic order is for Lacan the overarching structure of language and received social meanings within human culture. In order to achieve psychical differentiation and to enter life in society, human beings must take up a position as a *subject* within this order. For outside of the symbolic, there is only psychosis. The shift from the child's imaginary unity with its mother into the symbolic order, as we have previously seen, requires the intervention of a third person (the father), or term (language). By prohibiting the child access to the mother and her body, the law of the Name-of-the-Father operates to institute the threat of castration – the power backing this threat being symbolized by his phallus. The phallus, then, both serves to wrench the child away from its desire for the mother (which must be repressed) and stands for entry into the symbolic. That is to say, the position that an individual takes up as a gendered-subject within the symbolic order is *necessarily tied to a fundamental loss* – the loss of the maternal body. And it is because of this loss of the maternal body that human sexuality is understood as being created within a *lack*, leaving the phallus – with its status as the 'transcendental signifier' – to stand in for the divided and incomplete human subject at the level of sexual division.

'The selection of the phallus', Mitchell comments, 'as the mark around which subjectivity and sexuality are constructed reveals, precisely, that they are constructed in a division which is both arbitrary and alienating'.[7] Thus the phallic constitution of sexual division enables the child to repress its desire for the mother, and to make reference to objects outside and beyond this imaginary realm. The crucial point, though, is that the child's capacity for symbolization, individuation, and meaning are always outstripped by this prior imaginary experience. In short, the phallus functions to provide a fantasized scenario of coherence and unity which is belied by the lack, loss and absence of the missing object of desire. This lack, which in Lacanian terms *is* the unconscious, is understood as structuring all human experience and gender-identity.

It is important to note that this description of the function of the phallus in Lacanian theory is conceptually situated as a structure which is *neutral* on questions of gender. As a 'veiled' and 'lacking' object, the phallus is what permits the labyrinth of possible sexual determinations to come into existence through the effects of phantasy. The phallic signifier is at the very root of sexual phantasy, serving to repress that constitutive lack suffered by the subject. The important critical point here is that, since the concept of the phallus is connected to the lack of the imaginary order, and hence prior to sexual division, it serves to inform the structure of desire *for both sexes*. That is to say, even though the male sex has the anatomical penis, neither sex can actually *possess* the phallus – a point strongly stressed by Mitchell and other feminists. Accordingly, human subjects of both sexes are equally split and fractured; the sexual relation thus being understood as a doomed, frantic search for the power conferred by the phallus.

As Mitchell deftly argues in Lacanian vein, however, this potentially neutral phallus is in reality centred within the patriarchal sexual relations of modern societies. The phallus which symbolizes entrance into the socio-symbolic order of modern culture is thus far from neutral in its effects. Instead, it actually positions males and females within deeply asymmetrical and unequal gender relations. There are two factors here which distinguish this patriarchal functioning of phallic law. The first concerns the links between language and the place of the father; the second the visual perception and organization of the phallus. First, the break-up of the imaginary child–mother dyad, as we have seen, arises through the symbolic imposition of language. Yet the bounds of this symbolic differentiation operate exclusively around the place of the father. The mother is initially only centred in the child's unconscious at the level of the imaginary order; she does not achieve a differentiated status (and even then only a partial one) at the level of the symbolic until relatively late in the child's development. Difference is thus connected to the father, as representative of language and the outer, symbolic world. And it is this equivalence between language and the place of the father which Mitchell argues is fundamental to the *patriarchal nature* of the symbolic order. Second, the phallus, while conceptually distinct from the penis, comes to signify for the child through a *visual distinction* between the sexes. Put simply, the *real* symbols of sexual difference have somehow become tied to phallic prestige. Lacan outlined this tie between the penis and phallus in the following way:

> It can be said that this signifier is chosen because it sticks out the most in the real of sexual copulation, and also the most symbolic in the literal (typographical) sense of the term, since it is equivalent there to the (logical) copula. It might also be said that, by virtue of its turgidity, it is the image of the vital flow as it is transmitted in generation.[8]

This visual tie between penis and phallus is vital to the replication of patriarchal power, serving as it does to subjugate female sexuality. Since sexuality is constituted in a one-sided masculine fashion, women are consequently understood to be excluded from the phallus and, most significantly, its idealized power. The symbolic prohibition in modern society, Mitchell argues, 'only comes to be meaningful to the child because there are people – females – who have been castrated in the *particular sense* that they are without the phallus'.[9]

According to this Lacanian view, then, the phallus is a privileged signifier which has become connected on a *representational plane* to the penis – this linkage being the benchmark of male privilege and domination under patriarchy. Moreover, since difference can only signify itself in relation to some other term, the primacy of the masculine phallic position necessarily renders 'woman' an adjunct term, as something outside and Other. In the symbolic order, female sexuality is not something with 'positive' content. Femininity only acquires meaning by way of its difference from masculinity. Mitchell points out here that this is the meaning of Lacan's scandalous claim that 'Woman', as some kind of essence or eternal being, does not exist. Structured entirely as the negative of the masculine phallic position, femininity becomes an endless series of masks and fabrications which women and men spend their lives seeking out. In the same fashion that human subjects forever seek an imaginary, impossible self-unity, so too the field of sexual relations is revealed by Lacanian theory as containing an impossible aim. The category 'woman' operates as an idealized Other, entirely separate from particular females, that men and women fantasize as a potential site of desire, fulfilment, joy and wholeness. Female sexuality is thus an *imaginary supplement* to that lack which informs the structure of subjectivity.

To summarize Mitchell's claims so far:

1. The theories of Freud and Lacan are important to feminist concerns since they offer a radical deconstruction of the psychic and symbolic dimensions of the constitution of sexuality, femininity and gender-identity.
2. In contrast to essentialist notions of a pre-given sexual 'nature', Mitchell argues it is the Oedipus and castration complexes which *create* sexual division. The bifurcation of sexuality arises from the structuring of imaginary fantasies, in which individuals come to live asymmetrical and unequal subject-positions as men or women within patriarchal societies.
3. It is through language and the symbolic that the child is subjected to the law of the Name-of-the-Father, which operates to institute sexual difference, prohibition, meaning and individuation by the threat of castration.
4. This shaping of the subject, which breaks up an imaginary unity with the mother, arises from lack, which is allied with the function of the phallus. The value of having or not having the phallus is caused by its imaginary representation of unity and power – attributes which in reality have been forever damaged by the effects of castration.

The critical force of this analysis in wider social and cultural terms can be easily specified. A radical feminist politics, for Mitchell, implies interrogating and subverting those rigid masculine, phallic phantasies that are so central to our systematically unequal gender relations. The construction of sexuality in phallocentric culture, particularly of women's objectification as the Other, requires an informed political critique. To that end Mitchell's ongoing analysis of the political, social, and economic oppression of women has consistently stressed that sexual identity is formed upon a shifting and uncertain unconscious terrain. The upshot of this in political terms is that, while the phallus may stand for entry into the symbolic, neither sex can actually possess it once and for all. Consequently, the existence of patriarchal power and unequal gender relations is deeply rooted in a symbolic distortion or fiction which it is the task of feminism to undo. And it is for this urgent political reason that Mitchell has long insisted that 'new structures will gradually come to be represented in the unconscious. It is the task of feminism to insist on their birth. Some other expression of the entry into culture than the implication for the unconscious of the exchange of women will have to be found in non-patriarchal society.'[10]

To criticize Mitchell's account of sexual difference for relying on the phallocentric assumptions of Freud and Lacan entirely misses the valuable concern of these theories with our unequal sexual world. As Mitchell defends her position: 'if psychoanalysis is phallocentric, it is because the human social order that it perceives refracted through the individual human subject is patro-centric. To date, the father stands in the position of the third term that *must* break the asocial dyadic unit of mother and child.'[11] Whether the father must stand as this third term in his current ideological form, and whether a non-patriarchal symbolic order is at all possible, are highly vexed questions in feminist psychoanalytic theory – as we shall see below. The point I wish to raise here, however, is that Mitchell's own theory and its claims to critical status are unsatisfactory in several important respects. To begin with, there are grave difficulties in this account of sexual difference in accounting for the possibilities of meaningful social and political struggle. While the unconscious is rightly treated as the locus of our unstable sexual identities, its rigid positioning within language, conceived along structuralist lines, would appear to straightjacket political opposition to the symbolic order. If, as Mitchell claims, women entirely repress their unconscious sexuality and become symbolically fixed in relation to the phallus as the lacking Other, as men's object of desire, it is extraordinarily difficult to understand what motivates feminist strategy in the first place or how radical politics can ever destabilize the rigidity of the symbolic. In Lacanian terms, the problem is that femininity can be critically deconstructed, revealing the sexual masks conferred by the phallic signifier, but it is impossible to ultimately undo the power and ideology of the symbolic order itself since this would lead human subjects and society to psychic ruin. Indeed, in an interview, Mitchell subsequently acknowledged the ramifications of this impasse by admitting that Lacanian theory does not 'ultimately get us beyond the dilemma of the relationship between patriarchy and capitalism'.[12]

It is this strong emphasis in Lacanian theory on the determining force of the Law of the Father and the symbolic order which leads Mitchell's work into a kind of double bind. On the one hand, unconscious sexuality and repressed desire are highlighted as a potentially liberatory medium for the reconfiguration of self-identity and gender relations. This repressed field is open-ended and fluid and always returns to subvert the symbolic order and the subject. Yet, on the other hand, how we might ever discover the nature of repressed sexuality cannot be fathomed within Lacanian theory since it is understood as presymbolic. And, in Lacanian logic, this *pre-symbolic* field cannot be thought, or acted upon, without entering psychosis. 'Inasmuch as women are associated with the presymbolic', Jane Flax comments, 'they appear as the repressed within Lacan's theory'.[13]

These impasses of Lacanian theory have led some feminists to approach questions of feminine sexuality, gender relations and women's oppression from a different direction. From the late 1970s, particularly in French feminist theory, attention begins to shift from a preoccupation with language and the symbolic as constitutive of subjectivity to a concern with the nature of the imaginary order, and specifically with those psychic contradictions that work upon language. Many important questions thus begin to be raised. These include: is the symbolic order really so rigid and monolithic? Can femininity be defined only as the negative pole of masculinity? And is it possible to denote a feminine specificity without essentializing woman?

Rewriting Sexual Difference: The Limits of the Body in Cixous and Irigaray

Developed in the French post-structuralist context of the 1970s and 1980s, the theoretical writings of Hélène Cixous and Luce Irigaray dispute the definition that female sexuality has no content. They criticize Freudian and Lacanian views that female sexuality is only construable in modern culture as something Other, as lack, the dark continent, a failed sense of masculinity. In elaborating a problematic view of female desire as a ground of critique they claim that, while phallic law is undeniably the foundation of existing power relations, it is necessary to speculate on the 'otherness' of the feminine. The vital feminist task is to explore and valorize women's difference from men in order to go beyond the repressive confines of phallocentric culture. To do this Cixous and Irigaray, in differing theoretical ways, look to the female body itself – to the rhythms, flows and sensations of female sexual pleasure – as a means to disrupt women's inscription within male-dominated gender relations. In particular, they focus on certain subversive dimensions of women's relationship to phallocentric language, contending that it opens a path to an expressive female subjectivity, or at least suggests the possibility of such an opening. It is of course possible, they warn, that such a position of critique might be ultimately subsumed within the prison-house of patriarchal discourse. But the alternative to not challenging the patriarchal symbolic order, they argue, is simply to condemn women to silence, to their current status as man's Other. In the writings of Cixous and Irigaray, despite certain divergences, there are two central aspects of their elaboration of a genuine feminine subject-position. The first concerns the female imaginary (centring on the female body and problems of psychic differentiation), the second the nature of the symbolic (centring on phallic systems of representation and writing).

In the work of Cixous and Irigaray a vision of female sexuality is portrayed that is open-ended, dispersed, multiple. They speak of a feminine/female libidinal economy that is inclusive, discontinuous, plural. This heterogeneous form of female sexuality is understood to cut through and subvert the continuous, linear organization of male rationality and its rigid insistence upon genital monosexuality. According to Cixous and Irigaray, the pre-Oedipal mother–daughter relationship is of key importance to understanding the fundamental sexual differences between women and men. Whereas male sexuality in its current forms depends upon a strong repression of the mother, the complicated trajectories of the daughter's 'love-objects' are understood to leave the mother less repressed. In this view women's sexuality, in contrast to men's experience, is more closely interwoven with the mother's body and desire. 'No woman', writes Cixous, 'piles up as many defences against their libidinal drives as a man does. You don't prop things up, you don't brick things up the way he does, you don't withdraw from pleasure so "prudently".'[14] The privileged pre-Oedipal relation of the daughter to the mother's love constitutes a complex feminine position, a sexuality that is in the end neither subjective nor objective. Female sexuality is never simply phallic in orientation, centred only on the release of orgasmic tension, but is located in the '*jouissance*' of the body. In Cixous's words, woman has the 'capacity to depropriate unselfishly, body without end, without appendage, without principal "parts" ... Her libido is cosmic, just as her unconscious is worldwide.'[15] In her essay 'This sex which is not One', Irigaray describes the multiplicity of sensations in the female body arising from the many elements of her sexual organs – vagina, clitoris, cervix, lips, breasts.[16]

One way of understanding this libidinal multiplicity of feminine sexuality in the work of Cixous and Irigaray is as an attempt to reconfigure the Lacanian imaginary, that pre-Oedipal order which is prior to sexual difference and language. Through recasting the imaginary constitution of subjecthood, especially women's privileged relation to this order, Cixous and Irigaray seek to refute the view that sexuality is monistic and that sexual difference arises only from lack. As Cixous puts this: 'What's a desire originating from lack? A pretty meagre desire.'[17] But if the imaginary is granted a more creative role in these post-Lacanian accounts of subjectivity and gender relations, it is still emphasized that this order is a principal site of distortion and alienation. The imaginary, unconscious forces of splitting, disavowal, and negation are constituted through their inscription in the phantasies of the patriarchal symbolic order. In general terms, then, what Cixous and Irigaray are claiming is that this potentially expressive sexuality of woman's pre-Oedipal experience suffers violence under phallic law – casting her outside of the symbolic, representation and language. The crucial point is that the *mother–daughter relationship of the pre-Oedipal imaginary phase cannot be symbolized under patriarchy.* As Irigaray argues, women are consigned to 'drives without any possible representatives or representations'.[18] Women are unable to establish a symbolic identification with the mother *as a woman*, as an independent human being with her own separate desires and intentions. Instead, women can only identify at a symbolic level with the maternal function itself.

Interestingly, this issue of women's problematic relation to individuation is also taken up in the influential feminist work of Nancy Chodorow. Chodorow's critique of the current gender system focuses on the point that women 'mother', tracing in particular the impact of this upon female sexual development. On this view, the consequences of the familial division of labour are an extreme splitting of psychological capacities produced in the sexes. 'Mothers', Chodorow writes, 'tend to experience their daughters as more like, and continuous with, themselves. Correspondingly, girls tend to remain part of the dyadic primary mother–child relationship itself ... By contrast, mothers experience their sons as a male opposite. Boys are more likely to have been pushed out of the preoedipal relationship, and to have had to curtail their primary love and sense of empathic tie with their mother.'[19] For Chodorow, then, mothering has different consequences for the sexes – it being likened to a form of 'gender imprinting'. From this angle, the problem of individuation for women is the following one: if women are unable to identify with anything but the maternal function itself it is because women's primary sexual location is inscribed within mothering.

But while there are certain thematic similarities between Chodorow's critique of mothering and the work of Cixous and Irigaray, the issues confronted in each are in fact quite different. Chodorow's work on the reproduction of mothering, though explicitly drawing on psychoanalysis, avoids tackling the difficult issue of the unconscious construction and acquisition of sexual identity. Instead, she replaces the concepts of the unconscious and bisexuality with a sociological account of 'gender roles'. By contrast, Cixous and Irigaray are concerned to unearth the unconscious roots of sexuality. Their work, in short, focuses on the intertwining of the unconscious imaginary *and* the socio-symbolic order. In so far as women's difference and sexual location is grounded in a confusion and merging of imaginary boundaries, existing forms of femininity are understood as a *symptom* of patriarchal oppression – what Irigaray calls woman's 'dereliction', the failure to attain individuation and differentiation.[20] Yet, as a cultural and political critique, Cixous and Irigaray are not claiming that the plural and multiple organization of the female libidinal economy should be simply celebrated in its own right, separate from symbolic forms. This is an important aspect of their work, and its neglect by critics has led to the oft-repeated charge of biological essentialism. While it is certainly the case that many of the political arguments developed by Cixous and Irigaray appeal to the potentially liberatory character of a specific female imaginary – as we shall see – they also stress that, at present, such pre-Oedipal modes of experience are a sign of phallic oppression. This point is brought out perhaps most clearly by Irigaray:

> there is no possibility whatsoever, within the current logic of sociocultural operations, for a daughter to situate herself with respect to her mother: because, strictly speaking, they make neither one nor two, neither has a name, meaning, sex of her own, neither can be 'identified' with respect to the other ... How can the relationship between these two women be articulated? Here 'for example' is one place where the need for another 'syntax', another 'grammar' of culture is crucial.[21]

This urgent need for a feminine grammar clearly suggests the centrality of symbolic mediation within gender relations. Accordingly, the fundamental problem becomes: how might it be possible to construct from the female imaginary a non-patriarchal symbolic order?

These issues, however, are yet further complicated in the work of Cixous and Irigaray. On the question of patriarchy, they argue that the term 'woman' is structured through masculine discourses of philosophy, of metastatements, as well as phallocentrism. In developing this view their analyses are particularly indebted to Jacques Derrida's critique of the Western philosophical tradition. Following Derrida, they contend that male-dominated philosophical categories have been inseparable from binary oppositions (logocentrism), which thereby fix and delimit the differences of language from a male position. Cixous in particular has stressed how oppositions such as activity/passivity, culture/nature, logos/pathos, and others, are related to the opposition man/woman. She suggests that, by structuring conceptual thought in this way, woman's difference is at once neutralized and repressed by philosophy. Patriarchal logic organizes the other as the same. Woman is defined as man's mirror, his 'reflection'. By pointing to this oppressive closure of difference in masculine discourse, Cixous and Irigaray claim that feminist attempts to create a non-sexist and non-oppressive society must be situated on the philosophical/symbolic plane as much as the psychic/sexual level. As this critique is expressed in *The Newly Born Woman*: 'The logocentric plan had always, inadmissibly, been to create a foundation for (to found and fund) phallocentrism, to guarantee the masculine order a rationale equal to history itself.'[22]

Given the inner logic of this linkage, it is perhaps difficult to envisage how women might ever escape from the repressive confines of patriarchal discourse. Yet it is precisely in this context that Cixous and Irigaray call for a return to the female body. In order to reconfigure the categories of sexual difference, they urge women to create and develop a specific *feminine language* which evades patriarchal regulation. Despite certain divergences in their approaches, the chief theme here is that the body is the site of a truly feminine specificity which is the potential source of an alternative symbolic order. Variously designated as the 'female imaginary', the 'alternative female unconscious', or the 'feminine libidinal economy', Cixous and Irigaray, in differing theoretical ways, identify this specificity as radical and subversive since it is constituted prior to the language (and, hence, the Law of the Father) in pre-Oedipal modes of experience. As a libidinal space prior to the symbolic, then, this pre-Oedipal femininity is viewed as a mode of pleasure and difference which is present to varying degrees in female speaking and writing. For Cixous, it is by writing from the feminine body that 'woman will affirm woman somewhere other than in silence, the place [currently] reserved for her in and through the symbolic'.[23] And in a similar fashion, Irigaray argues that through certain strategies of writing – designated as 'womanspeak' – woman can seek to recover a libertory relationship with her 'morphology' or 'form'. The speaking/writing woman then involves both a threat to phallocentric discourse, through refusing to allow her body to be appropriated as a sexual object for men, and offers political emancipation by the creation of new representations for female subjectivity.

The postulation of a truly feminine/female libidinal economy by Cixous and Irigaray has fuelled recent debates in feminist theory concerning biological essentialism; the political edge of which has centred on whether some form of essentialism is necessary to affirm the specificity of female subjectivity, or whether it is ultimately reactionary and regressive.[24] But whether biological essentialism actually renders human capabilities unalterable or not, the argument has been put that such charges against the work of Cixous and Irigaray are misfounded in any event. Margaret Whitford contends that Irigaray's positing of a feminine specificity does not urge feminists to ignore the complexities of the symbolic field.[25] In Whitford's view, Irigaray's work should rather be seen as attempting to promote a change in the symbolic status of women, as currently defined within male discourses of power. Accordingly, feminists who adopt this standpoint are not simply celebrating the 'feminine' for its own sake, but are concerned to expose and reconfigure the position of feminine sexuality at the level of the symbolic. Against this description, however, certain problems must still be noted. It can be argued, for example, that whatever the symbolic mediations governing the production of new social representations of woman's subjectivity, it is still a psychically and analytically distinct *female imaginary* which is seen by Cixous and Irigaray as the ultimate driving force for change. A kind of essentialism is consequently operative here, conflating what are in fact complex constructions of sexuality and subjectivity into a *pre-existent* foundation of the feminine. Such a standpoint, in psychoanalytical terms, appears to ride roughshod over the arbitrary nature of sexual division. As Jacqueline Rose has argued, the contention that there is a distinct female imaginary threatens to undermine the precise object of psychoanalytic enquiry – the actual *construction* of sexuality and subjectivity.[26] The obvious danger here is the following one: in assuming that there is a truly female imaginary which is prevented expression in male-dominated culture, this position risks falling into biologism and thereby reinforcing traditional gender divisions. For if feminine sexuality is ultimately derived from the body, then surely it is also placed under severe limits and constraints by it as well. Through displacing attention from the complexity of the psychic and social construction of sexual division in this way, this position mirrors certain aspects of the idealization of the 'feminine' in the post-Freudian theories which were noted above.

Many of the same reductionistic problems in the work of Cixous and Irigaray appear in their use of the concept of the symbolic; their case tending to push to one side its more enabling features for a single-minded insistence on the patriarchal homogenization of this order. From this angle, it is because the male-dominated symbolic is such a rigidly monolithic, non-contradictory region that feminine sexuality is seen as almost entirely repressed. At its worst, this view implies that all women are equal victims of the law, uniformly helpless before the regulatory powers of the phallic order. What this 'global' portrayal of the symbolic overlooks, however, are the very real differences of inequality which affect women's specific experiences of oppression and symbolic violence. It simplifies the complex and subtle ways in which the socio-symbolic order organizes certain power effects differentially *among* women, according to political categories such as class and race. These structuring properties of

gender-identity are vitally important, I believe, since their fragmentation and division across socio-symbolic space represents a major
obstacle to the formation of feminist political action in the first place.
The work of Cixous and Irigaray entirely glosses over these inequalities among women, divisions that promote competition and envy,
and replaces it with a global appeal to the female imaginary and the
transformative effects of feminine writing. Yet the very terms of this
appeal can lead us to question exactly how many women are socially
situated to engage in such 'revolutionary activity' as writing from the
body? And, in any event, is a transformation in gender relations really
just a matter of connecting the plural and multiple field of the female
imaginary to writing in the symbolic realm? Cixous and Irigaray
certainly develop a particular vision of feminine sexuality, but it is
only purchased at the expense of totalizing 'woman' and the imaginary forms of feminine sexuality. As Toril Moi warns of the political
dangers of this case: 'It is, after all, patriarchy, not feminism, that
insists on labelling women as emotional, intuitive, and imaginative,
while jealously converting reason and rationality into an exclusively
male preserve.'[27] It is undeniably the case that feminism is right to
insist upon the arbitrariness and ambiguity of sexual division. But the
point is that, without an equal concern for the differing symbolic
organization of women's individuation and differentiation, claims for
the intuitive, inconsistent nature of feminine sexuality are simply
likely to be drawn back into cultural stereotypes of femininity
currently prevalent in male-dominated gender relations.

Kristeva on the Semiotic Foundation of Female Sexuality

Unlike Mitchell, and Cixous and Irigaray, Kristeva's relationship to
feminism is ambiguous.[28] Kristeva's theoretical project has often
been criticized by feminists for its detachment from concrete political
concerns, its inability to take sides, and for its less than committed
stance towards the women's movement. Moreover, Kristeva herself
has maintained a distance from feminism and has often criticized
certain sectors of the women's movement for their complicity with
phallocentric modes of political discourse. But while such ambiguity
is undeniably a problem for a clear feminist politics, Kristeva's work
has sought to situate itself at a point of transition in respect of the
analysis of femininity and feminine sexuality. In this respect, she has
argued that neither liberal nor socialist accounts of women's oppression serve as a useful point of orientation in the late modern age.
Criticizing the efforts of Cixous and Irigaray to delineate a truly
feminine language as essentialistic, Kristeva suggests that a more
complex psychoanalytic approach to these issues is demanded:

The desire to give voice to sexual difference, and particularly the position of the woman-subject within meaning and signification, leads to a veritable insurrection against the homogenizing signifier. However, it is all too easy to pass from the search for difference to the denegation of the symbolic. The latter is the same as to remove the 'feminine' from the order of language. In this case, does not the struggle against the 'phallic sign' and against the whole mon-logic, mon-theistic culture which supports itself on it, sink into an essentialist cult of *Woman* ... In other words, if the feminine *exists*, it only exists in the order of significance or signifying process, and it is only in relation to meaning and signification, positioned as their excessive or transgressive other that it *exists, speaks, thinks* (itself) and *writes* (itself) for both sexes.[29]

Kristeva is thus insistent that sexual difference is only intelligible by reference to the symbolic, and that to define woman's feminine essence can only lead to a reinforcement of traditional gender divisions. How then does Kristeva redefine the connections between femininity and the symbolic order without sliding into determinism? And what is the relation between the socio-symbolic order and the disruption of gender relations in Kristeva's work?

In one sense, Kristeva's theoretical project can be understood as an attempt to revise the scope and structure of the Lacanian imaginary and symbolic orders. Against more deterministic interpretations of Lacanian theory, Kristeva elucidates the problem of a productive and heterogeneous symbolic order/language, the focus of which she terms the 'subject-in-process'.[30] As we shall see, this Kristevan subject is at once structured by and subversive of the symbolic law. The ability of human subjects to subvert symbolic meaning is understood as deriving from a radical irruption of early bodily drives; designated as a pre-Oedipal sexuality that is existent in both sexes. Kristeva's elaboration of this open-ended and mobile imaginary foundation of the self centres on both masculine and feminine drives. This approach accordingly differs from that of Cixous and Irigaray in that the subversive qualities of femininity are not in any way linked to gender. The disruptive potential of the imaginary dimension of selfhood, which Kristeva argues can destabilize traditional gender divisions, is available to both women and men. Accordingly, before we approach how Kristeva theorizes questions of feminine sexuality, it is necessary first to examine her views on the constitution of human subjectivity.

Language and the Subject-in-Process

Kristeva's most detailed account of the relations between subjectivity, the imaginary, and processes of signification are given in her doctoral dissertation, *Revolution in Poetic Language*, which was published in 1974. This study begins with a critique of modern structural linguistics. Examining the Saussurean conception of language as a differential system of elements, Kristeva argues that structuralist approaches to cultural production are necessarily problematic since they treat processes of signification as fixed and homogenous. As she observes, this static conception of language is 'helplessly anachronistic when faced with the contemporary mutations of subject and society'.[31] In order to comprehend the indeterminacy and displacements of language, then, Kristeva claims it is necessary to break with the Saussurean concept of *langue* and to replace it with a theory of the *desiring subject*. Such a theory, she argues, must be in radical contrast to the notion of a transcendental ego posited by traditional philosophy. Drawing on Freudian and Lacanian theory, Kristeva argues for the importance of decentred subjectivity; viewing consciousness, not as some pre-given 'substance', but as the result of symbolic positioning. Her project, then, is to connect the 'empty signifiers' of traditional linguistic theory to the field of psychical life and unconscious processes.

Kristeva elucidates this problematic of decentred subjectivity by recasting the Lacanian imaginary and symbolic orders into the corresponding modalities of the *semiotic* and the *thetic*. The former of these registers, the semiotic, refers to pre-Oedipal modes of experience and to the existence of oral and anal libidinal drives. In this early pre-self register of the semiotic, the small infant experiences itself as an array of passions and bodily capacities which are multiple and discontinuous. It is through the child's relationship with the pre-Oedipal mother and her body that this heterogeneous flow of libidinal drives are gradually ordered, or 'gathered together', within a social framework. As Kristeva theorizes this ordering of the drives:

> Discrete quantities of energy move through the body of the subject who is not yet constituted as such and, in the course of development, they are arranged according to the various constraints imposed on this body – always already involved in a semiotic process – by family and social structures. In this way the drives, which are 'energy' as well as 'psychical' marks, articulate what we call a chora: a non-expressive totality formed by the drives and their stases in a motility that is as full of movement as it is regulated.[32]

Appropriated from Plato, the concept of the chora in Kristeva's work designates this *ordering* of the drives. It is important to note, however, that this ordering pre-exists the establishment of self-identity (the subject/object split) and thus the constitution of sexual difference.

For Kristeva, this semiotic dimension of subjectivity is intimately connected to the somatic aspects of language which are outside representation, such as the rhythmic and breathing patterns of speech, tones of expression and silences.

Mapping the emergence of signification, that realm of received social meanings, Kristeva posits a splitting of this semiotic dimension. The split which produces this positioning of the subject is termed the thetic order, and is likened to Lacan's account of the symbolic. Following Lacan, Kristeva claims that the formation of selfhood in the mirror stage, as well as the later trajectories of Oedipal development, results in a transition from the heterogeneous realm of the semiotic into the structured terms of thetic law. That is to say, the shift from the semiotic to the thetic constitutes the human subject within a structured set of temporal and spatial socio-historical meanings. But whereas for Lacan entry to the symbolic implies a radical break-up and separating out of the imaginary order, for Kristeva the semiotic continues to exert a more pervasive influence upon the imaginary foundations of subjectivity. As she observes, 'the thetic is not a repression of the semiotic chora but is instead a position either taken on or undergone'.[33] It is this potential proximity of subjects to the semiotic which grants Kristeva a plausible route out of the strict determinism of the Lacanian symbolic and the law of patriarchy, as we shall shortly see. The central point to note here is that it is this entwinement of the semiotic and thetic in Kristeva's framework that underlies processes of signification. Thus the imaginary dimensions of the semiotic are important, Kristeva contends, because all communication and signification contains certain levels of disruption by these early bodily drives. The semiotic dimension of subjectivity is always implicit in symbolic exchange, articulating the displacements of libidinal drives in tonal rhythms, slips, discontinuities, silences. In sum, then, the Kristevan subject is at once structured and heterogeneous, subjected to the law but ruptured by the boundless play of semiotic drives. This postulate is fundamental to Kristeva's work and is crucial to its heuristic strength.

The Relationship between Language, Femininity and Feminism

In one sense, these nodal categories of the constitution of the subject – semiotic, chora, thetic – represent Kristeva's attempt to develop a rigorously anti-essentialist theory of sexual difference. From the foregoing outline it should be clear that Kristeva entirely rejects any linkage of the feminine with traditional gender terms. The semiotic, as we have seen, is associated with the pre-Oedipal phase – centred around the mother and her body – and is thus *prior* to sexual difference. Accordingly, whatever its disruptive and subversive potential, this pre-self experience of the semiotic is non-gender specific. For Kristeva, the semiotic is a *mode of being* that exists in all human subjects and, consequently, either gender can be 'feminized' in a radical fashion.

But what does this mean exactly for theorizing asymmetrical gender relations? Kristeva presses her theory of subjectivity into a powerful account of the replication of patriarchy and our unequal sexual world. While arguing that there is a complex structuration of the semiotic and thetic in all signifying processes, Kristeva claims that patriarchal social relations generate many destructive and pathological consequences for the semiotic. The patriarchal symbolic order as Kristeva uses the term involves the domination of the 'Law of the Father' and a marginalization of the semiotic, and specifically the place of the mother. At the political and ideological level, Kristeva claims that post-industrial capitalism has hollowed the creative cultural forms of subjectivity into the vulgarity of the mechanistic quality of the commodity itself. Decentred by the operations of a global economic system, the 'fiction' of scarcity is said by Kristeva to be deeply implanted within our subjecthood, thereby positioning subjects within highly competitive and conflictive social relations. To maintain this high dosage of economic rationalism, there is a need for the continual strengthening of the more repressive aspects of the thetic order, the Law of the Father. In short, modernity has induced a widespread schizoid-paranoid disorder, levelling and equalizing all semiotic experience into the rigid structures of the symbolic order itself. As Kristeva observes, 'in the State and in religion, capitalism requires and consolidates the paranoid moment of the subject: a unity foreclosing the other and taking its place'.[34] Central to this suppression of the diffuse network of semiotic drives is the reorganization of subjectivity into the system's official male ideal of the 'centred, self-directing agent'. This separates human subjects out from the semiotic, the libidinal body, and their relation to the pre-Oedipal mother.

Kristeva's analysis of this repressive *positioning* of the semiotic by the patriarchal symbolic order connects to the oppression of women in modern culture in several associated ways. Most significantly, it is both the semiotic and women that are subjected to marginal status under patriarchy, to the periphery of society. 'As the feminine is defined as marginal under partriarchy', comments Toril Moi, 'so the semiotic is marginal to language'.[35] The political problem then for Kristeva is the recovery, the rebirth, the rediscovery of the semiotic. Her project seeks to forestall thetic closure, insisting that the disruption of the semiotic chora can undermine centralized power structures and traditional gender divisions. To explain this, Kristeva characterizes the *jouissance* of semiotic experience as breaking up and subverting symbolic categories and meanings.[36] Through the operations of the signifying chain, the individual subject is understood as deriving unconscious pleasure from going beyond the organized significations of the symbolic. Kristeva terms this the 'unstable symbolic'. In her words:

> Though absolutely necessary, the thetic is not exclusive: the semiotic, which also precedes it, constantly tears it open, and this transgression brings about all the various transformations of the signifying practice that are called 'creation' ... This is particularly evident in poetic language since, for there to be a transgression of the symbolic, there must be an irruption of the drives in the universal signifying order, that of 'natural' language which binds together the social unit. That the subject does not vanish into psychosis when this transgression takes place poses a problem for metaphysics, both the kind that sets up the signifier as an untransgressable law and the kind for which there exists no thetic and therefore no subject.[37]

Kristeva's project is presented in this passage as transcending deterministic interpretations of the symbolic and of approaches that mistakenly posit the body or primary processes outside of signifying practices. Created in the space of imaginary contradiction, the 'subject-in-process' for Kristeva encompasses semiotic drives, symbolic meanings, and the socio-historical world in which these are embedded.

Kristeva, then, turns to these semiotic aspects of language as a potential political means of undermining the symbolic order, social institutions and traditional gender divisions. In order to make intelligible the ways in which semiotic processes are released into the symbolic, Kristeva outlines certain connections between social reorganization and the anal drives of expulsion, negation and rejection. Rereading Freud's essay 'Negation' in semiotic vein, Kristeva argues there are important links between the negative symbol and the unconscious expression of destructive wishes. For Freud, negation is often a last-ditch effort to deny certain traumatic aspects of psychical reality. 'Negation', Freud wrote, 'is a way of taking cognizance of what is repressed; indeed it is already a lifting of the repression, though not of course an acceptance of what is repressed'.[38] Linking these aspects of negation with the pulsional pressure of semiotic processes, Kristeva contends that expressions of self-dissolution and rejection, structured by Eros and Thanatos, ensure a continuous movement and contradiction between subject and society. Kristeva has developed several studies of these processes of semiotic dissolution, the method of which she terms 'semanalysis', although it might be noted that she never adequately clarifies the specific relation between semiotic rupture and modern society. She has examined certain semiotic infusions between feminism and temporality, motherhood and reproduction, and the politics of exile and marginality. But the most sustained outline of semiotic transgression appears in her studies of male French Symbolist writers – Mallarmé, Céline, Artaud, Lautréamont. Briefly put, she argues that these avant-garde artists press received social meanings to their utmost limit, in which semiotic forces disrupt the material properties of linguistic signs. For Kristeva, these writings embody a radical, indeed revolutionary, disruption of the symbolic which unconsciously forces subjects to confront the sensible certitude of their ideological existence. In advocating this view, of course, Kristeva shares certain affinities with her former mentor Roland Barthes, who claimed that 'a text of jouissance imposes a state of loss. It is a text that discomforts, unsettles the reader's historical, cultural, psychological assumptions.'[39] In Kristeva's theory, however, the irruption of the semiotic chora works not only in a negative fashion. It also works to create new forms of subjectivity and symbolic meaning; essential operations for the 'subject-in-process'.

In political terms, then, the relationship between Kristeva's order of the semiotic and feminism is an ambiguous one. On one side, women and the semiotic forge certain connections through their marginal status under patriarchal language; on the other, 'woman' has no privileged access to the semiotic and, indeed, appears as merely an ideological misrecognition. In an interview, Kristeva has sought to separate out this distinction between 'woman' and the political problems of 'real' women:

> The belief that 'one is a woman' is almost as absurd and obscurantist as the belief that 'one is a man' ... Therefore we must use 'we are women' as an advertisement or slogan for our demands. On a deeper level, however, a woman is not something one can 'be' ... By 'woman' I understand what cannot be represented, what is not said, what remains above nomenclatures and ideologies.[40]

At the theoretical level, Kristeva adheres strongly to the Lacanian view that 'woman' does not exist. The political alternative therefore becomes a question of how women and men can redefine themselves through the semiotic, and thereby break down existing gender divisions of modern society. Indeed, as Kristeva argues in 'Woman's Time', modern feminism needs to embrace the ethical problem of how it might be possible to bring out the singularity of every individual in a manner that will enhance her capacity for symbolic and sexual identifications.[41]

The Politics of Semiotic Transgression: Subverting Gender Norms

In many ways Kristeva's effort to reconfigure the imaginary and symbolic dimensions of subjectivity, and her insistence on the repression of the semiotic within male-dominated culture, must be considered as one of the most important feminist contributions of post-structuralist thought. Throwing new light on the 'dark continent' of femininity, Kristeva's stress on the powers of women and men to consistently disrupt phallocentric discourse – through the semiotic chora, the ambivalence of affect, the unstable symbolic – marks a step towards a new feminist politics, a step beyond the frameworks of liberal or socialist politics. Her emphasis on the primary capacity of the subject to grasp semiotic forms, and attendant deconstruction of deterministic interpretations of the symbolic, recasts feminist understandings of asymmetric gender relations. The central feminist political problem is not that the feminine self is entirely determined by the symbolic (as with Mitchell), nor is it the need to go beyond the limits of the symbolic itself (as with Cixous and Irigaray). The political problem for the Kristevan subject is rather that of combining the semiotic/symbolic in new form, in a manner that satisfies the particularity of the individual.

However, it must be noted that Kristeva has not been as evidently successful in articulating the specific connections between the 'subject-in-process', as concerned with the disruption of the symbolic through semiotic forces, and her more concrete political concerns. While situating the political context of the poetic texts she examines in an illuminating fashion, the complex ways in which semiotic libidinal drives undo certain repressions and pathologies of self, gender and society are never truly specified. In basing the radicality of her social theory on the view that poetic language contains a semiotic pressure that dislodges the reader's ideological assumptions, Kristeva implies that social and political structures can also be disrupted and broken apart in a comparative manner. Yet it must surely be questioned whether the semiotic disruption in poetic language can be formally equated with the transformation of gender relations in the spheres of politics and society. For *what* is so significant about the break-up of the structures of language in these texts when they appear to carry little impact on wider social relations? The problem here stems from the analogy Kristeva posits between texts and social practices. Social practices, and particularly social constructions of gender, are not simply homologous to textual/discursive structures, but rather are traversed by historically dense relations of unconscious force and power, situated within concrete social institutions.

This inevitably raises serious questions about Kristeva's political programme. In comparison with Lacan's theory, as we have seen, Kristeva develops a more dialectical view of the relation among semiotic drives, language and the law. Yet, for a number of commentators, the political implications of Kristeva's rejection of the linguistic determinism of the Lacanian symbolic order are less than clear. It has been suggested that for Kristeva received social meanings can only be questioned and challenged through a dissolution of consciousness into the disruptive, heterogeneous flow of semiotic drives. As White argues, Kristeva accords little moral or ethical autonomy to the human subject and thereby moves dangerously close to promoting some kind of political anarchism.[42] In Kristeva's work, White comments, an exclusive emphasis on the semiotic pressures of contradiction and rupture, of the sadistic excesses of negation, leads to a fundamental neglect of symbolic contexts in which all social transformation is embedded. The consequences of this are a reinstatement of fixed binary oppositions. The semiotic is the space of flux and heterogeneity, the symbolic of repressive social meanings.

Such a judgement, however, is in fact more appropriate to the work of certain postmodernist thinkers – such as Jean-François Lyotard and Gilles Deleuze – than of Kristeva. Kristeva's critique of semiotic rupture is opposed to the postmodern celebration of the dispersal of the libidinal economy itself. In fact, her work shows that any simple prioritization of the libidinal economy is a specious political programme for change, a program in which there would no longer be a self to claim emancipation. As we have seen, one of the most persistent themes in Kristeva's writings is the impossibility of transcending the symbolic domain. The field of language and received social meanings cannot simply be expected to evaporate. And it is for this reason that the semiotic and symbolic modalities, while separated, are not posed in oppositional terms. Kristeva, then, is a good deal more prudent about the symbolic negotiation of semiotic transgressions than is often claimed. Yet although she clearly sees symbolic mediations within the disruptive potential ascribed to semiotic expression, it is less clear in what the politics of this subversion consists. One major difficulty here, I think, is that her account obscures the fundamental significance of critical reflexiveness in processes of self and social transformation. For exactly what aspects of the self are at work in Kristeva's topology? Are a person's transgressive actions, for example, to be viewed as resulting from the semiotic play of libidinal drives, the chora's displacements of rhythms and sounds, or as motivated by the intentions of consciousness? In a social and political context, Kristeva's account of semiotic subversion bypasses some of the most important problems concerning the complex ways in which subjects critically reflect and act upon, not only gender norms, but politics itself.

In her more recent work, Kristeva has developed a kind of solution to these problems. *Tales of Love*, *In the Beginning was Love*, *Black Sun* and *Strangers to Ourselves* argue for the capacity of human subjects to elaborate diverse imaginary forms and to question and transform symbolic experience.[43] In these works Kristeva stresses that the semiotic is not only disruptive of language and representation, but is fundamental to enlarging the imaginary and symbolic possibilities of human subjects. In discussing this imaginary constitution and dissolution of psychic space, she points out that the semiotic is principally centred around those 'archaic' dimensions of subjectivity which precede the mirror stage in Lacan's work. This focus is important, it should be noted, since it allows Kristeva to avoid the impasses of specular identity discussed in Chapter 4, and to transcend the implicit determinism of Lacan's theory of the symbolic. Conceptualizing this primordial experience of the pre-self, Kristeva points out that human infants are only at first capable of separating from the mother through certain semiotic forms such as voice, colour, taste, the skin surface, and so on. These semiotic affects and drives are a product of the imaginary capabilities of human subjects and are formed in a non-specular way. Kristeva describes this first grasping of the self as the 'zero degree' of the psyche, and links it with Freud's categories of 'primary identification' and the 'father of personal pre-history'.[44] This 'father' of the child's pre-history is understood in Lacanian terms as the mother's desire for the phallus; which thereby prefigures the symbolic intervention of a third term into the child–mother dyad. The imaginary father functions to effect a preliminary split with the mother and refers the child to certain ego-ideals prior to the establishment of an object-relation proper.[45] By replacing the plenitude of imaginary completeness with a subjective void – which it is the function of narcissism to screen over – the operation of primary identification is seen as inseparable from the emergence of ego formation, self-organization and self-love. In sum, primary identification is for Kristeva that point in which affects and ideals combine to produce the first grasping of a structuration of subjectivity.

In linking the operation of primary identification with the creation of psychic space in this way, Kristeva contends that subjectivity is an 'open system' – a term she borrows from modern biology. The subject's capacity for identification, or more precisely, pre-identification, lies at the root of both the loss of the self and all subsequent reworkings and innovations of psychical organization. This point is of some considerable importance in respect of the criticisms which I have raised against Kristeva's work. The relationship between the subject, the imaginary object of desire and the Other (the social dimension of idealization) is fundamental in Kristeva's later works for any project of self-realization and autonomy. This schema is the cement which holds together human subjectivity and is at the heart of all innovation, contradiction, development, pleasure. On the basis of this entwinement of ego identity, the other and the social code, Kristeva speaks of a 'true process of self-organization', 'libidinal auto-organization', psychical life as 'open systems connected to each other'. Of particular interest to the development of free and open human relations is the way Kristeva configures the complex relations between semiotic subject and social code. She writes:

To say that the systems operating in transference are 'open' implies not only interaction, but also the opening up of each system into its heterogeneous components ... Man as a fixed, valorized entity finds himself abandoned in favor of a search, less for his truth ... than for his innovative capacities. The effect of love is one of renewal, our rebirth. The new blossoms out and throws us into confusion when libidinal auto-organization encounters memory-consciousness, which is guaranteed by the Other, and becomes symbolized ... In a semanalytic interpretation, it would amount, for the amorous and/or transference discourse, to a permanent stablization-destablization between the symbolic (pertaining to referential signs and their syntactic articulation) and the semiotic (the elemental tendency) of libidinal charges toward displacement and condensation, and of their inscription, which depends on the incorporation and introjection of incorporated items; an economy that privileges orality, vocalization, alliteration, rhythmicity, etc.[46]

This reconceptualization of subjectivity around the concept of primary identification in Kristeva's later works, however, is still to some degree in conflict with her feminist and political concerns. For it is as if having rewritten subjectivity as an open and innovative process, and having rejected a deterministic view of the symbolic, Kristeva is unable to recognize that many of her conceptual terms imply that women and men are doomed to remain enclosed within the boundaries of the patriarchal symbolic order. Whatever the more creative aspects attributed to the subject through primary identification, it might be argued that Kristeva's stress on 'the father of personal pre-history' simply reinscribes the paternal metaphor at the heart of the subjective field. What is at stake in this linkage of self-formation with the 'imaginary father', from the viewpoint of writers like Cixous and Irigaray, is that it reproduces existing ideological divisions about women and men. Mothers occupy the undifferentiated space of pre-Oedipal love; while fathers, even in imaginary form, occupy the symbolic space of differentiation which brings the self into being. It should be stressed, of course, that for Kristeva this 'father of personal pre-history' is less the actual father than his structural position, represented in the mother's desire for the phallus. But, even so, the troubling point in Kristeva's work is the unavoidable suggestion that the creativity and productivity of psychical life can only unfold within a symbolic order that is inherently patriarchal. The question then which needs to be posed is this: why does Kristeva, having insisted on the innovative and productive nature of the imaginary, make no attempt to question the specific ways in which psychical creation may alter the patriarchal symbolic? More specifically: why does she fail to consider the possibilities for a fundamental rupture within traditional gender divisions caused by the psyche as an 'open system', which in turn would surely affect the socio-symbolic constitution of self-identity?

Kristeva is reluctant to raise these issues, I believe, since to do so would involve a thoroughgoing revision of the Lacanian concept of the symbolic and the origins of psychical reality and self-identity. As we have seen, Kristeva connects the constitution of the self to the symbolic function of the imaginary father – elaborated through the child's primary identification with the mother. I want to claim that, although an advancement over Lacan's version of specular selfhood, this position is still theoretically limited. It is futile to attempt to derive the conditions of psychical reality from the characteristics of the symbolic matrix of society. To complement the Lacanian emphasis on the primacy of the symbolic with an accentuation of the significance of the semiotic (and, specifically, primary identification) is unsatisfactory unless it is understood that the imaginary is the capacity of the psyche to create and elaborate representational forms. This demands acknowledging, with Freud, that the constitution of the ego arises not through the instantiation of the symbolic (though symbolic forms are always present), but from the child separating out a self from its 'original narcissistic investment'. This process of self-production arises from the profoundly imaginary dimensions of the primary unconscious. The upshot of this, in political terms, is that the gender norms which engage the unconscious investments of human subjects are, in turn, open to the articulation of the imaginary and thus to social transformation and development. I shall confront the implications of this, as well as other issues, in the following, concluding chapter.

7 Social Theory and Psychoanalysis in Transition

The Possibilities of the Social Imaginary

Throughout this book I have been concerned to develop certain arguments about the relevance and utility of psychoanalysis for social theory. By focusing on contemporary contributions to our understanding of this relation, I have argued that psychoanalysis is of major importance for rethinking central problems in social theory today – problems concerning self-identity, power and ideological domination; sexual difference and gender; and the question of human subjectivity and the theory of the unconscious more generally. In this concluding chapter, I shall summarize and try to place these issues in the context of my critical discussions of the foregoing theoretical approaches, in an attempt to move beyond their limitations. It should be stressed, however, that this outline of my position must remain tentative and incomplete at this stage. It is intended as a prelude to the development of a framework for rethinking social theory and psychoanalysis, a framework which I shall develop in a subsequent work.* It is thus to these preliminary considerations that I now turn.

Self-Identity and the Imaginary in the Modern World

One of the major contributions of psychoanalysis to social theory is that it directs our attention towards the complex ways in which ideological relations of domination and power interlace with the repression of the self. At issue are the modes of repression by which modernity produces *fragmentation, marginalization* and the *destruction of difference*. In contemporary critical theory, as we have seen, social and political forces are identified as the central determinants of internal deformation, fragmentation and immobilizing repression. The radical mutations brought about through the transition from market to monopoly capitalism have hollowed the emotional core of psychic interiority and instituted new social and ideological determinants of personal identity. The 'centred' and 'unified' subject is still an ideological necessity of the political system, but is now shown to be constituted to its roots by the manipulation of unconscious forces – through a web of intricate relations that are entirely opaque to everyday consciousness. By contrast, in Lacanian and post-structuralist thought a more formalistic politics is affirmed. According to these approaches, repression and subjective deformations are the result of the entry into language as such. The fictive sense of subjecthood which is at once implanted and disrupted through 'mirror misrecognitions' (Lacan), 'ideological interpellation' (Althusser), or the 'antagonistic structure of symbolization' (Laclau/Mouffe/Žižek), locates individual subjects within an order of others from which the self is always excluded or alienated due to the impossibility of transcending the 'wall of language'. The human subject is therefore *always* seen as fragmented, never identical with itself, at once constituted and deformed along a chain of unstable signifiers.

Here I shall evaluate this recasting of self and self-identity developed in the foregoing theoretical standpoints. In order to approach these issues I shall retrace their analyses of the ways in which hegemonic modes of power interlace with unconscious experience and therefore with the self. In doing so I shall argue that the devaluation of the creative, imaginary features of psychic processes in these approaches carries serious deficiencies for their theorizing about modern culture and social life. The question therefore arises as to how the potentially transformative elements of the imaginary and the self should be reconnected to the social field. In this respect I shall argue that the imaginary is inscribed within socio-symbolic forms in both libertory and repressive ways, while also maintaining an autonomous role for the imaginary in the psychical reorganization of the self and social relations.

Let us, then, take stock of the social implications of psychic fragmentation, of the radical split between the conscious life of the ego and the unconscious, of reason and desire, by returning to the arguments developed in the critical theory of the Frankfurt School. In Marcuse's and Adorno's analyses of bourgeois society, there is an attempt to locate historically the origins of the fragmentation and disintegration of the subject. Through a mapping of Freudian psychoanalysis on to the fundamental themes of *Dialectic of Enlightenment*, the humanization of unconscious drives, resulting in the transformation from blind instinct to the conscious self, is held to release the subject from its enslavement to Nature. But, in a tragic irony, the unconscious drives enabling this autonomy undergo a violent repression that reduces the subject to inner division, isolation, and repetitive compulsion. The forging of the ego thus reveals its

Janus-face in the repression of unconscious drives as the price of individuation and self-control. This ambivalently emancipatory and repressive forging of the self is most clearly discerned by Marcuse and Adorno in the dialectic of the Oedipus complex. In the Oedipal drama, it is claimed, the emergence of self-identity and autonomy are internally tied to the perpetuation of domination since they rest upon a prior acceptance of paternal authority. The dialectic of submission and resistance to the father both constitutes and painfully splits the human subject – a splitting that inscribes a compulsive drive for self-preservation at the heart of the unconscious.

For Adorno, the psychic costs of these repressions are particularly grave. The compulsive features of the subject, expressed as the yearning for identity and unity, are inherently self-contradictory, perpetuating the repression and damage of those aspects of the self that are non-identical. As regards modernity, Adorno is acutely sensitive to the intensification of these costs imposed by the forging of a 'unified' and 'responsible' subject. The law of capitalist social relations surreptitiously organizes the individual subject into an 'identity', violently and manipulatively suppressing those aspects of non-identity from consciousness. And the more this process becomes totalized, the more inherently pathological it becomes. 'For Adorno', as Terry Eagleton comments, 'the self is rent by an internal fissure, and the name for the experience of it is suffering'.[1] The transition from the liberal epoch of bourgeois society to late capitalism affects this suffering in quite specific ways. Due to the increasingly instrumental and commodified nature of capitalist social processes, the subject is held to forgo self-awareness in order to effect the 'senseless renunciations' demanded by late capitalism. This elimination of ego identity and the subject's measure of autonomy leads to a withdrawal into the unconscious and into sealed, narcissistic illusions of self-containment. Culminating in feelings of personal emptiness and powerlessness, this proliferation of pathological narcissism is viewed by Adorno as the final response of a 'subjectless subject' trying to retain some level of self-worth and integrity. Withdrawing into the unconscious, the psyche becomes subject to direct social mediation. For Adorno, the 'totally administered society' increasingly manipulates unconscious processes, progressively liquidating the individual subject's capacity for individuation, emotional reciprocity, human understanding.

As with Adorno, Marcuse's analysis of modernity posits a rapid disintegration of the autonomous ego. Premised on the alleged social integration of contemporary culture, human consciousness and reflectiveness are increasingly repressed, rendered culturally redundant. In a rationalized world of commodified culture and depersonalized social relations, subjects can no longer express a measure of autonomy and spontaneity. Like the structure of the culture industry in which they are administered, human subjects today are increasingly 'one dimensional'. It is for this reason, as we have seen, that Marcuse pronounces the obsolescence of the Freudian subject – once radically divided between the conscious life of the ego, the law of the superego and the recesses of the unconscious. In conditions of modernity, such divisions begin to blur and erode. Speaking of an 'automization' of the psyche, Marcuse argues that the modern subject is a passive and administered product of social determinants. As all public spheres become more and more saturated with practices of consumption, so too the individual subject becomes integrated around the dictates of 'commodification'. Increasingly dependent on feelings of narcissism and acquisitiveness that are shaped by capitalist social processes, Marcuse argues, human autonomy and spontaneity have been effectively corroded. And while he ultimately traces the possibility of collective resistance and political emancipation to the internal dynamics of these psychical processes – as previously discussed – he finds little possibility of redemption offered in the current cultural spheres of capitalist society, which only promote and intensify 'repressive desublimation'.

From a standpoint which focuses upon the creative features of psychic processes and intersubjectivity, however, these emphases in Adorno's and Marcuse's work appear highly questionable. A concern with the intersubjective realm, with the recognition that the other person is central to the formation of the self, pinpoints many of the central weaknesses of the Frankfurt School's rather solitary, monadic conception of the human subject. From such a standpoint, as discussed in Chapter 2, Adorno's and Marcuse's key premise that all ego development is *a priori* self-defeating is faulty. As the work of Wilden, Whitebook and others demonstrates, the constitution of the self occurs, not through a monadic repression of innate forces, but through a complex and intricate repression of unconscious drives that are formed in our relations with others. From this angle, then, existing modes of repressed desire are a product of social organization – a theme I shall return to later in this chapter. The implications of this, as we have seen, are considerable. It highlights that the result of ego development is not necessarily inner compulsion and self-mutilation, as Adorno and Marcuse believe, but also individuation and autonomy. The Oedipus complex need not be viewed as a process which leads to a uniform, repressive introjection of the law. Though the Oedipus complex undeniably instantiates secondary repression, an intersubjective focus also stresses that it is a crucial affective and social interaction from which individuation and autonomy flow. On this view, the father in the Oedipus complex can be just as much a partner in emotional and affective understanding, as he is some 'model' which is repressively internalized.[2] The result of such a recognition, at the theoretical level at least, is an escape from the fate of fragmentation that is implied by an autonomy that can only be constituted by the concomitant introjection of a repressive authority.

It is partly from an extended critique of these issues, as we have examined in Chapter 3, that Habermas develops a more differentiated account of the intersections between subjectivity and contemporary social processes. Like the early Frankfurt School, Habermas argues that the increasing penetration of a rationalizing, bureaucratizing logic into the life-world has degraded human experience and autonomy. The development of anonymous systems of administration and economy, so Habermas argues, increasingly reaches into every cultural sphere, thereby colonizing consciousness and the affective resources essential to expressive subjectivity. Yet because Habermas sees subjectivity as characterized by a high potential for autonomy and accords the sphere of the affective a strong capacity for resistance, he rejects the view that social and cultural affairs have been subjected to complete systemization and administrative control. Contending that contemporary societies are marked by a high degree of differentiation, Habermas finds modern selfhood inscribed between spaces of autonomy and dislocation, unity and fragmentation.

It is for this reason, as we have seen, that Habermas analyses the dynamics and procedures of intersubjectivity, of everyday linguistic practice, to reach down to the immanent features of cognitive and affective interactions. Baldly stated, Habermas's belief is that language – however distorted and deformed in social terms – always has autonomy, consensus and understanding as its normative basis; a basis from which current social life might be potentially transformed. The major question concerning the possibilities for collective autonomy in contemporary capitalist societies is the extent to which human beings can reverse the pathological colonization of the life-world by systems reproduction. The key to an emancipatory outcome, argues Habermas, depends on the practice of bringing internal pathologies and institutional constraints to critical self-reflection. In this model, discourses about needs and motives unfold in this communal process of self-reflection, as repressed desires and phantasies are reintegrated into social discourse. This vision of autonomy developed by Habermas, however, is certainly not without problems. It is a vision, as I previously argued, that displaces some of the most vital issues about human needs, affects and desires in favour of dominant, masculinist ideals about 'rationality'. By conceptualizing the affective and unconscious features of the self as a 'barrier' or 'distortion' to free communication, Habermas recoils from examining the profoundly imaginary and sexual dimensions within which individual and collective identities are actualized. This vision of emancipation misses the point that unconscious needs, aspirations and desires are as much a productive underpinning of the dialogic process as they are a barrier to its realization.

In emphasizing that the constitution and reproduction of subjectivity is intricately bound up with our relation to others, certain parallels might be noted here between some of Habermas's concerns and the perspectives developed by Lacan. For, as with critical theory, Lacan is primarily concerned to elucidate the narcissistic and illusory features of self-identity and, like Habermas, sees internal pathologies and distortions as emerging from the dialectics of intersubjectivity. Yet in contrast to Habermas's rather uncritical reliance on ego-psychology and cognitive-developmental theory, it can be argued that Lacan's work provides a much richer and detailed analysis of the (de)formations of the subject. Tracing the fissures and ruptures through which consciousness passes in order to achieve a sense of selfhood, Lacan's work intricately maps the specular lures and traps which lie at the centre of the intersubjective domain. From these decoys of imaginary experience, the subsequent entry into language, as we have seen, is said to render the subject forever alienated from human relationships. 'Language', Lacan remarks, 'is constituted in such a way as to found us in the Other, while radically preventing us from understanding him'.[3]

It is at this point that we once more encounter the importance of Lacan's essay 'The mirror stage as formative of the function of the I' in his analyses of the misrecognition inherent to human subjectivity. As discussed in Chapter 4, Lacan argues that a sense of selfhood is only slowly and precariously established when the infant, still largely uncoordinated, finds a coherent image of itself reflected back from another. For Lacan, the key feature of this process is that, in forming an integrated self-image, the human subject is led to *misrecognize* and *misperceive* itself. This is because the formation of the ego is principally narcissistic in character; it provides an illusory apprehension of unity that has not been objectively achieved. The subject is destined to be forever 'alienated' from the image with which it identifies since, in reality, its experiential world is still structured within a sense of turbulence and asymmetry which it has known since birth. According to this standpoint, then, the ego provides a narcissistic buttressing of fictive, imaginary completeness which, always precariously, 'covers over' the fragmentations and anxieties of the psyche. As Lacan puts this, the structure of the ego 'neglects, scotomizes, misconstrues'.[4]

In post-Lacanian social theory, as examined in Chapter 5, this narcissistic *mis*-recognition is made the centrepoint of the individual subject's relation to society as a whole. According to Althusser, ideology is best read in Lacanian vein, as a sort of 'imaginary assemblage' which at once generates a map of social reality and subjects human beings to social positions within material institutions. With the work of Laclau and Mouffe, and Žižek, this tendency to approach the relations between self and ideology as a 'decentred process' is further dramatized. Through a reworking of the Lacanian concept of the real as a fundamental source of social antagonism, a systematic effort is made to redefine social and political interests as a locus of contingency, lack and linguistic uncertainty. The only answer to this imaginary mystification of human subjectivity, as we have seen, lies in those critical attempts to penetrate to the real of human desire and knowledge – to that elusive realm beyond the imaginary and symbolic planes.

Ambiguity, contradiction, dispersal, and oscillation: these are the dangerous reaches of psychic structures in current social processes. From the level of the individual right up to that of society as a whole, these tendencies toward fragmentation have their explanation in a blending of disturbed narcissism, the increasing flux and decomposition of social meanings, the mirror-like illusions of the imaginary, and the like. From these images of fragmentation, there immediately arises a host of social and political questions. Among the most important for social theory are the following: are these fragmentations of human experience intrinsically connected to the imaginary and language as such (as Lacanian and post-structuralist theories suggest), or do they spring from recent changes in social and political relations? In what ways, exactly, do these tendencies toward fragmentation express themselves today in cultural and social forms? And, as a matter of historical periodization, are these tendencies toward fragmentation best considered as features of modernity or of postmodernity? Clearly, it would be impossible to discuss the many ramifications of these issues in the detail demanded in this study. Instead, I shall focus on the key claim of the foregoing approaches that the fragmentation and dispersal of the human subject has become totalized, and is thus the key psychic feature of modern social processes. From the vantage point of recent social thought, such broad generalizations about the self and self-identity are highly questionable. It is wrong, I want to argue, to see the socio-symbolic order of modern societies as intrinsically alienating and repressive of the self's imaginary capacities. Rather, the imaginary is of central significance – I shall claim – for engendering symbolic forms of self-expression, both liberatory and repressive. It should be emphasized, however, that the following discussion is by no means exhaustive. My critical remarks are intended to be primarily suggestive, raising certain alternatives and possibilities which require, in my view, further research and analysis.

The themes of fragmentation and dispersal developed in critical theory, Lacanian-orientated social theory, and post-structuralism do not lead, I argue, to an adequate theory of the self, social processes, or of their relation to one another. Drawing on psychoanalytic theory to demonstrate that the human subject is radically fractured and decentred, the foregoing approaches project from this, in their varying ways, an *inverse* level of *social incorporation*. The human psyche is seen as obediently ordered into the more systemic modes of the requirements of the social system, traumatically divided between an imaginary unity and turbulent fissure. In the critical theory of the Frankfurt School, this incorporation is traced as the end result of the social and ideological manipulation of the unconscious. In Lacanian and post-structuralist thought, the subject is more universally destined for a symbolic introjection of the law – by which it is inserted into pre-given social and political 'positions'. Characterized this way, then, a conception of society is presented which stresses the homogeneity of symbolic forms and the *destruction* of the powers of the imaginary. And it is because of the all-pervasivness of this omnipotent law – either that of consumer society or the signifier itself – that freedom and autonomy remain obscure and unknowable from these standpoints. Autonomy, in short, can only be imagined as the recovery of an inner realm of the self, as in the individualism of Marcuse and others. Or it becomes conflated back into the very notion of fragmentation. Discontinuity is viewed as a state of authenticity and psychic escape from the imposed, repressive categories of the symbolic, as in the post-Lacanian work of Laclau and Mouffe, and Žižek.

Yet it is mistaken, as I have previously argued, to see the fundamental asymmetry of the self in terms of a repressive symbolic order and the capture of the imaginary on the one side, and the fragmentation and dispersal of desire on the other. Such a view can have no proper grasp of the imaginary of human subjectivity, an imaginary which continually transforms social life in both liberatory and repressive ways. In reducing the imaginary to an empty universal of ideology, these approaches are unable to confront issues of how given cultural phenomena change or of how development interlaces with historically specific modes of subjectivity. Consider in this respect the nature of social movements. The international significance of social movements in recent decades, particularly feminist, peace and ecological movements, suggests that the innovative and creative dimensions of human subjectivity have not been repressed in anything like the manner suggested by these approaches. As a collective process of self-reflection upon human needs, social movements articulate alternative imaginary forms which oppose dominant social and political relations. In this respect, the role of the imaginary is of a double kind. By elaborating alternative imaginary representations to hegemonic forms of self-constitution, these movements supply a clear illustration of the creation of new ways of thinking, feeling and acting in the social domain. At the same time, in becoming part of social life, these imaginary forms may act to fracture the very hegemonic modes of cultural representation they oppose – thus generating the possibility of an alternative future. This linkage of the imaginary to potential transformations in social life is precisely what has taken place in the women's movement, in the worldwide struggle against nuclear weapons, and in ecological programmes of action.

From this angle, it can be seen that the imaginary dimensions of the self are complex and crosscut the symbolic dimensions of modern societies. This point is of fundamental significance to grasping the nature of the self and self-identity. The transformative possibilities opened out through the imaginary, however, cannot indicate how such forms and representations might be actualized in any given social context. This depends rather, as I have argued, on the social, political and economic structures in which these imaginary forms are embedded. In relation to the theoretical deficiencies of the foregoing approaches to these issues, then, their difficulty lies not so much in a failure to anticipate these transformative properties of the psyche. As we have seen, the 'return of the repressed' (Marcuse), the 'inadequation between signifier and signified' (Lacan), and the 'disruption of the real' (Laclau/Mouffe/Žižek) all testify to diverse possibilities for social transformation. The point is rather that they neglect the crucial imaginary means through which symbolic structures are either consolidated or disrupted, and that this feature of psychic processes demands sustained critical attention.

This line of criticism should not be taken as denying the more destructive and oppressive features of modernity as they impact upon the self. The increasing influence of bureaucratic logic and rigid symbolic forms – to mention only two features of current social relations identified by these theoretical standpoints in the construction of self – play a vital role in securing the ideological legitimation of specific power structures in contemporary society. Interpreted as a process of 'social incorporation', however, they delineate an approach to ideological consciousness that is far more rigid and inflexible than the internally differentiated social formations that exist in the modern world. In contrast to providing a general cultural diagnosis, I believe that these approaches are best seen as a *phenom-enology* of particular modes of self-identity and the self in modernity. Interpreted this way, they offer a view of the tendencies towards narcissism and fragmentation of self that is not so much wrong, but rather only partial. The creation of narcissistic and rigid self-identit-ies in the face of a standardizing socio-symbolic order is only one overall *mode* of self-constitution in modern social life. The reasons for this relate to a theme discussed throughout this book – the rich and diverse range of *imaginary forms* in the constitution of the self. The foregoing approaches tend to lose sight of these imaginary modes of representation, thought, and feeling as they are manifested within society and culture. This does not mean, as is sometimes claimed, that these standpoints simply evade consideration of the dynamics of subjectivity and self-identity. It will not do to dismiss these theories as denying the existence of historically determinate meanings, subjectivities, intentions, and so on. For what is common to critical theory, Lacanian-inspired thought, and certain versions of post-structuralism, as we have seen, is their attempt to prise open the repressive structuring of self-identity, and thereby to lay bare the oppressive weight of political and social practices that maintains its force at the level of psychic processes. However, where these stand-points are grossly deficient is in their neglect of the *active* and *creative* features of imaginary experience by which men and women image themselves and each other in modern social life. It is simply inade-quate to imagine that society reaches out and colonizes a fragmented psychic space, restructuring a diffuse network of libidinal drives. These standpoints fail to accord due recognition to the active dimen-sions of subjecthood; to the point that ideological and social fields are rewritten and changed within the indeterminacy of subjectivity, even though modern subjects are decentred and dispersed. To claim otherwise means that variations in institutionalized forms of power, systems of domination and modalities of law as they affect the self are screened from social analysis and critique. All socio-symbolic forms are viewed as equally oppressive and coercive forces upon the self.

The idea of the atomization and disintegration of the self in the face of modern social institutions is familiar enough today, having been much popularized by the cultural criticism of writers such as Sennett and Lasch.[5] Many of these themes about the 'death of the imaginary' have also been reproduced in diverse stands of modern social theory. Jean Baudrillard refers to the postmodern imaginary as a 'simulacrum' of endless repetition; Roland Barthes to an imagina-tion dispersed through our 'civilization of the image', and Jacques Derrida to the imagination as the effect of a linguistic 'play of *différance*'.[6] According to these images of our late modern (or post-modern) social universe, the imaginary is not simply in a state of crisis but is rather swallowed up as an effect of language, the symbolic, the text. 'After imagination', as Richard Kearney writes of postmodernist thought, 'there is no reality. Only the limitless play of pastiche.'[7] If the views developed in this book command any credence, such interpretations about the modern imaginary are certainly questionable. While it is not altogether wrong to speak of the discontinuity and fragmentation of the imaginary, I have argued that it is mistaken to see these tendencies as objectively 'implanted' at the heart of subjective life. As modern social life becomes increasingly differentiated, with individuals forging new cultural spaces in the shaping of their lives, the imaginary continues to exert a fundamental influence upon individuation and the self. In this connection, I wish to suggest some alternative lines of thought for rethinking the crisis of the imaginary in the modern world. The first consideration is primarily sociological, concerned with refiguring the relations between self and society. The second is more psychoanalytic in character. It concerns how best to approach new configurations of the imaginary in the present age.

In certain strands of recent social thought there have been a number of interesting attempts to challenge the currently preeminent image of modernity as 'incorporative'. Through reworking certain basic assumptions about self and society, the lived experience of modernity is configured as an immensely complex and subtle phenomenon – one that continually crosscuts symbolic modes of collective organization. There is now a rapidly growing literature about this, and it is not my intention to offer a detailed analysis of it here. Rather, in passing, I shall simply note two important discussions about modernity, concentrating only on those analytic points that are directly relevant to the issues raised in this book. *Nomads of the Present*, by Alberto Melucci, provides a reconsideration of how deep-seated contradictions of contemporary social life reshape the self.[8] The fissures and contradictions of modernity, argues Melucci, provide a setting for individual experience which at once enhances and restricts self-expression. In advanced society, social systems and large-scale organizations increasingly infiltrate and manipulate existing opportunities for individuation. But at the same time, paradoxically, these conditions offer new cultural resources to individuals – such as leisure, knowledge and money – and thus often promote an extension of the autonomy of the self. Rejecting the view that modern social processes flatten out the self by atomization, Melucci argues that psychic processes of self-definition must be seen as crucial to the unfolding of social life. As he puts it, 'The conscious production of one's own identity – self-identification – is a necessary condition for enabling the individual to establish social bonds, and to locate him- or herself as one of the poles in a relationship of solidarity or conflict.'[9] Similarly Anthony Giddens, in *Modernity and Self-identity*, argues that the reflexivity of the self means that social life is placed within a setting of 'indefinite extension' – at once enhancing and restrictive.[10] Referring to the creation and reproduction of self-identity as a process of 'unification and fragmentation', 'dispersal and reappropriation', and 'displacement and re-embedding', Giddens portrays modernity as a complex dialectic of powerlessness and empowerment. In the terms of Giddens and Melucci, then, the experience of modernity simultaneously threatens to rend itself into disorder and dispersal and yet is actively reappropriated and coordinated through the reflexivity and creative powers of human beings.

Such an emphasis upon the self-production of social life, I believe, is important for social theory, providing it with a fruitful framework for rethinking the relations between self and society. As regards psychic processes, however, this stress on the contradictory orientation of modern institutions raises important issues about the imaginary and self-identity. How are we to account for this split, for example, between subjective dispersal and the reappropriation of the grounds of human agency? How are we to understand the fact that the human subject is continually decentred and outstripped by modern social processes on the one hand, and that individuals have created new ways of forging social involvements, of personal intimacy, and of developing a core of meaningful selfhood on the other hand? Is it just a matter of saying that the subject is caught between, and subjected to, conflicting dimensions of symbolic codes which cannot be reconciled?

If the arguments about the creativity of the psyche I have developed in the preceding chapters are right, it is essential to recognize that imaginary and symbolic representations interlace in contradictory and conflicting ways at every level of society. The role of the imaginary, to be sure, plays a constitutive role in social life – representations and traces of affect are 'immanent' in social relations – and, from this angle, symbolic codes draw upon the creativity of the social imaginary. That the imaginary is an ineliminable feature of symbolic organization and of every social activity indicates its importance for the development of self and self-identity, but this significance is fundamentally different in scope from that proposed in critical theory and Lacanian-inspired theoretical work. The symbolic is certainly an order that goes beyond the schemata of imaginary phantasy. But to say that it is forced upon the imaginary, by which the subject is repressively inscribed in society, is equivalent to abolishing the deeper structures of subjectivity. The symbolic, on the contrary, depends upon the continual structuring of the imaginary, grasped as the transformation of a virtual order of 'phantasized objects' into a matrix of common, social forms. This does not prevent us from conceiving symbolic codes as crucial to the reproduction of social relations of domination, relations that escape the 'control' of individual actors. But it does highlight that imaginary forms are *deeply embedded* in all symbolic modes of repression. No doubt the *forms* of the imaginary as they interlace with the symbolic are indefinite – ranging across states of disintegration, destruction, and hate to empathy, containment and love. But the central point is that the symbolic and imaginary are always irreducible; any transformation in cultural symbolic representations requires a corresponding imaginary reorganization of the self.

Consider in this regard the destructive and pathological effects of technological knowledge and rationalization in modern culture. It has been widely argued that the influence of reifying bureaucratic logics, and the ever-increasing rationalization of all aspects of day-to-day social life, have produced the wholesale manipulation of the imaginary. Just as the self is increasingly controlled by new technical arrangements and administrative methods, so too the imaginary is stripped and reduced to a purely mechanical system of reproduction. Yet while capturing certain aspects of the *content* of symbolic forms of large-scale bureaucracies and modern organizations, the central tenets of this view are plainly inadequate. Actually to dwell within a selfhood constructed upon the dull conformity of bureaucratic assimilations, or to see other human beings as no more than mechanical 'objects' or 'things', involves not the destruction but the *radical involvement of the imaginary*. From a psychoanalytic viewpoint, the constitution, reproduction and disruption of all symbolic forms, whether of local or global meaning, must derive their source from this imaginary. This is true even in destructive political contexts where the gap is tightened between symbolic possibilities and social reality. It is certainly the case that many cultural and symbolic representations draw upon, and reshape, the imaginary in corrosive and destructive ways – what Castoriadis has termed modernity's 'second-order imaginary', one that is lacking any 'flesh of its own'.[11] But as a general point it remains the case that, whatever the imaginary borrows from symbolic forms, such representations always point beyond their own enclosure. Repression of the constitutive elements of the imaginary can never be complete. Autonomization of the imaginary by debilitating symbolic forms is always open to counter-reaction – as the overturning of the repressive bureaucratic economies of Eastern Europe and the Soviet Union clearly demonstrates.

Perhaps more than ever, the structure of the imaginary is today being transformed. The globalizing effects of modernity – generated through institutional transformations such as mass communications, new technologies and capitalist world commodification – intensifies and radicalizes the organization of the imaginary by the symbolic order. In doing so these practices might be seen to restructure the imaginary in negative forms – as a 'second-order imaginary', as it were. Yet the degree to which the imaginary is being inscribed within standardizing socio-symbolic forms is certainly not uniform or a one-way process. Nor can an inscription of such forms into the tissue of imaginary experience institute the 'destruction' of this constitutive psychic order. To what degree the psychical organization of the self will resist these standardizing influences of modernity in the future is unknown. But whatever transformations occur between self and society will crucially depend upon the imaginary dimensions of human subjectivity.

Sexual Difference and Gender Complexity: Problems of Contemporary Debate

Psychoanalysis, as we have seen, shows how gender relations and our sexual world are asymmetrical and unequal by providing a focus on the deep psychic roots of the emergence of separation, differentiation, and the construction of sexual difference. Schematically, a child of either gender faces the complex task of separating from a narcissistically merged connection with the mother to a socially demarcated relation between self and other, subject and object-world. This process of differentiation, it has been argued, locates the constitution of the self within the frame of gender issues. In this section, I will retrace various psychoanalytic lines on the construction of gender identity, unconscious sexuality and sexual difference. I will focus in particular on two areas of psychoanalytic debate on human sexuality – areas that form a common preoccupation among contemporary feminist theory and particular strands of feminist politics. These concern those social forces, and the question of their political reformulation, that shape the symbolic organization of women's sexuality; and the consequences of the privileged status of the father's position, as bearer of the phallus, in the constitution of sexual identity. In deconstructing contemporary approaches to these issues, particularly Lacanian and post-Lacanian arguments, I will suggest that an attention to the constitutive imaginary dimensions of human sexuality throws into question some widely held assumptions about gender determination and the fixity of our current gender system.

The theories examined in this book on the reproduction of sexuality in its dominant forms, both psychoanalytic and feminist, engage in different ways with the Freudian discourse on feminine sexuality. Three key aspects of Freud's views need to be re-emphasized in this connection. First, that human sexuality is profoundly imaginary in character. Gender identity, and the institution of sexual difference, goes beyond any natural or biological division. Second, Freud posits a 'psychic bisexuality' for the infant. Instituted modes of sexuality are established through an *ordering* of the psyche in the Oedipus complex, forged through a relation to the phallus itself. According to Freud, the development of heterosexuality in the girl is a by-product of a failed sense of masculinity – the Oedipal discovery that both she and the mother lack the phallus. As such, the adoption of femininity only occurs when the girl turns away from the mother to her father, hoping to receive the missing phallus by becoming the father's sexual object. Third, the development of both feminine and masculine sexual identifications is precarious and fragmentary; any normative mode of sexualization is belied by the flux of the unconscious and sexuality.

In psychoanalytical terms, the important content of these claims is that the Oedipus complex institutes a set of social and historical laws that are foundational to gender and individuation. The violent breakup of the child–mother dyad by the intrusion of a third party – the *place* of the father – brings the individual psyche into received cultural meanings and social institutions. It would be unwise to suppose, however, that one could ascribe any invariable characteristics to this ordering of the psyche. We are dealing less with some immutable 'law' – I shall claim – than with the *creation* of a gendered social individual, the form and content of which does (and is always open to) change. Thus despite the sexist and ideological assumptions which permeate Freud's account of sexual difference, most notably the equations of masculinity with activity and femininity with passivity, it is also clear that this theory captures dominant aspects of the contemporary gender system. As Juliet Mitchell argues, these dominant sexual ideologies are the work of a culture in which masculinity is the hegemonic site of sexual agency, and femininity the 'object' of desire. Destabilization of such repressive and rigid polarities is thus a common meeting point for both psychoanalysis and feminist social theory.

In Lacanian feminism, as we have seen, this sexualization of the subject is conceived as being linguistically structured. In contrast to the plenitude of the imaginary realm, understood by Lacanians as an order of misrecognition and specular traps, the symbolic intervention of the paternal law is the cultural basis that founds the social link. That is to say, individuals constitute themselves as human subjects only through entry into the symbolic order of language. This transition from the precariousness of imaginary traps (that inmixing of bodily illusions, *jouissance* and alienation) to the constitution of a symbolic gender-identity occurs through the function of the phallus, as a 'veiled' imaginary object. The phallus intervenes into the two-term relation between mother and child, referring the latter to a place *beyond* the imaginary order – the symbolic place of the father. By instituting a break in this imaginary dyad, the phallus stands for that moment of sexual division at the level of the subject itself. It represents a founding differential mark of sexual identification, from which the small infant perceives the cultural value of having or not having the phallus. The polarity of 'masculine' and 'feminine' attributes exist, then, only in so far as they are structured linguistically at the level of the unconscious. In Lacanian terms, if 'woman' is defined as something other within existing social relations it is because of the male-dominated form of this sexual/linguistic structure, and not because of any innate attributes of femininity.

On a more sociological plane, Lacanian feminists argue that the privileged position of the phallus in representing desire accounts for the desexualization of the feminine and the splitting of unequal sexual roles in the current gender system. The instantiation of the Law of the Father enjoins human subjects to a symbolic realm of language and culture, which in consequence entails a shift away from the maternal body and the feminine. This is so, in the present social context, since the structuration of the symbolic is secured in a one-sided masculine fashion. Women take primary care of children, while men are the embodiment of the outside, symbolic world and phallic dominance. In political terms, then, the cost of the rudiments of language, logic and symbolization means that the feminine is left either outside or beyond the social. The law of the father triumphs over the loss of the maternal body, leaving the memory of the feminine as a *linguistic construction*, somewhere always beyond the closed circuit of the symbolic – returning only in states of *jouissance*. From this angle, the painful dilemma of women's oppression is all too clear. The repression and devaluation of the feminine, which necessarily follows from the idealization of the symbolic father and the power of the phallus, leads to the objectification of women in culture. Defined as other through the phallic sign, women are unable in general to achieve a sense of sexual agency, being located instead as an imaginary reflector for male desire. Yet, however politically troubling this situation may be, Lacanian feminism makes the argument that it is only by acknowledging the power of the phallus in representing desire that women may eventually seek to destabilize and undo the psychic underpinnings of patriarchy.

As I have argued in previous chapters, however, there are important objections to this Lacanian account of gender determination.

While Lacanian theory offers a suggestive view of women's desexualization and objectification in contemporary culture, it is still open to
the objection that the central premise of an all-determining
symbolic/linguistic structure sets up in advance the situation it
intends to explain. By collapsing the constitutive imaginative dimensions of human sexuality into a symbolic ordering by an ahistorical
'law', the political forces that affect gender relations are fudged into
a certain social inevitability. In ranking unconscious representations
and sexuality as simply the byproduct of a law that makes no room
for social and historical variables, nor its political reformulation in
less repressive forms, Lacanian feminism takes up a reactionary political stance. We need to look more closely at some of the ideological
assumptions at work here. As we have noted, there is no pre-
discursive reality in Lacanian-inspired accounts of sexuality and the
unconscious. (As Lacan theorizes this impossibility: 'How return,
other than by means of a special discourse, to a prediscursive
reality?') According to Lacanian feminism, sexualization and the
unconscious are only constituted once the paternal law of sexual
difference has been effected. Yet notice that this privileging of the
symbolic shifts Freud's postulate of an originary bisexuality to the
very domain of culture itself. The dialectic between the creation of
representations, drives and affects through phantasy on the one hand,
and their subsequent entwinement within social reality on the other,
is lost from view. The imaginary is now little more than an *effect* of
the symbolic. Thus, given this theoretical assumption, it is perhaps
not surprising that the imaginary relation to the maternal body in
Lacanian theory must by definition be devalued and unthinkable. In
respect of gender issues, this raises serious political dilemmas. If
femininity in its hegemonic forms actually arises from the cultural
instantiation of desexualization, what precisely is the ontological
status of the imaginary representations which this law affects and
structures? What are the deep psychic roots of feminine passivity?
Where, exactly, does this 'lack' of feminine sexual agency originate?
Does it arise through a relation to the maternal position itself? Or is
it only constituted through the paternal cultural injunction?

The work of post-Lacanian feminists, such as Cixous and Irigaray,
suggests that we cannot answer such questions concerning the reproduction of the current gender system by recourse to the symbolic law
alone. According to Cixous and Irigaray, as we have seen in Chapter
6, Lacan's thought neglects fundamental pre-Oedipal modes of imaginary experience which structure psychical differences between
women and men. Of key importance in this connection is the unsym-
bolized mother–daughter pre-Oedipal relation. In their view, the
imaginary is not simply an empty receptacle of distorted images (as

with Lacan), but is rather a productive site of identifications and bodily connection with the pre-Oedipal mother. The constitution of human sexuality thus arises from this more fluid and interrelational imaginary domain, and not simply through the instantiation of the symbolic law. Yet, although sexuality unfolds through this pre-Oedipal imaginary, and hence exists *prior* to the mark of symbolic difference and the law, Cixous and Irigaray find the same reinstatement of male domination within this psychic register – a register from which the girl child is forced, or is rather prevented, from recognizing *herself.* The central difficulty here, in both psychic and cultural terms, is that the girl child is unable to separate from her mother and, by extension, to establish individual difference more generally. As we have seen, the girl's failure to achieve individuation and symbolization is analysed by Cixous and Irigaray as resulting from the phallocentric organization of language itself as it affects the imaginary domain. Within the existing male parameters of symbolic discourse, there is simply an absence of any cultural representations from which daughters might identify with their mothers as autonomous and creative agents. Instead, the central determinants of women's experience can only be drawn from, and constructed around, the *maternal function itself.* Unlike the boy child who can appropriate phallocentric discourses with which to symbolize his loss of the maternal body, the girl's more fluid and less split-off imaginary representations of the pre-Oedipal mother leave her permanently mourning a lost object that repeatedly proves resistant to symbolization. Women, as Irigaray comments, are consigned to 'drives without any possible representatives or representations'.[12] Despite this gloomy portrayal of feminine sexuality, however, it is actually women's more fluid self which holds out the liberatory promise for confronting, and unsettling, the male-dominated symbolic order of patriarchy. Unlike the closed circle of the Lacanian symbolic, which both structures and secures sexual difference, Cixous and Irigaray argue that there is a place prior to the law – women's pre-Oedipal imaginary, female specificity, and feminine writing – which can destabilize and free human beings from existing phallocentric appropriations of sexuality.

Interestingly, many of these same themes are taken up in the recent psychoanalytic social theory of Jessica Benjamin. For our purposes, Benjamin's work serves as a useful point of comparison to the work of Cixous and Irigaray since she approaches the question of women's individuation and autonomy from a theoretical position that draws from, yet refashions, the critical theory of the Frankfurt School. Of those aspects in Benjamin's work most relevant to the issues under consideration here, there are two key arguments developed about women's sexual subjectivity. The first involves an attack on the Lacanian and post-Lacanian concept of maternal 'lack'. According to Benjamin, the girl child does suffer extreme problems in separating from the imaginary mother – but this is because the infant constructs powerful representations of her, and not because the mother always exists at some self-same level of 'lack'. Drawing on the research of Chasseguet-Smirgel, Benjamin argues that the Lacanian-inspired view of 'woman as castrated and powerless – a catalogue of lacks – is the exact opposite of the little child's unconscious image of the mother'.[13] Rather, the unconscious representations and affects that the child forges in relation to the mother are so strong and powerful that they actively lead to a desire *for* symbolic differentiation and individuation. The second argument concerns the father and the social and political forces structuring his symbolic role. According to Benjamin, if we are adequately to understand the immense difficulties the girl child has in separating from the pre-Oedipal mother, the process of separation must be seen as further complicated by the 'father–daughter relationship'. Building on a line of thought established by critical theory for the analysis of unconscious processes, Benjamin argues that it is grossly reductionist not to recognize the interaction of social and political forces within existing symbolic representations of the father, and of the enormous role of advanced capitalism in securing conditions for, and reinforcing, paternal dominance as a constitutive cultural force. In this connection, Benjamin criticizes the post-Lacanian tendency to see the father as only the possessor of a phallus; a possession that at once signifies exclusion and is linguistically sedimented as a point of sexual failure for women. Rather, Benjamin suggests that the repudiation of feminine sexuality occurs less through some ahistorical categorization of the gendered self in language than through a repressive social and institutional interaction between the symbolic father and the infant. As Benjamin expresses this:

> The father's own disidentification with his mother, and his continuing need to assert difference from women, make it difficult for him to recognize his daughter as he does his son. He is more likely to see her as a sweet adorable *thing,* a nascent sex object. Consequently we see that little girls often cannot or may not use their connection with the father, in either its defensive or constructive aspects (that is, to deny helplessness or to forge a sense of separate selfhood).[14]

Thus, there is a fundamental debate about the psychical *and* social factors that result in the derogation of female sexual agency and individuality, as well as the possibilities for restructuring these existing features of gender differentiation. For writers such as Cixous and Irigaray, the reproduction of women's oppression is crucially tied to the structuration of the imaginary by the male-dominated symbolic order. The penetration of male-dominated phantasies into the very tissue of imaginary experience, organized and reinforced by phallocentric language and discourse, means that women are unable to attain differentiation. Moreover, the only viable route out of these political realities for women, contend Cixous and Irigaray, is through glimpses (and the reformulation) of an authentic feminine imaginary, a femininity that can disrupt and undermine the phallocentric structure of language. Yet, for writers such as Jessica Benjamin, currently repressive gender arrangements can be challenged in forms other than purely defensive ones. Rather, for Benjamin, it is necessary for psychoanalytic social theory to confront the point that psychical differentiation is fundamentally *affected* by concrete social and political practices that sustain sexual hierarchy and inequality. From this angle, Benjamin seeks to show that existing cultural symptoms and pathologies – that mothers cannot figure for their children as models of separation and agency, that fathers cannot emotionally connect with their children, and so forth – deeply infuse central key categories of psychoanalytic theory itself; and which must, therefore, be challenged. In this connection, she argues, it is necessary to think through new liberatory forms for individuation and gender autonomy. It is necessary to trace out possible circumstances in which women might articulate a new relation with their mother, a relation in which the mother is perceived as an autonomous sexual *subject*; and of how women might establish a paternal identification that allows for a full expression of feminine desire and agency.

Certainly there have been important changes in the structure of gender division in recent decades. Trends such as the breakdown of rigid family roles, changes in parenting patterns, and so on, are indicative of broader changes in the quality of emotional and social relations. Yet, as Benjamin explicitly acknowledges, the intractability of the existing gender structure, and particularly the phallocentric splitting of 'masculine' and 'feminine', highlights that psychical reality and the social field are not commensurate entities. In my view, Benjamin's critique of the perpetuation of these dominant representations of desire is important for several reasons. First, her focus on the social and political forces that affect women's desexualization highlights once again one of the central theoretical deficiencies of Lacanian and post-structuralist theories of sexual difference: their grounding in an absolute and formal view of language which deems all existing gender relations as inherently repressive, thus allowing no room for salience or fluidity in gender relations. Second, and most importantly, Benjamin's approach analyses gender hierarchy and relations of inequality in a manner that accords fundamental weight to the constitutive imaginary dimensions of unconscious sexuality. This is highly significant since it enables us to recognize the active features of the human subject's construction of individuation, and of the complex processes through which the self intertwines with phallocentric dominance as a central social force. From this angle, the urgent feminist political task is to enquire further into these active and constitutive imaginary features of human sexuality, and of how they might be critically deployed to challenge existing constructions of gender and the self within symbolic structures. In this connection, the aestheticizing of the feminine recommended by post-Lacanian feminists such as Cixous and Irigaray would appear at best a limited political strategy. The political task in modern culture is surely more complex. It demands a destruction of polarized sexual terms within gender relations as well as the reintegration of masculine and feminine aspects of the self.

It is precisely this privileging of the determining force of language that suggests the correctness of Kristeva's attempt to reintegrate the subject's deeply unconscious, affective experience into the analysis of gender relations. Reformulating the Lacanian imaginary as an order of affects constituted through a pre-self relation with the maternal body, Kristeva's account of the semiotic aims to identify certain possibilities of language which escape the control of paternal law. Exploring the possibility of semiotic subversions, through disruptive pleasures of poetic language and maternity, Kristeva argues that this affective level of bodily experience provides a basis for transformations of self, gender and social relations. Her ascription of radical transformative value to the semiotic itself, however, raises important political difficulties. As we have seen, whatever the more enabling aspects of semiotic subversion, it remains unclear in Kristeva's work how human subjects might ever creatively reflect and act upon such bodily expressions of repressed selfhood. The central political problem in this respect, as I previously argued, is that the semiotic remains inevitably located with the boundaries of paternal law, and that no reflective or critical capacity is really attributed to subjects in order finally to subvert hegemonic gender norms.

Let me summarize the central points of my argument so far. I have argued that the foundational basis of the symbolic for gender-identity in Lacanian and post-Lacanian feminist thought, that is, the phallus as the instituting mark of sexual identification, acutely delimits the social and cultural transformation of sexuality with which feminism is most explicitly concerned. The fundamental problem in Lacanian-orientated accounts of gender relations lies not so much in their emphasis on the structuring power of the symbolic – clearly some level of symbolic intervention is essential for the very articulation of subjectivity – but rather in the assumption that this is a one-way process of psychic organization. That the profoundly imaginary dimensions of human sexuality are only *constituted* as the *effect* of a pre-given symbolic/linguistic structure particularly exemplifies this problem. Such deterministic emphases in Lacanian theory erase the imaginative self-creation of sexuality – at once psychical and social – and thus imprison feminist discourse in reactionary cultural categories. Nor are the various post-Lacanian attempts to locate a feminine sexuality prior to the social-historical field promising as alternative political strategies. The critical task for psychoanalytic social theory is not to seek for the glimmerings of human sexuality outside of the social-historical world. Rather, the critical task, I want to argue, is to rethink those constructions of the imaginary and phantasized aspects of sexuality (constitutive psychical resources that Freud uncovered in the erotogenicity of the surface of the human body) and the constituted forms of sexuality in the socio-symbolic world. In particular, it is necessary to trace out the intertwining of these aspects of human sexuality and to consider the critical possibilities for intervention in gender construction. From this angle, the following questions arise: what critical strategies exist for exposing the rift between sexuality as phantasmatic and the cultural contingency of gender norms? In what ways can the imaginary dimensions of human sexuality rewrite the possibilities for gender transformation? And how can the undifferentiated state of imaginary sexual pleasure be usefully politically employed in the day-to-day lives of gendered subjects?

The role of the imaginary in emancipating ourselves from male domination is unfortunately controversial, and is still rejected by many. But here I want to suggest that a rethinking of the concept of the imaginary and the primary unconscious might lead to a better understanding of alterations in the representation of desire and gender. We have seen that, in contrast to 'essentialist' theories of gender difference, the symbolic categories of 'men' and 'women' are organized and shaped *through* the imaginary, via processes of internalization and identification with others. The imaginary refers to that emergence of representations of the self and gender-identity that evolves through the subject's immersion *in* the social-historical world. In the current gender system, there can be little doubt that the imaginary encounters a social and political field which is occupied by the male-dominated phallus. Yet while the imaginary production of the gendered self certainly emerges within these symbolic structures, it is not (as much contemporary theory mistakenly assumes) simply created by them. And since this imaginary order of the self is not identical with symbolic categories, we can reject the view that sexual identity and gender can be assigned a universal and determined set of meanings. Whether or not the current symbolic organization of gender is profoundly oppressive (which it surely often is), however, is not really of decisive significance in this context. The point is that we can envisage circumstances in which imaginary representations of self restructure existing modes of the symbolic organization of gender – thereby significantly altering human relations to sexuality.

Consider in this regard the way the women's movement has contributed to profound alterations in the representation of sexuality in recent decades. Among other things, female sexuality has been profoundly reshaped by women actively rejecting the rigid family roles which traditionally have confined their agency to the functions of maternity. The important point about women's collective action, for our purposes at any rate, lies with those alterations in the representation of sexuality which made possible this rejection of female subordination in the first place. It seems difficult to suppose that such changes in gender relations could have been brought about if the imaginary, and its alleged structuring by language, is determined in the way that contemporary theory suggests. Rather, it is clear that the creativity of the psyche has entered here through a socio-symbolic *alteration of representation*. The imaginary underpinning of women's political mobilization has both influenced social policies and in turn has been reshaped by new institutional resources. That is, women's collective action in society has, among other things, led to the institutional redefinition of the objectives and aims of the women's movement. This is clear, for example, in the shift from the 1970s, when an essential female subjectivity was posited against male domination, to the growing tendency today for women's movements to support a plurality of female subject positions (such as sexual, work and political identities). At a theoretical level, then, it can be said that processes of imaginary transformation establish new symbolic possibilities from which a variety of gender issues come to be addressed anew. At the current juncture, we do not know how individuals will respond to recent changes in the representation of sexuality – especially if the relationship between child and mother continues to be transformed, and the mother is fully perceived as an autonomous sexual *subject*. There might be a profound reshaping of existing sexual organizations, gender identities and practices, and perhaps even of those public domains traditionally associated with male-dominated 'rationality'. But whatever these possible sexual worlds, gender transformation presumes the centrality of the imaginary organization of the self.

Subjectivity and the Unconscious: Towards an Affirmative Model of Psychical Production

The position I have sought to develop in this book regarding the profoundly imaginary character of the unconscious comprises several features. Through a detailed examination of Freud's writings in Chapter 1, I argued that the primary unconscious is a constitutive source of representations, drives and affects essential to the formation and continuation of the self. Such an originary capacity to evoke unconscious representation, I suggested, is at once the condition of human agency and autonomy, and a potential source of repression and deformation. For it is within these deep, affective elements of the unconscious imaginary that subjectivity 'opens out' to the self, to others, to reason and to social reality. This 'opening out' of the unconscious occurs within specific symbolic forms of society and politics. The simultaneous empowerment and repression of the self which this signals is not, however, some secondary reordering of psychic processes. Rather, the imaginary dimensions of the unconscious are deeply embedded in, and elaborated through, asymmetrical relations of power which structure modern institutions and social life. As such, the social field figures in this account, not simply as a force which is external, but as a productive basis which constitutes human subjects at the deepest unconscious roots of their lived experience. Yet it would be a mistake, as I have argued throughout, to understand the impact of the social field upon the psyche as all-enveloping and unifying. On the contrary, the psyche and social field interlace in complex, contradictory ways. In this connection, I have argued that human subjects are never passively 'shaped' by symbolic and cultural forms, but actively engage with, and creatively interpret, such significations in the light of their representational activity. The upshot of this, in political terms, is that the unconscious engenders different styles of self-constitution which are enabling/autonomous, alienating/repressive, or some blending of the two. As regards social critique, I have suggested that an attention to the unconscious dimensions of ideology offers the possibility of disclosing certain repressive relations between modes of self-identity and forms of social power.

These ideas on the relation between psychical production and the social field are different in several key respects from the foregoing theoretical standpoints examined in this book. In elaborating these ideas, however, I do not wish to suggest that these approaches ought to be wholly dismissed, since no doubt they contain certain elements of interest. In this connection, I have argued that there are many important and promising themes concerning subjectivity and the unconscious which the foregoing theories investigate. Yet if the ideas I have developed in this study are right, there are important respects in which these theoretical approaches are substantially inadequate. In the remainder of this chapter, I will summarize these conceptual confusions and raise some further considerations about the alternative model of psychical production which I have outlined thus far.

Perhaps a useful way to proceed is by returning to that conceptualization of subjectivity and the unconscious which has most influenced contemporary social theory: Lacanian psychoanalysis. As we have seen, Lacan's innovation lies in his attempt to 'rewrite' psychoanalysis in ways relevant to the analysis of language. According to this literal interpretation, the unconscious is 'structured like a language'. Drawing on structuralist and post-structuralist theories of language, Lacan analyses the unconscious as an endless movement of signifiers – with each signifier bearing the trace of an entire chain or code of signifiers. Through processes of metonomy (displacement) and metaphor (condensation), signifieds or 'stable meanings' for Lacan are nailed down *(points de caption)*. Such meanings, however, are constantly understood to be fading or evaporating due to the fracturing effects of repression. And since the unconscious just *is* this unstable network of signifiers, Lacan views the generation of unity or self-identity as a narcissistic illusion which is properly the function of the imaginary order. On this view, as discussed in Chapter 4, subjectivity is radically split between the imaginary, narcissistic dimensions of the ego and the place of the 'true subject' or 'subject of the unconscious'. The imaginary plenitude of specular selfhood, formed during the mirror stage of development, is forever unsettled by the disruptive power of the unconscious – an order which is constituted for Lacan only with the insertion of the subject into the symbolic. That is to say, the 'scission' effected by the symbolic and language radically disrupts the narcissistic fullness which the subject was previously granted from its own mirror-image. The cost of gaining access to language and symbolization, then, is a crucial decentring of the subject. This is so, according to Lacan, since the small child unconsciously learns that the words available to it only have meaning to the extent that others (that is, prior generations) have endowed them with significance. The symbolic order, then, does not in fact grant us with the means to satisfy our own desires, but actually places us within an *order* of others.

It is possible to characterize more precisely this relationship between language and the formation of the unconscious by recalling the ontological privilege that Lacan accords to 'lack'. For Lacan, there is something eternally unsatisfying about the placing of human demands upon others – and hence desire more generally. Desire is always lacking; it never matches its object, and continually goes awry. On this view, imaginary phantasies are constructions of concealment, through which the infant seeks an escape from the painfulness of 'lack'. Yet the free-floating mirror-images of this imaginary realm must be partially transcended, as we have seen, if the infant is to avoid psychosis and enter received social meanings. This is the very function of the symbolic and language, which tears the infant away from the imaginary and constitutes her or him as a subject. According to Lacan, therefore, the human subject is an effect of language, or, more precisely, an 'effect of the signifier'. Unlike certain versions of post-structuralism, however, this does not simply imply the 'death of the subject' itself. On the contrary: it is in the *spacing* of these linguistic differences that Lacan locates the 'subject of the unconscious'. Lacan's central thesis is that the small child delivers its unarticulated demands and desires, in order to be understood by others, to the differential system of language. However, in so doing, these desires are thereby placed within the differences of language, thereby actually preventing the expression of desire and throwing the subject back onto its fundamental sense of 'lack'. Thus, Lacan equates the unconscious with the gap or spacing that separates one word from another, of meaning from meaning. As Lacan puts this, 'the exteriority of the symbolic in relation to man is the very notion of the unconscious'.[15] And it is because the unconscious is on the outside – that exterior space which can never be reached – that the subject finds itself returned to the deep-rooted realm of 'lack', without fully adequate words or symbols. Hence, for Lacan, the human subject itself represents 'the introduction of a loss into reality'.[16]

Lacan's reconceptualization of the unconscious has been tremendously influential in modern social theory. As we have seen, many social and political theorists have embraced Lacan's work, notwithstanding its essentially pessimistic view of modern culture, with a fervour that has blinded them to the vulnerable theoretical premises upon which it rests. The reasons for this can now be discerned without too much difficulty. Lacan's work confronts in a sophisticated theoretical manner a problem which is central today in social theory: how the individual subject is constructed in and through cultural discourse and the social field. By treating the unconscious as that elusive point at which linguistic articulation at once succeeds and fails, Lacanian doctrine provides a complex picture of the human subject *and* society – a picture which emphasizes both the centrality of symbolic structures in the life of the subject, as well as the disruption caused to these structures through the fracturing effects of the unconscious. The importance of this model of the unconscious lies, then, in its *problematization* of subjectivity itself. Against deterministic accounts which posit a fixed human nature or certain synthetic qualities of the self (as in ego-psychology and certain versions of object-relations theory), Lacanian doctrine emphasizes that subjectivity is constructed only through a continuous process of articulation via the other person. However, as I hope to have shown in Chapter 4, the theoretical premises which inform Lacan's critique of subjectivity and the unconscious are highly questionable and, ultimately, unsatisfactory. It is necessary briefly to retrace these weaknesses in order to justify the claim that social theory ought to abandon Lacan's model of the unconscious.

There are two principal reasons to suppose that Lacanian-orientated theoretical work is inadequate for the study of social action. The first concerns the undercutting of the unconscious by 'lack'. On this view, the imaginary is no more than a construction of concealment, papering over that painful 'lack' which lies at the heart of human subjectivity. As I argued earlier, however, there is good reason to suppose that 'lack' cannot pre-exist the organization of psychic space, but can only be constituted through the investment of desire. The problem, in brief, is that Lacanian doctrine mistakenly inverts the relationship between the unconscious and object-loss. Any lacking object can only come to exist *as* lacking to the extent that it is invested through representations, drives and affects. The first part-object which is privileged in psychoanalytic theory, the breast, is at once present *and* absent (or at least always potentially absent) and is forged through an originary relation to the unconscious. Yet having bracketed the unconscious to those secondary formations of language and symbolic residues, Lacanian theory has no coherent way of conceptualizing this. Instead, the imaginary character of psychic processes is reduced to little more than a 'sideshow' – always and everywhere filling in that 'lack' in the subject's being. In social and political terms, the consequences of this ontological privileging of 'lack' are the levelling and homogenizing of culture, creativity and self-fulfilment. Cultural association, whether at the level of personal relationships or the more general level of social collectivity, is rendered a blank-fiction, the 'suturing' effects of deeper forces. As such, social critique is likewise stripped of any ethical dimension. All social practices, from culturally enhancing ones to the most politically destructive, leave human subjects inherently dissatisfied. But while this view may capture certain phenomenological features of late capitalism, it fails to deal with the fundamental drive of the unconscious for pleasure, satisfaction, fulfilment. Lacanian doctrine, as Cornelius Castoriadis writes, offers a conceptual focus only on 'the citizen walking in the street – who is full of unrealizable desires, and even of unsatisfied needs, all of which are respectable, important and decisive. But this is not what is at issue in the psychoanalytical perspective. *In psychical reality all desires are not fulfillable, they are always fulfilled.*'[17]

The second reason concerns Lacan's structuralist interpretation of the unconscious. I have argued that Lacan's conceptualization of the conscious/unconscious dualism as a linguistic relation culminates in aporias. My comments here only focus on certain problems and issues which have been analysed more fully in preceding chapters. Briefly put, Lacan's argument for a purely 'literal' understanding of the unconscious appears vulnerable when we consider the centrality that Freud ascribes to representation in the work of the primary processes. Freud outlined time and again that the unconscious, while its region of existence is beyond the grasp of direct description, is unaware of negation, time or contradiction. And it is for this reason that he argued it is impossible to accord the phenomenon of language a place within the workings of the unconscious. For Freud, language is found only within the secondary processes. The conscious-preconscious system of secondary processes comprises 'word' and 'thing' presentations, while an 'unconscious presentation is the presentation of the thing alone'.[18] And it is due to this separation that traditional structures of thought are powerless before the opacity of the unconscious. Accordingly, it is unlikely, in my view, that the work of unconscious representation can be comprehended or usefully analysed by being assimilated to structural linguistics.

In opposing Lacan's interpretation, I refer again to an important passage from the sixth chapter of *The Interpretation of Dreams*, a passage in which Freud contrasts the specificity of unconscious processes with the secondary modes of waking language. 'The unconscious', Freud remarks, 'is not simply more careless, more irrational, more forgetful and more incomplete than waking thought; it is completely different from it qualitatively and for that reason not immediately comparable with it. It does not think, calculate or judge in any way at all; *it restricts itself to giving things a new form.*'[19] It is this capacity for the forming of representation which most specifically characterizes the unconscious as irreducible to structural causation. That is to say, the capacity of the unconscious to create representation presupposes more than the mere 'condition' of being within language. In short, there is a 'dynamic unconscious'. This should not imply the existence of some 'hidden' substance, like a bodily kidney or heart. Rather, it designates that deep realm of the psyche which only makes itself known through the distortions it inflicts on consciousness. And it is from this primordial capacity of the psyche to create representation upon which the human being's ability to use language rests.[20]

To review. Rejecting the currently fashionable view that the unconscious is linguistically structured also entails rejecting the presupposition of 'lack' upon which this rests. What, then, should replace this conception of subjectivity and the unconscious?

I have suggested in this study that an account of the psyche that casts the conscious/unconscious dualism as the capacity to create representation would have as its central presupposition the *affirmative character* of psychical production. That is to say, unconscious representation does not cover over, or stand in for, a 'lack' or 'gap' which is taken to lie at the centre of subjectivity. (This standpoint does not imply, it should be emphasized, that psychical reality never encounters absence. What I am suggesting, though, is that for an object to be experienced as absent or lacking it must have first been invested with desire.[21]) The general point is rather that unconscious representation attains significance through its own material and organization. A central clue as to what occurs here is provided by Freud's linkage of the first longed-for satisfaction with the representational or phantasmatic nature of the unconscious itself. According to Freud, unconscious representations are not so much wish-fulfilments as fulfilled wishes. These fulfilled wishes, however, should not be understood as desire in some sense attaining or subsuming its object. For, as we have seen, the objects of unconscious desire are essentially contingent and replaceable. On the contrary, the real source of pleasure at the level of the unconscious is the *work of representation as such*. When the libidinal drives achieve representation the unconscious reaps pleasure – regardless of whether the actual 'object' pleases or frustrates at the level of consciousness. And this is one reason why the very experience of pleasure is so tantalizingly obscure; it is itself a *swerving* of representational forms in the libidinal economy.

The significance of an affirmative view of psychical reality is that it directly confronts what Lacanian theory in fact ignores: that the organization of unconscious representation is the central means of procuring satisfaction within personal and social relations. That is to say, social practices and ideologies are always structured in and through *representation*. To raise such considerations is to focus attention toward the social and political dimensions of the imaginary investment in pleasure. This focus does not, however, 'bring in' a dimension of experience external to unconscious mechanisms. For political and cultural influences had been there from the beginning. The unconscious pleasures attained through states of representation are always organized within the power relations of specific forms of social and institutional life. The reproduction of representational systems of all kinds, from images of sexuality in film and television to the medicalization and technical control of sickness and death in modern social life, touch deeply upon our unconscious investments; gratifications which are mutually imbricated with our existing systems of power. Once this is recognized, I argue, we can begin to look at the *forms* in which social ideologies draw upon the unconscious economy of human subjects. On this basis it is possible to look at economies of pleasure, compromise formations and defence mechanisms which intersect with the reshaping of a variety of social practices and institutions. It is possible to evaluate the quality of individuality and community, tracing the complex trade-offs between imaginary investments and social reality. At the same time, since this approach does not see subjectivity as the 'filling-in' of a 'lack', social practices are understood as deeply conditioned by the imaginary forms of the unconscious. That is to say, subjectivity is accorded its due place in social analysis. Social ideologies are not simply 'implanted' into a lacking subject; rather, the reproduction of states of representation depend upon engaging the affective investments of human beings.

The problem that must be confronted, then, concerns the complex, dialectical interplay between the imaginary dimensions of the unconscious and the structuring of states of representation. In this study, I have not tried to formulate a systematic account of this dialectic, but rather have suggested ways of thinking about the unconscious and its relation to action, social structures and institutional life. An adequate account of the unconscious in relation to the social field, I think, should focus on three central levels, each of which is only methodologically distinguishable. The first concerns the profoundly imaginary character of unconscious representation. It must be recognized that the unconscious imaginary is the creative work of representation as such. To grasp the primary unconscious is to grasp the imaginary way subjectivity 'opens out' to self-identity, others, reason, society and political engagement. The second concerns the interlacing of these imaginary forms with symbolic states of representation, as the productive site of social and cultural ideologies. This level focuses on the intertwining of imaginary forms (drives, image-production, originary narcissistic investments) with broader social influences of pleasure (symbolic representational forms). It must be recognized that subjects are never passively determined by such symbolic forms, but rather actively interpret (or, as Winnicott says, 'find') social significations through their representational activity. The third level is that of concrete ideological relations of power and domination. It must be recognized that the imaginary and symbolic forms through which human subjects derive pleasure are structured within culturally specific social and political relations.

What I am suggesting, then, is that it is mistaken to sever the unconscious and repressed desire from concrete relations of social and political power. For we live in a world in which fundamental matters of moral significance, such as our existential relation to birth, sexuality and death, are endlessly deferred and repressed from critical self-reflection. This 'forgetfulness' itself is unconsciously driven, structured within broader encompassing social ideologies and political forces. This is certainly the case in those domains of mass culture marked today by crippling forms of oppression. As the writings of Adorno and Marcuse make clear, the self is increasingly rendered an 'object' in mass culture, an entity 'eroticized', subject to commodification and 'repressive desublimation'. As a result, it might be argued, aggression and hatred in modern culture goes underground, resurfacing as the 'return of the repressed' – and one obvious articulation of this is the ever-threatening possibility of nuclear self-destruction. Clearly, these are extremely complex issues. But my argument is that a theory which posits the unconscious as the result of the entry into language as such can only provide a limited understanding of the links between psychical and social reality. Such a focus is the end-point of the problem, as it were, rather than the beginnings for social critique. To recognize, however, that unconscious desire is deeply buried, sedimented in social practices and systems of domination, offers an alternative kind of strategy for social analysis. It is one that recognizes that the maintenance and transformation of our existing systems of power are closely related to the possibilities for the expressive and affective articulation of the self. That is to say, it takes the fulfilment and emotional well-being of human subjects as its overriding concern.

Summary

A few summary comments on the foregoing points might be useful at this stage. I have outlined certain theoretical and substantive problems – problems that were analysed in some considerable detail in previous chapters – in Lacanian-orientated and post-structuralist approaches to the unconscious and social relations. In an attempt to move beyond these limitations, I have suggested several respects in which the unconscious might be reconceptualized for developing a more adequate conception of human subjectivity for the purposes of social and political analysis. I compare the basic premises of Lacanian and post-structuralist theories with this alternative position, which I call an affirmative model of psychical production (see Table 7.1).

Table 7.1 Psychical production: comparisons between the Lacanian/post-structuralist model and an affirmative model

Lacanian-inspired post-structuralist model	Affirmative model of psychical production
Defines the unconscious as an organized structure, conceived as a differential system of linguistic elements.	Defines the unconscious as a distinct psychic system that produces representations, drives, affects.
Defines the imaginary as alienating and illusory concealments, generated by a deeper ontological 'lack'.	Sees the unconscious imaginary as a constitutive and creative feature of psychic life; a feature that engenders both active object-involvement and object-loss.
Views the self as narcissistic object of imaginary misrecognition, decentred by determining power of the symbolic.	Treats modes of self-identity as the interlacing of imaginary representational activity and symbolic forms, involving both autonomy and heteronomy.
Sees alienation of the self as intrinsically connected to entry into symbolic order of language as such.	Traces libertory and repressive paths of self-identity as deeply embedded in asymmetrical relations of power.
Defines self-transgression in the aesthetic force of *jouissance*, of absence, the real order.	Defines individual and collective autonomy as transformed relation between conscious intention and unconscious representation; sees the imaginary as crucial to such reorganization to the economy of the self.

Some Connections and Implications

We can explore some possible implications of this affirmative model of psychical production by considering a specific example. Let me very briefly focus on some theoretical connections concerning the issue of racism, an issue that has been discussed in previous chapters.

Racism is perhaps one of the most complex destructive forms of social categorization. On the one hand, 'race' is an empty marker – a category whose attributes depend on largely superficial differences. On the other hand, the psychic investment in these differences forged through racist ideology is widespread across social division and has been one of the major causes of human suffering in the modern world.

The contribution of psychoanalytic theory to the interpretation of this phenomenon, as previously suggested, focuses upon how unconscious dynamics of subjectivity are deeply inscribed with broader social forces which contribute to the reproduction of racism. In Lacanian and post-Lacanian accounts of racist ideology, the key categories of explanation comprise certain primordial mirror-illusions – through which the internal divisions of desire are constituted – within antagonistic relations between self and other. On this view, aspects of self and non-self are structured linguistically through reference to the Other, in which fundamental lines of social division are drawn and established. Racist fantasies are thereby understood as a displacement of the self's internal otherness, lack and fragmentation onto this Other, an enemy which functions as an external container of anxiety.

Yet while Lacanian theory is right to stress that racist ideology establishes linguistic markers or boundaries between self and others, it would be a mistake to see this as the sole characteristic of racism. To the white racist, a black person is not simply a collection of non-white characteristics; and similarly, for the anti-Semite, the Jew is not merely some unbearable 'marker of difference' from the non-Jewish world. Racism tends to be promoted by deeper affective identifications, desires and affects than Lacanian-inspired social theory recognizes. In this connection, one of the most striking features about Adorno's study of anti-Semitism is its discovery of 'reversals of affect' in racist fear. Paranoid beliefs of a 'Jewish conspiracy', Adorno argues, transfer affects of identificatory admiration with Jews into affects of hate against Jews. In this way, the danger of the Jew for the anti-Semite inverts a disguised identification with the imagined power of the hated object. That is to say, Jews are constructed as a viable target of hate and aggression through projective delusions and mass paranoia. 'The out-group, the chosen foe', writes Adorno, 'represents an *eternal challenge*'.[22] This thesis may very well be valid for the phenomenon of racist ideology as a whole. As we have seen, however, the analysis of these trends developed by Adorno and others in critical theory tends to link psychic dispositions to social configurations in a reductionistic fashion – severing the contradictory ways in which imaginary representations of the self interlace with the broader encompassing symbolic forms of modern culture.

While these approaches raise some important questions about the links between unconscious processes and racial attributions, the crux of the matter lies elsewhere. For the issue of the alienation of desire, manifested either through language or social manipulation in the above discussion, does not raise the basic question about the *fulfilment* of unconscious pleasure embedded in racist practices. Theories which fail to call into question the imaginary forms of unconscious pleasure attained in racist ideology cannot comprehend the pain and repression they cause to their subjects, nor their intertwining in the network of broader social relations. In contrast, the unconscious mediation of racist ideology, I suggest, comprises two related dimensions. The first concerns the specific form of imaginary representations, driven and overdetermined by unconscious processes of condensation, displacement, reversal of affect, and so on. What is at stake here are the destructive and pathological modes by which the self constitutes a 'dehumanized other'; an out-group invested with hate and denigration. Unconscious pleasure and fulfilment, it should be made clear, are centrally involved in any such representational configuration. Rustin expresses this well:

> Expressions of prejudice, rejection, or distaste fulfil active, albeit unconscious, emotional needs for those who make them – they get rid of something unwanted or uncomfortable out of the self, where they cause mental conflict and pain, into some external container, whose pain is either disregarded as of no account or, worse still, has a perverse value for those who project it in its visible existence outside the self. One can easily see how social groups made to receive the projections of collectivities superior to them will be filled with the desire to push them on to some group still more vulnerable than they, and thus how maltreatment is passed down the social status ladder from group to group. Racism can thus be seen to involve states of projective identification, in which hated self-attributes of members of the group gripped by prejudice are phantasied to exist in members of the stigmatized race.[23]

This passage captures (albeit implicitly) the *representational pleasure* inherent in all racist attribution. The significance of these projective mechanisms is not simply that they unify destructive affects of hate around the targeted object. The point is rather that such representations and affects provide unconscious pleasure and gratification; as a 'deep affective structure' for the continuity of the self. And it is precisely because of the representational pleasure attained through projection that racism has so often proved intractable in the face of reasoned arguments and anti-racist strategies.

The reproduction of such psychical states connects directly to the second dimension of analysis: the entwinement of the unconscious and broader encompassing social influences. No doubt the perpetuation of racist attitudes often 'filters through' social groups and classes – from one out-group to another, as it were – in the manner that Rustin's characterization suggests. Yet, at a theoretical level, such an understanding of culturally displaced affect provides only a limited grasp of the psychic and social processes of racism. The central problem of this view is its implication that racism is perpetuated through an actual 'passing on' of the threat of the other; thus ignoring the point that the social escalation of racist ideology occurs through the medium of phantasy. Perhaps more important, then, is that all unconscious forms of racist fear are centred within broader encompassing socio-symbolic *fields of representation*. That is to say, there is a connecting track between the production of individual phantasy on the one side, and the control of fields of representation within social institutions and political relations on the other. From this angle, it can be readily acknowledged that existing imaginary *forms* of racism are structured within historically specific social processes. Racism in the twentieth century, for example, has firmly embedded unconscious processes within institutionalized forms of Western colonialist domination, imperialism, economic oppression, and so on. Social orders founded upon racial domination, such as Nazi Germany and South Africa, construct human relations through deep imaginary valorized states of hate, greed and destruction. And, in turn, these imaginary forms 'feed back' into the social field to produce exclusion and marginalization. Indeed, the link between unconscious processes and social relations of racism have often spiralled into a complete rejection of the unpredictability and diversity of modernity itself. In this connection, one of the most interesting aspects of Theweleit's analysis of the sexual fantasies of men in the Fascist Freikorps of Weimar Germany concerns their inability to tolerate any forms of difference or emotional ambivalence. 'The monumentalism of Fascism', writes Theweleit, 'would seem to be a safety mechanism against the bewildering multiplicity of the living. The more lifeless, regimented and monumental reality appears to be, the more secure the men feel.'[24] So, too, unconscious dynamics of racism can provide a defence against the complexities of modern social life. The general point, then, is that all forms of unconscious representation and phantasy are shaped by, yet actively reshape, broader social fields of representation. Recognizing this dual nature of representational forms is crucial, I believe, for theorizing forms of imaginary pleasure, the network of social relations they are embedded in, and the restructuring of those relations which they help constitute.

Social Critique and the Mediation of Human Needs through Psychoanalysis

The question of social critique poses the final issue of this study: human needs and their relation to social transformation. The social-theoretical contributions examined in the foregoing chapters offer only limited and partial accounts of the relation between self-transformation and political community. In differing conceptual ways, as we have seen, these approaches posit that deployments of power or language are inseparable from the repression of the self, thereby closing down the possibilities for the practical intervention of social critique. Ideology either processes the self through the reifying dynamics of 'self-preservation' (critical theory), or deposits the subject at the self-same position of 'lack' and 'misrecognition' (Lacanian-inspired theory and post-structuralism). Yet the idea that our capacity for self-transformation and critical reflection is fully contaminated by either narcissistic illusions or the drive for self-preservation is weak precisely in respect of providing a critique of this vulnerability. Moreover, the social and political premises of these approaches, I have argued, are unduly negative. Lost is the sense in which human needs and desires intersect with the social field in conflictive ways; lost is the sense in which specific forms of social and political organization either encourage or inhibit the restructuring of human social relationships. This is not to deny, of course, the diverse liberating impulses which inform these theoretical approaches. Rather, it is to claim that these approaches ultimately fail to conceptually illuminate the processes through which the self might be liberated from politically destructive relations of conflict and antagonism.

A more concrete conception of self-transformation and collective autonomy can be discerned only by rethinking the radical nature of the unconscious imaginary and its relation to human needs. While unconscious desire certainly always separates out from biological needs within the domain of culture, I have suggested that social critique should install itself precisely at this point of differentiation. For it is because of the existence of certain transhistorical human needs – such as infantile helplessness, the need for warmth and nourishment, separation and individuation, attachment, and so on – that a vital nexus arises between the material interests of human beings and the creative space in which unconscious desire and symbolization unfolds. These transhistorical human needs, while certainly always historically and socially mediated, provide something of a baseline for social critique and political judgement.[25] This should not imply, however, that human needs are some final 'court of appeal' in the regulation of human affairs. As we have seen, destructive and hateful states of psychic development are also central to the shaping of the self; and clearly any theory which automatically privileges such needs runs the risk of promoting a destructive cultural order. Rather, the general point, as Habermas has argued, is that human needs are central to any energizing vision of collective autonomy as well as the subjective desires of individuals. From this angle, human needs are bound up, as it were, with the highest cultural and political values which human beings can attain – as the ongoing communal search for new forms of subjectivity, autonomy and freedom demonstrate. It is important to stress in this context that social critique cannot legislate in advance as to how human needs and their symbolic elaboration will develop. Like subjectivity itself, the expression of human needs is not fixed in this way. In any politics which places human relationships, dispositions and needs centrally at stake, as the history of the women's movement illustrates, renewing attention to shifting, and often uneven, needs and desires is an ongoing process of critical self-reflection. 'The fundamental political question', as Terry Eagleton has argued, 'is that of demanding an equal right with others to discover what one might become, not of assuming some already fully-fashioned identity which is merely repressed'.[26]

Such a stress on the creative self-transformation of human needs is clearly at odds with the foregoing theories, based as they are upon the subject's lack of critical reflexiveness. By stressing the creative character of psychic processes in the forging of the self and in social life more generally, I have sought to highlight the radical involvement of critical self-reflection in processes of cultural resistance and transformation. The imaginary and social activity are linked, I have suggested, through the ability of human beings to critically reflect upon the deeper sources of their representational activity, sexuality, selfhood, needs and feelings. These reflexive achievements, which entail a *transformation* between the conscious self and unconscious representation, are certainly presupposed within the clinical practice of psychoanalysis itself. The aim of psychoanalysis, as Freud tirelessly repeats, is to encourage women and men to reflect, and become more conscious of, their imaginary forms of self-representation. As regards social critique, it is this aspect of critical self-involvement which suggests the very possibility of interpreting, and hence seeking to reshape, the links between human experience and social institutions. On this basis, social critique is concerned to trace out the *partially* mystified ways in which human agency is repressed, or displaced in others. And in doing so it contributes at a more general level to emancipatory claims for the quality of individuality and the quality of political community.

A more comprehensive treatment of the relations between human reflexivity and unconscious representation, and the broader connections with social and political transformation, will have to confront head-on the question of the imaginary character of human subjectivity. In conclusion, though, it should be emphasized that the capacity of the subject for critical self-reflection, of placing social boundaries in question, is only a *possibility* of human social relationships – which, in turn, is linked to the question of *alternative futures*. At the current juncture of world history, where the future of modernity is pitted against an unparalleled capability for nuclear destruction on the one hand, and the possibility of ecological disaster on the other, only the most myopically optimistic would claim that our capacity for reflexivity and autonomy is predestined. Certainly, the twentieth century has provided some of the most brutal examples of terroristic social orders in which even the last glimpses of human reflectiveness and affectivity appear to have been all but obliterated. Yet while the possibilities for individual and collective autonomy are certainly far from predestined, the lesson offered from psychoanalysis is double-edged. While the theory of the unconscious demonstrates the human subject to be non-identical, internally pitted against itself, it equally finds within the recesses of the psyche the seeds of creativity, innovation, self-renewal. In short, the possibility of an alternative future. As concerns the pursuit of this goal, Paul Ricoeur comments:

> the fact of being conscious can neither be suppressed nor destroyed. For it is in relation to the possibility of becoming conscious, in relation to the task of achieving conscious insight, that the concept of a psychical representative of an instinct becomes meaningful. Its meaning is this: however remote the primary instinctual representatives, however distorted their derivatives, they still appertain to the delimitation of meaning; they can in principle be translated into terms of the conscious psychism. In short, psychoanalysis is possible as a return to consciousness because, in a certain way, the unconscious is homogeneous with consciousness; it is its relative other, and not the absolute other.[27]

It is in seeking to understand this 'relative other' of the unconscious, both what is non-identical in ourselves as well as in other human beings, that subjectivity, autonomy and desire may be more fully realized and thus transformed. The nature of the unconscious does not betoken irreversible repression, but is rather intrinsic to the search for self-identity, human autonomy and political community.

Notes and References

Preface

1. Jeffrey Prager, *Presenting the Past: Psychoanalysis and the Sociology of Misremembering* (Cambridge, MA: Harvard University Press, 1998), p. 140.
2. See Zygmunt Bauman, *Postmodernity and its Discontents* (Cambridge: Polity Press, 1998), pp. 1–4.
3. See, for example, Frederick Crews's rhetorical essay 'The unknown Freud', *New York Review of Books*, 18 November 1993, pp. 55–66; and, more recently, F. Crews (ed.), *Unauthorized Freud* (New York: Viking, 1998).
4. Tom Wolfe, 'Sorry, but your soul just died', *Forbes ASAP*, 2 December 1996, p. 218.
5. Anthony Elliott, *Subject to Ourselves: Social Theory, Psychoanalysis and Postmodernity* (Cambridge: Polity Press, 1996).
6. See, for example, the reviews by Janet Sayers, *Sociology*, Vol. 27, No. 4, 1993, pp. 714–16; Steve Pile, *Environment and Planning D: Society and Space*, Vol. 11, 1993, pp. 607–8; Jennifer L. Pierce, *Contemporary Sociology*, No. 4, July 1993, pp. 763–4; Alberto Paolini, *Thesis 11*, No. 37, 1994, pp. 172–6; Nick Stevenson, 'Contraflows in Critical Theory', *Critical Sociology*, Vol. 21, No. 1, pp. 121–30.
7. Anthony Elliott (ed.), *Freud 2000* (Cambridge: Polity Press, 1998; New York: Routledge, 1999).
8. Andrew Scull, 'The end of Freud?', *Times Literary Supplement*, 30 October 1998, pp. 9–10. The quotations are from p. 10.
9. For summary discussion of this research see Jay Greenberg, *Oedipus and Beyond* (Cambridge, MA: Harvard University Press, 1991); Anthony Elliott, 'The affirmation of primary repression rethought', in A. Elliott and S. Frosh (eds), *Psychoanalysis in Contexts: Paths between Theory and Modern Culture* (London and New York: Routledge, 1995), pp. 36–52.
10. The rise of the concept of intersubjectivity in psychoanalysis has been palpable during the 1990s, and is especially evident in American relational theory. 'Intersubjectivity', as the inter-

subjective psychoanalysts Robert Stolorow and George Atwood write, 'brings to focus *both* the individual's world of inner experience *and* its embeddedness with other such worlds in a continual flow of reciprocal mutual influence'. *Contexts of Being: The Intersubjective Foundations of Psychological Life* (Hillsdale, NJ: Analytic Press, 1992), p. 18. See also Jessica Benjamin, 'Recognition and destruction: an outline of intersubjectivity', in her *Like Subjects, Love Objects: Essays on Recognition and Sexual Difference* (New Haven, CT: Yale University Press, 1995).

11. Jessica Benjamin, *Shadow of the Other* (New York: Routledge, 1998), p. 93. The following reference is also to this page.

12. See Anthony Elliott and Charles Spezzano, 'Psychoanalysis at its limits: navigating the postmodern turn', *Psychoanalytic Quarterly*, 1996.

13. I develop such a line in *Subject to Ourselves: Social Theory, Psychoanalysis and Postmodernity* (Cambridge: Polity Press and Cambridge, MA: Blackwell, 1996). See also Stephen Frosh, *Identity Crises* (London: Macmillan, 1991) and James M. Glass, *Shattered Selves: Multiple Personality in a Postmodern World* (Ithaca, NY: Cornell University Press, 1993).

Introduction

1. I should strongly emphasize that the position I develop in this study is not an attempt to 'integrate' German and French perspectives on these issues; perspectives which, in any case, are largely contradictory. Nor is it an attempt to uncover the central weaknesses of these standpoints through an assessment of other psychoanalytic approaches – although references are made to developments in objects-relations theory, Kleinian theory and self-psychology. I have chosen against such an interpretative strategy since the traditions of thought under review here, especially Lacanian theory, have developed powerful critiques of psychoanalytic approaches which privilege the ego or self. My own view, therefore, is that it is necessary to demonstrate that an adequate understanding of the relations between the psyche and social field is impossible from within the social-theoretical perspectives under consideration because of their vulnerable and unquestioned ideological assumptions. It is only once this is shown that a more fruitful approach may be developed.

2. See Terry Eagleton, *The Ideology of the Aesthetic* (Oxford: Basil Blackwell, 1990), Chapter 14. For excellent theoretical accounts of the impasses of post-structuralism see Manfred Frank, *What is NeoStructuralism?* (Minneapolis: University of

Minnesota Press, 1989) and Peter Dews, *Logics of Disintegration* (London: Verso, 1987).

3. The classic account of these problems is now surely Paul Ricoeur, *Freud and Philosophy: An Essay on Interpretation* (New Haven, CT: Yale University Press, 1970).

4. The 'primary unconscious' refers to the constitutive mechanisms of the primary processes – condensation, displacement, considerations of representation, and the transfer of affect. See Sigmund Freud, 'The unconscious', *The Standard Edition of the Complete Psychological Works of Sigmund Freud* [hereafter *SE*], trans. J. Strachey (London: Hogarth Press, 1953–73), Volume XIV. The primary unconscious is discussed in Chapter 1.

5. This aspect of the work of Castoriadis, which I draw on considerably throughout this study, is most fully presented in *The Imaginary Institution of Society* (Cambridge: Polity Press, 1987).

6. The institutional parameters of these developments as they impact upon subjectivity have been fruitfully developed in the writings of Anthony Giddens. See for example *The Consequences of Modernity* (Cambridge: Polity Press, 1990) and *Modernity and Self-identity* (Cambridge: Polity Press, 1991).

Chapter 1

1. See Talcott Parsons, 'Psychoanalysis and the social structure', *Psychoanalytic Quarterly*, 19, 3 (1950), pp. 371ff. For a more recent outline of this approach see Robert Bocock, *Freud and Modern Society* (Berkshire: Van Nostrand Reinhold, 1976), and his *Sigmund Freud* (London: Tavistock, 1983).

2. Freud writes that unconscious processes 'are not ordered temporally, are not altered by the passage of time; they have no reference to time at all'. 'The unconscious', *SE*, XIV, p. 187.

3. Sigmund Freud, *The Interpretation of Dreams*, SE, V, p. 600.

4. Sigmund Freud, 'Formulations on the two principles of mental functioning', *SE*, XII, p. 225.

5. Juliet Mitchell, *Psychoanalysis and Feminism* (London: Penguin, 1974), p. 6.

6. Sigmund Freud, *An Outline of Psycho-analysis*, SE, XXIII, p. 154.

7. Freud, 'The unconscious', pp. 161–215.

8. Sigmund Freud, *The Ego and the Id*, SE, XIX, p. 15.

9. Sigmund Freud, 'Repression', *SE*, XIV, p. 147.

10. Ibid., p. 148.

11. Freud, 'The unconscious', p. 166.

12. Freud, *The Interpretation of Dreams*, SE, IV, p. 160.

13. Ibid., *SE*, V, p. 507.

14. Ibid. p. 525 (my emphasis). This quotation, however, is from Cornelius Castoriadis's translation of the original German which contains the phrase 'without any definite endings'. The English and French translations omit this vital remark: see Castoriadis, *The Imaginary Institution of Society*, (Cambridge: Polity Press, 1987) pp. 279–81 and his comments at n.7, p. 401.
15. Freud, *The Interpretation of Dreams*, SE, V, p. 37.
16. Freud, 'The unconscious', p. 177.
17. Castoriadis, *The Imaginary Institution of Society*, pp. 274–91 (my emphasis).
18. Ibid., p. 282.
19. Cornelius Castoriadis, *Crossroads in the Labyrinth* (Cambridge, MA: MIT Press, 1984), p. 22.
20. For a fuller discussion of Freud's account of the ego as a physical energy se J. Laplanche and J.B. Pontalis, *The Language of Psychoanalysis* (London: Hogarth, 1985), pp. 130–43.
21. Freud, *An Outline of Psycho-analysis*, p.188 (original emphasis).
22. Sigmund Freud, 'Psycho-analytic notes on an autobiographical account of a case of paranoia', SE, XII, pp. 60–1.
23. Sigmund Freud, 'Two encyclopedia articles', SE, XVIII, p. 257.
24. Jean Laplanche, *Life and Death in Psychoanalysis* (Baltimore, MD: Johns Hopkins University Press, (1976) p. 73.
25. Sigmund Freud, 'Mourning and melancholia', SE, XIV, p. 255.
26. Freud, *The Ego and the Id*, p. 30.
27. Richard Wollheim, *Freud* (London: Fontana, 1971), p. 189.
28. Sigmund Freud, *Civilization and its Discontents*, SE, XXI, pp. 105–6, n.3.
29. Juliet Mitchell, *The Selected Melanie Klein* (London: Penguin, 1986), p. 26.
30. Laplanche and Pontalis, *The Language of Psychoanalysis*, p. 286.
31. The phantasy of castration is said to operate in different ways in the case of males and females. Whereas the boy develops castration anxiety as a result of the fear which accompanies his phantasized sexual activities, in the case of the girl the absence of the phallus is experienced as a wrong suffered under the law. See Laplanche and Pontalis's discussion of these differences in *The Language of Psychoanalysis*, pp. 56–9.
32. The classic objections to the Oedipus complex were outlined in the 1920s by Bronislaw Malinowski in *Sex and Repression in Savage Society* (New York: Humanities Press, 1927).
33. Freud, *The Ego and the Id*, p. 34.
34. Freud, '*Civilization and its Discontents*', p. 77.
35. Sigmund Freud, *New Introductory Lectures on Psycho-analysis*, SE, XXII, p. 67.

254 SOCIAL THEORY AND PSYCHOANALYSIS IN TRANSITION

36. This concept has been further developed by Julia Kristeva for understanding the processes by which the individual subject is inserted into the symbolic order: see 'Freud and love: treatment and its discontents', in her *Tales of Love* (New York: Columbia University Press, 1987) pp. 26–9.
37. Philip Rieff, *Freud: The Mind of the Moralist* (Chicago, IL: University of Chicago Press, 1979), pp. 159–60.
38. Sigmund Freud, 'My contact with Josef Popper-Lynkeus', *SE*, XXII, p. 221.
39. Rieff, *Freud*, pp. 59–60.
40. Terry Eagleton, *The Ideology of the Aesthetic* (Oxford: Basil Blackwell, 1990), p. 273.
41. Russell Jacoby, *Social Amnesia* (Boston, MA: Beacon Press, 1975), p. 128.
42. Freud, *New Introductory Lectures*, p. 77.

Chapter 2

1. For a general discussion of the integration of psychoanalysis into the theoretical work of the first generation of critical theory see Martin Jay, *The Dialectical Imagination* (Boston, MA: Little, Brown and Company, 1973), Chapter 3; David Held, *Introduction to Critical Theory* (London: Hutchinson, 1980), Chapter 4.
2. Theodor Adorno, 'Sociology and psychology', *New Left Review*, 46 (1967), p. 78.
3. See H. Dubiel, *Theory and Politics* (Boston, MA: MIT Press, 1984).
4. For an overview of the concepts of the 'totally administered world' and 'administered subject' as the common denominator in the theoretical works of Marcuse and Adorno, see Axel Honneth, 'Critical theory', in A. Giddens and J.H. Turner (eds), *Social Theory Today* (Cambridge: Polity Press, 1987), p. 371.
5. Herbert Marcuse, *Eros and Civilization: A Philosophical Inquiry into Freud* (London: Ark, 1956), p. 31.
6. Cf. Marcuse's 'Critique of neo-Freudian revisionism', printed as the epilogue of *Eros and Civilization*, pp. 238–74.
7. Max Horkheimer and Theodor Adorno, *Dialectic of Enlightenment* (London: Allen Lane, 1973), p. 54.
8. Marcuse, *Eros and Civilization*, p. 17.
9. Ibid., pp. 11–12.
10. Ibid., p. 16.
11. Ibid., p. 12.
12. Ibid., p. 37.

13. Ibid., pp. 35ff.
14. Herbert Marcuse, *Five Lectures: Psychoanalysis, Politics and Utopia* (London: Allen Lane, 1970), pp. 8–9.
15. Marcuse, *Eros and Civilization*, p. 47.
16. Theodor Adorno, 'Zum Verhaltnis von Soziologie und Psychologie', *Soziologische Schriften*, 1 (1955), vol. 8. References in this study are to the English translation by Irving N. Wohlfarth, 'Sociology and psychology', 'Freudian theory and the pattern of Fascist propaganda', repr. in A. Arato and E. Gebhardt (eds), *The Essential Frankfurt School Reader* (New York: Continuum, 1985), pp. 118–37; and 'Die revidierte Psychanalyse' [Revisionist psychoanalysis], 1 (1955), *Gesammette Schriften, Soziologische Schriften*, vol. 8, pp. 20–41.
17. Martin Jay, *Adorno* (London: Fontana, 1984), p. 90.
18. Theodor Adorno, *Negative Dialectics* (New York: Continuum, 1973), p. 349.
19. Adorno, 'Sociology and psychology', p. 86.
20. Ibid., p. 87.
21. Adorno, 'Freudian theory and the pattern of Fascist propaganda', p. 136.
22. The following overview refers to Adorno's account of the dialectic of the 'ego and non-ego' in 'Sociology and psychology', p. 87ff.
23. Ibid., p. 95.
24. Held, *Introduction to Critical Theory*, p. 133.
25. Adorno, 'Sociology and psychology', pp. 87–8.
26. Ibid., p. 95.
27. Marcuse, *Eros and Civilization*, p. 99.
28. Herbert Marcuse, *One-dimensional Man: Studies in Advanced Industrial Society* (Boston, MA: Beacon, 1966), pp. 74–7.
29. Adorno, 'Sociology and psychology', p. 85.
30. Marcuse, *Eros and Civilization*, p. 94.
31. Gilles Deleuze and Félix Guattari, *Anti-Oedipus* (New York: Viking, 1977).
32. A summary of these trends is given in J. Laplanche and J.B. Pontalis, *The Language of Psychoanalysis* (London: Hogarth Press, 1985), pp. 220–2.
33. Ibid., p. 221.
34. Lacan's distinction, which I examine in Chapter 4, highlights that biological needs have no *determining* role in processes of repression. It thus allows us to comprehend the difficulties in Freud's interpretation of the connections between biological needs and libidinal drives in the following passage from his '*New Introductory Lectures on Psycho-analysis*', (1933) *SE*, XXII:

> The sexual drives are noticeable to us for their plasticity, their capacity for altering their aims, their replaceability ... and their readiness for being deferred ... We should be glad to deny these characteristics to the self-preservative drives, and to say of them that they are inflexible, admit of no delay, are imperative in a very different sense and have a quite other relationship to repression and anxiety. But a little reflection tells us that this exceptional position applies, not to all ego drives, but only to hunger and thirst, and is evidently based on a peculiar character of the sources of these drives. (p. 97)

Freud's confusion about the place of the functions of self-preservation is particularly evident. In contrast to the sexual drives, which because of their plasticity are unconscious *desires*, the forces of hunger and thirst, in Lacan's scheme, are classified as biological *needs* due to their instinctual rigidity. Such needs, however, play no *determining* part in the specific social-historical structuring of the representational process or of the specific configurations of repression. Against Marcuse and Adorno, this is properly the *creative* place of unconscious desire. For a fuller treatment of these issues see Anthony Wilden, *System and Structure* (London: Tavistock, 1973).

35. Anthony Wilden, 'Marcuse and the Freudian model: energy, information and phantasie', *Salmagundi*, 10/11 (1969), pp. 196–245.
36. Ibid., pp. 221–2.
37. See Fredric Jameson, *The Ideologies of Theory* Vol. 1, *Situations of Theory* (London: Routledge, 1988), pp. 109–10.
38. The results of such research are summarized in Anthony Giddens, *The Constitution of Society* (Cambridge: Polity Press, 1984), pp. 239–42. The views I develop here directly draw on Giddens's arguments that social theory should avoid postulating such homologies between the increasing complexity of social life on the one hand and intensified levels of psychological repression on the other.
39. Jean Laplanche, 'Notes sur Marcuse et la psychanalyse', *La Nef*, 36 (1969), p. 133.
40. Wilden, 'Marcuse and the Freudian model', p. 221.
41. Julia Kristeva, *Tales of Love* (New York: Columbia University Press, 1987), pp. 9–10.
42. See Jessica Benjamin, 'The end of internalization: Adorno's social psychology', *Telos*, 32 (1977).
43. For a review of these materials see Held, *Introduction to Critical Theory*, p. 372.

44. See Melanie Klein, 'On the development of mental functioning' (1958), in *Envy and Gratitude and Other Works* (London: Virago Press, 1988), pp. 236–46.

45. For a discussion of the deficiencies of Marcuse's account of the institutional processes of social reproduction see Claus Offe, 'Technology and one-dimensionality: a version of the technocracy thesis?', in R. Pippin, A. Feenberg and C. Webel (eds), *Marcuse: Critical Theory and the Promise of Utopia* (London: Macmillan, 1988), pp. 215–24.

46. See Anthony Giddens, *Profiles and Critiques in Social Theory* (London: Macmillan, 1982), pp. 154ff.

47. The sociological research which highlights the pervasiveness of social differentiation and fragmentation has been extensively developed; here I refer only to the most important texts. Such findings were initially reported in Michael Mann, 'The social cohesion of liberal democracy', *American Sociological Review*, 35 (1970), pp. 423–39; and *Consciousness and Action among the Western Working Class* (London: Macmillan, 1973). A more recent theorization of these complex interconnections between social differentiation and the ideological field is John B. Thompson, *Studies in the Theory of Ideology* (Cambridge: Polity Press, 1984).

48. Thompson, *Studies in the Theory of Ideology*, p. 63.

49. A useful discussion of the effect of unconscious mechanisms upon the social divisions and tensions of race and gender is Stephen Frosh, *Psychoanalysis and Psychology: Minding the Gap* (London: Macmillan, 1989), Chapters 4 and 5.

50. A useful overview on this evidence is given in Telos's symposium on narcissism and contemporary social processes: *Telos*, 44 (1980).

51. Otto F. Kernberg, *Borderline Conditions and Pathological Narcissism* (New York: Jason Aronson, 1975); Heinz Kohut, *The Restoration of the Self* (New York: International Universities Press, 1977).

52. Joel Kovel, *The Radical Spirit: Essays on Psychoanalysis and Society* (London: Free Association Books, 1988), p. 194.

53. Christopher Lasch, *The Culture of Narcissism* (London: Abacus, 1979).

54. Jürgen Habermas, *The Philosophical Discourse of Modernity* (Cambridge: Polity Press, 1987); Jessica Benjamin, *The Bonds of Love: Psychoanalysis, Feminism and the Problem of Domination* (London: Virago, 1990); Anthony Giddens, *Consequences of Modernity* (Cambridge: Polity Press, 1990) and *Modernity and Self-identity* (Cambridge: Polity Press, 1991).

55. Jürgen Habermas, *The Theory of Communicative Action*, Vol. 1: *Reason and the Rationalization of Society* (Cambridge: Polity Press, 1984), p. 382.

Chapter 3

1. Herbert Marcuse, *Reason and Revolution: Hegel and the Rise of Social Theory* (London: Routledge and Kegan Paul, 1969), p. 433.
2. Marcuse, *Eros and Civilization: A Philosophical Inquiry into Freud* (London: Ark, 1956), p. 224.
3. Herbert Marcuse, *Counter-revolution and Revolt* (Boston, MA: Beacon Press, 1972), p. 17.
4. Marcuse, *Eros and Civilization*, p. 19.
5. Ibid., p. 143.
6. Ibid., p. 202.
7. Ibid., p. 235.
8. Ibid., p. 151.
9. L. Kolakowski, *Main Currents of Marxism*, Vol. 3: *The Breakdown* (New York: Oxford University Press, 1978). Cf. D. Kellner, *Herbert Marcuse and the Crisis of Marxism* (London: Macmillan, 1984), Chapter 10.
10. Herbert Marcuse, 'Philosophy and critical theory', in *Negations: Essays in Critical Theory* (Boston, MA: Beacon Press, 1968), p. 19.
11. Marcuse, *Eros and Civilization*, pp. 18–19.
12. J. Laplanche and J.B. Pontalis, 'Phantasy and the origins of sexuality', *International Journal of Psycho-Analysis*, 49, 1 (1968), pp. 1–18. Translated from *Les Temps Modernes* (1964), the English version employs the word 'fantasy' throughout the article. However, in keeping with Marcuse's work and current psychoanalytic commentary, I have altered the translation to 'phantasy' for the purposes of this study.
13. Ibid., p. 16.
14. Fredric Jameson, *Marxism and Form* (New Jersey: Princeton University Press, 1971), pp. 113ff.
15. Michel Foucault, *Power/Knowledge: Selected Interviews and Other Writings 1972–77* (Brighton: Harvester Press, 1980), p. 59.
16. Michel Foucault, *Discipline and Punish* (Harmondsworth: Penguin, 1977), p. 174.
17. Michel Foucault, *The History of Sexuality: An Introduction* (London: Penguin, 1979). Throughout this study, references to this work refer to Volume 1 of Foucault's genealogy of the social construction of sexuality.
18. Ibid., pp. 81–2.

19. Ibid., pp. 152–3.
20. See, for example, Charles Taylor, 'Foucault on freedom and truth', in *Philosophy and the Human Sciences* (Cambridge: Cambridge University Press, 1985).
21. Cf. Peter Dews's interesting argument that Foucault's elevation of the 'body and its pleasures' implicitly moves towards the concept of the subject. *Logics of Disintegration* (London: Verso, 1987), p. 168.
22. See Jürgen Habermas, *The Philosophical Discourse of Modernity* (Cambridge: Polity Press, 1987), Chapter 5.
23. Jürgen Habermas, *Communication and the Evolution of Society* (London: Heinemann, 1979); *The Theory of Communicative Action*, 2 vols (Cambridge: Polity Press, 1985–86).
24. Quoted in John B. Thompson, *Studies in the Theory of Ideology* (Cambridge: Polity Press, 1984), p. 291.
25. Habermas draws mainly from Lorenzer's *Symbol und Verstehen in Psychoanalytischen Prozess* (Frankfurt: Suhrkamp Verlag, 1970). For an English translation of his work see 'Symbols and stereotypes,',in P. Connerton (ed.), *Critical Sociology* (Harmondsworth: Penguin, 1976), pp. 134–52.
26. Jürgen Habermas, *Knowledge and Human Interests* (London: Heinemann, 1972), p. 285.
27. Jürgen Habermas, 'On systematically distorted communication', in Connerton, *Critical Sociology*, p. 360.
28. Ibid.
29. Habermas draws specifically from the work of Sanford, de Levianta, and G. and R. Blanck, as well as from traditional ego-psychologists such as Harry Sullivan and Erik Erikson.
30. A useful summary of Habermas's interpretation of cognitive-developmental psychology is T. McCarthy, *The Critical Theory of Jürgen Habermas* (Cambridge: Polity Press, 1978), pp. 344–57.
31. Jürgen Habermas, 'Consciousness-raising or redemptive criticism', *New German Critique*, 17 (1979).
32. Ibid., p. 58.
33. Habermas, *Communication and the Evolution of Society*, p. 93. This is what Habermas has called, going beyond Kohlberg, Stage 7 of moral consciousness.
34. Ibid., p. 94.
35. A valuable critical collection of essays on Habermas's work is John B. Thompson and David Held, *Habermas: Critical Debates* (London: Macmillan, 1982).
36. Joel Whitebook, 'Reason and happiness: some psychoanalytic themes in critical theory', in R.J. Bernstein (ed.), *Habermas and Modernity* (Cambridge: Polity Press, 1985), pp. 140–60.

37. Ibid., p. 155.
38. Ibid., p. 156.
39. Russell Keat, *The Politics of Social Theory* (Oxford: Basil Blackwell, 1981).
40. Ibid., p. 107.
41. A useful summary of these objections to Habermas's work is contained in M. Jay, 'Habermas and modernism', in Bernstein, *Habermas and Modernity*, pp. 134–7.
42. Jürgen Habermas, 'A reply to my critics', in Thompson and Held, *Habermas*, p. 235.
43. Iris Marion Young, 'Impartiality and the civic public', in Seyla Benhabib and Drucilla Cornell (eds), *Feminism as Critique* (Cambridge: Polity Press, 1987), p. 70.
44. Nancy Fraser, 'What's critical about critical theory?: the case of Habermas and gender', in Benhabib and Cornell, *Feminism*, pp. 31–56.
45. Seyla Benhabib, *Critique, Norm and Utopia: A Study of the Foundations of Critical Theory* (New York: Columbia University Press, 1986).
46. Ibid., pp. 340–1.

Chapter 4

1. The principal works by Lacan that I have drawn upon for this chapter are his *Ecrits: A Selection* (London: Tavistock, 1977); *The Four Fundamental Concepts of Psychoanalysis* (Harmondsworth: Penguin, 1979); *The Seminar of Jacques Lacan*, Vol. 1: *Freud's Papers on Technique 1953–54* (Cambridge: Cambridge University Press, 1988); and *The Seminar of Jacques Lacan*, Vol. 2: *The Ego in Freud's Theory and in the Technique of Psychoanalysis 1954–55* (Cambridge: Cambridge University Press, 1988). For valuable introductory overviews to Lacan see B. Benvenuto and R. Kennedy, *The Works of Jacques Lacan* (London: Free Association Books, 1986); and Malcolm Bowie, *Lacan* (London: Fontana, 1991).
2. For an interesting treatment of the influence of Kojéve's interpretation of Hegel upon Lacan, see Peter Dews, *Logics of Disintegration* (London: Verso, 1987), Chapter 2.
3. See Judith Butler's comments concerning Lacan's misinterpretation of Hegel in *Subjects of Desire: Hegelian Reflections in Twentieth-century France* (New York: Columbia University Press), 1987: 'In disregarding the comedy of errors that mark the Hegelian subject's travels, Lacan unjustifiably attributes Cartesian self-transparency to the Hegelian subject' (p. 196).

4. Sigmund Freud, 'On narcissism', *SE*, XIX, p. 29.
5. D.W. Winnicott, 'Mirror role of mother and family in child development', in *Playing and Reality* (Harmondsworth: Penguin, 1980). Winnicott discusses the 'other' as a cognitive and emotional being, rather than as a surface, in the constitution of the self.
6. Jacques Lacan, 'The mirror stage as formative of the function of the I', *Ecrits*, pp. 1–2.
7. Bowie, *Lacan*, p. 21.
8. Lacan, 'The Mirror Stage', p. 2.
9. Jacques Lacan, 'The subversion of the subject and the dialectic of desire in the Freudian unconscious', in *Ecrits*, p. 315.
10. Lacan, 'The mirror stage', p. 4.
11. Quoted in Ellie Ragland-Sullivan, *Jacques Lacan and the Philosophy of Psychoanalysis* (Chicago: University of Illinois Press, 1986), p. 91.
12. Benvenuto and Kennedy, *The Works of Jacques Lacan*, p. 174.
13. Lacan, 'The subversion of the subject and the dialectic of desire', p. 311.
14. Jacques Lacan, *Ecrits* (Paris: 1966), p. 444.
15. See Ferdinand de Saussure, *Course in General Linguistics* (London: Fontana, 1974).
16. Quoted in Ragland-Sullivan, *Jacques Lacan*, p. 106.
17. Jane Gallop, *Reading Lacan* (Ithaca, NY: Cornell University Press, 1985), p. 20.
18. Butler, *Subjects of Desire*, p. 191.
19. Jacques Lacan, 'Agency of the letter in the unconscious', *Ecrits*, p. 166.
20. Malcolm Bowie, 'Jacques Lacan', in J. Sturrock (ed.), *Structuralism and Since* (Oxford: Oxford University Press), 1979, pp. 130–1.
21. Jacques Lacan, 'The function and field of speech and language in psychoanalysis', *Ecrits*, p. 66.
22. Ibid., p. 68.
23. Ibid.
24. Claude Lévi-Strauss, *The Raw and the Cooked* (London: Cape, 1970), p. 12.
25. The principal text in which Lacan analyses the objectivist claims of 'structuralism-as-code' is the 'Seminar on "The Purloined Letter"', *Yale French Studies*, 48 (1972), pp. 39–72.
26. Lacan, *Seminar*, Vol. 2, pp. 30–1.
27. Bowie, *Structuralism and Since*, p. 134.
28. Quoted in Dews, *Logics of Disintegration*, p. 82.
29. Ibid., p. 79.

30. Julia Kristeva, *Revolution in Poetic Language* (New York: Columbia University Press, 1984), p. 44.
31. Quoted in Ragland-Sullivan, *Jacques Lacan*, p. 93, (my emphasis).
32. Castoriadis has waged a critical attack against Lacanian theory and analysis for many years now. The outline of his critique that follows here, with which I have a great deal of sympathy, is developed in *The Imaginary Institution of Society* (Cambridge: Polity Press, 1987).
33. Ibid., p. 3.
34. See Cornelius Castoriadis, *Crossroads in the Labyrinth* (Cambridge, MA: MIT Press, 1984), Chapter 2.
35. Ibid., p. 57.
36. As with Freud, narcissism is understood in the writings of Kohut and Kernberg, not as an ontological given, but as an imaginary relation to the self and its objects that is potentially open to critical reflection, alteration, and change. For a useful overview of what Kohut calls the 'lines of narcissism', see M. Elson (ed.), *The Kohut Seminars on Self-psychology* (New York: Norton, 1985); and Otto Kernberg, *Borderline Conditions and Pathological Narcissism* (New York: Jason Aronson, 1975).
37. See Manfred Frank, *What is NeoStructuralism?* (Minneapolis: University of Minnesota Press, 1989), Chapters 19 and 20; and Dews, *Logics of Disintegration*, Chapter 3.
38. Frank, *What is NeoStructuralism?*, p. 309.
39. Dews, *Logics of Disintegration*, p. 88ff.
40. Ibid., p. 90.
41. Jacques Lacan, *The Four Fundamental Concepts of Psychoanalysis*, trans. A. Sheridan (Harmondsworth: Penguin, 1979), p. 103.
42. Castoriadis, *The Imaginary Institution of Society*, pp. 288–91.
43. Jacques Lacan, 'Seminar of 21 January 1975', in J. Mitchell and J. Rose (eds), *Feminine Sexuality: Jacques Lacan and the Ecole Freudienne* (London: Macmillan, 1982), p. 165.
44. For excellent critical overviews of Lacan's application of structural linguistics to the unconscious see the following studies: David Macey, *Lacan in Contexts* (London: Verso, 1988); Cornelius Castoriadis, 'Psychoanalysis: project and elucidation', in his *Crossroads in the Labyrinth*; Paul Ricoeur, *Freud and Philosophy: An Essay on Interpretation* (New Haven, CT: Yale University Press, 1970), whose following statement I believe is close to my position on Lacan:

    If we take the concept of linguistics in the strict sense of the science of language phenomena embodied in a given and

therefore organized language, the symbolism of the unconscious is not *stricto sensu* a linguistic phenomena. It is a
symbolism common to various cultures regardless of their
language; it presents phenomena such as displacement and
condensation which operate on the level of images, and not
that of phonemic or semantic articulation. (p. 399)

See also Jacques Derrida's criticisms of Lacan's structuralist
tendencies: 'Le facteur de la verite', in *The Post Card* (Illinois:
University of Chicago Press, 1987).

45. Fredric Jameson, *The Ideologies of Theory*, Vol. 1: *Situations of Theory* (London: Routledge, 1988), p. 88.
46. Lacan, 'Agency of the letter in the unconscious', p. 161.
47. See Jean-François Lyotard, 'The dream-work does not think' and 'Beyond representation' in Andrew Benjamin (ed.), *The Lyotard Reader* (Oxford: Basil Blackwell, 1989). Note also Lyotard's suggestive dig at Lacan, correcting the view that Freud was concerned above all with linguistic operations in the psyche, in the following footnote: 'Freud devotes five pages to displacement as against twenty-six to condensation, *ninety-five to considerations or representability*, and twenty to secondary revision', (p. 53, n.23 (my emphasis)).
48. Sigmund Freud, *The Interpretation of Dreams*, SE, V, p. 507 (my emphasis).
49. Lyotard, 'The dream-work', p. 19.
50. Ibid., p. 51.
51. Ibid., pp. 22–3.
52. Ibid., p. 27.
53. For an excellent critique of Lyotard's position on the unconscious as it relates to the destruction of secondary elaborations of language see Dews, *Logics of Disintegration*, Chapter 4.
54. Sigmund Freud, 'The unconscious', SE, XIV, pp. 201–2.
55. My approach to the following issues concerning society and the symbolic owes a good deal to Castoriadis, whose views I have examined in Chapter 1. See Castoriadis's discussion of the appropriation of the social by the psyche in *The Imaginary Institution of Society*, pp. 308–20.
56. Quoted in Frank, *What is NeoStructuralism?*, pp. 304–5.
57. Lacan, *Ecrits*, p. 67.
58. Lacan, *Seminar* , Vol. 1, pp. 191–205.
59. Ibid., p. 201.
60. Sigmund Freud, *Introductory Lectures on Psycho-analysis*, SE, XVI, p. 345, (my emphasis).
61. See Sigmund Freud, *The Ego and the Id, SE*, XVI.

264 SOCIAL THEORY AND PSYCHOANALYSIS IN TRANSITION

62. D.W. Winnicott, *The Maturational Processes and the Facilitating Environment* (London: Hogarth Press, 1965); and *Playing and Reality* (Harmondsworth: Penguin, 1974).
63. Winnicott, *Playing and Reality*, p. 97.
64. Ibid., p. 83.
65. Ibid., p. 13.

Chapter 5

1. For comprehensive overviews of Althusser's theoretical work, see Ted Benton, *The Rise and Fall of Structural Marxism* (London: Macmillan, 1984); and Gregory Elliott, *Althusser: The Detour of Theory* (London: Verso, 1987).
2. Louis Althusser, 'Idealogy and idealogical state apparatuses' and 'Freud and Lacan', both reprinted in Louis Althusser, *Essays on Ideology* (London: Verso, 1984).
3. Althusser, 'Idealogy', pp. 38–9.
4. Louis Althusser, *Lenin and Philosophy and Other Essays* (London: New Left Books, 1971), p. 160.
5. Althusser notes of this distance between the specular 'I' and the subject of the unconscious: 'the real subject, the individual in his unique essence, has not the form of an ego, centred on the 'ego,' on consciousness or on 'existence' ... [rather] the human subject is decentred, constituted by a structure which has no 'centre' either, except in the imaginary misrecognition of the 'ego,' i.e. in the ideological formations in which it recognizes itself.' 'Freud and Lacan', pp. 170–1.
6. Louis Althusser, *For Marx* (London: Allen Lane, 1969), pp. 234–5.
7. Althusser, 'Freud and Lacan', p. 161.
8. Althusser, 'Ideology', p. 35.
9. See Chapter 2, n. 46.
10. John B. Thompson, *Ideology and Modern Culture* (Cambridge: Polity Press, 1990). p. 90.
11. Ernesto Laclau and Chantal Mouffe, *Hegemony and Socialist Strategy: Towards a Radical Democratic Politics* (London: Verso, 1985).
12. Ibid., pp. 97–8. Laclau, it should be noted, had previously developed a reconceptualization of the Althusserian theory of interpellation in his *Politics and Ideology in Marxist Theory* (London: New Left Books, 1977).
13. Laclau and Mouffe, *Hegemony*, pp. 105ff.
14. Ibid., p. 113.
15. Ibid., p. 114.

16. See Jacques Lacan, *The Four Fundamental Concepts of Psychoanalysis* (Harmondsworth: Penguin, 1979), Chapter 5.
17. Ibid., p. 88, n.1. Laclau discusses his appropriation of Lacanian thought in an interview 'Theory, democracy and socialism', in Ernesto Laclau, *New Reflections on the Revolution of our Time* (London: Verso, 1990), pp. 209ff.
18. Laclau and Mouffe, *Hegemony*, pp. 191–2.
19. Slavoj Žižek, *The Sublime Object of Ideology* (London: Verso, 1989).
20. Ibid., p. 175.
21. Slavoj Žižek, 'Beyond discourse-analysis', in Laclau, *New Reflections*, pp. 251–2.
22. Žižek, *The Sublime Object of Ideology*, p. 43.
23. Ibid., p. 124.
24. Ibid., p. 125.
25. Slavoj Žižek, 'Eastern Europe's republics of Gilead', *New Left Review*, 183 (1990), p. 56.
26. Žižek, *The Sublime Object of Ideology*, p. 127.
27. See Jessica Benjamin, *The Bonds of Love: Psychoanalysis, Feminism and the Problem of Domination* (London: Virago, 1990).
28. Terry Eagleton, *Ideology: An Introduction* (London: Verso, 1991), p. 209.
29. Ibid., p. 214.
30. See Jean Laplanche, *Life and Death in Psychoanalysis* (Baltimore, MD: Johns Hopkins University Press, 1976), Chapter 3.

Chapter 6

1. Simone de Beauvoir, *The Second Sex* (London: Jonathan Cape, 1953), p. 16.
2. Juliet Mitchell, *Psychoanalysis and Feminism* (Harmondsworth: Penguin, 1974). The alternative theories to Freud on sexuality that Mitchell examines are those of Wilhelm Reich and R.D. Laing.
3. Juliet Mitchell, 'Freud and Lacan: psychoanalytic theories of sexual difference', in *Women: The Longest Revolution* (London: Virago, 1984), pp. 248–77.
4. Ibid., p. 253.
5. Sigmund Freud, 'Some psychical consequences of the anatomical distinction between the sexes', *SE*, XIX, p. 256.
6. See Mitchell, *Women*, esp. pp. 265–74. For an account of the pervasiveness of these approaches in feminism today, see Nancy Chodorow, *Feminism and Psychoanalytic Theory* (Cambridge: Polity Press, 1989), Chapter 8.

7. Mitchell, *Women*, p. 256.
8. Jacques Lacan, *Ecrits: A Selection* (London: Tavistock, 1977), p. 287.
9. Mitchell, *Women*, p. 266.
10. Mitchell, *Psychoanalysis and Feminism*, p. 415.
11. Mitchell, *Women*, p. 274.
12. 'Feminine sexuality: interview with Juliet Mitchell and Jacqueline Rose', *m/f*, 8 (1983), p. 7.
13. Jane Flax, *Thinking Fragments: Psychoanalysis, Feminism, and Postmodernism in the Contemporary West* (Berkeley: University of California Press, 1990), p. 106.
14. Hélène Cixous, 'Sorties', in F. Marks and I. de Courtivron (eds), *New French Feminisms* (Brighton: Harvester Press, 1980), p. 95.
15. Hélène Cixous, 'The laugh of the Medusa', in Marks and de Courtivron, *New French Feminisms*, pp. 259–60.
16. Luce Irigaray, 'This sex which is not One', in Marks and de Courtivron, *New French Feminisms*, p. 100.
17. Cixous, 'The laugh of the Medusa', p. 262.
18. Luce Irigaray, *This Sex which is not One* (Ithaca, NY: Cornell University Press, 1985), p. 189.
19. Nancy Chodorow, *The Reproduction of Mothering: Psychoanalysis and the Sociology of Gender* (Berkeley: University of California Press, 1978), pp. 166–7.
20. See Luce Irigaray, *Ethique de la différance sexuelle* (Paris: Minuit, 1984), pp. 72ff.
21. Irigaray, *This Sex which is not One*, p. 143.
22. Hélène Cixous and Catherine Clément, *The Newly Born Woman* (Minneapolis: University of Minnesota Press, 1986), pp. 64–5.
23. Ibid., p. 93.
24. For a valuable guide to the critical controversy over biological essentialism and feminism, see the essays by L. Jardine, R. Braidotti, M. Whitford and G. Spivak in Teresa Brennan (ed.), *Between Feminism and Psychoanalysis* (London: Routledge, 1989).
25. Margaret Whitford, *Luce Irigaray: Philosophy in the Feminine* (London: Routledge, 1991).
26. Jacqueline Rose, *Sexuality in the Field of Vision* (London: Verso, 1986), pp. 78–81.
27. Toril Moi, *Sexual/Textual Politics* (London: Routledge, 1985), p. 123.
28. For a comprehensive overview of Kristeva's career, see John Lechte, *Julia Kristeva* (London: Routledge, 1990); and, from a

feminist angle, the best introduction to Kristeva is still Toril Moi, *Sexual/Textual Politics*, Chapter 8.

29. Julia Kristeva, cited in Toril Moi (ed.), *The Kristeva Reader* (Oxford: Basil Blackwell, 1986), p. 11.

30. Like the Freudian view of subjectivity as split and fractured by desire, Kristeva speaks of a subject 'in process', 'on trial', 'in question'.

31. Quoted in Moi, *Sexual/Textual Politics*, p. 152.

32. Julia Kristeva, 'Revolution in poetic language', in Moi, *The Kristeva Reader*, p. 93.

33. Ibid., p. 104.

34. Quoted in Judith Butler, *Subjects of Desire: Hegelian Reflections in Twentieth-century France* (New York: Columbia University Press, 1987), p. 232.

35. Moi, *Sexual/Textual Politics*, p. 166.

36. Like Lacan, Kristeva uses the term *jouissance* to denote sexual and sensual joy; but she also seeks to broaden its reference to designate the *total* human dimensions of all transgressive experience. On this point, see L.S. Roudiez's introductory comments in Kristeva's collection of essays, *Desire in Language* (Oxford: Basil Blackwell, 1982), pp. 15ff.

37. Kristeva, 'Revolution in poetic language', p. 113.

38. Sigmund Freud, 'Negation', *SE*, XIX, p. 143.

39. Roland Barthes, *Pleasure of the Text* (London: Jonathan Cape, 1975).

40. Julia Kristeva, 'Woman cannot be defined', in Marks and de Courtivon, *New French Feminisms*, pp. 137–8.

41. Julia Kristeva, 'Woman's time', in Moi, *The Kristeva Reader*, p. 210.

42. A. White, 'L'Eclatement du sujet': *The Theoretical Work of Julia Kristeva*, University of Birmingham Centre for Contemporary Studies, Stencilled Occasional Paper, no. 49, 1977.

43. Julia Kristeva, *Tales of Love* and *In the Beginning was Love: Psychoanalysis and Faith* (New York: Columbia University Press, 1987); *Black Sun: Depression and Melancholia* (New York: Columbia University Press, 1989); *Strangers to Ourselves* (New York: Harvester, 1991).

44. According to Kristeva,

at some point in his life the human being is fascinated by his image. But it is possible only if this human being is capable of some separation from his mother and is capable of grasping some imaginary forms, which is the zero degree of the third between the infant and the mother. And this zero degree is not a word used by Freud; I use the word, Freud speaks of about the father of pre-individual history, which is not grasped as a real person by the infant but like a sort of symbolic instance. ('Julia Kristeva in conversation with Rosalind Coward', ICA Documents, 1 (1984), p. 22)

45. In describing the subject's pre-identification with the 'father of personal pre-history', Freud asserts that primary identification is the 'original form of emotional tie with an object', 'Group psychology and the analysis of the ego', SE, XVIII, p. 107.
46. Kristeva, *Tales of Love*, pp. 15–16.

Chapter 7

* See Anthony Elliott, *Subject to Ourselves* (Cambridge: Polity Press, 1996); Anthony Elliott, *New Directions in Social Theory* (Cambridge: Cambridge University Press, forthcoming).
1. Terry Eagleton, *The Ideology of the Aesthetic* (Oxford: Basil Blackwell, 1990), p. 348.
2. See Jessica Benjamin, *The Bonds of Love: Psychoanalysis, Feminism and the Problem of Domination* (London: Virago, 1990), Chapter 4.
3. Lacan, quoted in Peter Dews, *Logics of Disintegration* (London: Verso, 1987), p. 79.
4. Jacques Lacan, 'Aggressivity in Psychoanalysis', *Ecrits: A Selection* (London: Tavistock, 1977), p. 22.
5. Richard Sennett, *The Fall of Public Man* (Cambridge: Cambridge University Press, 1977); Christopher Lasch, *The Culture of Narcissism* (London: Abacus, 1980) and *The Minimal Self* (London: Picador, 1985).
6. Speaking of the 'irreference' of postmodern culture, Baudrillard in *Simulations* (New York: Semiotext, 1983), writes of the imaginary: 'It bears no relation to any reality whatsoever, it is its own pure simulacrum' (p. 11). The futility of Baudrillard's account of the circles of mirror-play are plain from a psychoanalytic angle – even if many in social theory are still 'lost' in these writings. The human subject cannot become caught within an imaginary circle – one without any reference to social reality – without entering psychosis.
7. Richard Kearney, *Poetics of Imagining: From Husserl to Lyotard* (London: HarperCollins, 1991), p. 177.
8. Alberto Mellucci, *Nomads of the Present* (London: Hutchinson, 1989).

9. Ibid., p. 129.
10. Anthony Giddens, *Modernity and Self-identity: Self and Society in the Late Modern Age* (Cambridge: Polity Press, 1991).
11. See Cornelius Castoriadis, 'The imaginary in the modern world', in *The Imaginary Institution of Society* (Cambridge: Polity Press, 1987), pp. 156ff. The view of the imaginary I am proposing here is substantially indebted to the work of Castoriadis.
12. Luce Irigaray, *This Sex which is not One* (Ithaca, NY: Cornell University Press, 1985), p. 189.
13. Benjamin, *The Bonds of Love*, p. 94.
14. Ibid., p. 109.
15. Lacan, quoted in Dews, *Logics of Disintegration*, p. 83.
16. Jacques Lacan, 'Of structure as an inmixing of an otherness prerequisite to any subject whatever', in R. Macksey and E. Donato (eds), *The Structuralist Controversy: The Languages of Criticism and the Sciences of Man* (Baltimore, MD: Johns Hopkins University Press, 1975), p. 193.
17. Castoriadis, *The Imaginary Institution of Society*, p. 296.
18. Sigmund Freud, 'The unconscious', *SE*, XIV, p. 201.
19. Sigmund Freud, *The Interpretation of Dreams*, *SE*, V, p. 507 (my emphasis).
20. For example, to be able to imagine or image a heart within the inscription of the letters I have used in the above example.
21. According to the standpoint I am proposing, there is an infinite range of 'lacking' objects which the psyche may create. But there is no initial 'lack'. In terms of the linkage between desire and representation, what the psyche will always search to image is that which is unrepresentable – namely its psychical state prior to separation, in which the pleasure principle reigned supreme. On this point Castoriadis offers a useful lead:

> What is missing and will always be missing is the unrepresentable element of an initial 'state' ... This initial desire is radically irreducible not because what it aims at does not find in reality an object that embodies it, or in language words that state it, but because it cannot find in the psyche itself an image in which to depict itself. Once the psyche has suffered the break up of its monadic 'state' imposed upon it by the 'object', the other and its own body, it is forever thrown off-centre in relation to itself, orientated in terms of that which it is no longer, which is no longer and can no longer be. *The psyche is its own lost object.* (Castoriadis, *The Imaginary Institution of Society*, pp. 296–7)

22. T.W. Adorno, E. Frenkel-Brunswick, D. Levinson and R. Sanford, *The Authoritarian Personality* (New York: Norton, 1982), pp. 324–5.

23. Michael Rustin, *The Good Society and the Inner World: Psychoanalysis, Politics and Culture* (London: Verso, 1991), p. 68.

24. K. Theweleit, *Male Fantasies* (Cambridge: Polity Press, 1987), p. 218.

25. For interesting psychoanalytic accounts of the links between human needs, aspirations, desires and political norms, see Joel Kovel, *The Radical Spirit: Essays on Psychoanalysis and Society* (London: Free Association Books, 1988); Alan Davies, *The Human Element* (Harmondsworth: Penguin, 1988); and Richard Wollheim, *The Thread of Life* (Cambridge: Cambridge University Press, 1984).

26. Eagleton, *The Ideology of the Aesthetic*, p. 414.

27. Paul Ricoeur, *Freud and Philosophy: An Essay on Interpretation* (New Haven, CT: Yale University Press, 1970), p. 430.

Index

Oedipus complex 31–6, 39–40
  female 32–3, 185–6, 191
  and individuation 226
  Lacan and 133
  in linguistic terms 123–4
  Marcuse and Adorno and 5, 52–3,
    55, 60, 68–70, 214, 215–16
  and sexual division 185, 226
oppositional attitudes 73
oppression 72
  see also repressiveness
Other 123–4, 154–5, 164, 174–5,
    179, 209, 217, 244
  concrete 108
  as mirror 9
  self and 28–9, 64–5
  unknowable to self 110
otherness 116
  of language 121, 122
overdetermination, symbolic 160–2,
    169–70

parapraxes 14
parental-object identification 39
parenting patterns, changes in 231
Parsons, Talcott 93
past, shaping present 42
paternal law see Law of the Father
patriarchal, symbolic order 193
patriarchal law 183, 184
patriarchy 35, 182, 191–2, 196
performance principle 52, 54, 79,
    80, 81
phallocentrism 197, 229, 231, 232
phallus
  and 'lack' 128, 189, 191, 192
  and male domination 190, 229
  mother's desire for 208, 210
  phallic authority 31–2
  phallic law 6, 189
  and sexual division 188–9, 190,
    191, 225, 226, 227
phantasy 17, 20, 24, 117
  blocked 85, 86
  objects 131
  origin of 85–6
  positive and negative features
    86–7

and reality 79–81
  sexual 189
  and social representation 246
  and social transformation 83,
    84–5, 86
Piaget, Jean 97
place of the father 189–90, 227
Plato 201
pleasure 2, 16, 17, 19, 64, 245
  and pain interplay 24
pleasure principle 22, 28, 50, 60, 62
Poe, Edgar Allen 140–1
Pontalis, J.B. 35, 63, 85–6
'post-ideological condition' 2
post-Lacanian theory 178–81, 218
  feminist 8, 228
  and ideology 146
post-Marxism 159–65, 176
post-structuralist theory 9, 41, 76,
    147, 213, 219
  identity 161
  and Lacanian theory 166
  and language 151
  repression 20, 22, 221
  see also Althusser
postmodernism 2, 3, 9, 68, 207, 222
power
  destructive relations of 4, 9
  sexist 182
  social 40, 43–4, 45, 66, 72,
    87–91, 92, 109
pre-mirror period 116
pre-Oedipal stage 34, 70, 112,
    200–1
  femininity 197, 202
  mother-daughter relationship
    194–5, 196, 228–9, 230
  mothers 210
preconscious/conscious system 16,
    28, 137
prehistory, collective 35
primal repression 19, 22
primary unconscious 4, 10, 20, 22,
    233
projection 30
psyche
  analogy with State 38–9
  automization of 59, 215, 222

transformation *see* change
transitional objects 142–3
truth 127, 165

unconscious 2, 10, 14–26
and alternative social order 5
collective thought 124
and creativity 10, 44
distorting meaning 21, 136, 217
and dreams 20
fulfilled wishes 133
and identity 50
imaginary nature of 9
as 'lack' 189
and language 6, 10, 98, 100–2,
119–20
manipulation of 57–8, 59, 60,
71, 78, 91, 92, 96
mechanisms 21
nature of 12, 15, 18, 26, 96,
102, 110, 118–19, 133–9
object a 130–1
primary 4, 10, 20, 22, 233
primary processes 6, 15–16, 21,
134–5, 136
and rationality 102
and reality 16
representation 3, 10, 15, 16, 21,
25–6, 27
and repression 14, 15, 16, 19,
103–4
and self-actualization 74, 80
and sexual identity 184–5
and social power 100
in social theory 4, 40
structuralist approach to 7, 10
subject of 123, 129
as symbolic system 123
transformative work 21

utopian ideals 78, 79, 82–3, 86, 98,
105, 108, 109

values
social and cultural 179–80
see also morality
voyeurism, and exhibitionism 28

Weber, E.H. 46
White, A. 207
Whitebook, Joel 101, 102, 215
Whitford, Margaret 197, 197–8
Wilden, Anthony 64–5, 67, 215
Winnicott, D.W. 114, 142–4, 241
Wollheim, Richard 30
woman
castrated/powerless 230
as the Other 182, 190–1, 192,
193, 227
'womanspeak' 198
women
female libido 194, 196, 197
inequalities among 198–9
oppression 182, 183, 193, 227
subjectivity 182, 229
women's movement 248
and ideology 177–8
and representation 234
'word-presentations' and 'thing-
presentations' 137–8, 239
work practices, repressive 71

Young, Iris Marion 106

Žižek, Slovoj 7, 146, 166–70,
172–81, 213, 218, 219

*Index compiled by
Sue Carlton*